"For the growing number of pastors, artists, and lay leaders who love the arts but are unsure of their role in ministry, Michael Bauer here provides just what is needed. Though historically and theologically informed, his *Arts Ministry* focuses on the practical issues of making the arts an integral part of the worship and ministry of the church. With ecumenical sensitivity Bauer employs multiple case studies and addresses many potential pitfalls in encouraging a more holistic and multisensory worship. This is the book to put in the hands of your church's worship committee, or to assign in seminary or college ministry courses."

— WILLIAM DYRNESS
Fuller Theological Seminary

"This is a book of ideas and insights. It explores the context in which the church engages in a wide spectrum of the arts, it reflects on the resources at hand, and it provides a framework for conceiving and crafting an arts agenda that is comprehensive, responsible, and timely."

— QUENTIN FAULKNER
University of Nebraska

The CALVIN INSTITUTE OF CHRISTIAN WORSHIP LITURGICAL STUDIES Series, edited by John D. Witvliet, is designed to promote reflection on the history, theology, and practice of Christian worship and to stimulate worship renewal in Christian congregations. Contributions include writings by pastoral worship leaders from a wide range of communities and scholars from a wide range of disciplines. The ultimate goal of these contributions is to nurture worship practices that are spiritually vital and theologically rooted.

Published

Arts Ministry

Nurturing the
Creative Life of God's People

Michael J. Bauer

William B. Eerdmans Publishing Company
Grand Rapids, Michigan

Wm. B. Eerdmans Publishing Co.
2140 Oak Industrial Drive N.E., Grand Rapids, Michigan 49505
www.eerdmans.com

Library of Congress Cataloging-in-Publication Data

Bauer, Michael J., 1956-
Arts ministry: nurturing the creative life of God's people / Michael J. Bauer.
pages   cm.   — (The Calvin Institute of Christian worship liturgical studies)
Includes bibliographical references.
ISBN 978-0-8028-6928-9 (pbk.: alk. paper)
1. Christianity and the arts.   2. Church work.   I. Title.

BR115.A8B38   2013
253'.7 — dc23

2013009748

To my parents,
who surrounded me with beauty,
and taught me the value of a liberal education

Contents

Contents

Contents

Preface

It is a truism that books are not the product of one person's work; they are the product of a community. Several different communities have had a role to play in the current study.

First, I am deeply grateful for the work of countless writers, working particularly in the past thirty years, who have taken various aspects of this topic seriously. Without the efforts of scholars like Wilson Yates, Don Saliers, William Dyrness, Frank Burch Brown, Janet Walton, Nena Bryans, and so many others that I do not have space to name, this book would not have been possible.

Next, I am thankful for my teachers and my students, who have prepared and sharpened my thinking about the various issues considered in these pages. Without their influence this book would be significantly weaker. I am also keenly aware of the contributions made by my colleagues in arts ministry, people who have freely shared their own gifts in the development of various church arts ministries and participated with me in sacred arts projects over the course of many years.

There are a number of specific people who have had a more direct role to play in the process of writing this book. To Stephan Casurella, Quentin Faulkner, Joan Koneck-Wilcox, Barbara Ostermann, William Dyrness, Lisa DeBoer, and Lara West go my sincere thanks for your insightful reading of the manuscript and your comments on my work. I am also grateful to the many people who have facilitated the various small case studies that are scattered throughout these pages. Countless others also responded to requests for information about their own ministries and generously gave of their time to help this book become a reality. Many equally worthy ministries could have been featured in these pages. I thank them all for their gracious responses and wish them well as they continue on their path as arts ministers.

I owe a special debt to John Witvliet for his encouragement and for his including this book in the Calvin Institute of Christian Worship Liturgical Study Series, and to my wonderful, patient editor, Mary Hietbrink, as well as to Jon Pott, Linda Bieze, Jeffry Lewis, Victoria Fanning, Kevin van der Leek, Willem Mineur, and the entire staff of William B. Eerdmans Publishing Company for their outstanding work on this publication.

Finally, I would be remiss in not acknowledging the very personal contributions made by three special people:

My mother, who was a superb musician, and early in life a faculty member in the Music Department at Oshkosh State Teacher's College (now the University of Wisconsin, Oshkosh); she taught me piano for twelve years, kept our house full of music at all times when I was growing up, and then began her own exploration of the organ, studying for seventeen years at the Eastman School of Music.

My father, a retired professor in the School of Education at the State University of New York, Geneseo, and the finest teacher I have ever known; he introduced me to philosophy and taught me to value excellence.

My wife, Marie Rubis Bauer, the Director of Music Ministry, Archdiocese of Omaha/Cathedral Organist, Saint Cecilia Cathedral — a magnificent organist, choral conductor, harpsichordist, and church musician; she has shown me how to actually do all the things I teach, and cheerfully supported me throughout the process of writing this book.

Introduction

At St. Michael and All Angels Episcopal Church in Mission, Kansas, Kenneth Walker, Director of Music and the Arts, worked for years with a wide variety of parishioners to foster the development of the Horizons Arts Ministry. Not long after coming to this parish in 1989, he noticed a variety of talented people in the congregation who didn't know each other:

> Some were professional artists, some were refined amateurs, some were just adding a new dimension to their lives. What was obvious to me was that there was no central gravity to share accomplishments or to pursue new experiences. Each person came to church for worship, and many also came for parish community events, but all went their own ways in the arts. There was little venue to discuss or discover together what art is and why it matters to spiritual life.

One of their first events was a parish-wide art show. "Parishioners responded enthusiastically," Walker recalls, "and the fellowship hall was filled on every wall and table with paintings, carvings, needlework, stained glass, flower arrangements, calligraphy, photography — anything that a parishioner made could be shared." That first year began a series of events that continues to this day. He notes that Horizons Arts Ministry is more than a "presenting organization":

> It seeks to engage faith, Christian community, and outreach. We've been investigating a book study series and, in addition to occasional lectures, we've done video brunches after church with film topics such as the

Gospel of Mark and Hildegard von Bingen. Our annual series of events varies with concerts, monthly exhibits, lectures, dinners (sometimes a beautiful feast is an art form in itself), and children's encounters. We have had world-renowned musicians, such as the organist of St. Paul's, London, and we have had grassroots ministries. . . . We've had a children's encounter with the Kansas City Ballet as well as a puppet workshop where children made their own puppets as part of a celebration of God's Creation.

The ministry thrives when it grapples with the ambiguity and mystery involved in the relationship between God, humanity, and the arts. "I believe we're on the growing edge when we aren't sure what all the questions are," he says. "It is that very uncertainty that builds faith and motivates us to search in art and life for the horizon where God and humanity join in an unending line of union."[1]

The "search in art and life for the horizon where God and humanity join" animates this book. Articulating some of the specific questions that arise when we unite art and ministry in the context of this search is one of the central purposes of this book. It is my hope that focusing sustained attention on these questions will lead to growth and expose the reader to a rich new palette of options for the development of faith and ministry. In so doing, I propose not only to study but to celebrate what I see as an exciting path through the emerging landscape of arts ministry, a path that holds the promise of a future ultimately defined not by artists or ministries, but by the Triune God, who promises to make "all things new" (Rev. 21:5).

There are many models of arts ministry encompassing a variety of creative ventures accomplished by individual artists, churches, and organizations. My own experience of the efforts of creative laypeople, trained artists, and arts organizations provided the inspiration for writing this book. As you will see, there is no shortage of remarkable ideas. Here is just a small sampling:

- Christ the King Presbyterian Church in Boston has an arts ministry that features art exhibitions, theatrical and musical performances, poetry readings, lectures and "Opus 99" — Friday evening coffeehouses involving visual art, poetry, and music.[2]

---

1. Kenneth Walker, interview with Marie Rubis Bauer, 6 October 2006.
2. For further information, see http://www.ctkcambridge.org.

- Partners for Sacred Places is "the only national advocate for the sound stewardship and active community use of America's older religious properties."[3]
- St. Gregory the Great Roman Catholic Church in Chicago sponsors an artist-in-residence program involving an iconographer, musicians, and a theatre company — all dedicated to fostering the relationship between art and evangelism.[4]

After encountering these and many other contemporary examples, we need to remind ourselves that arts ministry is nothing new. It is as old as the Judeo-Christian tradition itself. When Bezalel and Oholiab fashioned the tabernacle (Exod. 31:1-11), they acted as arts ministers, as did Miriam when she danced by the side of the Red Sea (Exod. 15:20-21), and Paul and Silas when they sang together in prison (Acts 16:25). As long as there has been a community of faith, there have been creative people eager to share their gifts, to enliven ritual, and to enhance the day-to-day lives of the people of God.

What *is* new is the sheer number of arts ministries embedded within the institutional fabric of churches, and the exponential growth in sacred arts organizations that has occurred in recent years. The success of these ministries in their own local settings suggests that the church is starting to get it. The stodgy old church — the "we couldn't possibly do it that way" church — is starting to wake up and realize the power and possibility inherent in arts ministry.

This book is an attempt to lay a foundation for that vital work by grounding it in the insights derived from the rich history of writing in the field of Christianity and the arts. As I delve into this material, there are some factors that will necessarily color and bias my approach. It is perhaps best to mention these at the outset, so the reader will have some basis for making an informed judgment about the book. They fall into three categories: Christianity, art, and culture.

The Christian tradition encompasses two thousand years of rich diversity as well as common practice. In order to be true to this history, I have made a sustained effort to maintain an ecumenical perspective and make this book relevant to a wide range of believers — Orthodox, Roman Catholics, mainline Protestants, and evangelicals. This concern comes partially as

---

3. For this quote, as well as further information, see http://www.sacredplaces.org.
4. For further information, see http://www.stgregory.net.

the result of a career spent teaching church music at a state university where sensitivity to ecumenism and interfaith dialogue is at a premium.

Arts ministry is an important tool to help people cross boundaries, including denominational and theological boundaries. There are some aspects of arts ministry that apply everywhere. A truly ecumenical approach to arts ministry suggests the ability to imaginatively enter into alternative artistic and theological worlds. It helps us re-think our own viewpoints in light of new sensibilities gained from other religious and artistic traditions.

Yet arts ministry also has distinctive applications within individual religious traditions. Protestant, Roman Catholic, and Orthodox believers all have their own histories with respect to art, their own ritual patterns, and their own ways of integrating art into their individual and corporate lives.[5] In light of this fact, it is important to note that I am a mainline Protestant. After being raised for some years as a Catholic, I became Protestant while still a young person. I attended a Methodist seminary, and now, after working as a minister of music in a wide variety of Protestant traditions, I serve an Episcopal church. I look forward to reactions to this material from those who hail from other traditions and can speak to it from the perspective of their own habits of thought.

The word "art" can refer to so many different things. It can apply to the various fine arts, to the wellspring of human creativity located in human crafts, and to the simple products of everyday creative ventures produced by people living out their lives in light of their creation in the image of God. Art has many facets and many different faces. As is the case with faith, there is much that is held in common across the wide spectrum of artistic expressions. There is also much that is peculiar to one art form that is not shared with other artistic disciplines or genres.

Neither I nor anyone else is equally adept or knowledgeable in each of these disciplines. I was trained as a musician — specifically, as an organist, a choral conductor, and a harpsichordist. I have performed, taught in a university setting, and served as a church musician for most of my career. As I have read, taught, lectured, and written about Christianity and the arts, I have increasingly come to view this as my real field. While I still spend most of my energy and time doing the same things I did in the past, I now view music under the broad umbrella of Christianity and the arts.

---

5. For an excellent comparative study of the role of the arts in these three traditions, see William Dyrness, *Senses of the Soul: Art and the Visual in Christian Worship* (Eugene, Ore.: Cascade Books, 2008).

Nonetheless, these pages betray a natural predilection toward viewing arts ministry in terms of music. I beg the forgiveness of artists in other disciplines and look forward to seeing the different ways they will find to translate this material into concepts and forms that are instructive for their own work.

I must mention one other artistic factor at the outset. My own training was in classical music. While I have had some truly enjoyable experiences with popular culture — playing in rock groups and directing a small ensemble that led the music for a "contemporary service" — I have a definite bent toward music and art that has stood the test of time, as well as contemporary artistic expressions that are derived from classical traditions. Popular culture forms an extraordinarily important dimension of arts ministry today. While not ignoring them in any way, I do not intend to offer a thoroughgoing critique of popular cultural materials. It seems to me that it makes more sense to speak from my own tradition and what I know best. I leave it to others more knowledgeable than I to translate this material into terms that speak clearly to those whose energies and faith are enlivened by the products of popular culture.

Arts ministry occurs everywhere: at every time and every place touched by the Christian tradition as well as in settings that are not specifically Christian. The church has a rich artistic heritage to share with the world. Artists are continually re-invigorating the church and the surrounding culture with fresh ideas and innovative artistic forms. As they have opportunities to integrate this material into their own ritual life and ministry, churches and individual artists discover that the wide panoply of cultural traditions represented in Christendom serves as a tremendous resource for faith and practice. Cross-cultural fertilization is imperative in twenty-first-century Christendom.

Nonetheless, just as Jesus was born into a particular cultural milieu, so every author writes from a specific cultural vantage point. My own perspective is that of a middle-aged, white, male, middle-class American writing in the first quarter of the twenty-first century. Although this book aims at trans-cultural, cross-cultural (and even counter-cultural) sensitivity, the text undoubtedly bears something of the values and ideology that come from my personal vantage point and history. I have no doubt that it would be immeasurably enriched by the perspectives of women, the offerings of those who hail from other places and times, and insights arising from representatives of different ethnic and cultural traditions.

To help us overcome the limitations of our personal religious, artistic, and cultural backgrounds, we need to see and experience arts ministry in different settings and from different perspectives. This is why there are a number of short descriptions — case studies — of arts ministries scattered throughout the pages of this book. (See the list following this introduction.) They include arts ministries in the context of institutional churches, universities, museums, and sacred arts organizations. Not all the organizations pictured are explicitly Christian, nor are they all formally involved in arts ministry. Nonetheless, the work they do contributes to the understanding, appreciation, and practice of art in the context of the Judeo-Christian tradition. My hope is that they will inspire similar efforts and creative ideas about how to grow arts ministry in the soil of the church and the surrounding culture. These are all examples that were active at some point during the writing of this book. As with any program or project, they each have their own histories and trajectories that do not remain static as time unfolds. Thus, what is described here may no longer reflect the current status of any individual ministry or institution at the time you are reading this book. Nonetheless, they remain potent models that have the power to excite the imagination and show us what is possible.

This book is divided into nine chapters. You can read it from cover to cover, or select isolated topics to pursue as they attract your interest and attention.

Chapter One opens with a description of various individual arts ministries to offer a glimpse of what arts ministry might look like in different settings. It continues by defining important terms related to arts ministry and distinguishes arts ministry from the wider field of Christianity and the arts. This leads to a definition of arts ministry, followed by a description of the natural constituencies who relate to arts ministry.

Chapter Two considers the need for arts advocacy in the church and examines the various arguments *against* arts ministry that have come down to us through the ages. This is done as a means of helping us construct a positive argument *for* arts ministry throughout the remainder of the book.

Chapter Three examines the relationship between arts ministry and God. It discusses different ways in which we encounter God through the arts, focuses on God as the source of arts ministry, and concludes with an overview of transcendence and immanence as two different lenses through which God's beauty is perceived in the world.

Chapter Four considers arts ministry and human formation. It looks at the question of human identity as it evolves throughout the life of the believer and discusses the role that art plays in this process. It goes on to examine the relationship between arts ministry and the mind, the spirit, and the body as discrete topics that, taken together, define a holistic approach to arts ministry.

Chapter Five broadens the topic of arts ministry by looking not just at its relationship to the individual, but at its relationship to the world as a whole. After considering the model of the arts minister as servant, it examines arts ministry under four headings: evangelism, community, social justice, and the cosmos.

Chapter Six focuses on human creativity as it develops in and through arts ministry. An introduction contrasting creativity and destruction is followed by a study of the imagination in Christian life and witness, a description of the meaning and significance of human creativity, and a preliminary attempt at the development of a theology of creativity.

Chapter Seven discusses the relationship between arts ministry and worship. This is treated under three headings: worship as art, artful worship, and the arts in worship.

Chapter Eight seeks to foster a provisional theology of arts ministry. In so doing, it considers three general topics: art as meaningful communication, the question of beauty, and the task of making artistic judgments in the church.

Finally, Chapter Nine considers questions related to the development of arts ministry in the church. This is divided into the broad categories of theory and practice. It includes a discussion of how to lay the foundations for arts ministry and how to grow arts ministry once these foundations have been solidified.

The actor and dancer Judith Rock writes,

> Theology and the arts are architectures of meaning, fragile structures through whose doors and windows we glimpse the mystery of our being. Hungry to hear and see some part of the truth about ourselves, we go to church, the synagogue, the theatre. Each time, we hope to be called by name, to be surprised, reminded of who we are and whose we are. The artist and the theologian share the task of inviting us across these mysterious thresholds.[6]

Consider yourself invited.

---

6. Judith Rock, quoted in Nena Bryans, *Full Circle: A Proposal to the Church for an Arts Ministry* (San Carlos, Calif.: Schuyler Institute for Worship and the Arts, 1988), p. 46.

Case Studies

Case Studies

CHAPTER ONE

An Introduction to Arts Ministry

We want to give our church songs not yet sung, images not yet imagined, words not yet forged into poems, dances not yet rehearsed in our muscles and bones, and all the other dazzling testimonies to the creative power of God at work here within the creation. We long to bring the warmth and disclosure of art to worship; to bring a joy beyond words to the celebration of the sacraments; to incarnate the pain and sorrow of the reality of crucifixion; to proclaim a promise of resurrection that evokes hope from the whole being, not merely the intellect.

Nancy Chinn, *Spaces for Spirit: Adorning the Church*

A Celebration

Amen! These stirring words are an appropriate beginning to a book about the role of the arts in ministry. Nancy Chinn echoes the sentiments of many laity, clergy, artists, and arts organizations in the church today. Christian life is integrated and whole. It involves the body, the mind, and the spirit. As the twenty-first century progresses, many Christians throughout the world are living and worshipping in full color. Rejoicing in the dance of life that springs from the artist's brush and the poet's pen, they find themselves enlivened and connected in new and unexpected ways to God, to other people, and to creation itself. The psalmist proclaims,

They shall celebrate the fame of your abundant goodness,
and shall sing aloud of your righteousness. (Ps. 145:7)

Anecdotal evidence suggests that this celebration is happening all
around us. In his excellent study entitled *All in Sync: How Music and Art
Are Revitalizing American Religion,* Robert Wuthnow writes,

> The influence of music and art on spirituality is becoming increasingly
> apparent. Church members, recognizing the spiritual implications of
> the arts, are overwhelmingly interested in them. In most churches, mu-
> sic and art play important roles in worship and in the social life of the
> congregation.[1]

Individuals and churches alike are experiencing the abundance and
richness of Christian life lived creatively in radical openness to the artistic
gifts and talents with which they have been endowed. Under these circumstances, a return to black-and-white worship or ministry is no more palatable than would be a return to watching black-and-white movies or going
back to living in the gray buildings of the Eastern Bloc under communist
rule.

Clearly something is changing — not for everyone yet, and not in the
same way in every church or for every parishioner. But a foundation has
been laid that enables the church as a whole to move forward into an increasingly exciting and variegated future, a future built on two thousand
years of tradition and yet still refreshingly new.

Throughout history, Christians have been formed and shaped by rich
theological and liturgical traditions that give meaning and significance to
their lives. One of the values that contemporary believers inherited from
their forebears is an emphasis on the left brain, on reason and rationality.
Christianity developed in a Greco-Roman culture that valued the life of
the mind. While this approach has much to offer, the traditional stress on
reason means that the creative dimension of Christian living — the right
brain — often goes unnoticed, or at the very least underappreciated.

For contemporary Christians, relying exclusively on intellect and reason as a means of relating to God and neighbor is no longer enough. Rational argument simply does not provide sufficient motivation to make peo-

---

1. Robert Wuthnow, *All in Sync: How Music and Art Are Revitalizing American Religion*
(Berkeley and Los Angeles: University of California Press, 2003), p. 134.

ple get out of bed, ignore the beauties of nature on a Sunday morning, and go to church. Parishioners cannot go through the motions anymore, sitting in the pew with a sense of boredom, their spirits heavy. It is not that they want to turn off their minds so much as they want to turn on their senses — to experience the power of sight, taste, touch, gesture, line, color, sound, texture, rhythm, and metaphor.

This "great awakening" of the senses involves a quality of exploration and experimentation in the contemporary church that extends to every nook and cranny of Christian life. "Out-of-the-box thinking," valued for so long by secular culture, has now become an important resource in worship and ministry. The genie of creativity is out of the bottle, and there is no way to put it back.

The name that is increasingly given to this movement in the church is *arts ministry*. This is a term I first encountered in Neena Bryans' seminal book *Full Circle: A Proposal to the Church for an Arts Ministry*.[2] In a sense, the book you are reading is an attempt to extend the work that Bryans began in 1988.[3]

Before trying to give this term a technical definition, it seems more appropriate to introduce an image. This is, after all, the way artists work. My image of arts ministry is really very simple. For the past seventeen years my wife and I have maintained a garden at our home, consisting primarily of perennial flowers and plants. Our garden provided me with this image and continues to nourish my thinking about arts ministry to this day.

Arts ministry reminds me of a rose. As human beings we want roses in our lives. Sometimes that is all we really need. Whether it is a single rose or an entire bouquet, there are times in life when roses have the capacity to change us, to heal us, to bring us up from the depths of our existence and remind us that despair is not all there is.

Roses inspire us visually, charm us with their scent, recall for us the thorny ambiguities of life by their touch, and serve as powerful symbols of love, beauty, and mortality. Roses are not easy to grow. They require constant attention. Preparing the soil, pruning, watering, ensuring exposure to the proper amount of sunlight, and watching for disease can keep the

2. Nena Bryans, *Full Circle: A Proposal to the Church for an Arts Ministry* (San Carlos, Calif.: Schuyler Institute for Worship and the Arts, 1988).

3. It is in Nena Bryans' book that I first encountered the Nancy Chinn quotation that heads this chapter and the Judith Rock quotation that concludes the preface.

gardener very busy. It is easy to make a mistake. But when all goes well, the results can be stunning.

Roses come in many different varieties and serve many different purposes, helping us form deep and lasting associations with the events, people, and places of our lives. They arrive at our doorstep on Valentine's Day, adorn our sanctuaries on Sunday morning, go home with our families at baptism, process down the aisle with our brides, and blanket our caskets at the end of life. "Lo, how a rose" . . . indeed! Their hold on us transcends rational categories. We are simply and completely captivated by their beauty and reminded of the God who is the source of beauty itself.

Roses serve as a wonderful metaphor for arts ministry. They point to what we can become if we open ourselves to the possibilities of life and submit to the direction of the Holy Spirit with imagination, discipline, and love. They command us to stop and cast a contemplative gaze on our surroundings, to attend to the details of life, to search for the presence of the invisible in the midst of the visible. Roses serve as markers along the way, helping us experience exhilaration and lament. They appear in many different places under many different guises. We cultivate them, and they, in turn, shape us.

In advance of having a formal definition of the term "arts ministry," roses will have to do. In fact, after I have articulated a formal definition, you will see that roses trump any definition I could formulate. They demonstrate eloquently the inherent superiority of metaphor over discursive arguments.

Arts Ministry: A Walk in the Rose Garden

> Footfalls echo in the memory
> Down the passage which we did not take
> Towards the door we never opened
> Into the rose garden.
>
> T. S. Eliot, "Burnt Norton," *Four Quartets*

If arts ministry may be compared to a rose, then there is an entire rose garden of options available to the prospective arts minister. Just as there are seemingly endless species of roses, so there are innumerable manifestations of arts ministry. It is up to the gardener to cultivate the possibilities. Here are just a few varieties to whet our appetites and give us some hint about what arts ministry might look like in different settings.

4

The Cathedral Arts Project
Omaha, Nebraska

The Cathedral Flower Festival

Flowers for a Sacred Space

The end of January in Omaha, Nebraska, can be cold and forbidding. What better time for the Cathedral Arts Project to break the gloom of winter with a pageant of color and aroma as it sponsors its annual flower festival. Some thirty florists from the surrounding area, along with the Cathedral Floral Guild, design and install floral arrangements throughout Saint Cecilia Cathedral, the magnificent Spanish Romanesque Roman Catholic cathedral that sits at the top of 40th Street overlooking a wide swath of greater Omaha. (Since their inception in 1986, flower festivals have often been based on annual themes. Examples include "Saints and Seasons," "Flowers and Quilts," and arrangements commemorating the 400th anniversary of Christopher Columbus's voyage to America.) Each year, from 10,000 to 13,000 visitors stream through the cathedral during the weekend, viewing the lovely arrangements and taking in the sounds of ongoing concerts that fill the space with music.

Origins and Mission

The Cathedral Arts Project (CAP) is a non-profit organization that was formed in 1985. Brother William Woeger, Founder and Executive Director of CAP since its inception, describes its goal:

> The core mission of CAP is to bring visual and performing arts to the setting of historic Saint Cecilia Cathedral. We are about promoting the humanities within the context of "cathedral culture." This is an exploration between spirituality and the arts, and the cathedral is the context for that dialogue.*

CAP attempts to revive the medieval notion that a cathedral is not only a place for worship but also serves as a center for the cultural life of an entire region. Thus, while CAP has strong ties to Roman Catholic tradition, it maintains a broadly ecumenical outlook.

Performing Arts

Throughout its history, CAP has sponsored a wide variety of concerts, ranging from the religious music of Dave Brubeck to the medieval music ensemble "Anonymous 4," from "Chanticleer" and the "Vienna Boys' Choir" to the "Omaha Symphony," from "Opera Omaha" to organ recitals on the Cathedral's magnificent dual-temperament Martin Pasi organ. In addition, there have been fully costumed concerts representative of San Marco in Venice in 1610, Salzburg in 1776, El Escorial in Spain, and the Cathedral de las Americas.

CAP has also sponsored jazz on the lawn and month-long jazz workshops featuring local artists. It coordinates visiting college and university choirs who enjoy the experience of singing in the exceptional acoustical surroundings of the cathedral.

*Brother William Woeger, interview with Marie Rubis Bauer, February 2004.

Visual Arts

The Sunderland Art Gallery

In recent years CAP has developed two important outlets for the presentation of visual art. The ambulatory behind the main altar in the cathedral was originally the setting for up to five annual shows of artworks by regional artists. Beginning in the year 2000, a permanent collection was assembled in this space focusing on art of the colonial period from Spain, Mexico, Bolivia, Peru, and the Philippines, selected to complement the architectural style of the cathedral.

In 2003 this gallery was augmented with the opening of the Cathedral Cultural Center. This lovely center, housed in the former cathedral high school, includes a museum that details the history of the archdiocese, and the Sunderland Gallery, which features rotating visual art shows, often with explicitly sacred themes. CAP sponsors a docent program to provide educational opportunities in conjunction with its visual arts offerings.

The offerings sponsored by CAP represent an extensive and innovative approach that integrates the arts into a beautiful cathedral center. It is a model that could easily extend to local parish churches as well.

A Visual Sermon → painting

It was time for the sermon at Crossroads Church, a small Reformed Church of America congregation in Overland Park, a suburb of Kansas City. As the preacher rose to present the sermon, so did Jean Singer, a local painter who was a member of the congregation. Jean had previously prepared a garden scene on canvas. Into that scene she painted the outline of a human figure.

As the sermon proceeded, Jean continued to work on the piece from a position just in front of the preacher. At one point in the sermon the preacher spoke about human alienation and the results of our expulsion from the Garden. As he spoke these words, Jean forcefully defaced the painting she was creating with a sweeping gesture of her arm. Pastels went flying out of her hand onto the floor, and the figure no longer looked human. At this moment a noticeable gasp went up from the congregation.

The preacher continued, noting that this was not the end of the story, reminding the congregation that God was working in and through history with a plan of redemption. Jean calmly picked up her pastels and began to work again, re-forming the images in her painting, evoking the age-old story of Christians being shaped into the image of Christ.

An Enacted Prayer → acted out prayers from congregations

The Northwestern College (Orange City, Iowa) Drama Ministry Ensemble was presenting drama at a worship service. When it came time for the prayers of the people, the ensemble's director, Jeff Barker, took prayer requests from the congregation. One woman spoke about her friend, who was seriously ill with cancer. The friend was separated from loved ones and dealing with her health problems more or less alone. The actors heard this story for the first time as the woman spoke. Jeff quickly looked for volunteers from his ensemble to play different roles in the drama. He then offered a brief introduction, ending with the words "This *is* our prayer."

Three of the actors played the role of the Triune God. Others took the parts of the sick woman, doctors, caregivers, and family and friends who were far off. Without words the ensemble proceeded to dramatize this woman's story, surrounding her with the prayers of her loved ones and the healing touch of God. They focused on the work of doctors and nurses, depicted her as she asked why this was happening, and finally, at the end of the prayer, enacted the moment when she was re-united with those she loved.

A Danced Resurrection →dancing w/ reenacting resurrection

Three dancers from the Omega Dance Company at the Cathedral of Saint John the Divine in New York took their places in the center of the choir at the chapel of Princeton Theological Seminary. Edward Lawrence, a powerfully built, graceful dancer, played the role of Jesus while dancing *Resurrection*, Larry King's stirring organ work. The work was performed during a worship service that focused on four central human relationships: the relationships we have with ourselves, with God, with other people, and with the world around us.

As the dance opened, Jesus was lifeless. Kara Miller and Janet O'Faolain, portraying the two women at the tomb, danced slowly around him. Soon a reiterated motive in the music signaled the beginning of the resurrection. This motive grew in intensity as all three dancers started to move in tandem, leaping, embodying the vitality and joy of the Easter story.

Eventually the music died down again, with fragments of the original resurrection theme continuing softly, almost in the background. Earlier, two long bands of white fabric had been attached to the top of the organ case at the front of the sanctuary. At this moment, the women gradually unraveled the material, using it to connect the top of the organ with Jesus' arms and torso. On one foot, almost weightless, Jesus began to move slowly with the material, forging a physical connection with the music, creating the appearance of a graceful, dancing butterfly.

Theology in Stone → theology + architecture

A dozen members of Trinity Lutheran Church in Lawrence, Kansas, met on Saturday morning to participate in an adult education class on the relationship between church architecture and theology. It was the second of two Saturday-morning forums on this topic. At the first session the class was presented with an overview of the history of church architecture, illustrated with slides projected on a large screen in the fellowship hall.

Today the class sat together around a long table. One of the books that served as a source for the discussion was *Theology in Stone: Church Architecture from Byzantium to Berkeley* by Richard Kieckhefer.[4] In this work, Kieckhefer outlines three models of church architecture: sacramental space, evangelical space, and communal space.

These three concepts, along with a few basic theological implications, were introduced in the first hour. After this the class took a field trip, traveling to local churches to see examples of each of the three models. Finally, they returned to their own sanctuary to look with fresh eyes and consider anew what it said to them about God and one another.

Poetry and the Spirit → Poetry + church

Peggy Rosenthal, author of *The Poets' Jesus: Representations at the End of a Millennium*[5] and other works on sacred poetry, sat on a chair in front of some twenty workshop participants. She handed out copies of a poem to everyone and invited one young woman to read it aloud:

> The year relents, and free
> Of work, I climb again
> To where the old trees wait,
> Time out of mind. I hear
> Traffic down on the road,
> Engines high overhead.
> And then a quiet comes,
> A cleft in time, silence
> Of metal moved by fire;
> The air holds little voices,
> Titmice and chickadees,
> Feeding through the treetops
> Among the new small leaves,
> Calling again to mind
> The grace of circumstance,
> Sabbath economy

4. Richard Kieckhefer, *Theology in Stone: Church Architecture from Byzantium to Berkeley* (Oxford: Oxford University Press, 2004).

5. Peggy Rosenthal, *The Poets' Jesus: Representations at the End of a Millennium* (Oxford: Oxford University Press, 2000).

In which all thought is song,
All labor is a dance.
The world is made at rest,
In ease of gravity.
I hear the ancient theme
In low world-shaping song
Sung by the falling stream.
Here where a rotting log
Had slowed the flow: a shelf
Of dark soil, level laid
Above the tumbled stone.
Roots fasten it in place.
It will be here a while;
What holds it here decays.
A richness from above,
Brought down, is held, and holds
A little while in flow.
Stem and leaf grow from it.
At cost of death, it has
A life. Thus falling founds,
Unmaking makes the world.

Wendell Berry, *A Timbered Choir* (1983)[6]

Following this, someone else read the poem; then yet another reader stepped forward. After several participants read the poem aloud, Rosenthal suggested that all the participants name one word or short phrase that struck them in some way. They were instructed not to discuss the word or phrase, simply to name it. A variety of phrases soon followed: "the grace of circumstance," "all labor is a dance," "a richness from above," "a cleft in time," "unmaking makes the world."

After a while, Rosenthal encouraged the participants to engage their intellects. She led them through an analysis of the poem, unpacking its various images and tracing together the different levels of meaning that were present. Finally, the poem was read aloud once again.

As many readers will notice, Rosenthal was applying the ancient principle of *lectio divina* (sacred reading) to this poem. In so doing, she made

6. Wendell Berry, *A Timbered Choir: The Sabbath Poems, 1979-1997* (Washington, D.C.: Counterpoint, 1998), pp. 56-57.

this venerable technique available to the participants as a source and vehicle for their own poetic, spiritual, and aesthetic journeys.

These vignettes each represent a different expression of arts ministry. Notice the sheer variety present here. The examples occur both within and outside of worship. They incorporate different art forms and relate to other ministries within the church. They engage the participants on cognitive, affective, spiritual, and physical levels. This brief listing doesn't even scratch the surface of what is possible. There are probably as many approaches to arts ministry as there are artists, churches, and organizations that practice it. In fact, one of my principal goals in writing this book is to suggest different models of arts ministry in the hope that this will inspire similar efforts and foster the development of entirely new ideas.

Arts Ministry: Defining Terms

As we begin to unpack the idea of arts ministry, it is important from the very beginning to understand the way in which I am using this term. There are three aspects of arts ministry that briefly need to be named and discussed before we can proceed: *the arts, human creativity,* and *ministry.*

Samuel Laeuchli claims that the very definition of art is precarious. He says, "There is no general consensus as to what art is."[7] Strictly speaking, this is true. Nonetheless, I believe that in the day-to-day lives of parishioners there is a generally agreed-upon starting point for our discussion. When most people think about arts ministry in the church, they turn their attention first to the fine arts (conceived, admittedly, in terms of their own experiences with them). The "fine arts" traditionally include music and dance, the visual arts and architecture, and the literary and dramatic arts, among which are poetry, literature, theatre, and film. These are perhaps the most obvious expressions of arts ministry. In her classic work *Christ and the Fine Arts,* Cynthia Pearl Maus suggests that

> The purpose of the fine arts is to help us to see, to feel, and to appreciate the world in which we live. They are concerned, not with prosaic facts, but with the poetic joy of discovering beauty wherever it may be found.

7. Samuel Laeuchli, *Religion and Art in Conflict* (Philadelphia: Fortress Press, 1980), pp. 9-10.

In the landscape, the sea, the sky, the human soul, and many another source, the fine arts discover and picture for those of us who would otherwise be inarticulate, the love, the light, the beauty of God so richly incarnate in Jesus Christ.[8]

Historically, the fine arts have been an important source of creative enrichment for both congregations and individual Christians. This presents both an opportunity and a problem. The sheer quantity and quality of sacred art is staggering. Collectively, the Christian community is the recipient of efforts by artists such as John Bunyan, Albrecht Dürer, Benjamin Britten, Robert Bresson, W. H. Auden, and Madeleine L'Engle. In addition, local churches are blessed with the ongoing work of painters, writers of icons, poets, musicians, actors, dancers, and other artists who come from their own ranks. Considered as a whole, the Judeo-Christian artistic tradition offers a virtually endless supply of creative material from which it is possible to weave a unique fabric of arts ministry in the setting of the local parish. This is the opportunity.

Many people, however, have a vision of arts ministry that is confined almost exclusively to the fine arts. They are limited in their thinking by this traditional classification and by their own associations with the word "arts." This is the problem. It should be noted that on a practical level this problem tends to function somewhat differently in Roman Catholic, Orthodox, and Protestant settings. At the risk of greatly oversimplifying these distinctions, I note that the Roman Catholic tradition has both a long-standing commitment to the fine arts and a parallel tradition of private devotional art that springs organically from the life of the people. Art in the Orthodox tradition, by contrast, is centered on the icon, church architecture, and sung choral liturgy. This artistic tradition is governed by a series of conventions (especially in regard to the visual arts) that are consistently taught and practiced down through the ages. By definition this tradition has an "orthodox" understanding of art that aligns it with the formality implicit in the categories of the traditional fine arts. Finally, Protestants tend to be influenced by the surrounding culture and its art forms. This includes both the art of popular devotion and high art, both popular culture and the classical fine arts, depending on the dominant cultural milieu at any particular place and time.

8. Cynthia Pearl Maus, *Christ and the Fine Arts* (New York: Harper & Brothers Publishers, 1938), p. 2.

[handwritten margin note: CHANGE + FLEXIBILITY IN CHURCH]

Given these diverse approaches, I believe it is important to paint with a broad brush. This suggests being open to artistic forms and styles produced outside the academic framework of Western culture. Churches, arts institutions, and individual believers will come to their own conclusions about what is most appropriate and fitting within their own setting. At this point it is enough for us to gradually become aware of the potential range of options and approach the topic of arts ministry with open minds and hearts.

Next we consider the importance of fostering human creativity in the church. This extends our task beyond specific artistic disciplines to encompass what it means to live as creative people. In her book *The Creative Call,* Janice Elsheimer reminds us that "all of us were given the gift of creativity. Some are more artistically talented in certain areas than others, but even if our talent is as seemingly mundane as keeping a beautiful yard or a lovely home, we all have simple gifts we can choose to either develop or bury."9

From the very beginning of this discussion it is critical to note that arts ministry is not just a matter for the specialists. It cannot be left to the professional artists, those who write about theology and the arts, or museum directors. It is too important for that. Arts ministry is, at its root, a fundamentally *egalitarian* pursuit. Everyone has a part in it. Everyone has a creative dimension to their lives, whether they are aware of it or not. This is not a stance in opposition to aesthetic standards or a call for anyone who wants to sing a solo on Sunday morning to be given a platform for their need for self-expression. It is simply a way of saying that no one should be intimidated by the notion of arts ministry. No one should shy away from participating because they think that they lack a creative impulse in their lives. Sometimes the flames of creativity need to be rekindled, to help us recall what we once knew implicitly, but the creative impulse lives inside of all of us simply because we are all made in the image of a Creator God.

Finally, ministry is the context within which these various artistic and creative gifts are nourished and nurtured. In his book *Creative Ministry,* Henri Nouwen shows us the scope and ultimate meaning of ministry: "Ministry is not an eight-to-five job but primarily a way of life, which is for others to see and understand so that liberation can become a possibility."10

9. Janice Elsheimer, *The Creative Call: An Artist's Response to the Way of the Spirit* (Colorado Springs: WaterBrook Press, 2001), p. 41.

10. Henri J. M. Nouwen, *Creative Ministry* (New York: Doubleday, 1978), p. xxiii.

"Ministry" is a charged word. It used to be associated primarily with Protestantism. Since the Second Vatican Council in the 1960s it has been used in the Roman Catholic tradition to similar effect. In his book *Theology of Ministry,* Thomas Franklin O'Meara provides the following definition:

> Christian ministry is the public activity of a baptized follower of Jesus Christ flowing from the Spirit's charism and an individual personality on behalf of a Christian community to witness to, serve, and realize the kingdom of God.[11]

Jesus came not to be served but to serve (Matt. 20:28). Arts ministry must similarly adopt an attitude of service if it is to be an effective witness to Jesus Christ. This is sometimes difficult for artists who assume an autonomous stance toward the world. When we adopt a servant model of ministry, we say that all we do must be directed toward the end of uplifting, supporting, or enhancing someone other than ourselves. Arts ministry accomplishes this as it uses art to glorify God, identify with the sufferings of God's people, and exhibit the real condition of God's world. In the process, arts ministry also works on the artist to engender growth and renewed commitment to core Christian values.

Being a servant means being active. Thus arts ministry involves an active public presence in the world. The art we employ in this ministry must be shared. It is not a private affair that no one sees or hears. It is true that living a creative life is the ground of arts ministry. Being is related to doing. If we live creatively, our artistic products will more likely be creative and, in turn, responsive to the hopes, needs, and dreams of the people whom we serve. Thus, taking time to be creative ourselves and encouraging the creativity of the people in our care are both critically important. But that is not enough.

11. Thomas Franklin O'Meara, *Theology of Ministry* (New York: Paulist Press, 1983), p. 142. Note that this is not a universally held definition. Harold Best writes, "To an authentic Christian, ministry is simply another word for living a life of constant worship and witness. So don't separate ministry out as if it brings special luster or mystique to the ordinary act of service, whether through your art or your daily chores" (quoted in Michael Card, *Scribbling in the Sand* [Downers Grove, Ill.: InterVarsity Press, 2002], p. 126). Joseph J. Allen writes, "*Ministry means service.* In a sense, that is *all* it means. Whether one is in the ministry of the clergy or of the laity, it means only that he is to serve as one appointed by God." See *The Ministry of the Church: Image of Pastoral Care* (Crestwood, N.Y.: St. Vladimir's Seminary Press, 1986), p. 13.

So often, Christian life consists of attending worship and praying or reading the Bible at home. A rich interior life lived in connection to the Holy Spirit provides an important foundation for all our activities in the world. Arts ministry, however, calls the artist to be both contemplative and active. Arts ministers are called to share the fruits of their inner life as it is expressed in their artwork. As O'Meara reminds us, "The public characteristic of ministry challenges any rechanneling of Christian service into liturgy alone or into inner piety."[12]

Arts ministry uncovers the hidden gifts and talents embedded in the congregation and the community and brings them to light. It reveals them for all to see and experience. It helps members of the community of faith live fuller, richer lives by exposing them to the beauty of human creativity in all its variegated forms. In so doing it forges a partnership between action and contemplation, between our private creative life and our public presence in the world.

The arts, human creativity, and *ministry* thus form the foundation for our consideration of arts ministry. The purpose of the book you are reading — and, indeed, the ultimate purpose of arts ministry — is to explore the intersections between these three terms. *Arts ministry happens when we integrate the arts, human creativity, and ministry in the context of our own individual and corporate lives, both within our own churches and in the various institutions and organizations that are dedicated to fostering the sacred arts.* Like panels of an altar triptych, they not only speak to the viewer but also carry on a holy conversation with one another. As Nouwen reminds us, in the course of this conversation, liberation occurs.

This book is meant to be a practical study of arts ministry. The intended audience is first and foremost the church, not the academic community. Nonetheless, the book will be grounded in the work done by those who have thoughtfully addressed this topic in the past, many of whom come from academia. As we will see, during the past fifty years an extraordinary number of books have been written about the intersection between Christianity and the arts. This includes theological and historical studies as well as art criticism itself. It is now time for the Christian arts community to go beyond the classroom and the library, to translate this excellent academic material into a form where it is accessible and useful for arts ministry in the local church and for individual Christian artists of all kinds. These are central goals of this study.

12. O'Meara, *Theology of Ministry,* p. 137.

More than anything, though, this book is a celebration. It celebrates the continuing creative activity of God in the church. It invites us to "taste and see the goodness of the Lord," and not only to taste, but to employ all our senses and all the creative gifts with which we are endowed in the service of a loving and gracious God. In the inspiring words of Madeleine L'Engle,

> Feel! Touch and see
> how gracious the Lord is!
> Taste, hear, smell, feel and see
> how gracious the Lord is![13]

Christianity and the Arts

As we continue to refine our thinking, we must examine the different contexts within which arts ministry functions. First of all, it is important to recognize that arts ministry is one subcategory within the larger field of Christianity and the arts. "Arts ministry" and "Christianity and the arts" are not identical terms. The success of our inquiry into arts ministry requires that we first understand something about the relationship between these two terms.

Let's start by looking at the field of Christianity and the arts. This is a broad, interdisciplinary enterprise that includes both a practical (artistic) and a theoretical (or theological) dimension. We will consider each in turn.

The Practical Dimension: The Sacred Arts

When I refer to the practical dimension, I mean the way in which the various sacred arts have developed throughout thousands of years of Judeo-Christian history. This focuses our attention on artistic products themselves. While attempting to fully recount this history is impractical here, there are several important points to be made as we consider the contribution that sacred art makes to Christianity as a whole and specifically to arts ministry.

13. Madeleine L'Engle, "After the Saturday Liturgy at Montfort," in *The Weather of the Heart* (Wheaton, Ill.: Harold Shaw, 1978). p. 89.

First, we should note the sheer diversity and depth of the artistic traditions that have emerged from the Judeo-Christian experience. Faith and art have been joined together from the very beginnings of the Judeo-Christian story. This history is revealed first of all in Scripture. We can trace the story of sacred art back to

- Bezalel (Exod. 31:1-11) and Jubal (Gen. 4:21), the "fathers" of visual art and music;
- Miriam (Exod. 15:20-21) and David (2 Sam. 6:5, 14), who danced before the Lord;
- and Jesus himself — a carpenter and a consummate storyteller.

The Bible is the locus for the creation of a wealth of sacred art. We think immediately of Solomon's temple and the extravagant, elaborate architectural and ornamental design that God planned for this space (1 Kings 5–6; 2 Chron. 3–5). Levitical musicians filled the temple with sacred music: singing and the sounds of trumpets, percussion, harps, wind and string instruments (1 Chron. 25:6-7).

As we have seen, dance was also a part of the biblical mix. Miriam's intuitive response to the parting of the Red Sea was to dance. With similar devotion and enthusiasm, David (along with some 30,000 men of Israel!) danced before the Ark of the Covenant as it was carried to Jerusalem. So, too, Saul was met with dancing as he returned from battle with the Philistines (1 Sam. 18:6).

The extraordinary wall paintings in the third-century Jewish synagogue at Dura-Europos, unearthed from the Syrian desert, suggest that the visual arts played a greater role in the life of the Jewish people than we might have expected, particularly given the extraordinary sensitivity to the problem of idolatry that is present throughout the Hebrew scriptures.

Poetry and narrative are also central features of biblical literature. In fact, it is hard to imagine anything like the Judeo-Christian tradition emerging without them. In regard to poetry, we rightfully think first of the Psalms, but we should not ignore the rest of the biblical canon. Many people are surprised when told that fully one-third of the Hebrew Bible is poetic. Likewise, narrative is present throughout the biblical canon. Narrative carries the stories of God's activity and human response: stories of faithfulness and betrayal, of love and anger, of promise and possibility. The engaging and provocative quality of the stories that Jesus tells brings alive the message he is trying to convey.

Built on this biblical base, the Judeo-Christian artistic tradition grew to become the focal point of Western culture until at least the end of the Renaissance era. Perhaps the high point of this activity was the medieval cathedral, an architectural witness to the glory and grandeur of God. Within the walls of the cathedral, medieval people experienced music, visual art, drama, poetry, literature, and dance. Here the full panoply of human life was present as human creativity and the arts were integrated into the everyday lives of the people of God. This holistic lifestyle and worldview were based on a theological foundation born of the union between the transcendental properties of truth, goodness, and beauty.[14]

While ensuing eras witnessed an ever-widening sacred-secular rift, sacred artworks of depth and genius were continually produced in great numbers even in the most secular of times. In the age of Enlightenment, we find the metaphysical poets, Christopher Wren's churches, the oratorios of Handel, and the cantatas of Bach. During the nineteenth century we encounter neo-Gothic churches, grand requiems, and the transcendental poetry of Gerard Manley Hopkins. Half a world away, the Shakers danced their way through worship, presenting us with a model that is enticing even today.

The twentieth century took this foundation and built a great edifice on it, stretching from Schoenberg's expressionism early in the century to the mysticism of Arvo Pärt and John Tavener at its conclusion, from the tapestry of Graham Sutherlund to the prophetic sculpture of Stephen De-Staebler and the richly illuminated St. John's Bible, from T. S. Eliot's *Four Quartets* to the Sabbath poems of Wendell Berry, from Le Corbusier's chapel at Ronchamps to the Rothko Chapel in Houston, from the seminal religious dances of Ruth St. Denis to the mature, incarnational movement of Carla DeSola. In seeming defiance of the prevailing spirit of secularism, the sacred arts seem to have flourished like so many oases in a vast desert.

Diversity has been the order of the day not only in the Western world but also outside the West, where art and faith form a partnership that helps explain the vitality of Christianity in the developing world. Whether it is dance in African Christian worship or visual art and lively music in Latin America, the arts have often been close to the heart and soul of the people. It could be argued that there is an even more profound connection between the arts and ministry in the non-Western world than has been achieved in the West. In many cases the history of these art forms and of

---

14. This will be discussed further in Chapter Eight.

their role in ministry has not yet been written. They are nonetheless significant and will, no doubt, be influential in the future development of Christianity and the arts in the West as well as in their own cultures.

Next we note the contributions to the Judeo-Christian artistic tradition that have been and continue to be made by "secular" artists whose work serves both the church and the synagogue. The development of a secular arena in Western culture means that people of faith are not the only ones who practice the sacred arts. There is no creedal "litmus test" for sacred artists. Ralph Vaughan Williams, one of the great composers of English cathedral music in the twentieth century, editor of several hymnals, and author of such well-known tunes as *Sine Nomine* ("For All the Saints"), was an agnostic. He is in good company. Many great artists have created works for the church without sharing its fundamental theological assumptions.

In most cases these artists were, first and foremost, products of the Western artistic and intellectual tradition. The metaphors and images that arose in sacred art from earlier centuries went a long way toward defining the scope and character of the "great conversation" that became the hallmark of the Western tradition itself. Had they ignored these creative sources arising from the Judeo-Christian tradition, secular artists would, in effect, have cut themselves off from their own artistic heritage.

Furthermore, through repeated treatment by different artists over time, individual metaphors and iconic forms created in the church achieved a symbolic resonance and depth that became irresistible to later secular artists. Even if they did not accept the intellectual framework behind this art, it was nonetheless important for secular artists to be in dialogue with the Judeo-Christian tradition, and to express their own realization of these important themes.

As we have seen, sacred artworks were produced for use *in the context of worship* and for various purposes *outside of worship*. Similarly, sacred art has been produced for use both *within* and *outside* of the church. This seems self-evident, but it is an important point to bear in mind as we develop a vision of arts ministry. Much sacred music was intended for concert use. Visual art was created for homes or galleries. Full-length theatre is rarely performed in the church and even less often in worship. Sacred poetry is frequently published in collections and often plays a greater role in the personal devotional life of individual believers than it does in the gathered community.

In fact, the purposes for which individual artworks have been employed are fluid over time, evolving with the changing perspectives of the church and the surrounding culture. Good examples of this are liturgical vessels. Chalices and patens were created for utilitarian purposes in the liturgy, only to find their way into museums where they are now admired as objects of aesthetic satisfaction and delight.

Finally, we note the important role that the arts play in illuminating the religious character of Christian culture at any given time in history. In order to comprehend fully the spiritual and theological identity of any group of Christians, it is important to know their art. The arts show us both the public posture and the inner spirituality of the people of God in ways that transcend what we learn from canonical, theological, or liturgical documents.

As Alejandro Garcia-Rivera points out, "There exists a type of theology that could be called 'living' as opposed to 'textual.' 'Living theology' has its home in symbols, images, and songs. Theology lives in the music, imagery, and cultural symbols of those who must live out that which 'textbook theology' attempts to understand."[15] Wilson Yates adds, "The arts provide a means for encountering the 'soul' of a culture and its spiritual condition. They do this not through detached reflection upon it but through an imaging, a revelation, a participation in it."[16]

What can we learn about arts ministry through this brief examination of the sacred arts? First, we need to recognize the breadth and depth of the tradition of Judeo-Christian sacred art as a potent source for artistic expression in the church today. This is particularly important in our era, when the significance of historic sacred "fine" art is so often challenged by advocates of "contemporary" worship. When all of the resources used for worship in a local congregation have been created in America during the last twenty-five years, the assembly is no longer connected to this tradition. This impoverishes their worship and their spiritual formation. It removes vital metaphors, images, and narratives that have been developed in many different cultures through repeated presentation and refinement over the course of centuries.

Second, we learn that it is artworks that matter, not the intentions or theology of the artist. Attempts to "fence the table" of Christian artistic expression by accepting only the products of theologically orthodox artists eliminates much of the great sacred art produced for the church's use.

15. Alejandro Garcia-Rivera, *A Wounded Innocence: Sketches for a Theology of Art* (Collegeville, Minn.: Liturgical Press, 2003), p. viii.
16. Wilson Yates, *The Arts in Theological Education* (Atlanta: Scholars Press, 1987), p. 107.

Third, we discover that, just as it's not a good idea to worry about the artist's theology, so it's also not a good idea to worry about the original purpose for which artworks were employed. Negative associations are, from time to time, formed regarding artworks. These change over time. An excellent example is the organ. In the early years of the Christian era, it was played in public spaces in the Roman Empire, perhaps as accompaniment to the martyrdom of Christians. Understandably, this caused unfortunate associations in the minds of early believers. Centuries later it was baptized and put to work as the chief musical instrument of the church. The church discovered that the very instrument originally associated with pagan ideals could be instrumental in bringing a sense of life and vitality to worship.

Finally, we learn that the arts give us clues about our personal identity, and the identity of our collective cultural presence in the world as we work out our salvation before God "in fear and trembling." They hold up a mirror to us, show us where we have failed, and give us an honest reading of our progress.

The Theoretical Dimension: Theological Aesthetics

Alongside this practical activity in the sacred arts there has been a parallel tradition of scholarship by theologians and artists who seek to understand the role of beauty and the arts in Christian living. Often called "theological aesthetics," this body of literature provides an intellectual foundation for the field of Christianity and the arts.[17] I am using the term "theological aesthetics" in its broadest possible context, to denote the full range of writing and thinking about the role of the arts in relation to Christian faith and practice. This writing encompasses both technical, carefully reasoned argument and passionate, emotionally charged discourse.

A classic example of theological aesthetics comes from Augustine's *Confessions,* where Augustine recounts his struggles over the question of whether or not to sing in church:

---

17. Cf. the works of T. S. Eliot, Wassily Kandinsky, Karl Barth, Paul Tillich, Hans Urs von Balthasar, John Dixon, Mircea Eliade, Nicholas Wolterstorff, H. R. Rookmaaker, John and Jane Dillenberger, James Martin, Frank Burch Brown, Edward Farley, Jeremy Begbie, and Alejandro Garcia-Rivera.

When I recall the tears I poured out on hearing the Church's songs in those first days of my recovered faith, and how even now I am not moved by the singing but by the things sung, when they are sung with clear voices and fitting modulation, I again recognize the great utility of this institution.

Thus do I waver between the danger of sensual pleasure and wholesome experience. I am inclined rather to approve the practice of singing in church. . . . However, when it so happens that I am moved more by the singing than by what is sung, I confess that I have sinned, in such wise as to deserve punishment, and at such times I should prefer not to listen to a singer.

See how I stand! Weep with me, and weep for me. . . . O Lord my God, graciously hear me, and turn your gaze upon me, and see me and have mercy on me, and heal me. For in your sight I have become a riddle to myself, and that is my infirmity.[18]

Augustine's vacillation between his attraction to beauty and his fear of the power of beauty is symptomatic of a larger dialogue in the field. It acts as a sort of verbal icon, illuminating for us the history and trajectory of the great conversation about faith and art that dates back to the very beginning of Judeo-Christian history. This conversation generates almost as many questions as there are questioners. Do we or do we not employ art in the service of faith? If so, how do we integrate art into worship, or evangelism, or catechesis? What role will art play in the lives of individual believers, nonbelievers, cultural institutions, educational institutions, and the local church? How does human creativity express the beauty of God? How are aesthetic standards derived from biblical principles? Is there a relationship between classical aesthetic standards and works of devotional art? The questions multiply over time like the various themes and voices in the exposition of a great symphonic movement. Many different authors have contributed their voices to this dialogue.[19] During the past century we have witnessed an extraordinary rise of scholarly interest in the entire field of theological aesthetics. In addition to books, this dialogue has flourished recently in periodicals, as well as in universities and seminaries that are ac-

18. Augustine, *The Confessions of St. Augustine,* trans. John K. Ryan (New York: Doubleday, 1960), pp. 261-62.

19. John Chrysostom, Augustine, John of Damascus, Pseudo-Dionysius the Areopagite, Albertus Magnus, Thomas Aquinas, Abbot Suger, Bernard of Clairvaux, Martin Luther, Ulrich Zwingli, David Hume, and Jonathan Edwards, to name but a few.

tively involved in educating students in the history, theory, and practice of the arts in a Christian context.

The relationship between theological aesthetics and artistic activity in the church is complex and varied over the course of history. Both the theory and the practice of what I am calling the field of "Christianity and the arts" are important foundations for arts ministry. It is critical that they remain in dialogue with one another. Without solid theological foundations, arts ministry runs the risk of idolatry or triviality. Without proper grounding in artistic practice, arts ministry risks a loss of standards, reliance on kitsch, and irrelevance in the wider culture. At different times and places in the past, theological aesthetics and artistic practice have alternately assumed a primary role in the larger arena of Christianity and the arts. Within this arena, the academy often privileges scholarly dialogue, whereas the local church turns its attention to the creation and reception of actual artworks. My hope here is to help forge a renewed partnership between the two by examining the different ways they intersect in the context of arts ministry.

A good analogy to help us understand the relationship between the field of "Christianity and the arts" and "arts ministry" is to think about the dual meanings of the word "church." We often think of the church as a building, a physical structure. In this metaphor I will use the church building to represent Christianity and the arts. The foundations of the building are the various principles developed in the area of theological aesthetics. The walls and ceiling of the building are the different art forms themselves: the visual arts and architecture, dance and music, the literary and dramatic arts. The metaphor extends to the entire complex, including the sanctuary (where worship occurs), the fellowship hall (where community is formed), and the education wing (where human formation is the central concern).

By contrast, arts ministry is represented by the *ecclesia,* the church, this time defined as the unique community of people who inhabit the building and carry out the artistic and creative work of the kingdom. The people who come into the building rely on the foundations. The walls and the ceiling need to be strong, and the environment needs to be beautiful in order to support their work. But they understand that ultimately it is the coordination of divine and human activity within the walls that enables ministry and worship to prosper.

Toward a Definition of Arts Ministry

It is finally time to offer a provisional definition of arts ministry:

Arts ministry is an attempt to help human beings incorporate beauty into their individual and corporate lives in an appropriate fashion. It fosters the creative and artistic dimension of the life of God's people, who are empowered by the Holy Spirit to manifest the full meaning of their creation in the image of God (the *Imago Dei*).

This definition of arts ministry guides the current study. It is more suggestive than it is exhaustive. Much like other definitions that are written early in the history of various disciplines, it is probably excessively wordy.[20] Perhaps this is necessary at first. Note that it does not refer specifically to programming or even to the church. Rather than talking about liturgical dance ensembles or drama troupes, it focuses on the broader goals of integrating creativity and beauty into human living. Let us look at the definition in greater detail.

First, it claims that arts ministry has something to do with beauty. This will cause many readers to pause momentarily. Beauty is a concept that is out of fashion today. Postmodernism has not been kind to this fundamental human concern. Over the course of many centuries, the phrase "beauty is in the eye of the beholder" has led to more popular confusion than any amount of theologizing can solve. For the present, suffice it to say that I'm talking about beauty, not prettiness. While "prettiness" may be in the eye of the beholder, to a great extent "beauty," a more objective term, is not. In Philippians 4:8, Paul says, "Finally, brothers, whatever is *true,* whatever is *noble,* whatever is *right,* whatever is *pure,* whatever is *lovely,* whatever is *ad-*

---

20. Here's an example: in the foreward to their book *Sing with Understanding: An Introduction to Christian Hymnology* (Nashville: Broadman Press, 1980), pp. 7-8, Harry Eskew and Hugh T. McElrath point out two quite different definitions of a hymn:

(a) "A Christian Hymn is a lyric poem, reverently and devotionally conceived, which is designed to be sung and which expresses the worshipper's attitude toward God or God's purposes in human life. It should be simple and metrical in form, genuinely emotional, poetic and literary in style, spiritual in quality, and in its ideas so direct and so immediately apparent as to unify a congregation while singing it." *The Hymn Society,* 1937

(b) "The hymn may be regarded as a congregational song." *The Hymn Society,* 1978

mirable — if anything is *excellent* or *praiseworthy* — think about such things."[21] It is in this sense — in the context of truth, nobility, righteousness, and excellence — that I am speaking of beauty.

The definition further suggests that we are dealing not only with beauty, but with its appropriate role in human living. Once again, I offer a charged word. What is *appropriate* to one person in one cultural or historical context may be totally *inappropriate* for someone else. I have already suggested the organ as a case in point. The reason I speak about the appropriate role of beauty is simply to acknowledge what the biblical writers have claimed all along — that there are inappropriate uses of beauty.

It is impossible to travel far down the path of theological reflection on the arts without running into the notion of idolatry. To contemplate the use of beauty, it is first of all necessary to acknowledge the potential for its misuse. Golden calves abound in the history of Christian art and in the concerns of those who write about it. It is worth noting that the Bible spends significantly more time talking about idolatry than it does talking about beauty. Evidently idolatry was an important concept for the biblical authors. The author of Deuteronomy reminds us of that:

> They made him jealous with their foreign gods
> and angered him with their detestable idols. (Deut. 32:16)[22]

Whatever we think the "appropriate" use of beauty should be, in light of this warning from Deuteronomy it appears that it would be neither safe nor smart to ignore the question.

My definition of arts ministry goes on to speak of the "creative and artistic dimension of the life of God's people." As we have already seen, all people have a calling to be creative, each in his or her unique way. Living a creative life is itself a work of art. In this sense creativity is a constant factor in our culture. It impacts us from Sunday morning through Saturday night. For some people this concern for creative living may be augmented by a more specific focus on one of the fine arts.

In any case, we should note that the creative or artistic dimension of living is not just a matter for individuals; it relates to the corporate lives we live as well. Christian communities have a collective identity. As we unite

---

21. This verse is quoted from the *New International Version* (Grand Rapids: Zondervan Bible Publishers, 1985), italics mine.

22. *New International Version.*

our individual creative gifts, we form a whole that is both greater than and somewhat different from the sum of its parts. We are reminded of Paul's image of the Christian community resembling a body whose parts all co-operate in the furtherance of its common life.

This is happening all around us. Christian communities can be alternately stagnant or vibrant. Either they live creatively into a future of promise and new possibilities, or they slowly die by remaining exactly the same week after week. We can easily confirm this through our own experience with the local church. Focusing attention on the "creative" dimension of the life of God's people is a way of saying that growth matters, both for individuals and for churches. By its very nature, growth is creative, since it involves leaving behind an older approach in favor of trying something new. This is central to the meaning of arts ministry in the church.

The foregoing definition of arts ministry also suggests that by engaging in creative, artistic living, we are realizing the full meaning of the *Imago Dei* (our creation as human being made in the image of God). At the time that human beings were fashioned by God, Genesis tells us that we were unique. We were the one example in the created order of a species made in God's image.

Throughout history there has been much debate regarding the meaning of this concept. While it probably functions on more than one level, one thing is certain: at the time in the biblical narrative that this phrase was uttered, there was very little that could be said about God other than the fact that God was the Creator of the universe. "In the beginning, God created. . . ." As such, it is not too much of a stretch to think that, whatever else it means, at a minimum our creation in the image of God made us a creative people in imitation of a Creator God.

Living creatively, living artistically, is thus one means by which believers and communities can claim the *Imago Dei* for themselves. It signifies their attempt to be the people God created them to be, growing and developing authentically and holistically, "in sync" with their calling.

Finally, note the active words in the definition: "to *help* human beings incorporate beauty into their lives . . . it *fosters* the creative and artistic dimension of the life of God's people . . . *empowered* by the Holy Spirit. . . ." "Helping," "fostering," "empowered" — these are words that denote ministry at its core. They are pastoral words.

Henri Nouwen suggests that ministry "is the unconditional commitment to be of service."[23] *Arts ministry is what happens when the church*

---

23. Nouwen, *Creative Ministry*, p. 55.

takes the resources of art and theological aesthetics from the field of Christianity and the arts and employs them unconditionally in the service of God's people. The resulting ministry develops both the arts and human creativity itself.

It is worth repeating our definition one more time:

> Arts ministry is an attempt to help human beings incorporate beauty into their individual and corporate lives in an appropriate fashion. It fosters the creative and artistic dimension of the life of God's people, who are empowered by the Holy Spirit to manifest the full meaning of their creation in the image of God (the *Imago Dei*).

Beauty, appropriateness, creativity, artistry, authenticity, and ministry itself — all are part and parcel of what it means to engage in arts ministry. They are enacted in the fullness of the relationship between arts ministry and its parent field of Christianity and the arts. As this relationship grows throughout the church, there is hope for renewed vitality and commitment, and the promise of a future that will connect with the deeply felt passions and concerns of the people of God.

Who Is Involved in Arts Ministry?

As God's people engage in arts ministry, who will be involved? Among a variety of different alternatives, I would like to focus on five categories of people or organizations that frequently participate in arts ministry. These include untrained laity, trained artists, local churches, educational and cultural institutions, and sacred arts organizations.

Laity → no training

Untrained laity represents the largest group of participants in arts ministry. These are people in the pews who have no formal training in the arts and whose chief desire is to be connected to arts ministry through their appreciation of the fine arts, or through enhancing the creativity of their own lives. It includes those who cultivate artistic interests outside the church: attending concerts or plays and visiting their local museums.

It is, unfortunately, all too easy to ignore untrained laity when we are administering arts ministries. This ends in irrelevancy when no one is present to witness a beautifully executed program. It is also possible to overemphasize the role of untrained laity, leading to programming that is too safe and devoid of any prophetic character. Perhaps the best solution is to respect laity. Involve them in the planning process. Treat them as thoughtful people who want to be addressed in their own language. Take into account their native interests. Understand that they are capable of growing. They neither need nor want to remain perpetually in a state of artistic adolescence.

Artists → ppl with experience

Artists, like laity, come in many different packages. Artists have the capacity to help us stop and pay attention to the details of the world around us. As Langdon Gilkey points out, they say to us, "Stop, look, and see what is real, and be."[24] Sometimes, as in the case of dancers, they literally *embody* a word of truth for our lives, drawing back the veil and showing us something of God's holiness and mystery. Artists have a highly developed sense of intuition that is an important resource for those seeking to develop their spiritual lives and theological insights.

It is also good to remember that artists do not have a special pipeline to God that makes them somehow inerrant. Nor do they necessarily have much theological education. This can be a problem when, as so often occurs, they are thrust into situations in the church where they are called on to exegete Scripture or interpret a theological concept.

The arts can extend the range of theology beyond the limits of discursive language. This is one of their great strengths. Many artists take this to mean that they can also stretch the orthodox theological tradition, taking it down new and previously unforeseen paths. While this is certainly true, the artistic products that are created must be judged using the same theological criteria that would be employed elsewhere in the church. Theologians often exercise creativity in their own theologizing. It is incumbent upon artists who wish to do the same to seek out theological education, so that they acquire the intellectual and theoretical resources that are needed in order to interpret the Christian tradition with insight and depth.

24. Langdon B. Gilkey, "Can Art Fill the Vacuum?" in *Art, Creativity, and the Sacred,* ed. Diane Apostolos-Cappadona (New York: Crossroad, 1989), p. 187.

Redeemer Presbyterian Church:
Valuing the Connections between Faith and Art

Two Members of an Actor's Vocation Group

It would be difficult, if not impossible, to encapsulate in these few lines the breathtaking array of arts ministries offered by Redeemer Presbyterian Church in New York City. Their statement of purpose hints at the priorities that guide this visionary ministry:

> Redeemer's Arts Ministries seek to build communities of artists where they can know and *be known* by God and one another; provide opportunities for artists to *create* in Christ-centered community, for the benefit of the church and our city; lead the Redeemer congregation to *engage* with the art of New York City and with its artists, for the purposes of cultural renewal.*

The ministry impacts artists, the Redeemer congregation, and the surrounding culture. Luann Jennings, founding program director of the ministry, notes,

*Redeemer Presbyterian Church arts ministry, http://www.faithandwork.org/arts.php.

For artists, simply creating a context in which they can connect their faith and their craft is huge. We hear from many people who came to New York City from other parts of the country (or even from other churches and church traditions in this area) that it's been life-changing for them to be able to spend time with other Christians who are artists. The fact that we create times and ways to process specific issues and problems in integrating their faith with their work from a Biblical perspective is important, but we believe that creating communities of artists who love Christ is about the most important work we do.

For the congregation, it's important that they see that Redeemer values the arts and their impact on culture. The fact that we hold art exhibitions, dance programs, music programs, classes, "field trips" to arts events, etc., clearly sends the message that Redeemer believes that active, thoughtful engagement in culture is the best way to be God's people in it. "Cultural renewal" is one of the primary components of Redeemer's vision, and the Arts and Music ministries are vital ways in which we're working out that vision.*

Over the years, Redeemer has sponsored a wide variety of artistic ministries, including vocational groups that "gather regularly for fellowship, encouragement, and teaching among others working in the same industry."† Jennings continues,

It's important to us that the congregation hear that Redeemer values the arts, so we go out of our way to insure that our events get announced regularly, and that we are very "present" on the radar of our whole congregation. We believe that just being visible changes how our congregation views the arts and their impact on culture. We also have a number of programs that the congregation may attend — dance programs, art exhibition openings, and Open Forums.‡

*Luann Jennings, e-mail to the author, 6 June 2010.
†Redeemer Presbyterian Church arts ministry, http://www.faithandwork.org/arts.php.
‡Luann Jennings, e-mail to the author, 6 June 2010.

At the end of the day, artists need to be nurtured by the church. As Dorothy Lairmore reminds us, "Artists belong in the center of the church, not on the fringe, or as an afterthought or as a 'decoration.' If we are to create a more humane world, the Kingdom of God, we need the social imagination of artists from every persuasion to tell us the Truth!"[25]

There have been far too many situations in the church, as in the wider culture, where artists have been seen as peripheral to the real work of the institution. One of the goals of arts ministry must be to see that this does not happen.

A number of years ago I had dinner in New York City with several members of the Omega Dance Company from the Cathedral of St. John the Divine. Over the years this dance company has been one of the great sacred dance ensembles in the country. The dancers all had marvelous backgrounds from top-flight schools and superb resumés. At dinner our conversation turned to the problem of how difficult it is for liturgical dancers to piece together a living in the church.

I have never forgotten that evening. It is one of the reasons that this book was written. The great shame in this situation is not simply the inability of artists to make a living in the church. The great shame lies in what the church is missing. Our collective dance of life as the body of Christ is less graceful, less vital, and less insightful than it otherwise might have been. This is truly a cause for lament. To address this problem in any meaningful way, arts ministries would do well to remember artists, to celebrate their work, to support them, and to engage them in theological dialogue for the benefit of all.

The Church

Perhaps the most obvious context for the development of arts ministry is the local church. For arts ministries to develop, congregations must first recognize that arts ministry is a legitimate concern alongside other ministries in the church, ministries like social action, worship, education, and evangelism. This means that arts ministry is a candidate for staffing and funding just like these other ministries. In many congregations this would be a radical suggestion.

Traditionally the one art form that holds pride of place in the church is

25. Dorothy Lairmore, quoted in Bryans, *Full Circle*, p. 47.

music. Architecture is also more or less universal, because communities need to meet somewhere, but in terms of staffing and budget, music has led the way. The concept of arts ministry represents a challenge to the hegemony of music in the church. It extends the church's programs beyond the music ministry to include the other fine arts and human creativity itself. This has serious implications for staffing, programming, lay participation, and administration.

Practically speaking, a single individual with vision and initiative often initiates a new arts ministry. Frequently an arts committee is assembled to assist with this project. Arts committees then go about the task of planning and administering arts programs. In the midst of this important work it is good to bear in mind the long-range goal of institutionalizing arts ministries by ensuring that they have support in the church budget. If this is accomplished, there is the possibility for continued life after the original source of the vision is no longer active in the ministry.

The other important component of arts ministry in the church is activity on the denominational level. Denominations, working either nationally or regionally, have human resources, financial support, and networking capabilities that transcend those available at the local church. If arts ministry is to realize its full potential, denominations themselves must play a constructive role in this development.

Educational and Cultural Institutions

Throughout history there have been a number of different ways in which artists have learned their craft. Until the nineteenth century, apprenticeships were the most common form of learning. Gradually, in modern times, higher education has taken over as the dominant means of artistic training, at least for professional artists. Colleges, universities, conservatories, and institutes thus perform an important function as facilitators of arts ministry by teaching new generations of artists who go on to find their place as arts ministers in churches and in the wider culture.

Recently there have been a growing number of educational institutions, including prominent seminaries, that identify arts ministry as one of the key components of their mission.[26] This serves to heighten awareness

26. Prominent examples include the Graduate Theological Union, a consortium of California seminaries, the Yale Institute of Sacred Music, United Theological Seminary in Min-

of arts ministry by bringing together scholars and practitioners in a setting where dialogue and creative ventures are encouraged and supported. It also provides emerging arts ministers with a forum in which they can test out their own ideas and get a sense of the possibilities inherent in this growing field. The fruits of this labor will be seen in the careers of the students who emerge from these institutions. Their contributions to arts ministry will provide a testimony to the quality and depth of their own education and inspire new generations of arts ministers to continue in the same path.

A natural outgrowth of educating arts ministers is to embrace the broader goal of presenting art and educating the public. An important part of education involves guided exposure to the arts and the simple appreciation that results from this experience. Museums and concert halls are good examples of institutions that perform this function, enabling the general public to have direct contact with original works of sacred art that have the capacity to change them and help them to grow.

Sacred Arts Organizations

Finally, we should note the wide variety of independent sacred arts organizations active across the country. Virtually every art form is served by one or more organizations, and many denominations have arts organizations of their own.[27]

Artists who care passionately about the sacred arts often think they are working in a vacuum. They feel isolated and without support. Sacred arts organizations connect these artists to others who share their vision and their passion. In so doing they create new collegial relationships. This is enlivening for the artists and for the organizations alike. These organizations offer opportunities for continuing education, sharing ideas and resources, and building community between artists. They are an invaluable resource for the church universal and for individual parishes that seek to form arts ministries.

I do not want to suggest that this division between the different settings in which arts ministry occurs — between what happens in church, in

---

neapolis, the Luce Center for Religion and the Arts at Wesley Seminary in Washington, D.C., and the Brehm Center at Fuller Theological Seminary.

27. See the list of organizations in the appendices.

a museum or in a local art studio — is constructed of the same stone that we encounter in the medieval cathedral. Rather, it may be seen as a fluid grouping in which individuals who share common interests experience the arts and dialogue with one another as they go back and forth between these different settings, each of which augments and enriches the others. In the course of this conversation a unique community emerges, a community of common passion and dedication.

Conclusion

Arts ministry is noteworthy for the sheer diversity of its applications. It appears under many guises and serves many purposes. Overlooking a verdant artistic landscape that offers rich opportunities to exercise our creativity, we catch a glimpse of the potential of this approach to revitalize the church.

As individual churches launch new arts ministries, a constant refrain is heard. It is the voice of artists who lament the fact that they have never been asked to use their gifts in the service of the church. Their religious and artistic insights have never been required before. In place of their lament, arts ministry offers them an opportunity to celebrate the marriage of beauty and faith. This new opportunity is exciting to them and rarely requires anyone to twist their arms.

Artists jump at the chance to enter what has often been a strange and unforgiving world. In response to the efforts of these artists, churches have experienced the power and vitality that the arts bring to worship and to ministry. They have begun to sense the meaning and importance of creativity for their congregations.

The rose remains a potent symbol for this movement. We have now cultivated the ground. Next we will look at the various challenges involved with planting and caring for this rosebush in the soil of the church.

CHAPTER TWO

Skepticism about Arts Ministry

They admire the beautiful more than they venerate the sacred.

Bernard of Clairvaux, *Apologia*

An Apologetics of Arts Ministry

In the year 754 C.E., the Byzantine emperor Constantine V convened a synod at Hieria that issued the following decree:

> Supported by the Holy Scriptures and the Fathers, we declare unanimously, in the name of the Holy Trinity, that there shall be rejected and removed and cursed out of the Christian Church every likeness which is made out of any material and color whatever by the evil art of painters. Whoever in future dares to make such a thing, or to venerate it, or set it up in a church, or in a private house, or possesses it in secret, shall, if bishop, presbyter, or deacon, be deposed; if monk or layman, be anathematized, and become liable to be tried by the secular laws as an adversary of God and an enemy of the doctrines handed down by the Fathers.[1]

1. *The Seventh Ecumenical Council,* vol. 14 in *The Nicene and Post-Nicene Fathers,* Second Series, ed. Philip Schaff and Henry Wace (Grand Rapids: Wm. B. Eerdmans, 1956), p. 545. Note that this council was called by an iconoclastic emperor and attended only by iconoclastic bishops.

It's probably safe to say that arts ministry did not play a significant role in Constantine's chapel! As anyone who studies the history of the arts in the Judeo-Christian tradition knows, Constantine's chapel is hardly an isolated example. The roll call of visual artists, dancers, actors, musicians, and writers who have been criticized by churches either officially or unofficially is long and distinguished. It includes such eminent names as Bach, Caravaggio, Michelangelo, Messiaen, Bernini, and Flannery O'Connor.

With rare exceptions, the church has not accepted artists as full partners in ministry. In fact, the treatment of the arts and of artists themselves has varied wildly depending on the time, place, and art form in question. This is still true today. Many Roman Catholic bishops have banned liturgical dance and drama. Reformed churches often continue to view visual art in a negative light. Musical instruments are not allowed in worship services sponsored by the Church of Christ. These are just a few examples. A simple listing of historic instances of the church's ambivalent or even destructive attitude toward the arts would take up much of the remainder of this book.

On a more mundane level, within most congregations there are skeptics who recite their own version of the Seven Last Words: "We've never done it that way before!" Thus tradition itself — or at least the little slice of tradition that is bound to personal memory — becomes a barrier to creativity. The arts are singled out as especially worthy targets of such attacks. This is ironic, given the church's rich and abundant artistic heritage.

Theologians are also part of the problem. As Frank Burch Brown reminds us, "Christian theologians have insisted time and again that the association of the arts with the senses, with self-indulgence, with worldly entertainment, and with things purely fictitious can render the arts either trivial or dangerous."[2]

Clearly, anyone who attempts to foster arts ministry in the contemporary church has to take these various sensibilities into account. This has very real and direct implications for arts committees, arts ministers, and artists themselves.

It is not enough for committees to sponsor arts programs in the church and assume that they will be understood, appreciated, or funded. Likewise, artists need to do more than simply produce wonderful paintings, poems, or dances. As full partners in the task of fostering arts ministry, both those who administer arts programs and the artists who produce

---

2. Frank Burch Brown, *Good Taste, Bad Taste, and Christian Taste: Aesthetics in Religious Life* (New York: Oxford University Press, 2000), p. 32.

these programs must learn how to teach and how to argue persuasively for the inclusion of their discipline in the life of the church. They must participate in the development of an *apologetics of arts ministry*. One of the goals of this book is to marshal resources from the field of theological aesthetics in order to construct just such an argument.

Arts Advocacy in the Church

Teaching and public advocacy do not come easily to many artists for the simple reason that they spend much of their time working in private. Engaging with people and institutions is difficult work. It involves skills that artists typically do not learn in the course of their education. Producing artworks of depth and quality is certainly an important part of the artist's advocacy, but this by itself is not enough. Living in the midst of an inherently skeptical church, artists and all those who consider themselves to be arts ministers need to develop the ability to teach and to serve as spokespeople for their craft and apologists for the discipline of arts ministry.

There are several different requirements incumbent upon arts advocates. First, they must be willing to invest their time, a precious commodity for creative people. This means that they may be called away from their next painting or script to read a book about Christianity and the arts or to attend a conference that will help them come to a clearer understanding of the foundations of arts ministry. It means they will have to sacrifice time in the studio or the practice room in favor of time spent in meetings and preparing classes.

Next, they must acquire at least a minimal theological background. W. David O. Taylor discusses this problem. He worked for years as the arts minister of a church in Austin, Texas. Looking back on his efforts, he notes, "I assessed my work too heavily according to whether an artistic activity produced a positive or negative experience apart from any *theological* consideration. Very few of our conversations as artists revolved around a theological understanding of the church — or of worship — or of art — or of what it means to be human — and therefore of how we ought to see art properly serving the church, apart from whether an experience felt good or bad."[3]

In reality, the language employed in the debate about arts ministry is

---

3. W. David O. Taylor, "Introduction," in *For the Beauty of the Church*, ed. W. David O. Taylor (Grand Rapids: Baker Books, 2010), p. 20.

often theological, not artistic. In an ideal world, arts advocates might attend seminary at some point during their careers. Of course, this is impractical for most people. Nonetheless, with or without an academic theological education, everyone who advocates for arts ministry must learn something about *how faith impacts art* and *how art impacts the life of faith.* Above all, arts ministers must develop a vision for the role that this vital ministry can play in the church, in the wider culture, and in the lives of individual people.

One of the interesting features of the ongoing dialogue about the arts in the contemporary church is that theology is the central issue, yet these conversations generally occur between laypeople who possess little or no theological education and clergy who have little training in theological aesthetics. It is often the task of the arts advocate to introduce a theological component into discussions about the arts and an artistic component into theological debates so that arts committees, clergy, and parishioners alike have some basis for decision-making beyond personal preference.

In their role as advocates, arts ministers need to become increasingly comfortable speaking and writing about arts ministry. This is difficult for artists, who often specialize in nonverbal forms of communication. While not everyone may be comfortable preaching a sermon about Miriam's dance or leading a seminar about beauty, there are a variety of relatively simple ways that arts ministers can advocate for their positions. Brief bulletin or newsletter notes can engage the congregation in meaningful learning. Sometimes all that is required is recognizing the need for education and sponsoring programs that feature guest speakers who can address relevant issues.

In addition to acting as educators, arts ministers must also discover the characteristic traits of the various committees with whom they work in their local parish, learn about church polity (governance), and grow in their knowledge of when to lead and when to follow. If they are wise, they will use the intuitive gifts they developed as artists to become increasingly sensitive to the leadership of the Holy Spirit in their own lives. This will help them immeasurably as they traverse the winding path between developing a pastoral ministry that is responsive to the tastes of the congregation and a prophetic ministry that challenges the congregation to move beyond its comfort zone.

Periodically, it is important to be reminded that congregations include a wide variety of different people with diverse backgrounds and differing capacities to accept change. A key element in any successful pastoral min-

**Religious Art Show
Trinity Lutheran Church, Mission, Kansas**

A vignette from the Religious Art Show

In 1982, Trinity Lutheran Church sponsored its first Religious Art Show. The pastor of the church, Roland Boehnke, was a stained-glass artist himself. As he planned this initial show, his first step was to gather several members of the church who were artists. Together they became a steering committee for

istry is to develop relationships based on trust. This is no less true of arts ministry than of any other pastoral ministry in the church.

Mabel, that nice elderly woman who sits near the aisle in the third pew on the left every Sunday, has ideas, feelings, and a personal relationship with God that are nurtured and formed by her experiences in church. She is not just a piece of clay that can be tossed aside like a chalice that doesn't turn out quite right. Those who seek to foster arts ministry must take Mabel seriously. They must make an attempt to get to know her on a personal level. It is important to create works of art that speak to her in some way. It is also important to frame an argument that means something to Mabel, not just to the professional artist or theologian.

the juried show. They decided that the principal mission of the show would be "to provide a venue where artists could display their religious works of art."* Since that time, the show has been held for two weeks each year. The original members of the steering committee remained involved for the first twenty-five years of the show's existence.

One of Boehnke's first calls was to the Director of the Kansas City Art Institute, who offered to provide summer scholarships to the Institute that could serve as prizes for the winners. Initially there was an adult division and a children's division. The steering committee contacted all the artists they knew and art teachers at the local schools. Boehnke notes, "We were somewhat surprised at the interest that many people had in entering some of their best works of art in such a show." After a few years it became necessary to eliminate the children's division because the church could not accommodate all the entries it was receiving. Throughout its history, the show has accepted, on average, between 110 and 120 pieces of art each year, depending on the size of the individual submissions.

From the outset, Trinity Lutheran Church agreed to purchase one piece of art from the show each year. Thus, in addition to the annual enrichment of cultural life in the church and the community, a more permanent church collection has developed over time that enhances the beauty of the entire facility.

*This and the subsequent quotation come from Roland Boehnke's e-mail to the author, 4 November 2010.

If an apologetics of arts ministry has any chance of success, it must be both personal and holistic. That is, it must speak to the mind as well as to the affections. It must join sound intellectual thinking, clear presentation, and warm human sensibilities. It must be an argument that can hold out hope for the future in the midst of a church in which many parishioners are opposed to arts ministry. It must seek peaceful and honorable solutions to the culture wars that have gripped the church for so long. It must enable average parishioners to think that arts ministry makes it possible to actually *improve* their experience of "church," to bring them closer to God and to one another.

A good argument should not leave anyone — parishioner, artist, or leader — feeling that they are "singing the Lords song in a foreign land." It should embrace everyone in the community: skeptics, artists, church leaders, and the people in the pews. Finally, it must be an argument that is in some sense humble. It should not claim to have all the answers to questions that have been reverberating through the halls of church history for two thousand years.

After reading these requirements, the reader might well ask whether such an argument is actually possible. Can we construct an apologetic that speaks to everyone in the church equally well? The answer, of course, is "No." We no more live in a world of perfect solutions, perfect advocates, or perfect arguments than we live in a world of perfect artworks. Furthermore, even if we did, there is no guarantee that everyone would apprehend a perfect argument with "ears that can hear." Stubbornness, sin, and the insensitivity born of living in a society that doesn't value thoughtfulness all come into play. Remember that Jesus encountered obstinate people when he was traveling through Galilee teaching. They are still around today. It didn't stop Jesus from his advocacy of the kingdom of God, and it shouldn't stop us from advocating for arts ministry, either.

Like Jeremiah, arts ministers might say, "Ah, Lord GOD! Truly I do not know how to speak, for I am only a boy." God did not readily accept Jeremiah's protestations, replying, "Do not say, 'I am only a boy'; for you shall go to all to whom I send you, and you shall speak whatever I command you. Do not be afraid of them, for I am with you to deliver you" (Jer. 1:6-8). This suggests that arts ministers should trust God and be thoughtful. They should take time to learn what they need to know. They should not demonize Christians who are opposed to one or another of the arts; rather, they should enter into dialogue with them. They should take every opportunity to educate those with whom they work both within and outside of the church.

Martin Luther once said, "Nor am I of the opinion that the gospel should destroy and blight all the arts, as some of the pseudo-religious claim. But I would like to see all the arts, especially music, used in the service of Him who gave and made them."[4] It would be nice if everyone agreed with Luther. It would certainly make arts ministry much easier. But, as we all know, this is not the case. In subsequent chapters we will examine various aspects of arts ministry that will help us construct a persuasive argument for the inclusion of all the arts in the contemporary church. Before

---

4. Martin Luther, "Preface to the Wittenberg Hymnal," in *Luther's Works*, vol. 53: *Liturgy and Hymns* (Philadelphia: Fortress Press, 1965), p. 316.

doing this, though, we need to understand some of the major objections that we will face. This is the central focus of the current chapter. It makes no sense to construct a detailed apologetic until we know the questions and objections that have been raised throughout church history.

Among many possibilities, I will highlight four issues that have generated conversation and controversy over the centuries: idolatry, stewardship, morality, and distraction. Since arts ministry engages the arts in the service of the church, each of these arguments against the use of the arts in the church also, by definition, constitutes an argument against arts ministry itself.

Arguments against Arts Ministry

Idolatry

Idolatry is the oldest and perhaps the most persistent of these concerns. As such, it will require the most extensive discussion. The issue of idolatry has been raised repeatedly in church history, notably during the Eastern iconoclastic controversy of the eighth and ninth centuries and at the time of the Protestant Reformation. It has remained an important issue for virtually every Christian tradition since the sixteenth century, each in its own way, and it clearly has significant implications for the contemporary church.

In our own thinking about idolatry, we tend to jump immediately to stories that we first learned in the Old Testament, stories about the golden calf, *asherah* poles, and altars built in the high places surrounding Israel. In fact, societies throughout history have invented a wide variety of creative ways to express idolatry. This continues today. Neil Postman points out that "television is . . . a form of graven imagery far more alluring than a golden calf."[5] Richard Foster reminds us that, when other forms of idolatry are absent, the old favorites "money, sex, and power"[6] are always lurking in the background of every civilization.

Given the wide-ranging opportunities for idolatry that exist in human

---

5. Neil Postman, *Amusing Ourselves to Death: Public Discourse in the Age of Show Business* (New York: Penguin Books, 1986), p. 123.

6. Richard Foster, *The Challenge of the Disciplined Life: Christian Reflections on Money, Sex, and Power* (New York: HarperCollins, 1985).

culture, it is interesting that the arts seem to retain their status as important symbols of idolatry. What is it about the arts that both threatens and frightens Christians even in the twenty-first century?

The Meaning of Idolatry

To answer these questions, we must first learn more about the root meanings of idolatry. In their excellent study entitled *Idolatry,* Moshe Halbertal and Avishai Margalit suggest the following definition: idolatry is "any nonabsolute value that is made absolute and demands to be the center of dedicated life."[7]

They go on to present several different Old Testament approaches to idolatry that illustrate this principle. I would like to highlight three of their categories.

IDOLATRY AS THE WORSHIP OF OTHER GODS   This is expressed powerfully by the metaphor of marriage. God's relationship to Israel (and, by extension, to the New Israel) is often defined as a covenant of marriage. Thus, it is an exclusive relationship. Seen in these terms, idolatry is likened to a betrayal of the bonds of marriage. The book of Hosea in the Old Testament is a striking narrative that illustrates this metaphor. Hosea's wife has strayed, and the prophet is called to take her back — just as Israel strays and is accepted once more into the Lord's care and protection.

Today, the worship of other gods extends to any other priority in our life that becomes absolute: money, power, leisure, material things, art, and so on. The list is practically endless.

IDOLATRY AS FALSE BELIEF   It is possible to avoid worshipping false gods in any overt sense while continuing to focus our worship on someone other than the true God of the Judeo-Christian tradition. We can have the right intentions but err in our thinking about the nature or character of God. According to Maimonides, the great medieval Jewish scholar, this is most often expressed in the form of anthropomorphisms — reducing God to human proportions.[8] Harold Best says something similar: "The Israelites were not so much turning away from God as introducing things that

---

7. Moshe Halbertal and Avishai Margalit, *Idolatry,* trans. Naomi Goldblum (Cambridge, Mass.: Harvard University Press, 1992), p. 246.

8. Halbertal and Margalit, *Idolatry,* pp. 109-110.

would represent his presence and conform him to preconceived notions. The idols would reduce God to a recognizable size and make him referentially familiar. . . ."[9]

Maimonides notes that theology requires both abstract thinking and allegory. A straightforward, literal reading of Scripture without any room for allegory results in an inadequate theology — an inadequate understanding of who God is. In this scenario God seems to be made in our image rather than the other way around.

Many Christians today have adopted an intellectual posture that is similarly devoid of allegory. We need to be reminded that it is literally impossible to form a picture of God without the use of metaphorical or allegorical thinking. Every word or phrase, every image and name we give to God is, in fact, metaphorical. Since arts ministry employs metaphor and allegory at its very core, it is easy to see the impact it can have on our developing understanding of God.

AVODAH ZARAH Finally, we encounter the biblical notion of *avodah zarah,* which literally means "strange worship." The term *Avodah zarah* is frequently used in the Hebrew scriptures in connection with idolatry. This third and final category highlights the distinction between two different forms of idolatry: (1) the strangeness of the subject of worship — worshipping a God who is not the true God, and (2) the strangeness of worship itself: worshipping the true God in something other than the right way. It introduces a new twist on the notion of idolatry — not the worship of something that is false, but the false worship of something that is true.[10] This is an extraordinary concept that has many potential ramifications for contemporary thinking about worship. How do we define the right and wrong ways to worship God? Is any sincere attempt to worship appropriate? When Psalm 51:10 says "Create in me a clean heart, O God," does that mean that if our heart is clean, we are absolved of the actual effects of our actions in the world? Perhaps our heart is clean because we don't know enough to understand what we are actually doing. It is easy to see how the questions can multiply quickly when it comes to this form of idolatry.

---

9. Harold Best, *Unceasing Worship: Biblical Perspectives on Worship and the Arts* (Downers Grove, IL.: InterVarsity Press, 2003), p. 165.

10. Halbertal and Margalit, *Idolatry,* p. 3.

Idolatry and the Arts

How does all this relate to the arts? First, it is important to note that every piece of art — even abstract art or pure design — has a subject. By this I mean that there is *at least* one reference point — one fundamental idea or concept — that generates every work of art. These reference points constitute the subject of the work. Sometimes they will be easily recognizable because of their connection to an object in the external world, and sometimes they will be more obscure to the viewer, having been generated by an idea that the artist has in his or her mind.

By expressing this subject through the medium of a particular and personal stylistic language, artists manifest a worldview in their artwork. They imaginatively construct a new world and invite us to explore it. As they do so, we need to remember that the worldview of the artwork may or may not correspond to the worldview held by the artist. Artists have the freedom to construct works that reflect views with which they might not personally be comfortable. Yet art and artists are, after all, also part of the world in which we live. While artists may or may not take as their subject a literal reference point in the real world, there is ultimately no way to separate either the artist or the artwork itself from the *milieu* of life on this planet. Their means of working may involve fantasy, but ultimately they are speaking to the real-life situation of human beings living in the here and now.

In the final analysis, even though artists may not be consciously attempting to communicate with the audience, meaningful communication nonetheless occurs almost in spite of itself. This communication suggests various insights about God, human beings, and/or the cosmos.

At this point the question of idolatry becomes part of the conversation. Since art has a subject, involves meaningful communication, and suggests a worldview, it is open to criticism in terms of idolatry. The insights emerging from a work of art may point the worshipper away from God or, at the very least, away from the true God. They may enmesh the worshipper in strange or inappropriate ways of praising the true God. Thus, the arts have the potential to distort our vision of the divine and to provide the means for idolatry.

In any consideration of idolatry, there are two fundamental issues that need to be addressed: (1) whether or not to use the arts in the church, and (2) how to use the arts in the church. Throughout its history different segments of the church have had different concerns when it comes to the arts.

For some traditions — for instance, the Reformed tradition in connection with visual art — the church has spent much time debating *whether* to use the arts. In other instances, such as Roman Catholic liturgical documents during the last century, significant time and attention have been devoted to the question of *how* to utilize the arts.

Clearly, for arts ministers in the twenty-first century, both questions are important. In some local congregations the issue of whether or not to employ liturgical dance or drama in worship remains a vital and engaging topic. They don't seem to be able to move beyond the walls they have erected to keep these art forms at bay. Other churches use all the arts on a consistent basis, but face the ever-present issue of how to do this in the most appropriate fashion. The issue of whether to use the arts is central to the concerns voiced in this chapter. Later chapters will take up the question of how to use the arts in an appropriate fashion.

At the heart of the historic issue of whether to use the arts is the generative question: *Do the arts have a legitimate role to play in the life of faith?* This is the central question in the debates over idolatry in the church's artistic mission. Originally the question of idolatry was based on the Second Commandment: "You shall not make for yourself an idol, whether in the form of anything that is in heaven above, or that is on the earth beneath, or that is in the water under the earth. You shall not bow down to them or worship them; for I the LORD your God am a jealous God" (Exod. 20:4-5a).

In reference to this commandment, Neil Postman comments, "I wondered . . . as to why the God of these people [the Israelites] would have included instructions on how they were to symbolize, or not symbolize, their experience. It is a strange injunction to include as part of an ethical system. . . ."[1] Indeed, it is amazing that the question of how to image God was at the heart and center of Israel's religious tradition. Judging from the number of references of this kind in Scripture, the question of imaging the divine was much more important than ethical issues like murder or robbery. At stake for the Hebrews was the very nature of the God whom they worshipped and the way they engaged with this God in their daily lives.

For most readers, the Second Commandment remains the ideological basis for their understanding of idolatry. The quintessential scriptural example that illustrates this concern is the story of the golden calf. As you re-

---

11. Postman, *Amusing Ourselves to Death*, p. 9.

call (possibly from Cecil B. DeMille's *The Ten Commandments*), Moses (Charlton Heston) was up on the mountain receiving the law from God. Meanwhile, the Israelites, growing impatient for his return, fashioned a golden calf. They substituted this artistic product for Yahweh and made it the object of worship. This is idolatry in its most raw and gross form.

The Bible records the consequences of this decision. First, the two tablets of the law, which served as a sign of the covenant between God and Israel, were broken. This signified the shattering of Israel's relationship with God. As if that wasn't enough, next the golden calf was ground into powder, added to the drinking water, and the idolaters were forced to ingest the product of their idolatry. Finally, the Israelites were divided into those who supported the Lord and those who supported the idol. The Levitical priests were told to go through the camp and massacre all the idolaters.

Serious consequences indeed! When we read the pages of the Old Testament, it is evident that God cares deeply about the issue of idolatry. As the author of Deuteronomy reminds us, "Cursed be anyone who makes an idol or casts an image, anything abhorrent to the Lord, the work of an artisan, and sets it up in secret" (Deut. 27:15).

The church has continued to discuss the meaning of this story throughout its history. The reformers Karlstadt and Luther engaged in a significant dialogue about idolatry during the sixteenth century.[12] Karlstadt said that the presence of images in churches is wrong. It clearly violates the Second Commandment. Since Christ came to fulfill the Commandments, it cannot be abrogated. If we ignore the commandment regarding images, then why not ignore the commandments regarding murder, lying, stealing, adultery, and so on? In fact, since image proscription is near the beginning of the Ten Commandments, is it not *more* important than some of the others? Luther replied that removing images from the church simply out of a belief that the law calls us to do this is itself an idolatrous practice. It places law above gospel and refuses to acknowledge Christ's new law of love. Furthermore, requiring the removal of images turns iconoclasm into a work, and Luther was, above all, opposed to works-based righteousness. He thought that the commandment regarding images only applied to images of God that were worshipped, not to images per se.

Significantly, chapters 25-31 and 35-40 in Exodus, which precede and

---

12. For commentary on this controversy, see John Dillenberger, *A Theology of Artistic Sensibilities: The Visual Arts and the Church* (New York: Crossroad, 1986), pp. 62-63.

follow the story of the golden calf, are concerned with fashioning the various artistic elements required for Israel's worship. In these chapters God expressly lays out a plan for the construction of beautiful objects that are to aid in Israel's worship life. Craftsmen are called together and empowered with skill in the various arts. Precious stones are cut and set into place; luxurious garments are woven for the use of the priests. Later, in the story of the building of Solomon's temple, God commands that images of cherubim and seraphim and a wide variety of other natural and abstract forms be created from gold and other precious materials.[13] The sheer presence, specificity, and size of these narratives in the Hebrew scriptures suggests that the problem may be not with images themselves, but with their treatment by human beings. God evidently approves of artworks that are constructed well and used for appropriate purposes.

The key issue turns out to be the age-old question of veneration. In the Middle Ages, veneration was offered to images for religious reasons. The idea of veneration was, in fact, one of the principal debating points in the iconoclastic controversies of the eighth and ninth centuries.[14] Would the faithful understand that the veneration offered to images was transferred to the person or idea that the images represent, or would they confuse the image with reality and practice a form of polytheism?

This continued to be an issue in the clashes over idolatry during the Protestant Reformation. Luther's contemporary, Ulrich Zwingli, describes the practice of veneration as worshippers use images in their devotional life in Zurich:

Men kneel, bow, and remove their hats before them; candles and incense are burned before them; men name them after the saints whom they represent; men kiss them; men adorn them with gold and jewels; men designate them with the appellation merciful or gracious; men seek consolation merely from touching them, or even hope to acquire remission of sins thereby.[15]

13. Francis Schaeffer points out the presence of "purple pomegranates" in this passage — something that does not exist in the natural world; he says this means that God is calling for the creation of abstract art! See *Art and the Bible* (London: Hodder & Stoughton, 1973), p. 14.

14. The question under debate was whether or not the veneration offered to an image that was intended to be transferred to the archetype would confuse the faithful into thinking that the image itself was the object of veneration.

15. Ulrich Zwingli, quoted in Margaret R. Miles, *Image as Insight: Visual Understanding in Western Christianity and Secular Culture* (Boston: Beacon Press, 1985), p. 99.

To this day, the church is wary of veneration arising from artistic products. Wilson Yates points out the problems with "any image whose 'extraordinary power' leads to idolatrous belief and action — to an identification of the image as the object of worship rather than the means of worship."[16]

Worshipping God through Matter

At the heart of the issue of idolatry is the prior question of how God can be worshipped through material things at all. Is it possible to worship God using art forms that incorporate the "stuff" of this world?

John Calvin raises this question with his famous saying, *finitum non est capax infiniti* ("the finite cannot contain the infinite").[17] He says, "Whatever holds down and confines the senses to the earth is contrary to the covenant of God; in which, inviting us to Himself, He permits us to think of nothing but what is spiritual."[18]

Idolatry, for Calvin, is a diminution of God's honor. Building on earlier patristic thinking, Calvin notes that when the material and the spiritual are intermingled (except in the case of Christ himself), a loss of glory occurs. He suggests that idolatry results from our fallen humanity and the resulting tendency we have to create our own gods. In the end, the objective reality of God is denied. We attempt to bring God down to our own level, in the process domesticating the divine, limiting God to the traits we can perceive. As a result of this thinking, both Calvin and fellow Swiss reformer Ulrich Zwingli eliminated images from the walls of their respective churches.

Today, the elimination of images from worship spaces continues apace,

---

16. Wilson Yates, *The Arts in Theological Education* (Atlanta: Scholars Press, 1987), p. 99.

17. John Calvin, quoted in Carlos M. N. Eire, *War against the Idols: The Reformation of Worship from Erasmus to Calvin* (Cambridge: Cambridge University Press, 1986), p. 197.

18. Calvin, quoted in Eire, *War against the Idols*, p. 201. By contrast, Paul Avis says, "The Christian doctrines of creation, revelation, incarnation, sanctification, and consummation . . . are all of a piece. They presuppose that mundane, worldly, created realities can become the vehicles and means of divine presence and purpose. They affirm that the material, the human, and the historical can reflect the glory of God." See *God and the Creative Imagination* (London: Routledge, 1999), p. 9. See also the *Constitution on the Sacred Liturgy* from Vatican II, which says, "There is hardly any proper use of material things which cannot thus be directed toward the sanctification of men and the praise of God" (Second Vatican Council, *Sacrosanctum Concilium*, 5:59).

as "auditoriums" (places built for auditory — hearing — experiences) are constructed instead of sanctuaries (places built for their potential to sanctify the worshipper). Auditoriums intentionally omit symbolic imagery. If and when images are employed, they are generally more literal and are either projected into the space or acted out in the course of dramatic presentations. This is done for two reasons. First, there is a sincere desire on the part of the leaders of these congregations to engage in what they consider to be effective evangelism. This means that they want to avoid offending "seekers" who might have a prior history of alienation from traditional religious imagery. The second, and often unspoken, rationale is a general lack of comfort with symbolic or metaphorical approaches to theology. It is interesting to note that neither of these reasons relates to the historic questions of idolatry (for example, veneration), even though the resulting contemporary spaces look just as plain as if they had been built in sixteenth-century Geneva.

Writing in the eighth century, John of Damascus presents the other side of this debate. He says, "I therefore confess that matter is something made by God and that it is good; you, however, if you say it is evil, either do not confess that it is from God, or make God the cause of evils."[19] Theodore the Studite adds, "If merely mental contemplation were sufficient, it would have been sufficient for Him to come to us in a merely mental way."[20] He goes on, "The mind does not remain with the materials, because it does not trust in them: that is the error of the idolators. Through the materials, rather, the mind ascends toward the prototypes: this is the faith of the orthodox."[21]

This view begins by acknowledging that God made the universe and all that is in it. It implies that we should respect and honor creation, seeing in it the handiwork of the divine. It values the particular and the capacity of the particular to point toward the infinite. Further, it notes that Christ came into the world and shared our common lot, living as a human being amid other human beings, working with the "stuff" of this world as a carpenter, and later as the one who instituted the sacrament of the Eucharist using ordinary bread and wine. In so doing, Christ showed

19. John of Damascus, *On the Divine Images*, trans. Andrew Louth (Crestwood, N.Y.: St. Vladimir's Seminary Press, 2003), p. 70.

20. Theodore the Studite, *On the Holy Icons* (Crestwood, N.Y.: St. Vladimir's Seminary Press, 1981), p. 27.

21. Theodore the Studite, *On the Holy Icons*, p. 34.

The Museum of Contemporary Religious Art, St. Louis, Missouri

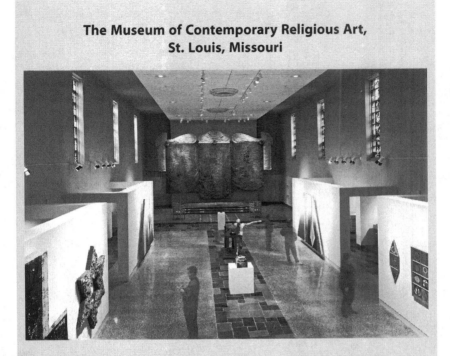

"Sanctuaries: Recovering the Holy in Contemporary Art" at the Museum of Contemporary Religious Art (MOCRA), Saint Louis University, in 1993. One can see works by (from left) Michael David, Daniel Ramirez, Michael Tracy (on the back wall), Seyed Alavi (on the pedestal), Ann McCoy (the freestanding altar), Stephen DeStaebler (the sculpture), and Bernard Maisner.

From 1985 to 1990, Fr. Terrence Dempsey was writing a doctoral dissertation at the Graduate Theological Union in Berkeley, California. The topic of his dissertation was "the re-emergence of spiritual and religious concerns in

us the value of the material world, redeeming it by his own presence and activity.

The debate will probably go on as long as the church has artists. Can the material realm be a fitting vessel to hold the divine? Even if it cannot rise to this level, can it hint at a transcendent presence in our midst? If so, arts ministry has tremendous potential; if not, we may be wasting our time.

American art of the 1980s."* This work became the basis for the development of the Museum of Contemporary Religious Art at St. Louis University.
Fr. Dempsey describes the origins and mission of the museum:

> It became clear to me that beginning in the late 1970s and continuing
> through the 1980s there was a growing interest among a large number of
> artists in creating work that explored the spiritual and religious dimen-
> sions. . . . In 1990 I joined the faculty of Saint Louis University to begin my
> duties as assistant professor of art history, as well as assistant director of
> Cupples House, a historic mansion on the Saint Louis University campus
> that served as the only museum on campus. While desiring to work at
> Cupples House, known primarily for its fine decorative art collections, I also
> had a desire to see if my doctoral research might [result in] an ongoing mu-
> seum, because I felt that something important had been going on in the
> art world at that time that was not being presented on a regular basis by
> any other museum or gallery. In 1991, I received permission to turn a large,
> 5,000-square-foot chapel on campus, formerly used by the Jesuits in train-
> ing for the priesthood and brotherhood, into the world's first interfaith mu-
> seum of contemporary art.
>
> The result of these efforts was the creation of the Museum of Contempo-
> rary Religious Art. Its mission is to be "a center for the ongoing dialogue be-
> tween contemporary artists and the world's faith traditions and to serve as a
> forum for interfaith understanding." Its ongoing exhibitions are comple-
> mented by lectures, symposia, performances, and other public presentations.

*This and subsequent quotations in this case study are taken from Fr. Terrence Dempsey's
e-mail to the author, 6 January 2011.

Art for Art's Sake

Since the eighteenth century, the struggle over the relationship between art
and God in Western culture has taken a new turn. Prior to this time, when
art was accepted as a legitimate expression of human creativity, it was seen
as a handmaid of the divine, a means of revealing the divine source of all
things to human beings. Art was in service to God. It exhibited something
of the nature and identity of the Triune God.

By contrast, in the eighteenth and nineteenth centuries, increasingly "art for art's sake" became the rallying cry of many Western artists. As a result, the arts themselves began to replace religion as a source of truth. Jacques Barzun describes the evolving relationship between these earlier religious and later secular functions of art: "This power of art to evoke the transcendent . . . is what has led artists and thinkers in the last two centuries to equate art and religion, and finally, to substitute art for religion."[22] Thus, for Barzun, art's original ability to function as a powerful theological and spiritual force in people's lives is the very trait that ultimately made it a possible surrogate (or idol) when the secular world was looking for something to take the place of God.

Nicholas Wolterstorff makes this explicit, noting that many contemporary people have substituted art for God and traded in the church bulletin for a museum catalog. This is veneration offered to sacred images for aesthetic rather than religious reasons. As Wolterstorff explains,

> Works of art become surrogate gods, taking the place of God the Creator; aesthetic contemplation takes the place of religious adoration; and the artist becomes one who in agony of creation brings forth objects in absorbed contemplation of which we experience what is of ultimate significance in human life. The artist becomes the maker of gods, we their worshippers.[23]

His response to this situation is no less telling:

> Art does not provide us with the meaning of human existence. The gospel of Jesus Christ does that. Art is not a way of rising to God. It is meant instead to be in service of God. Art is not man's glory. It displays man's

---

22. Jacques Barzun, *The Use and Abuse of Art* (Princeton: Princeton University Press, 1974), p. 26.

23. Nicholas Wolterstorff, *Art in Action: Toward a Christian Aesthetic* (Grand Rapids: Wm. B. Eerdmans, 1980), p. 50. Frank Senn adds another voice to this discussion: "The whole sacramental life of the church is predicated on the proposition that physical elements can be the means of grace by the word of God operating in, with, and through them. To ignore the potentiality of physical matter to convey the spiritual is to violate the very structure of human personality. Humanity cannot be less sensuous in its worship of God than God has been in his creation of the world and the salvation of his human creatures by means of the incarnation of his only-begotten Son." See *The Witness of the Worshipping Community: Liturgy and the Practice of Evangelism* (New York: Paulist Press, 1993), p. 32.

degradation as well as his dignity. The community of artists is not the new humanity. The community of Christ's disciples is that. Art is not man's liberating savior. Jesus Christ is that.[24]

In the church and the art world today, as was the case even in the eighteenth and nineteenth centuries, art for arts sake is by no means the only approach taken by artists or cultural institutions. There are, in fact, many different reasons that art is made and disseminated. It is made for commercial reasons; artists do, after all, have to eat. It is made for political reasons, to support one ideology over another. It is made for prurient reasons, to titillate the senses. One of the points of this discussion of idolatry is that all art (as well as anything else in the world) has the potential to be subverted and misused to become a "nonabsolute value that is made absolute and demands to be the center of dedicated life."[25]

Clearly the question of idolatry in the traditional biblical sense of the term is not going away. If arts ministry is to have a future, if it is to foster appropriate art within the church as well as to speak to the proper function of art in society, the many facets of this issue must be considered honestly, and the grounds for a response must be articulated in biblical, theological, and aesthetic terms.

Stewardship

Stewardship is the next issue over which skeptical Christians argue. In the classic expression of this argument, Bernard of Clairvaux says, "The church is radiant in its walls and destitute in its poor. It dresses its stones in gold, and it abandons its children naked. It serves the eyes of the rich at the expense of the poor."[26] Erasmus adds,

> I wonder sometimes what possible excuse there could be for those who spend so much money on building, decorating, and enriching churches that there is no limit to it. . . . What is the good of the vastly expensive

24. Wolterstorff, *Art in Action*, p. 196.
25. Halbertal and Margalit, *Idolatry*, p. 246.
26. Bernard of Clairvaux, quoted in Conrad Rudolf, *The "Things of Greater Importance": Bernard of Clairvaux's Apologia and the Medieval Attitude toward Art* (Philadelphia: University of Pennsylvania Press, 1990), p. 283.

organs. . . . What is the good of that costly musical neighbor when meanwhile our brothers and sisters, Christ's living temples, waste away from hunger and thirst.[27]

The arts have often been viewed as ornamental. They are nice, but hardly essential. As we know all too well, when a budget crisis occurs, they are often the first things to be cut.

Abbot Suger (the founder of Gothic architecture), writing in opposition to Bernard, says that if gold was used in the animal sacrifices in the temple, how much more should it be used for the celebration of the Eucharist: "One thing has always seemed preeminently fitting: that every costlier or costliest thing should serve, first and foremost, for the administration of the Holy Eucharist."[28] Where better to spend money than to adorn the worship of Christ?

Bernard and Suger both have good points to make. After hearing both their arguments, there may be yet another way to address the stewardship issue. Stewardship implies taking care that good priorities are followed when allocating our resources. Perhaps the real question is how to fund ministries that respond to social needs, while at the same time recognizing that the requirements of the human spirit are critical for contemporary people, requirements that are satisfied in part through the medium of the arts.

There are two different ways in which money becomes an issue in the development of arts ministry. The first is structural. However small, it is important to establish an institutional budget line right from the beginning of any attempt at arts ministry. This acknowledges the value of the work being done and enables future planning to occur. If an arts ministry always works ad hoc, going from program to program or worship service to worship service without any ability to plan, it will probably not last long. The second way that money intersects with arts ministry is through special projects and commissions. Throughout history, the church has taken upon itself the task of commissioning new artworks — churches, visual art, music, hymn texts, organs, and so on. Commissions often involve fundraising that is specific to the project at hand. It is incumbent upon the arts

27. Erasmus, quoted in Eire, *War against the Idols*, p. 44.

28. Abbot Suger, quoted in Erwin Panofsky, *Abbot Suger: On the Abbey Church of St.-Denis and Its Art Treasures*, trans. Erwin Panofsky (Princeton: Princeton University Press, 1946), p. 65.

minister to develop arguments that support both structural and project-specific fund-raising.

In my own experience, two arguments in particular stand out. They are both based on biblical principles. The first points to excellence as a biblical value. References to excellence, in the sense of doing things well, abound in Scripture. A cursory look at relevant passages yields examples like Exodus 31 and 35-40, which describe in detail the plans for creating the tabernacle. Here God says, "I have given skill to all the skillful, so that they may make all that I have commanded you" (Exod. 31:6). The building of Solomon's temple is chronicled in 1 Kings 6 and 7. For this project, Solomon hired Hiram of Tyre, a man who "was full of skill, intelligence, and knowledge in working bronze" (1 Kings 7:14). Psalm 33:3 enjoins us to "sing to him a new song; play skillfully on the strings, with loud shouts." In Philippians 4:8, Paul reminds us that "if there is any excellence and if there is anything worthy of praise, think about these things." Many other examples could be added to support this argument.

The second argument points to beauty as a biblical principle. Psalm 96:6 says, "Honor and majesty are before him; strength and beauty are in his sanctuary." The description of the art designed for the tabernacle is a sumptuous example of beauty fashioned for the worship of God:

> He made the curtain of blue, purple, and crimson yarns, and fine twisted linen, with cherubim skillfully worked into it. For it he made four pillars of acacia, and overlaid them with gold; their hooks were of gold, and he cast for them four bases of silver. He also made a screen for the entrance to the tent, of blue, purple, and crimson yarns, and fine twisted linen, embroidered with needlework; and its five pillars with their hooks. He overlaid their capitals and their bases with gold, but their five bases were of bronze. (Exod. 36:35-38)

This is echoed by images that come to us of the end of our journey, descriptions of the New Jerusalem:

> The wall is built of jasper, while the city is pure gold, clear as glass. The foundations of the wall of the city are adorned with every jewel; the first was jasper, the second sapphire, the third agate, the fourth emerald, the fifth onyx, the sixth cornelian, the seventh chrysolite, the eighth beryl, the ninth topaz, the tenth chrysoprase, the eleventh jacinth, the twelfth amethyst. And the twelve gates are twelve pearls, each of the gates is a

single pearl, and the street of the city is pure gold, transparent as glass. (Rev. 21:18-21)

Employing excellence and beauty as underlying biblical principles in support of arts ministry often means spending money — sometimes, as in the case a building a new sanctuary or commissioning a new organ, significant amounts of money. Not always, not in every circumstance, but the creation of artworks of true beauty and excellence will on occasion involve expensive materials that are fashioned by artists of true distinction. The history of art in the church is replete with examples of this practice, without which we would not have anything approaching our current Western artistic tradition. I say this not to discourage a small church or a fledgling ministry; I'm simply pointing to the fact that the Bible values excellence and beauty. It is reasonable to think that these values should underlie the choices we make in our own ministries. Lauren F. Winner cites one example of these values in practice:

Anglicans in South Carolina had a theology of beauty. They "understood earthly beauty to be a shadow of its divine original," and they preached sermons that "declared the beauty of holiness." In turn they built church buildings that expressed contemporary aesthetic virtues of "regularity, beauty, and stability." They filled those churches with fine crafted liturgical implements and paintings of angels that turned worshippers' imaginations to the supernatural. They worshipped in those spaces with music that, over the course of the colonial era, evolved from the simple lining out of Psalms to more elaborate church music, all of which aimed both to glorify God and to reflect God's glory.[29]

It is important to remember that the question of stewardship relates to so much more than money. The church is responsible for being stewards of the talents of its people and what Anthony Ruff calls the "treasury" of its cultural artifacts.[30] Cultural institutions like museums and concert halls are stewards of the artwork and artists they present and the artistic traditions they represent. Educational institutions that run programs for aspir-

---

29. Lauren F. Winner, "The Art Patron: Someone Who Can't Draw a Straight Line Tries to Defend Her Art-Buying Habit," in Taylor, *For the Beauty of the Church*, p. 78.

30. See Anthony Ruff, *Sacred Music and Liturgical Reform: Treasures and Transformations* (Chicago: Liturgy Training Publications, 2007).

ing artists are stewards of the students entrusted to their care, and church arts ministries are stewards of the artists who participate in their programs. These are just a few examples suggesting the full range of concerns that involve stewardship. Whether stewardship involves money or talent, time or the simple fact of stewarding the creation of a lifestyle that glorifies God, arts ministry has the joyful task and responsibility of uniting its goals and priorities with the charge given to all ministers, a charge embodied in the words of 1 Corinthians 4:1: "Think of us in this way, as servants of Christ and stewards of God's mysteries."

Morality

The next objection we will consider involves the question of morality. In a very real sense, the question of morality and the arts relates back to our earlier discussion of idolatry. The Christian scriptures expand the definition of idolatry and talk in terms of more complex behaviors than we saw earlier, behaviors that go beyond the blatant offering of worship to created images. Listen to Paul writing in Ephesians 5:5: "Be sure of this, that no fornicator or impure person, or one who is greedy (that is, an idolater), has any inheritance in the kingdom of Christ and of God." For Paul, immorality is idolatrous, impurity is idolatrous, and greed is idolatrous. These behaviors are idolatrous because they do not allow God to have the proper place of honor in human life. Thus, idolatry becomes a moral question.

Morality, as it is expressed in the New Testament, involves living in right relation to God, to other people, to creation, and to ourselves. Anything that causes these various relationships to be disordered is, by definition, an idol and leads to immorality. One specific instance of disordered relationships occurs when means and ends are confused with one another. This happens whenever people take things out of context so that they appear to be something other than what they really are. Thus a surprisingly wide range of activities becomes susceptible to the possible accusation of immorality. Misreading Scripture — taking selected passages out of context and reading meanings into them that are not supported by the wider biblical witness — could be considered a moral issue. Indeed, much evil in the world has resulted from poor exegesis of Scripture.

Means and ends are also confused when the claim is made that historic liturgical forms and patterns are somehow ultimate. The noted liturgical scholar James White takes issue with this when he says, "We do not yet have enough varieties of Christian worship."[31] Similarly, particular artists or artistic styles are sometimes held up as the incarnation of divine artistic sensibilities or celebrated as the only aesthetically approved or appropriate offerings to God. For example, some Roman Catholics have suggested that Gregorian chant and Renaissance polyphony are the only approved forms of church music. Similarly, Paul Tillich seems to think that only Expressionist art is truly religious. In truth, most churches express a narrow approach to this problem by the simple fact of their artistic choices. They admit only contemporary Christian music, only nineteenth-century paintings of Jesus, or only poetry that rhymes as acceptable expressions of religious sensibility.

Such judgments are, ultimately, moral judgments because they impact the human capacity to live in right relation with the divine and with other people in the surrounding culture. They can lead to ecclesiastical or cultural imperialism and destroy initiatives that would otherwise yield much fruit in God's kingdom.

The Morality of Artists

Another aspect of morality that relates to arts ministry is the personal morality of artists. This issue has been raised repeatedly in church history. It was particularly prevalent in the first several centuries of Christian history when the Roman theatre was in its heyday.

Cyril of Jerusalem writes,

> To this pomp of the devil belong the mania of the theatre, horse races, hunting, and all vanities of that kind. . . . Do not wish greedily to be concerned with the passions of the theatre, where obscene shows with actors are shamelessly presented. . . . All that belongs to the pomp of the devil.[32]

Art, by its very nature, requires sensitivity on the part of the artist. Emotions are frequently close to the surface. For many in the church, this has led to suspicions regarding sexual morality. The depiction of nudes in

31. James White, *A Brief History of Christian Worship* (Nashville: Abingdon Press, 1993), p. 179.

32. Cyril of Jerusalem, quoted in Johannes Quasten, *Music and Worship in Pagan and Christian Antiquity*, trans. Boniface Ramsey (Washington, D.C.: National Association of Pastoral Musicians, 1983), p. 135.

visual art, the portrayal of lascivious characters in drama, and the overt emphasis on the body in dance have all contributed to these suspicions. Many commentators note that John's Gospel admonishes us to worship the Lord in spirit and in truth. The flesh is not mentioned.

Three important points could be made here: (1) Sexuality, properly integrated into human living, is a wonderful gift from God. It is not something for which we have any reason to be ashamed. That said, it is also important to note that there *is* a distinction between sensuality and sexuality. Sensuality recognizes that human beings are sensate — they employ all five senses in their interactions with the world and with God. As people come to worship, they bring their entire being with them into the worship experience, including their senses. (2) Historically, Christian theology recognizes a holistic view of the human person. Christians are meant to develop the life of the mind, the spirit, the affections, and the body. Fragmenting this unity comes from a Platonic and Neo-Platonic view that emphasizes the value of the mind and spirit over the body. (3) Finally, the Incarnation of Christ put the divine stamp of approval on the human body. After the Incarnation, there could be no doubt anymore about the value and dignity of physical life.

This rationale is not put forward in order to suggest that insensitivity is acceptable. The need to be pastoral in ministry should take into account the sensibilities and traditions of the congregations we serve. Often, lengthy periods of education and gradual introduction to unfamiliar art forms are appropriate responses to these concerns.

It is important, once again, to recognize that artists are no different from anyone else. Just as work and ethics relate in the rest of life, so a connection should exist between artistic work and the ethical life of the artist. Jesus looks at the Pharisees and sees men who have refused to live by these standards. He says, "Woe to you, blind guides, who say, 'Whoever swears by the sanctuary is bound by nothing, but whoever swears by the gold of the sanctuary is bound by the oath.' You blind fools! For which is greater, the gold or the sanctuary that has made the gold sacred?" (Matt. 23:16-17). Jesus points out that the Pharisees have confused means with ends. They have not given the glory to God. They are clean on the outside, but rotting on the inside. They have not learned how to act justly, love mercy, and walk humbly with their God (Micah 6:8).

Does this mean that the church should value only artworks produced by women and men of high Christian calling, whose lives are examples of honesty and integrity? No. There is a distinction between the artist and the artwork. Artists, like all of us, stand in their own independent relationship with God. Artworks, whatever their source, have the capacity to speak to the human condition in ways that are either consonant or dissonant with the underlying theme of the gospel. Once they have been produced, they have a life of their own. They must be judged separately from the lives of those who produced them.

Nonetheless, the question of how artists model the gospel in their lives can be a legitimate question for the church. It is, in a sense, another instance of the issue of idolatry in a different form. The question is this: Do laity form cognitive associations between the illicit character of a particular artist and the artworks they produce such that the art itself is no longer helpful? In most cases, the answer is probably no, because the biographies of the artists are not sufficiently well-known among the laity to become a problem. However, there may be occasions when this is a valid issue. In these instances, as with other cases of association, time needs to pass, allowing the association to fade enough so as to permit the use of this art in church.

Distraction

The final source of skepticism is the capacity of art to distract. We all know people who attend a particular church solely for the purpose of experiencing the music, the lovely sanctuary, the visual art, or the beauty of the liturgy. Rather than transferring the worshipper's attention to God, art holds worshippers captive just as the siren song prevented Odysseus from continuing his journey home.

Bernard of Clairvaux offers a classic expression of this concern when he discusses the placement of fantastic imagery in the monastery:

> In the cloisters, before the eyes of the brothers while they read — what is that ridiculous monstrosity doing, an amazing kind of deformed beauty and yet a beautiful deformity? What are the filthy apes doing there? The fierce lions? The monstrous centaurs? The creatures, part man and part beast? The striped tigers? The fighting soldiers? The hunters blowing horns? You may see many bodies under one head, and conversely many heads on one body. On one side the tail of a serpent is seen on a quadruped; on the other side the head of a quadruped is on the body of a fish. Over there an animal has a horse for the front half and a goat for the

back; here a creature which is horned in front is equine behind. In short, everywhere so plentiful and astonishing a variety of contradictory forms is seen that one would rather read in the marble than in books, and spend the whole day wondering at every single one of them than in meditating on the law of God.[33]

In regard to the problem of distraction, often the real issues at stake are (1) whether an artwork fits its intended goal or purpose, and (2) whether the congregation has been adequately formed and prepared for the artwork. If the work is fitting and the congregation has been adequately formed and prepared, distraction is usually not a problem. In fact, under these circumstances, artworks typically focus *greater* attention on God, not the other way around.

The opposite of distraction is attentiveness and involvement. Different traditions achieve this in different ways. William Dyrness points out that Roman Catholics think that art, along with virtually everything else in the world, "creates an expectation of the presence of God."[34] It is potentially sacramental in its ability to point from the visible to the invisible. This hope and expectation arrest the attention of Roman Catholic believers as they encounter the artworks that surround them. Protestants, on the other hand, believe that it is ultimately their responsibility, with the assistance of the Holy Spirit, to remain attentive to God. The aesthetic environment in which they are placed can have either a positive or a negative impact on their devotional life. In any case, they are personally responsible for bringing their attention back to God when it strays. Orthodox believers, by contrast, do not rely nearly as much on their own imaginative capacities as they do on icons and the liturgy itself. They entrust the liturgy, along with its full range of artistic elements, to form them as believers.

The important point in this discussion is that, while the arts may have the capacity to distract us from God, they also very clearly have the power to focus our attention on the divine, to forge bonds with God that are enlivening and that lead us to new depths of spirituality and holiness.

---

33. Bernard of Clairvaux, in Rudolf, *The "Things of Greater Importance,"* p. 283.
34. William Dyrness, *Senses of the Soul: Art and the Visual in Christian Worship* (Eugene, Ore.: Cascade Books, 2008), p. 101.

Conclusion

Idolatry, stewardship, morality, and distraction are all issues that arts ministers face in the course of their work. Just as we are careful around the thorns on a rosebush, we should be careful how we handle these issues. Each is based on a legitimate concern that should be taken seriously by artists and arts committees alike. Nonetheless, they do not represent the whole story. That story begins with God.

CHAPTER THREE

Arts Ministry and God

Blessed is the mind which has gone beyond all beings and takes unceasing delight in the divine beauty.

Maximus the Confessor, *The Four
Hundred Chapters on Love*

Your face, Lord, has beauty, and this having is being. It is thus absolute beauty itself, which is the form that gives beauty to every form of beauty. O immeasurably lovely Face, your beauty is such that all things to which are granted to behold it are not sufficient to admire it.

Nicholas of Cusa, *On the Vision of God*

Experiencing God's Presence through the Arts:
What Is at Stake

Through the medium of the arts, the radiant, extravagant, abundant, and sublime presence of God is experienced both in the church and in the wider world. The well-known American monk Thomas Merton had one such experience while traveling in Rome. Prior to making a personal commitment to the Catholic faith, before any thought of monasticism entered his mind, Merton journeyed to Rome as a young man. He described what happened to him there in these words:

Things were going on as they usually did with me. But after about a week — I don't know how it began — I found myself looking into churches rather than into ruined temples. Perhaps it was the frescoes on the wall of an old chapel . . . that first aroused my interest in another and a far different Rome. From there it was an easy step to Sts. Cosmas and Damian, across the Forum, with a great mosaic, in the apse, of Christ coming in judgment in a dark blue sky, with a suggestion of fire in the small clouds beneath His feet. The effect of this discovery was tremendous. After all the vapid, boring, semi-pornographic statuary of the Empire, what a thing it was to come upon the genius of an art full of spiritual vitality and earnestness and power — an art that was tremendously serious and alive and eloquent and urgent in all that it had to say. And it was without pretentiousness, without fakery, and had nothing theatrical about it. Its solemnity was made all the more astounding by its simplicity — and by the obscurity of the places where it lay hid, and by its subservience to higher ends, architectural, liturgical, and spiritual ends which I could not even begin to understand, but which I could not avoid guessing, since the nature of the mosaics themselves and their position and everything about them proclaimed it aloud.

I was fascinated by those Byzantine mosaics. . . . And thus, without knowing anything about it, I became a pilgrim.[1]

Art can do that. Art has the capacity to awaken us to the presence of the divine. It opens our eyes to the reality of God's communion with us and, in so doing, functions as a sacramental presence in our midst.

Nonetheless, despite periodic transcendent encounters like Merton's, most of the time artists and arts ministers do not live on the mountaintop. They cannot remain long in booths they erect to behold the transfigured Jesus. Rather, they must come down and work on the day-to-day projects that are set before them.

Tasks in the everyday life of the church tend to revolve around practical matters. In the case of arts ministry, this means the focus is often on programming. Time is spent planning the next liturgy or special event, running administrative errands, communicating with artists, and publicizing programs. This is important work. Without these efforts, arts ministries would likely wither and die. There is, however, an attendant problem

---

1. Thomas Merton, *The Seven Storey Mountain* (New York: Harcourt, Brace, 1948), p. 108.

associated with this pragmatic focus. Often there is so much practical work to do that programs come to define the arts minister's identity. This runs the risk of missing the larger picture. It is unfortunate, because if arts ministers are here for the sole purpose of running programs, then they don't really have very much at stake.

To define what is at stake, it is important to view arts ministry in its larger context. As was indicated earlier, all human beings are involved in four primary relationships: their relationship with God (which they may or may not acknowledge), their relationship with themselves, their relationship with other people, and their relationship with creation itself. These are the different contexts within which arts ministry "lives, moves, and has its being." This is a way of saying that what is really involved in the development of arts ministry is our understanding of God, the formation of our true identity as human beings created in the image of God, and our interaction with the world around us. There can be no more important stakes than these.

Woven through our discussion of the relationship between arts ministry and God is the implication that God initiates an encounter with humanity that is subsequently embodied in one or more of the arts. The starting point for arts ministry is thus with God, not with institutions or even with artists themselves. God reveals something of the divine purpose and character to humanity and inhabits our world in ways that enable material reality to function as a point of contact with the transcendent reality that is above and beyond our everyday existence. This is the foundation for the revelatory and sacramental dimension of the arts. Wilson Yates expands on these ideas:

> To speak of *the revelatory and sacramental power of art* is to speak of its power to reveal reality, to make visible the invisible, to express meaning through its own symbolic forms and images while inviting participation in that reality through participation in the work itself. . . . art becomes a window that opens up to us that which lies beneath the surface — that which we do not perceive in the everyday routine of life — and invites us to experience at greater depth the reality of what is or the possibility of what might be . . . the work of art has the power to point to both the Divine and human activity, to the possibility of grace and wholeness and to the reality of our brokenness and need for rebirth. And it takes on a sacramental significance insofar as persons who participate in the work

as symbolic form are not only pointed to those realities but experience them.[2]

Langdon Gilkey adds, "Art opens up the truth hidden behind and within the ordinary; it provides a new entrance into reality and pushes us through that entrance. It leads us to what is really there and really going on. Far from subjective, it pierces the opaque subjectivity, the *not* seeing, of conventional life, of conventional viewing, and discloses reality."[3]

From the standpoint of the arts minister, there are several important points to be made here. In the course of salvation history, God discloses something of the character and mystery of the divine presence to human beings. We respond to this revelation in a number of distinctive ways, among which is our artistry. On the one hand, the art that is produced is ultimately a result of the gifts and inspiration first provided by God. On the other hand, this same art also serves as a medium through which God's presence is unveiled before our very eyes. It shows us that which was hidden both in the divine and the human sphere. Revelation is not mechanical or under the control of the artist. It is a gift of grace.

At the opening of John Calvin's monumental *Institutes of the Christian Religion,* Calvin says that we need only two kinds of knowledge: the knowledge of God and the knowledge of ourselves.[4] *The Constitution on the Sacred Liturgy* from the Second Vatican Council also affirms two central priorities: the glorification of God and the sanctification of human beings.[5] These foundational Protestant and Roman Catholic documents call us to deepen our relationship to God and to ourselves. In this spirit, we begin here by examining how we encounter God through the arts. We will follow this by looking at the beauty of God and conclude the chapter by examining transcendence and immanence as two primary lenses through which God's beauty is perceived in the world. Subsequent chapters will extend this focus to the relationship between arts

---

2. Wilson Yates, *The Arts in Theological Education* (Atlanta: Scholars Press, 1987), pp. 119-20.

3. Langdon B. Gilkey, "Can Art Fill the Vacuum?" in *Art, Creativity, and the Sacred,* ed. Diane Apostolos-Cappadona (New York: Crossroad, 1989), pp. 189-90.

4. John Calvin, *Institutes of the Christian Religion,* trans. Henry Beveridge (Grand Rapids: Wm. B. Eerdmans, 1983), p. 37.

5. *Constitution on the Sacred Liturgy,* in *The Documents of Vatican II,* ed. Walter M. Abbott, trans. Joseph Gallagher (New York: Guild Press, 1966), p. 142.

ministry and human identity and between arts ministry and the world around us.

Encountering God through the Arts

What are the categories that define how we encounter God using the arts? Do we meet God exclusively through "religious" works of art? Do some artistic experiences offer a more profound experience of the divine than others? Different authors approach these questions in different ways.

Olivier Messiaen

The twentieth-century composer Olivier Messiaen answered these questions in relation to music. Much of his response is also explicitly directed to other art forms, so he serves as a good source for our consideration. Messiaen identified three different types of music: "liturgical," "religious," and what he called "sound-color/dazzlement." These three categories exist in a hierarchical relationship, with liturgical at the bottom and sound-color/dazzlement at the top.[6]

Messiaen talks about liturgical music in relation to plainsong (chant). This is music created and performed specifically for use in worship. It is designed to fulfill a specific function, to play a particular role in the overall design and operation of the liturgy. Plainsong may, in fact, function as religious art or serve to dazzle as well, but this is not its primary mission. The primary mission of plainsong (and, I would add, of other art forms like architectural space and the art of reading Scripture) is to facilitate the proper and effective enactment of the liturgy.

Messiaen defines his second category, religious art, as "all art which attempts to express the divine mystery." It is evident that what he really has in mind is art with religious subject matter. As examples he cites Chartres Cathedral and works by Fra Angelico, Tintoretto, Chagall, and Bach, among others. Messiaen's "religious art" is what many might call "sacred art," art whose content centers on some sacred theme. It is found

6. For Messiaen's argument, see the talk he presented on 4 December 1977 at the Conférence de Notre Dame, quoted in Almut Rössler, *Contributions to the Spiritual World of Olivier Messiaen;* translation of the Conférence de Notre Dame by Timothy J. Tikker (Duisburg, Germany: Giles & Francke Verlag, 1984), pp. 57-66.

both within and outside of public worship. Ultimately, Messiaen believes that religious art "touches on the material, as well as spiritual, and finally finds God everywhere."

Messiaen labels his third category "sound-color/dazzlement." For the purposes of this discussion, Messiaen's final category might be called *contemplative* art, wording that he frequently uses in describing it. He says that this most sublime category will "give us dazzlement. Touching at once our noblest senses, hearing and vision, it shakes our sensibilities into motion, pushes us to go beyond concepts, to approach that which is higher than reason and intuition, that is to say FAITH." Contemplative art will "establish contact . . . with another reality: a rapport so powerful that it can transform our most hidden 'me,' the deepest, the most intimate, and dissolve us in a most high Truth which we could never hope to attain."[7] This is art at the height of its ability to be a vehicle for the transcendent God, art that works to transform human beings into the people they were created to be.

Messiaen's hierarchical approach reminds us that art can be a means of helping human beings ascend to ultimate union with God (the *anagogic* process), a notion that dates back to the early centuries of the church.[8] Messiaen believed that liturgical art, art with sacred themes, and art that helps in the process of bringing us to ultimate union with God represent three different ways that art reveals the divine. His development of these three categories is undoubtedly a result of the strong Roman Catholic commitment he maintained throughout his adult life.

Paul Tillich

Paul Tillich, one of the most important theologians from any era to address the relationship between art and faith, offers another perspective on the question of how human beings encounter God through the arts. He says that artists have the capacity to plumb the "depth dimension" (or "depth-content") of life, not simply depicting the surface qualities of exis-

---

7. Messiaen, quoted in Rössler, *Contributions to the Spiritual World of Olivier Messiaen*, pp. 65, 63.

8. See Robert O'Connell, *Art and the Christian Intelligence in St. Augustine* (Cambridge, Mass.: Harvard University Press, 1978), p. 16, where the author relates Augustine's position in these words: "The soul can arise to contemplation of the Supreme Beauty itself, dispense finally with all sense-intermediaries, and gaze directly upon the Archetypal Beauty of which the sense world is only pale imitation."

tence but struggling with the fundamental issues of what it means to be human: alienation, the fragmentation of social and cultural systems, grief, suffering, and anxiety. "Religious art" is art that expresses this "depth dimension," art that explores these basic issues through sound and color, light, texture, narrative, movement, and metaphor.[9]

Tillich defines religion as our "ultimate concern." He is not attempting to demonstrate how art presents a Christian response to the problems of human life; rather, he is suggesting that art should take ultimate questions seriously in order to be considered in any sense "religious." Thus, for Tillich, in contrast to Messiaen, religious art is primarily defined by the questions it asks rather than by its subject matter. Jeremy Begbie sums up Tillich's understanding of religious art by saying that, for Tillich, "Art is truly religious not when it employs traditional religious subjects, still less when it seeks a photographic depiction of reality, but when it probes beneath the surface of the finite and brings to light the ultimate meaning which lies beyond and beneath all things."[10]

Tillich goes on to suggest that religious styles of art are styles that depict this *depth dimension* of human living.[11] Art that is strictly for enjoyment, that doesn't have any of the angst or pathos associated with the human struggle to live in the midst of an often unkind and unforgiving world, does not, by Tillich's definition, possess religious style. He then proceeds to outline four possible relationships between religious style and religious content:[12]

> *Non-religious style, non-religious content:* Here the artwork is not using technical devices suggestive of pathos, and it is not explicitly about a religious subject. An example of this combination might be the Broadway musical *Oklahoma.*

9. Tillich says, "Only those styles which, in the portrayal of every object, give perceptibility to the depth-dimension of things can serve religious art in the narrower sense." See "On the Theology of Fine Art and Architecture," in *Paul Tillich on Art and Architecture,* ed. John Dillenberger (New York: Crossroad, 1987), p. 208.

10. Jeremy S. Begbie, *Voicing Creation's Praise: Towards a Theology of the Arts* (Edinburgh: T&T Clark, 1991), p. 20.

11. Tillich's "depth dimension" bears some resemblance to Noam Chomsky's and Heinrich Shenker's notions of the differences between surface and deep structure; see John Sloboda, *The Musical Mind: The Cognitive Psychology of Music* (Oxford: Clarendon Press, 1985), p. 13.

12. Paul Tillich, "Existentialist Aspects of Modern Art," in Dillenberger, *Paul Tillich on Art and Architecture,* pp. 93-99.

Non-religious style, religious content: Art in this category is pleasing and readily enjoyable. Although it isn't done in a religious style, it focuses on a religious subject. A good example is the Precious Moments Chapel outside Carthage, Missouri, a chapel that includes fifty-three sweetly painted murals by Samuel Butcher.[13]

Religious style, non-religious content: For Tillich, artworks in this category emerge from some form of historic or contemporary expressionism. Since most modern art has no formal religious subject matter, it isn't surprising that many of the works in this category come from the twentieth century. Tillich's classic example is *Guernica,* Picasso's famous painting depicting the horrors of war as it was visited on a small Spanish town in the 1930s. Here, even though the subject is war rather than God or faith, the work is deemed religious because its style expresses the "depth dimension" by showing the fundamental issues that arise from the grotesque dismemberment of human beings and human society as a result of a bombing assault from Italy and Germany, the first instance of "saturation bombing" in modern warfare.

Religious style, religious content: This is the most tenuous category for Tillich. He wonders aloud whether or not it is still possible for contemporary artists to create works that have both religious subject matter and also say something authentic about the human predicament. In the end, he admits that it is a legitimate option. Roualt's *Head of Christ,* or Benjamin Britten's *War Requiem,* written for the re-dedication of Coventry Cathedral in 1962, are both excellent examples of this category.

From the perspective of arts ministry, Tillich's four categories raise many interesting questions. As the church encounters God through the arts, what style or styles are most appropriate? Do *Guernica,* the Bartok string quartets, or the plays of Sartre have a place in the church as examples of "religious style"? Likewise, should the church be suspicious of many of the artistic products that have achieved widespread popularity: nineteenth-century hymnody like "In the Garden," paintings of Jesus by Warner Sallman that adorn so many church social halls, and contemporary worship that is always happy?

13. For an extended discussion of this chapel, see Frank Burch Brown, *Good Taste, Bad Taste, and Christian Taste: Aesthetics in Religious Life* (New York: Oxford University Press, 2000), p. 138.

It should be noted that Tillich has been widely criticized for his views, particularly his focus on expressionist art. His work grows out of a Protestant background and expresses his German intellectual upbringing. Perhaps Tillich's most important contribution to arts ministry is his notion of the "depth dimension." This idea can act as an important counterbalance to the shallowness of so much modern religious art, conceived and executed under the withering influence of twenty-first-century American culture.

Implications for Arts Ministry

What is true religious art? As human beings encounter God through the arts, is this encounter ultimately a function of liturgical purpose, subject matter, and contemplative possibility (as Messiaen claims), or style and depth (as Tillich says), or some combination of the two? As we have seen, a variety of different answers are possible. The practical implications of this answer for arts ministry are not to be taken lightly.

The parish that has the courage to answer the question in light of Tillich's categories will engage in a prophetic ministry that asks its people to think and feel in a deep and profound way. It will freely appropriate works that possess no overtly religious subject matter as long as they exhibit a "depth dimension" that deals with questions of ultimacy. This will challenge and alter the individual and communal life of the congregation in unforeseen ways.

The church that designs a ministry based on Messiaen's response to the question will likewise be changed, risking its future and identity on the uncontrollable movement of the Holy Spirit. It will begin with functional liturgical art, employ overtly religious art (defined by its subject matter) both within and outside of worship, and gradually open itself up to the mysterious and ubiquitous power of God as it engages the contemplative dimension of its religious life through art. The consequences of this decision will be just as significant and perhaps even more unpredictable.

Frank Burch Brown adds to our understanding of the practical ways in which human beings encounter God through the arts by suggesting a number of ways in and through which this encounter takes place.[14]

(1) First, he suggests that we can *dedicate* a work of art to God. Here the work of art becomes an offering whose purpose is to pay tribute to

14. Brown, *Good Taste, Bad Taste, and Christian Taste*, p. 117.

God, to show the artist's love and adoration for God in a tangible way, employing all the creative gifts given to the artist by God.

(2) Next Brown speaks of *addressing* an artwork to God. A poem, for instance, might become a personal prayer that expresses the heartfelt petitions of the poet in dialogue with the living God.

(3) We can also *consecrate* a work of art to God. Brown uses the example of a church building that we set apart for God's purposes.

(4) In addition, we can *receive or perceive* an artwork as coming from God. This means that those who appreciate art can acknowledge that the work has something to say to them about God's love, mercy, or judgment, that it points to transcendence itself, that it has the capacity to open their eyes and ears to the divine presence that is all around them.

(5) Finally, we can enjoy beauty alongside God. We can *share* our aesthetic appreciation for a beautiful artwork with God, rejoicing together with God in the same aesthetic qualities that originally emanate from the divine beauty itself.

Brown presents us with a compelling list. We can *dedicate* an artwork to God, *address* an artwork to God, *consecrate* an artwork to God, *receive or perceive* an artwork as coming from God, and *share* our appreciation of an artwork with God. As we explore these different possibilities, we experience the range of blessings that God intends for us through the medium of human creativity and the arts.

Recognizing that God Is Beautiful

In 1970 Ray Stevens wrote a popular song entitled "Everything Is Beautiful." The text of the chorus goes like this:

Everything is beautiful in its own way,
Like a starry summer night or a snow-covered winter's day.
Everybody's beautiful in their own way.
Under God's heaven the world's gonna find a way.[15]

I don't know if Ray Stevens had the medieval aesthetic tradition in mind when he penned those words, but he certainly expressed a central notion in

15. Ray Stevens, "Everything Is Beautiful," from the album *Everything Is Beautiful*, Barnaby Label (New York: CBS Records, 1970).

that tradition: everything is beautiful in its own way. The ultimate reason that everything is beautiful is that God is beautiful.[16] The question that we have dealt with earlier in the chapter — how we relate to God through the arts — is profoundly dependent on the nature of the God with whom we are in relationship. God's beauty is the key element in uncovering a rationale for artistic activity in the church and thus for speaking thoughtfully to this question. There are a number of scriptural passages that discuss the beauty of God. Among the most famous is Psalm 27:4: "One thing I asked of the LORD, that will I seek after: to live in the house of the LORD all the days of my life, to behold the beauty of the LORD, and to inquire in his temple."

All the beauty in the cosmos flows from this divine beauty, whether in nature or in the artifacts of human creativity. Roman Catholic and Orthodox traditions have been particularly sensitive to this idea. Saint Bonaventure says, "If the Likeness of God alone contains in the highest degree the notion of beauty, delight, and wholesomeness, and if it is united in truth and intimacy and in a fullness that fulfills every capacity, it is obvious that in God alone there is primordial and true delight and that in all of our delights we are led to seek this delight."[17]

Protestants have taken a somewhat different approach. Rather than extrapolating the beauty of nature or human artistry from divine beauty, Protestants tend to focus on God's gift of beauty to humankind and the gracious gift of artistic skill and inspiration to individuals in the church. This comes from a strong Pauline tradition that speaks of the church as the body of Christ and notes the diverse roles played by different part of the body. Certainly both the Roman Catholic/Orthodox and the Protestant ideas are important and not at all mutually exclusive.

Trinitarian Beauty

The beauty of God is seen in a variety of different ways in the different members of the Trinity.[18] The Father, the Son, and the Holy Spirit are all characterized by beauty. This extends not only to their individual actions

16. For an excellent discussion of the biblical language and categories of beauty and goodness, see William Dyrness, *Visual Faith: Art, Theology, and Worship in Dialogue* (Grand Rapids: Baker Book House, 2001), pp. 69-85.

17. Bonaventure, *The Soul's Journey into God*, quoted in *Theological Aesthetics: A Reader*, ed. Gesa Elsbeth Thiessen (Grand Rapids: Wm. B. Eerdmans, 2004), p. 86.

18. See Dyrness, *Visual Faith*, p. 92.

Artist-in-Residence Tanya Butler at Christ Church of Hamilton and Wenham, Massachusetts

***Triumphal Entry* by Tanya Butler**

"What does it mean to be an artist-in-residence at a church?" Tanya Butler was asked that question when she first agreed to become artist-in-residence at Christ Church (Episcopal) of Hamilton and Wenham, Massachusetts, from January through May of 2005.*

*For a full account of this residency, including the passages quoted here, see Tanya Butler, "Painting by Faith: An Artist Residency," Episcopal Church in the Visual Arts, http://ecva.org, 2005.

Clearly the answer to this question varies depending upon the artist and the church in question. For Butler, it began with conversations with members of the liturgical arts cooperative — visual artists, writers, poets, and dancers at Christ Church — and with the rector. One project that eventually emerged from these conversations was a series of eight icons created to reinforce the Gospel texts on consecutive Sundays beginning two weeks prior to Easter. Because of the church's support of ministries in a variety of foreign countries, these icons were painted in folk styles representative of native cultures, including an icon that Butler describes as "an African Christ displaying wounds carved into the surface and gilded. Painted on the image was an invitation to 'Feel my hands and side and believe.'" Apparently this admonition was taken literally, as many worshippers felt the wounds the first Sunday that the icon was displayed, partially wearing away the gold leaf. Another example is the *Triumphal Entry* pictured here. In addition to painting scenes from Gospel narratives, Butler also produced four acrylic paintings that hung behind the altar throughout the Easter season.

Following her experience, Butler had some important ideas to share with prospective artists-in-residence:

(1) A one-year time frame is optimal for the proper development of this type of residency.
(2) A written proposal and the full support of the clergy are essential.
(3) It is helpful to work alongside established ministries of the church and respond to their vision and concerns rather than simply presenting the artist's personal expression. This is part of what it means to work in community, allowing the residency to be the "work of the people" rather than just the work of the solitary artist. Working in community involves "stages of approval, organization, funding, and fabrication" that makes it different from the ordinary creative process employed by professional artists. Thus it requires patience on the part of the artist, patience that is amply rewarded as the work of the artist is integrated into the life of the parish.
(4) The residency should be as visible as possible, including such elements as "a public commissioning, organized prayer support, written and verbal announcements during Sunday services, bulletin inserts and articles in the church newsletter." In addition, it is helpful if sermons include periodic references to the visual imagery produced during the residency.

or roles in salvation history, but also to their inter-relations and to the very concept of a Trinitarian God. Jeremy Begbie suggests a comparison with music:

> Returning to the Trinity, instead of a chord, might it not be more appropriate to speak of God's life as three-part polyphony [three individual melodies that dialogue with one another], even, as . . . a fugue? This more readily suggests response, giving and receiving, particularity of the persons, even the joy of God. . . . Music can remind us that all the extraordinary patterns of interpenetration and resonance we have been tracing — within God, between the Son and the humanity of Jesus, and between us and God — all participate in a magnificent multi-voiced symphony of salvation, with the Incarnate Son at its heart. It is a symphony which has embraced dissonance at its most destructive, including the arresting dissonances and silence of Good Friday and Holy Saturday. Like all music, it is played out *for us* objectively, in time, in the incarnate life of Christ, and now, by virtue of the Spirit, it is played *in* and *through* us, catching us up in its manifold resonances. . . .[19]

The Father is the Supreme Artist and the author of creation. A popular biblical metaphor for this is to see God as a potter. Isaiah 64:8 reads:

> Yet, O LORD, you are our Father;
> we are the clay, and you are our potter;
> we are all the work of your hand.

Ambrose suggests a slightly different twist on the image: "Man has been depicted by the Lord God, his artist. He is fortunate in having a craftsman and a painter of distinction. He should not erase that painting, one that is the product of truth. . . ."[20]

The Son also has a distinctive role to play as an expression of the beauty of God. The Son is the perfect image (or icon) of the Father. Hebrews 1:3 reads, "He is the reflection of God's glory and the exact imprint of God's very being, and he sustains all things by his powerful word."

---

19. Jeremy Begbie, ed., *Beholding the Glory: Incarnation through the Arts* (Grand Rapids: Baker Book House, 2001), p. 150.

20. Ambrose, *Hexameron: Six Days of Creation: Six,* quoted in Thiessen, *Theological Aesthetics,* p. 41.

Even as the church acknowledges this relationship, it also proclaims that, in his role as the suffering servant, Christ is "not comely." There is nothing outwardly beautiful about Christ on the cross. In accepting his role, however, Christ opens up for us a new vision of beauty, redefining it as the beauty of the whole person.[21] Augustine penned these moving words about Christ:

> He then is "beautiful" in heaven, beautiful on earth; beautiful in the womb; beautiful in His parents' hands: beautiful in His miracles; beautiful under the scourge: beautiful when inviting to life; beautiful also when not regarding death: beautiful in "laying down His life"; beautiful in "taking it again": beautiful on the Cross; beautiful in the Sepulchre; beautiful in Heaven.[22]

Just as the Father and Son have important roles to play so, too, does the Spirit. The Holy Spirit has three different functions in relation to the beauty of God: (1) communicating God's beauty to the world, (2) inspiring the beauty of human artistry, and (3) an eschatological function that gives human beings "an anticipation of the restored and transfigured world which will be the fullness of God's kingdom."[23]

Beauty is not restricted to the Godhead. It flows freely to human beings as a gracious gift from God. There are strong biblical foundations that illustrate the divine connection to human artistry. We have referred previously to the critically important story of Bezalel. Here is the actual text:

> See, I have called by name Bezalel son of Uri son of Hur, of the tribe of Judah: and I have filled him with the spirit of God, with ability, intelligence, and knowledge in every kind of craft, to devise artistic designs, to work in gold, silver, and bronze, in cutting stones for setting, and in carving wood, in every kind of craft. (Exod. 31:2-5)

21. See Richard Viladesau, *The Beauty of the Cross: The Passion of Christ in Theology and the Arts, from the Catacombs to the Eve of the Renaissance* (Oxford: Oxford University Press, 2006), p. 9. The author notes that "in fact, the crucifixion frequently has been portrayed in a beautiful manner; the cross frequently is a beautiful object." The beauty of the cross will "expand our notion of the beauty of God, and indeed of 'beauty' itself."

22. Augustine, *Expositions on the Book of Psalms*, in Thiessen, *Theological Aesthetics*, p. 31.

23. Patrick Sherry, *Spirit and Beauty: An Introduction to Theological Aesthetics* (Oxford: Clarendon Press, 1992), p. 176. This work is a particularly fine study of the relationship between the Holy Spirit and aesthetics.

This is one of the most significant biblical passages about artistry. It connects wisdom, understanding, and knowledge to artistry. Furthermore, it says that Bezalel was "filled with the spirit of God." In fact, the name "Bezalel" means "in the very shadow of God." He is not only the first artist depicted in the Bible, but the first person who is said to be filled with the spirit of God.

Foundations

The beauty that originates in the Trinitarian God and flows from the throne of grace to human artists suggests in turn three foundational doctrines that undergird arts ministry in the church: creation, incarnation, and eschatology. While each doctrine implies a role for all three members of the Trinity, it is helpful to think of each person of the Trinity as having a special relationship to one of the doctrines.

Creation occurs through the agency of the Word. It directly involves the Spirit, who hovers over the waters. Nonetheless, as we see clearly on the ceiling of the Sistine Chapel, it is the Father who is most often associated with this doctrine.

The doctrine of creation provides the most fundamental biblical and theological foundation for the work of the artist. God creates. The material world — light and darkness, water, earth, and all that this implies — provides the starting point for the artistic enterprise. Without creation there would be no art.

It is not only the fact of creation that matters; it is the process. Order emerges from chaos, form from formlessness. Even that which appears to be random is part of a larger architecture that we are only now beginning to grasp. God values structures, patterns, and connections between things. These patterns yield meaningful relationships to those who study them. The amazing variety of the universe is somehow circumscribed by a fundamental unity. This suggests an aesthetic orientation to creation. Clearly, God values not only the form of the universe, but the resulting beauty. Note that the trees that God placed in the Garden had several different purposes. They were there to provide food and sustenance, but they were also "pleasing to the eye."

Finally, God commissions human beings to be creative. In the beginning, God models for human beings what it means to create. As we are fashioned in the image of a Creator God, the divine imprimatur is stamped on the fact and possibility of human creativity. Subsequently, God sends us out into the world and tells us to go and do likewise.

Incarnation, like creation, involves all three members of the Trinity, but here Christ is the focal point. The Incarnation has three important implications in terms of arts ministry. First, the Incarnation is God's affirmation of the *stuff* of this world. It is God's way of saying once and for all that matter and physicality are good. Thus Christian artists, who employ sound, texture, line, gesture, and color in their work, rejoice at the implications of the Incarnation. By means of this doctrine, their work is baptized; they are empowered to embody the truth in forms that captivate the eye and excite the imagination.

The second implication of the Incarnation is that God communicates with us in a language we can understand. So, too, the artist must establish a common language between his or her work and the intended audience, whether in or out of the church. This is an important point to keep in mind as we become involved in arts ministry. It is a warning not to get too far ahead of our congregations.

The third point to take from the Incarnation is that Christ was born in a manger to a father who was a carpenter and a mother who was a simple peasant girl. This authenticates our fundamental humanity. It says to the cook or the woodworker that what they do is important, that it is not only the highly trained artist, the genius in our midst, who matters. Ordinary human beings and the products they create are also receptacles of God's gracious charism.

Finally, our third doctrine, eschatology (the final goal and end of the divine economy), would not be possible without the full participation of the Father and the Son, but this doctrine has a special relationship to the Spirit, who guides us along the path on our journey to the promised kingdom. The Spirit fills us to overflowing with the divine presence as we take our seats at the banquet that has been prepared for us since the beginning of time.

Arts ministry gives us a foretaste of this heavenly banquet, hinting at the riches and ultimate beauty of life in the kingdom of God. It sets us on a road to the future, a road whose scenery is worth noting as we traverse its paths. This scenery includes the beauty of a single rose, the variegated landscapes of our remarkable planet, and the wonder of human creativity — beauty that we find alluring, that attracts us to God's truth and goodness and inspires us on our own journey through this world to the world beyond.

The Center for Liturgical Art, Concordia University, Seward, Nebraska

Amelia Hillman, a student at the Center for Liturgical Art, lays tiles for a mosaic intended for Alleluia Lutheran Church in Naperville, Illinois.

Educational institutions across the country provide a wide assortment of programs and projects that could be identified as arts ministry. One example is the work of the Center for Liturgical Art at Concordia University in Seward, Nebraska.

The Center for Liturgical Art opened its doors in 2004 as the result of an endowment given for the purpose of supporting the production of contemporary visual art in Lutheran churches. Mark Anschutz, the Center's managing artist, writes,

> As we have grown over the past years, we have expanded to working with other Christian denominations. We have also made art for schools, a retirement community, and a hospital. In addition, we have the added goal of educating Christians about the merits of strong and thoughtful liturgical art. By conducting workshops, sponsoring art exhibits, and supporting artistic mission work, we show people how to understand and embrace Christian art in their own faith lives.*

The Center consults with thirty to forty churches each year. They employ three full-time staff members: a managing artist, an operations manager, and a consulting artist. In addition, student workers take part in larger projects.

*Mark Anschutz, e-mail to the author, 9 November 2010.

Exploring Transcendence and Immanence

The question of how to structure an arts ministry relates directly to the manner in which God's beauty is perceived in the world. One approach to the question of perception is to acknowledge the fact that human beings tend to relate to God in one of two ways: either we focus on divine transcendence, the greatness of God, the sense in which God is bigger, more wonderful, and more powerful than we can ever imagine, or we encounter the immanent God dwelling within our hearts, closer to us than we are to ourselves.

This dialogue between divine transcendence and immanence defines quite different approaches to arts ministry, including everything from artistic expression right down to the details of programming. It would be hard to overestimate its importance.

Immanence and transcendence are, of course, not mutually exclusive. God is at all times and everywhere both transcendent and immanent. Furthermore, the same aesthetic experience can suggest the immanent dimension of God's presence for one person and God's transcendence for someone else. Immanence and transcendence are really two different emphases that from time to time have become more or less significant in different religious and artistic traditions. They relate to each other as a sort of divine counterpoint, one voice now taking the subject, then followed by the other. As in any contrapuntal piece of music, our attention should be focused not on the melody itself, but on the interplay between the two voices. We begin by looking at transcendence.

Transcendence

Biblical history is an appropriate place to begin our search for images of transcendence:

> In the beginning when God created the heavens and the earth, the earth was a formless void and darkness covered the face of the deep, while a wind from God swept over the face of the waters. (Gen. 1:1-2)

God appeared on the stage of history as the omniscient, mysterious, and all-powerful God, the very personification and image of transcendence. It is no accident that these initial passages in the book of Genesis have inspired countless composers, painters, and authors to reveal in art that which discursive speech alone could never hope to express: the mystery and wonder of creation.

The limitless divine power and authority over the affairs of this world, expressed so often as existing at the right hand of God, are encountered again and again in the pages of the Hebrew scriptures. The prototypical example of this in Israel's life is the story of God's deliverance of Israel from bondage in Egypt:

> The LORD drove the sea back by a strong east wind all night, and turned the sea into dry land; and the waters were divided. The Israelites went into the sea on dry ground, the waters forming a wall for them on their right and on their left. (Exod. 14:21b-22)

The Second Commandment, which stands at the juncture of religious and artistic life in ancient Israel, attempts to safeguard divine transcendence by explicitly forbidding any attempt to make images that could act as substitutes for God. This assures that worship is offered only to the transcendent God, rather than to merely contingent objects or images.

With the building of the temple in Jerusalem, we encounter what may be the quintessential Old Testament paradigm of transcendence, especially as it relates to the arts. God laid out an architectural blueprint for Solomon and specified the materials and the iconographic plan for the temple. Everything was to be splendid and awe-inspiring. The very best materials were employed: cedars from Lebanon, gold, olivewood, carvings of cherubim and palm trees. Hiram, one of the finest professional craftsmen in the entire region, was put to work fashioning bronze capitals and the great molten sea.

When the temple was finally completed, the glory of the Lord filled it and drove out all the priests. The connection between glory and transcendence was thus firmly established in the biblical corpus. This association continued throughout church history, with no more fervent advocate than the twentieth-century theologian and aesthetician Hans Urs von Balthasar.[24]

It is not accidental that when the temple was dedicated, formal worship began in Israel, and the Levitical choir was established to provide musical leadership. Formal worship, coupled with the idea of offering our finest artistic achievements to God, is a concept that is totally compatible with expressing divine transcendence.

Images of transcendence also begin to appear as one important element in Christian art. Various stories about miracles, often involving themes of deliverance, were painted on the walls of the catacombs. The raising of Lazarus and the story of Jonah and the whale were standard themes in early Christian iconography. This makes perfect sense in a church that was under persecution, where the very lives of its members were at risk.

It is interesting to note that the primary concerns the church fathers expressed about the arts were not condemnations of music, drama, or dance per se. Instead, their primary concern had to do with the connections between the arts and worldliness, the connection between actors or

---

24. Hans Urs von Balthasar, *The Glory of the Lord: A Theological Aesthetics* (Edinburgh: T&T Clark, 1982). In regard to the earlier tradition, see, in particular, the works of Pseudo-Dionysius the Areopagite.

singers and the lascivious ways of the flesh, between the eternal or transcendent God and the idols of the pagan temples.[25] They did not want to soil and demean God's transcendence by associating God with the base, immoral properties of the world, which they often connected with artists.

The architectural setting for medieval worship in both East and West was another powerful expression of transcendence. Even today, in the midst of this age of secularism, it is the rare person who can stand in the crossing at Notre Dame Cathedral in Paris without feeling an overwhelming sense of awe and majesty. This experience shows that divine power and transcendence are manifest not only in the intentional activity of God in salvation history, but also in the physical objects and holy places associated with the divine presence.

The connection between transcendence and place is embodied in the concept of sacred space. One of the ways a space becomes sacred is by serving as the setting where human beings experience the presence of God in unique and powerful ways. Liturgical legislation has often been enacted as a means of reinforcing the transcendent character of Christian worship that occurs in these worship spaces. Calls for solemnity and for the appropriate sanctity in both the arts and in liturgy itself form a constant refrain in church history.

Eastern Christians became particularly sensitive to transcendence as the heirs of a mystical, contemplative tradition whose full expression came to flower in the painting and veneration of icons, practiced in both private devotion and orthodox liturgy. The icon functioned as a way to safeguard divine transcendence. Rather than painting a realistic portrait of a saint or of Christ, the painter attempted to paint in such a way that the inner essence, or holiness, of the subject came through in the image. This was done precisely to avoid idolatry, to avoid confusing the painting itself with the reality of divine transcendence that lay behind it.

The image of Christ Pantocrator (Christ as judge) that adorns the ceiling of countless Byzantine domes is perhaps the most well-known symbol of transcendence. There is an other-worldly, timeless quality to this art that is akin to the mystical properties of both Western and Eastern chant. In relative terms, the East has focused more on divine transcendence than

---

25. See, for example, James McKinnon, *Music in Early Christian Literature* (Cambridge: Cambridge University Press, 1987), or Johannes Quasten, *Music and Worship in Pagan and Christian Antiquity,* trans. Boniface Ramsey (Washington, D.C.: National Association of Pastoral Musicians, 1983).

the West, creating a tradition where the immutable, unchanging quality of God acts as a conserving force, maintaining the traditional forms and structures of Eastern art and liturgy.

It would be easy to continue with many more examples, but the point has been made. Transcendence was a central feature of the Judeo-Christian artistic and liturgical tradition from the very beginning. In the twenty-first century, when the church seems to have lost its sense of awe and wonder as it makes its way through the maze of consumerism and instant gratification engendered by American culture, it is critically important that arts ministry attempts to recover transcendence as an integral element in the artistic life of both individuals and congregations.

Immanence

The second term in our theo-aesthetic equation is immanence. We turn once again to Genesis for the beginning of the story. The close connection we find in Genesis between divine immanence and divine transcendence is nothing short of astonishing. The transcendent God who appeared as a mysterious presence hovering over the face of the waters in the creation story is also the immanent God who walks with Adam in the garden in the cool of the day.

As the Hebrew scriptures continue, the transcendent God, the God who created the people of Israel, becomes more and more the God of individuals as well. The story of Yahweh's appearance to Elijah is a magnificent metaphor of the Old Testament dialogue between transcendence and immanence:

> He said, "Go out and stand on the mountain before the LORD, for the LORD is about to pass by." Now there was a great wind, so strong that it was splitting mountains and breaking rocks in pieces before the LORD, but the LORD was not in the wind; and after the wind an earthquake, but the LORD was not in the earthquake; and after the earthquake a fire, but the LORD was not in the fire; and after the fire a sound of sheer silence. (1 Kings 19:11-12)

This silence — sometimes translated as "a gentle whisper" — is a symbol of divine immanence. It reveals the Lord speaking personally and intimately with individuals. The heart, as opposed to the mind, is the primary vehicle for this communication.

The priestly tradition, so often associated with divine transcendence in Jewish worship, was joined on the pages of the Old Testament by the prophetic tradition. Artists, take note! Along with Amos, the prophetic tradition proclaims,

> I hate, I despise your festivals, and I take no delight in your solemn assemblies. . . . Take away from me the noise of your songs; I will not listen to the melody of your harps. But let justice roll down like waters, and righteousness like an ever-flowing stream. (Amos 5:21, 23-24)

Expressions of transcendence are of little importance if God is not present in the personal ethical decisions that shape and order human society. Thus, corporate, liturgical images of transcendence were set side by side with personal, sometimes pietistic images of immanence. The singing of the Levitical choir in the temple was balanced by the image of David as a pastoral musician calming the spirit of Saul.

The New Testament is the location of perhaps the most important image of immanence in human history: the Incarnation itself, *Dieu parmi nous,* "God among us." Just as the heavenly host appeared in the temple revealing the glory of God to Isaiah (Isa. 6), so now divine immanence is disclosed to simple shepherds by the singing of angels (Luke 2:8-15).

Immanence was also important in early Christian art. Here Christ was often pictured as a young shepherd boy. Immanence appears again and again in the art of popular devotional material and in folk traditions down through the ages. We see it in the intimacy of a sonnet, the naïveté of a Raphael Madonna and Child, and the gentle, repetitive cadences of a Taizé chorus.

Once again, we could continue with further examples, but the basic argument has been made.

The Ongoing Dialogue between Transcendence and Immanence

Early Christianity, as befits a religion whose liturgical practice was located in homes, tended to emphasize immanence. As imperial Rome took the reins of the faith, hierarchy became more and more important. This was expressed in ecclesiology, architecture, music, art, literature, and, eventually, in the social structure of feudal society. An appreciation for transcendence naturally accompanied these developments.

From the Renaissance to the present age, there has been an ongoing and passionate dialogue between transcendence and immanence. In the West, the Renaissance was the occasion for rethinking the concept of transcendence. In a very real sense, the divine power and authority that served as central features of transcendence were relocated within human beings. In this new worldview, transcendence was considered an expression of the human ability to reach beyond (to *transcend*) the limitations imposed by nature. Transcendence became incarnate not in Christ but in humanity itself. David no longer represented the reign of God over the Israelites in the person of a simple shepherd boy, as depicted in the catacombs. Instead, David became a symbol of the transcendence of the people over God, as seen in the Greek-god-like statue executed by Michelangelo. In the process, human beings, rather than God, became "the measure of all things."

At the time of the Protestant Reformation, divine immanence received new life. Probably the ultimate expression of the doctrine of immanence in the Protestant Reformation was Luther's theology. Luther refused to grant any distinction between sacred and secular culture; the entire world had the potential to reveal the divine presence. This opened the door to immanence.

Luther's thinking has particular significance for artists. For those who emphasize immanence, God is seen in and through artworks themselves. There is no better illustration of this shift than the art of Rembrandt and his colleagues working in northern Europe during the seventeenth century.

Rembrandt, though not a trained theologian himself, had a unique and compelling sensitivity to the Protestant emphasis on grace. He practiced a style of painting that conveyed the meaning of grace. As William Halewood points out, in Rembrandt's *Self-Portrait as the Apostle Paul,* the Apostle "gazes out directly at the viewer, with all of life's humbling experiences shared between them."[26] The portrait is bathed in a quiet, intimate light (using the so-called *chiaroscuro* technique) originating from within the figures themselves. This light is suggestive of the warmth, love, and forgiveness that is so characteristic of both Rembrandt's and Luther's vision of grace.

The rise of the Enlightenment in the seventeenth century signaled a turn in the direction of immanence, as the major thinkers of the day es-

---

26. William H. Halewood, *Six Subjects of Reformation Art: A Preface to Rembrandt* (Toronto: University of Toronto Press, 1982), p. 120.

chewed the notion of divine authority over the affairs of the world. None-theless, this was still the age of Baroque architecture, including buildings like the Church of the Gesù in Rome that attempted to overwhelm wor-shippers and catch them up into heaven.

In fact, the seventeenth through the nineteenth century is a difficult period of time to characterize because of the many conflicting tendencies that arise as the remnants of the old medieval worldview struggle with newer Enlightenment ideology. The resulting world of sacred art includes the Sanctus of Bach's Mass in B Minor and the pietistic hymn texts of both Joachim Neander (1650-1680) and Johann Freylinghausen (1670-1739); the neo-Gothic architecture of the ecclesiological movement, which stands (sometimes literally) alongside the intimacy of Victorian gardens; and the wild, awesome, almost mystical nature images from one of Gustave Courbet's paintings that offer a striking contrast to the simplicity of a Shaker meetinghouse.

Notwithstanding works like *La Sagrada Familia,* Antonio Gaudi's magnificent, unfinished church in Barcelona, or Benjamin Britten's *War Requiem,* the past century has witnessed a decided turn toward imma-nence. Due, in part, to the pervasive influence of popular culture, coupled with the breakdown of formal relationships in American society, most arts ministries today are located within ecclesiastical cultures that privilege im-manence over transcendence.

For arts ministers in the twenty-first century, it is vital that both tran-scendence and immanence have a place at the artistic table. Transcendence and immanence are irreplaceable expressions of the divine that must be given voice if an arts ministry is to be balanced and whole. Both are needed if art is to present an honest and authentic picture of the biblical God to the believer and to the world. In the context of the current ecclesi-astical milieu, this means that we need additional emphasis on an aesthetic of transcendence. The church is not in danger of losing its concern for a personal relationship with God, but the recognition of awe and wonder as intrinsic parts of that relationship is very much at risk.

Conclusion

All arts ministry begins and ends with God. As arts ministry is in dialogue with God, it has the potential to speak the truth to human beings. As it speaks the truth in beauty, it speaks a message that comes from a beautiful

God and expresses something of the divine character that is, at the same time, both immanent and transcendent. As it employs the language and categories of the depth dimension, it speaks meaningfully to our culture and our relationships with one another. Ultimately, that message is addressed to all of us and helps us become the people God created us to be.

CHAPTER FOUR

Arts Ministry and Human Formation

And I am sure that today also art, the work of art, can be a great symbol, a great meaningful sign: a symbol which, despite all difficulties and opposition, can remind human beings of the great heritage of the past, the future still to be won, of the meaning, value, and dignity of our life here and now; a symbol that can rouse our passion for freedom and truthfulness, our hunger for justice and love, our yearning for fellowship, reconciliation, and peace.

Hans Küng, *Art and the Question of Meaning*

How shall we be beautiful? By loving the One who is always beautiful. The more love grows in you, the more beauty grows: for love itself is the beauty of the soul. . . .

Augustine, *Psalmum XLIV Enarratio, Sermon*

In their own way literature and art are very important in the life of the Church. They seek to give expression to man's nature, his problems, and his experience in an effort to discover and perfect man himself and the world in which he lives; they try to discover his place in history and in the universe, to throw light on his suffering and his joy, his needs and potentialities, and to outline a happier destiny in store for him. Hence they can elevate human life, which they express under many forms according to various times and places.

The Pastoral Constitution on the Church in the Modern World

Human Identity

My wife, Marie, talks about the moment to this day. A number of years ago, we were in Rome together on a choir tour that she was leading. On a free day the choir took a bus out to see the catacomb of Calixtus on the Appian Way.

Entering a catacomb today is hardly the same experience as it would have been 1700 years ago. In one way, though, it may be even more powerful, for it helps us touch and feel for ourselves the presence of all those who have gone before us in the faith, stretching back some two millennia.

Catacombs are dark by their very nature. They take us under the earth and remind us of our own mortality. The walls are very high, the pathways are narrow, and the niches that once held the bodies of the faithful rise one above the other right to the ceiling, almost as if they were stretching and yearning for the day of resurrection. Occasionally the tunnels give way to rooms in which meals were eaten on the anniversaries of the death of the faithful departed. These rooms are also the primary locations of the artwork and symbols that have been celebrated as the foundations of Christian visual art.

After wandering for some time through this vast catacomb in the company of a young Italian guide, we came upon one such room. Marie turned the corner and immediately encountered a representation of Jesus on the wall. The moment took her breath away. All at once she felt a direct, existential connection to the ground of her own being in Christ. In that instant God was present to her in an unrepeatable and remarkable way. Jesus became real and tangible. The artwork took her out of herself and connected her to the source of her hope. It would not be too much to say that it reinvigorated her faith and her sense of God's presence in her life. It gave her a sense of her own identity as a child of God.

Who are we? As this story illustrates, art can help us ask and answer that question, one of the most difficult questions we will ever encounter. In this chapter we will consider the related questions of human identity and human formation, finally centering on the call to grow as the fundamental Christian mission in life, a holistic mission that involves the growth of the mind, the spirit, and the body.

We begin by examining the question of human identity. Human identity is a rich and complex phenomenon. Considering the various aspects of this issue taxes the imagination and occupies much of our time as we move from infancy through the various stages of our lives. We formulate different images of ourselves depending on the shifting personal and social contexts of our lives.

According to the Greeks, we are rational people. Shakers believe that we are a people who move with the dance of life. To romantics, we are bubbling cauldrons of emotion. Naturalists see us as an organic part of the cosmos. Meanwhile, an advertising executive may view human beings simply as economic units: potential consumers. We are also identified as members of different racial, ethnic, professional, and social communities: men, women, old, young, Caucasian, African-American, Hispanic, Asian, educated, white collar, blue collar, poor, rich, athletic, artistic, employed, unemployed, or retired. Obviously, none of these images tells the whole story. None of them circumscribes the human condition, even as it relates to one single individual. We are a complex and richly variegated people.

Nonetheless, we keep asking the question: Who are we? At our core, at our most profound depth, what makes us distinctive in the world? What defines us as individuals and as a species? Throughout history the issue of human identity has been one of the central topics entertained by philosophers, psychologists, theologians, anthropologists, artists, and ordinary people going about their business in the world.

Behind all the responses presented in arguments and images, behind Plato, Aquinas, and Freud, behind the personality traits from Myers-Briggs and the haunting human forms of Giacometti's sculptures, we continue to encounter and unpack one of the simplest and yet richest answers from the book of Genesis: "So God created humankind in his image, in the image of God he created them, male and female he created them" (Gen. 1:27).

Judeo-Christians have returned to this seminal account of human origins for millennia, seeking to understand who they are and whose they are. According to this primal narrative, our core identity as human beings is that we are made in the image of God (the *Imago Dei*). Our relationship to God the Creator, and to God the Sustainer of life (implying ongoing creative activity — *creatio continua*), grounds our identity as human beings. It is prior to and more fundamental than any other self-image we have.

There are many ways to interpret the concept of the *Imago Dei*.[1] We have already seen that one significant approach is to view the *Imago Dei* as

---

1. See the October 2005 issue of *Interpretation: A Journal of Bible and Theology*, entitled "Image of God," for a recent list of possible interpretations. See also Kathleen R. Fischer, *The Inner Rainbow: The Imagination in Christian Life* (Mahwah, N.J.: Paulist Press, 1983), Chapter Five.

an expression of human creativity, and thus of human freedom. Creativity and freedom are gifts given by the One who creates in pure freedom as an organic and irreducible part of the divine character. As creative people, we are endowed with the possibility of doing something new, of using our freedom to forge meaningful and potentially redemptive images of the world and to act based on those images.

We can also view the *Imago Dei* through the lens of humanity's fallen state. The image into which we were born is tarnished because of the choices we ourselves have made. The window of our creative soul is dirty. We who were formed and shaped out of chaos once again allow chaos to rule our lives and our creative output.

For artists and the creative process as a whole, this is particularly significant. First of all, artists wrestle with the products of their own imaginations. Much like Jacob, they can be injured in the process — emotionally and even physically (see Gen. 32:22-32). They find that what once seemed like a clear vision of the artistic product is now cloudy, and the way forward is uncertain. Artists struggle with raw materials that do not easily conform to the patterns and shapes they would have them take. Sound and gesture, wood and stone often seem recalcitrant and unruly as artists struggle to give them form and contour. Thus, the ultimate result of the Fall is the distortion and disruption of the creative process itself.

Fortunately, for the Christian tradition, that is not the end of the story. We hear and receive the Gospel message. The image is being restored again. The window is being cleaned. This is a direct result of grace (itself an aesthetic term — i.e., the grace of a dancer's line), experienced as we live into the *Imago Christi,* as we become more and more Christ-like by following the path of discipleship. This road leads inexorably toward a future in which our creativity will receive its fullest and most complete expression in the New Jerusalem, the city of amethyst and gold, whose radiance is the Lord, God Almighty. This means that as we live our lives in the here and now, we are a people living in between a creative past and a future of promised beauty.

In this in-between time, God calls us to live holistically. The *Imago Christi* (the "image of Christ" into which we are being redeemed) impacts every sphere of human life: our mind, our body, our spirit, our ethical life, our relationships, and our creative life. Holistic living is one of the keys to participating fully in the abundance that God intends for those who have been redeemed out of the pit. There is, in fact, a direct relationship between holistic living and holiness. Holistic living is a key element in the continued progress of the faithful toward fullness of life in the kingdom. As Augustine reminds us, "See that your praise comes from your whole being; in other words, see that you praise God not only with your lips and voices, but with your minds, your lives, and all your actions."[2]

A wonderful, whimsical illustration of the importance of holistic living comes from *The Wizard of Oz*, which functions as a sort of twentieth-century morality play. Good and evil are represented by the Wicked Witch of the West and the Good Witch of the South, Glinda. The heroine of the story, a saintly girl named Dorothy, is on a journey down a golden road, headed toward the Emerald Kingdom — quintessential eschatological imagery. She is accompanied by *everyman*,[3] in the person of three separate individuals: a lion seeking control over his will, a man of straw in search of his intellect, and the man Dorothy loved the most, a tin man looking for his affections. Conflated together, the lion, the scarecrow, and the tin man illustrate the human quest for wholeness, the desire that God has for us to live integrated lives, to grow increasingly closer to the true *Imago Dei* that lies deep in the heart of our humanity.

Historically, theologians have affirmed the importance of holistic living. The life of the will, the mind, and the affections are all important components of a fully functioning human being. The soul has often been viewed as the unity of these attributes, a unity that, under the guidance of the Holy Spirit, forms a well-ordered human life.

While this might be the ideal, it has not often been practiced in the Judeo-Christian tradition. There are many occasions in history where the body has been viewed as somehow less important and inherently more sinful than the mind or the spirit. The Puritans are a notable example of this way of thinking. Likewise, some eras were suspicious about the role of the spirit or the emotions in human living. In the late eighteenth and early nineteenth centuries, people who were too filled with the Holy Spirit or expressed their religiosity with too much emotion were given the derogatory title "enthusiasts." By contrast, during the Pietist movement in seventeenth-century Germany, and again in the late nineteenth century, emotions were emphasized at the expense of the intellect. Perhaps the current generation is another instance of this way of thinking.

2. Augustine, quoted in Philip H. Pfatteicher, *The School of the Church: Worship and Christian Formation* (Valley Forge, Pa.: Trinity Press, 1995), p. 41.

3. This is a reference to the fifteenth-century morality play that teaches lessons about how every person should live.

Human Formation: Who Will We Become?

In the midst of these conflicting historical swings toward one aspect or another of the human person, individual believers continue to make progress toward the abundant life of the kingdom. Progress along the yellow brick road that leads to the kingdom is, in real life, a function of growth. There is no way to walk the path of Christian discipleship except through growth. We do not have a fast-forward button that enables us to bypass the witch's castle and escape the hard times involved with growth.

As we grow in Christ, we become more and more the people that God created us to be.[4] We become increasingly authentic to ourselves and to the world around us. This process is often called "human formation." The Eastern Church calls it "theosis." John Wesley calls it "sanctification." Karl Rahner and Teilhard de Chardin identify it as "hominization." Whatever name we use, it is important to acknowledge that life is, indeed, a process. It is not static. Human beings are constantly changing and evolving throughout their lives in response to their own inner drives, the influences of the people and institutions around them, the dynamic impact of the cosmos itself, and the creative, sustaining work of the Holy Spirit.

Human formation and human identity exist in a symbiotic relationship. It is our capacity to make choices, to change and evolve in response to the vicissitudes of life, that creates our identity at any one point on the journey. As we assume and live into the identity that we have chosen, we soon realize that it does not provide sufficient answers or resources for every question or every circumstance in which we find ourselves. Under the guidance of the Holy Spirit, we leave our prior identity behind and submit to continued formation, continued change and growth. In the midst of this process, we gradually encounter the "I" that exists at the center of our lives, a person who is always on the move, a pilgrim passing through a land that is sometimes very foreign. Thomas Merton uses the traditional language of kenosis (self-emptying) to describe this process: "It is the renunciation of our false self, the emptying of self in the likeness of Christ, that brings us to the threshold of that true creativity in which God himself, the creator, works in and through us . . . this is creativity in a new and spiritual dimension, which is its full Christian dimension."[5]

4. As John Navone says in *Toward a Theology of Beauty* (Collegeville, Minn.: Liturgical Press, 1996), p. 19, "God is making humankind beautiful."

5. Thomas Merton, "Theology of Creativity," in *The Literary Essays of Thomas Merton*, ed. Patrick Hart (New York: New Directions, 1981), p. 370.

The Role of Arts Ministry in Human Identity and Human Formation

Art — and even more specifically, arts ministry — has the capacity to help us as we engage in the process of human formation, this process of self-discovery in which we are being known and named by God.[6] In conjunction with praise of God and service to the world, human formation is arts ministry's most important function. Used appropriately, art is a voice in the cultural wilderness calling us home, calling us to become more and more ourselves. Albert Rouet says, "Some sort of transfiguration then is at the heart of true art. It snatches persons beyond their limits to lead them out of everyday necessities and into what is truly necessary for a full and free humanity. This is grace."[7]

Arts ministers need to pay attention to the goal of human formation. They need to be reminded that art does not exist in the church simply to provide beautiful objects and experiences that will keep parishioners comfortable and secure. Indeed, it will often do the reverse. It has a way of comforting the disturbed and disturbing the comfortable. Art does this in order to assist God's people as they attempt to live into the *Imago Dei* in which they were created and the *Imago Christi* into which they are being redeemed. It is a form of ministry.

Arts ministry relates to the dual issues of human identity and human formation in a number of different ways: (1) art names us, (2) art relates us to the world around us, (3) art helps us to express our identity, and (4) art gives us tools for the journey.

Art Names Us

As patrons walk through the galleries of a museum and view the artworks hung on the walls or placed on pedestals before them, many people have a tendency to look immediately at the name of the artwork they are viewing. The name functions as a reference point that gives them an interpretive tool to use as they relate to this particular painting or sculpture. It may

---

6. Not everyone would concur. Harold Best writes, "Incipient idolatry comes from the idea that art and music possess the capability, by their presence and use, to shape behaviors." See *Music through the Eyes of Faith* (San Francisco: HarperCollins, 1993), p. 48. I often wonder how Best takes account of the story of David playing his harp to influence the behavior of Saul.

7. Albert Rouet, *Liturgy and the Arts*, trans. Paul Philibert, O.P. (Collegeville, Minn.: Liturgical Press, 1997), p. 141.

come as a surprise to realize that, just as the viewer is reciting the name of the work of art, so too the art is naming the viewer. In his book *Worship and Christian Identity: Practicing Ourselves*, Byron Anderson relates this phenomenon to hymn-singing:

> The singing of the hymn not only provides the means for person and community to express their faith but also proposes to them a way of meaning and being in the world. Singing the hymn commits us as persons and community to a vision of relatedness to God and one another no longer marked by rupture. Singing the hymn commits self and community to a stance of love and desire before God. . . . In doing so, we have gone beyond self-expression. Our singing of the hymn results, in a fashion, in the hymn "singing" us, naming us, identifying us as people of faith.[8]

As we are exposed to works of art in an arts ministry, we identify with (or perhaps react against) the individual artworks and become part of the artist's imaginative world. We encounter the artist's worldview and position ourselves in relation to it. This helps us locate ourselves and provides a sense of self-identity.

Naming is very important to people of faith. It was the first creative act by a human being in Scripture. Adam's act of naming the animals was an instance of performative language at work. That is, his words actually changed reality. The animals that God set before Adam received names that remained their names thereafter. We continue with this primal work of naming even today as we unpack the wonders of the universe or study the intricacies of the human genome. In like manner, when we are named by a work of art, there is a chance that our lives actually might change. As we become identified with the images we experience (particularly those experienced over a significant length of time), we have a tendency to conform our lives to the vision of humanity that they express.

Art Relates Us to the World

In and through artistic style, by means of formal elements as well as through subject matter itself, art provides us with metaphors of our relationships to one another, to God, and to the cosmos. These metaphors in-

---

8. Byron Anderson, *Worship and Christian Identity: Practicing Ourselves* (Collegeville, Minn.: Liturgical Press, 2003), p. 206.

crease the depth of our understanding regarding the nature and character of the lives we live. They enable us to stop and notice the everyday, mundane realities that we would otherwise pass by. They provide us with a new language of praise and lament. At the limits of discursive language we suddenly encounter a gesture that reveals something about hope, a brushstroke that lends new meaning to fragmentation, a melody that teaches us about yearning.

We do not experience these images in isolation. Arts ministry enables us to share them with one another. Thus our story intermingles with our neighbors'; our sense of anguish, joy, love, or despair is transported from the private realm to a place where it can be communicated to others who have had similar experiences. This enables us to forge bonds that bind us to the local community in which they are experienced and to the source of all human community in God.

Art Helps Us Express Our Identity

For many people, "identity" is not a matter for conscious deliberation. There is precious little time in the midst of busy schedules and modern technology to reflect on who we are or who we are becoming. Sometimes we need artists to help us reflect when we cannot do this for ourselves. Sometimes we need metaphor, we need to look out on a river and see what it really means. . . .

> The surface of the quieted river, as I thought in those old days at Squires Landing, as I think now, is like a window looking into another world that is like this one except that it is quiet. Its quietness makes it seem perfect. The ripples are like the slats of a blind or a shutter through which we see imperfectly what is perfect. Though that other world can be seen only momentarily, it looks everlasting. As the ripples become more agitated, the window darkens and the other world is hidden. As I did not know then but know now, the surface of the river is like a living soul, which is easy to disturb, is often disturbed, but, growing calm, shows what it was, is, and will be.[9]

Philip Pfatteicher reminds us, "The poets we value are important because they speak for us with words we could never find, and they help us

---

9. Wendell Berry, *Jayber Crow* (New York: Counterpoint, 2000), p. 20.

learn to speak for ourselves."[10] As this passage from Wendell Berry's *Jayber Crow* shows, it would be difficult to overestimate how significant this is in our lives.

Art Gives Us Tools for the Journey

In a very real sense, art acts as a means of grace. This is another way of saying that it is a sacramental and sanctifying presence in our lives. To suggest that art can be sacramental does not mean that it is a sacrament in any formal sense. It means that art has the capacity to hint at an underlying reality that transcends and grounds our normal, everyday experience. It does this by transfiguring and re-ordering the elements of everyday experience in new ways, revealing the depth and profundity that lies beneath the surface.

To experience the presence of God by means of an encounter with a work of art is to awaken the possibility of transformation. When we locate God in our midst, we are suddenly aware of new possibilities. Our love itself is deepened, and we look for ways to extend this love to the world around us.

Summary

It is important to recognize the power of art to help us experience the reality of brokenness and of redemption. It is important also to see how artists speak for us, how they provide a narrative context for our own stories, and how they name us and set us apart for the work of the kingdom.

Arts ministry is the systematic attempt on the part of the church to create an environment conducive to experiencing and reflecting upon and with art in these ways. It recognizes the need to be intentional about art and about human formation and to forge bonds between the two that are active in the lives of individuals and institutions.

How Does Art Help Us Grow toward God?

The specific question we need to address now is this: How does art, and specifically arts ministry, play a role in the growth of the human person to-

10. Pfatteicher, *The School of the Church*, p. 35.

ward God? I have made a claim that this is important. Like Ezekiel, we need to watch as more flesh is put on these bones and see if new life emerges (Ezek. 37:1-14). We will view this question under three headings: (1) Growth in Our Understanding: Arts Ministry and the Mind, (2) Growth in Our Relationship to God: Arts Ministry and Spirituality, and (3) Growth in Our Life as Embodied Spirits: Arts Ministry and the Body.

Growth in Our Understanding: Arts Ministry and the Mind

In his classic book *Christianity and Culture*, T. S. Eliot says, "We must treat Christianity with a great deal more *intellectual* respect than is our wont; we must treat it as being for the individual a matter primarily of thought and not of feeling."[11]

Clearly we are living in a time when intellectual formation is not a primary value in the Christian church. We may no longer be considered a thoughtful people. This is cause for lament. Church leaders have elected to keep the laity on a diet of milk their entire lives, rather than moving them to solid food. They have somehow decided that there is no connection between information and human formation, between understanding our faith and practicing it.

Only the human will seems to matter, and this is sustained by periodic emotional experiences in worship fostered, in large part, by the arts. In contrast to their role in the Middle Ages, when they were instruments of intellectual formation, now the arts are exclusively related to the production of human emotion. The arts thus become part of the problem rather than part of the solution. This situation has profound implications for artists, for individual believers, for the Christian community, and for the wider culture outside of the church.

Part of the problem may be that simple answers are given to complex questions. We have become intellectually lazy. We have lost sight of the biblical category of *sapientia* — of wisdom. How do we reconnect with wisdom? In 1 Corinthians 14, Paul says, "I will pray with my spirit, but I will also pray with my mind. I will sing with my spirit, but I will also sing with my mind." What does he mean by this? How can we "sing with our minds"? Does he simply mean that we need to pay attention to the words we sing, or is something more than this involved?

11. T. S. Eliot, *Christianity and Culture* (San Diego: Harcourt, Brace, 1939), p. 6.

The relationship between the arts and the mind is a topic that few church leaders would consider important. If pastors encounter laity who want to learn more about their faith, they do not immediately connect this intellectual curiosity with the arts. The notion that the arts can communicate meaning in the realm of theology, ethics, spirituality, or social justice would be far-fetched to many pastors and many laity alike.

Part of the problem is that not all of us are privy to the potential meaning conveyed by artistic language. For the arts to be intellectually meaningful, there must be a shared pool of common images and associations between untrained laity and artists. Many of these associations are learned. This means that, to some degree, education *in* the arts is important for learning and formation *through* the arts.

Does this mean that laypeople need to become trained artists? No. There's a difference between learning how to *make* art and learning how to *engage with* art. In order for art to disclose meaning, it is much more important that the laypeople learn the skills of engagement and appreciation than that they learn how to make art. Having said this, I should also emphasize that learning how to *make* art is one path that leads to *engagement* with art.

How do laypeople learn the skills of engagement? The first and most obvious way is simply by exposure — which ordinarily occurs through both active *experiences with* artworks and passive *learning about* artworks. Engagement means developing not only an understanding of the arts, but a taste for them. These two requirements are closely related, but not identical. The more that laypeople understand about art, presumably the more they will appreciate and, dare I say, even enjoy it. But prior to any education, laypeople must be willing to be exposed to the arts. They must be open and vulnerable, willing to be moved and willing to hear its message.

The culture in which we live often mitigates against this. It encourages exposure when the art originates in American popular culture, but it actively discourages contact with any other art form. This is increasingly true in the American church. To understand this, we need to briefly examine the cultural soil in which American Christianity is planted. What are the characteristics of American culture as they relate to the life of faith?

Neil Postman points out that we are a culture in danger of amusing ourselves to death. This is expressed most clearly through the medium of television. Television not only reflects and shapes our culture — increasingly, it *is* our culture. We don't have to worry about George Orwell's vision of totalitarian control that substitutes lies for truth. Instead, we simply trivialize the truth and make it entertaining. As Postman says, "Big Brother turns out to be Howdy Doody."[12]

What kind of people and culture are produced by television? Let's think for a moment about how television works. Most television viewing demands minimal comprehension. It aims at emotional gratification rather than intellectual stimulation and presents all experience under the rubric of entertainment. Even educational television is usually packaged as entertainment. The messages conveyed by television are brief and simple. Complexity is avoided. The information we receive comes in fragmentary and superficial forms. Ideas are presented without any context or sense of historicity; thus they lack internal coherence.

Stars are created by television, and it is the power of these stars that drives the commercial enterprise that, in turn, supports the medium. Stars sell the products on the commercials. Star broadcasters achieve the credibility that makes the evening news credible.

Finally, television viewing is an essentially individual experience. It usually occurs in the privacy of the home. Even when the family gathers to watch a television show together, the show rarely engages them in dialogue of any depth or profundity.

Marva Dawn sums this up and applies it to the church:

> Television revolutionized the structure of our thought. Whereas the printed page revealed a serious, coherent world . . . , television pictures the world in rapidly shifting images that destroy all the virtues formerly associated with mature discourse. . . . The loss of exposition must be a major concern for the Church, which tries to pass on faith to the next generation, teach creeds, set out the eminent reasonability of belief, and ground children in doctrines that will duly establish them for growth to maturity in truth and hope.[13]

In light of the pervasive influence of television and American popular culture, is it any surprise that neither laypeople nor clergy are motivated to

12. Neil Postman, *Amusing Ourselves to Death: Public Discourse in the Age of Show Business* (New York: Penguin Books, 1985), p. 111.

13. Marva Dawn, *Reaching Out without Dumbing Down: A Theology of Worship for the Turn-of-the-Century Culture* (Grand Rapids: Wm. B. Eerdmans, 1995), p. 23.

seek out the "depth dimension" that is expressed in so many works of art whose origins lie in what Nicholas Wolterstorff calls "our institution of high art"?[14]

Works that demand our attention, that call us to sustained reflection, are not valued because they simply demand too much effort. The effort to engage these works and hear what they have to say might be forthcoming, except that there is no commonly held assumption that they mean anything in the first place. If they are treated solely as a means of entertainment or diversion, there is no reason to expend the energy necessary to understand them when perfectly acceptable diversions are readily available.

Not all is lost, however. Great art appeals to people on many different levels. Westerners without any training whatsoever can still experience the vitality and joyful quality of the Bach Gigue Fugue, BWV 577, for organ. They can still be moved by the intense agony of Grünewald's *Isenheim Altarpiece*. They can still form a powerful connection with Van Gogh's sunflower or with a ballet performed by Baryshnikov. Perhaps this appeal may even be cross-cultural to some extent. That is still up for debate.

Our hope lies in the very integration that arts ministry seeks. Human beings are mind, spirit, and body. We represent a complex panoply of emotions and reason. At one and the same time we are ethical, rational, and aesthetic creatures. The path into any one of these areas can be through another area altogether. Our affections may be deeply moved by a performance of Dorothy Sayers' play *The Zeal of Thy House*.[15] This may, in turn, lead us to wonder about the nature and role of creativity in our lives. It may open up doors of intellectual inquiry that we would not have previously walked through, simply because we are now engaged emotionally with the drama.

As we integrate the different areas of our lives in and through our faith, it is important to remember that the intellect is one of the most remarkable and gracious gifts given to us by our creator. Using it, taking it out to a concert or for an occasional stroll through a museum, may in the end help us to become the people we were created to be.

14. Nicholas Wolterstorff, *Art in Action: Toward a Christian Aesthetic* (Grand Rapids: Wm. B. Eerdmans, 1980), p. 22.

15. Dorothy Sayers, *The Zeal of Thy House* (New York: Harcourt, Brace, 1937). The play was written for the Friends of Canterbury Cathedral.

Growth in Our Relationship to God: Arts Ministry and Spirituality

Frank Burch Brown asks an intriguing question: "What connection is possible between the taste for art and the thirst for God? Between . . . a love for the visibly artistic and a love for the invisibly Holy?"[16]

This raises the issue of the relationship between art, arts ministry, and spirituality. Spirituality makes real to us the ultimate fulfillment of human life. Joseph Pieper says that when we touch the core of all things, the foundation of all that is, we find our deepest satisfaction, the fullest achievement of human existence, the perfect expression of being alive.[17] We find abundant life. When this happens, we cannot help but celebrate. This celebration may have an individual dimension, but it is fundamentally corporate. We celebrate as the body of Christ, not as isolated individuals. I would suggest that the arts are at the heart of this celebration.

As we pursue this topic, we will ask two fundamental questions: (1) What resources do the arts provide that impact spirituality? and (2) How do these resources function in spiritual life?

Artistic Resources for Christian Living

Don Saliers points to the manner in which eschatological hope embodied in the arts acts as a resource for Christian living. He says,

> Where all that is creaturely will be permeated with light, dance, and song, there is the splendor of God's glory, there is Dante's *Paradiso* . . . "a new heaven and a new earth." Insofar as we experience the prefigurement of that reality in particular times and places, the art of liturgical celebration becomes congruent with the holiness of God and is lured by the beauty of the triune life of God, at once incarnate in human history, yet transcendent in glory beyond all created beings.[18]

Gaining a brief glimpse of the beauty of the divine and the ultimate end of our journey is important for two different but closely related reasons. First, it provides us with a vision that allures us. We anticipate the

---

16. Frank Burch Brown, *Good Taste, Bad Taste, and Christian Taste: Aesthetics in Religious Life* (New York: Oxford University Press, 2000), p. 96.

17. Joseph Pieper, *Only the Lover Sings* (San Francisco: Ignatius Press, 1988), pp. 22, 69.

18. Don Saliers, *Worship as Theology: Foretaste of Glory Divine* (Nashville: Abingdon Press, 1994), p. 216.

natural end of the Christian pilgrimage as a place of great beauty, providing lasting rewards that are abundant and fulfilling. Second, it engenders a sense of yearning within us to experience this beauty, a beauty that ultimately originates in the beauty of God.[19]

Not only does art give us a foretaste of future blessings; it also sanctifies the present moment by focusing our attention on the unnoticed beauty of the artifacts in our everyday world. Helping us attend to the minutiae of our lives in a new way redeems the individual moments and experiences of our lives. It gives us a new sense of meaning and purpose. Accordingly, it connects these experiences in the present with the ultimate beauty that is their ground and their eschatological hope.

Attending to minutiae and allowing them to enliven us isn't something that happens automatically. To varying degrees, many people in our culture fall into what Jon Michael Spencer calls the profane category.[20] They spend their days from nine to five working at tasks that they repeat over and over in numbing succession. These jobs are so stultifying that they kill any aesthetic sense, any capacity to relate to beauty, in these people. On the weekend many of these same people go to church. From a spiritual standpoint, their problem is that the life of the Spirit requires one of the same skills that we use when we encounter beauty: intuition. We intuitively follow the lead of the Spirit in much the same way that we intuitively know when something is truly beautiful.

Thus, one important function of arts ministry is to act as a training ground to develop the intuitive capacities of our congregations. As people become open on an intuitive level to the power of art, they will develop the capacity to become increasingly receptive to the gentle sway of the Spirit in their lives.

Art also requires discipline. Artistic creation (by the original artist), re-creation (by a performing artist), and engagement (by the congregation) all rely on a disciplined approach to the artistic process. This discipline is an analogy to spiritual discipline. It provides opportunities to practice disciplined behavior that can later be applied in the context of spiritual life.

19. See Brown's discussion of Psalm 42 in *Good Taste, Bad Taste, and Christian Taste,* pp. 97-98.

20. Jon Michael Spencer, *Theological Music: Introduction to Theomusicology* (New York: Greenwood Press, 1991), p. 15.

Labyrinth Ministry
East Liberty Presbyterian Church, Pittsburgh, Pennsylvania

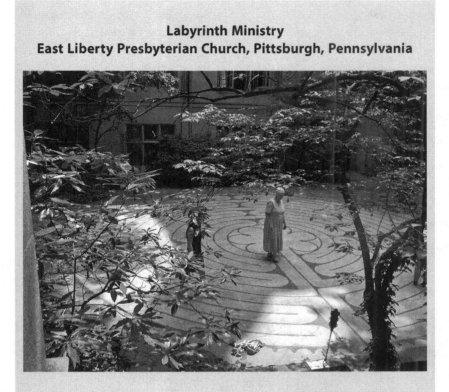

Walking the labyrinth in the courtyard at East Liberty Presbyterian Church

One of the traditional ways in which the arts and spirituality have intersected is through the practice of walking a labyrinth. Labyrinths have been part of the ministry at East Liberty Presbyterian Church in Pittsburgh, Pennsylvania, since 1996. The labyrinth ministry at this church has many facets. It includes (1) a public labyrinth that anyone can walk every Monday from 10 A.M. to 3 P.M., and every Wednesday from 10 A.M. to 9 P.M.; (2) an annual labyrinth event that includes walking the labyrinths, an orientation class on the history of the labyrinth, workshops, fellowship, and music; (3) a "loan program" that allows other churches and ministries to use the labyrinths here;

and (4) the use of labyrinths in connection with the various seasons of the liturgical year. The church describes its ministry as follows:

> The labyrinth is an ancient, sacred symbol found in many religious traditions throughout the world. During the Middle Ages, labyrinths were prominent in numerous cathedrals in Europe, where Christians walked floor labyrinths or traced their fingers along the carved ridges of wall labyrinths. For medieval Christians, the labyrinth was a symbolic pilgrimage: instead of taking a costly and dangerous pilgrimage to Jerusalem, worshipers made a symbolic journey on a cathedral labyrinth. The best known of these Christian labyrinths is in Chartres Cathedral in France, which was built during the thirteenth century.
>
> Today, modern pilgrims walk the labyrinth as one of many ways to pray and meditate. The winding path into the center and back out again is a metaphor for the journeys of life and faith. Unlike a maze, which has many paths and is a puzzle to solve, the labyrinth is a single path in and out and is designed to quiet the mind for prayer and meditation.
>
> Today we have four floor labyrinths, all on canvas. Three of the floor labyrinths are the 11-circuit Chartres pattern and are thirty-six feet in diameter. The fourth, in the Santa Rosa style with seven circuits or paths, is twenty-four feet. During the summer months when the weather permits, the labyrinth is placed outside in the beauty and serenity of our courtyard. Throughout the rest of the year and in prohibitive weather during the summer, the labyrinth is specially set up in our social hall or in the gymnasium, to reflect a calming and meditative ambience. The labyrinth has become an integral part of our diverse, multicultural ministry and a bridge for reaching Christian seekers and friends of all faiths.*

*East Liberty Presbyterian Church, http://www.cathedralofhope.org/programs/labyrinth ministry.html

How Do Artistic Resources Function in Spiritual Life?

Let us begin by identifying two different dialectics within which art and spirituality function: the transcendent/immanent dialectic, and the prophetic/pastoral dialectic.

We have already witnessed the dialectic between transcendence and immanence at work in the context of the human-divine relationship. Now it is time to examine its function as a means of human and spiritual formation.

Engaging with a transcendent God through the arts often involves a particular spiritual methodology. The artist is charged with the task of being open to God. God, in turn, reveals to the artist a direct insight regarding the divine character. Subsequently the artist embodies this insight in an artwork. As individual people encounter the artwork, they are transported beyond themselves to contemplate the nature of the divine. In this way, art becomes a means for them to grow in the direction of contemplative union with God, a union beyond all images. As they come to the final stages of this journey, they can discard art, since it now stands in the way of total union with God.

Patrick Sherry speaks of Clement of Alexandria, who believed that "Earthly beauty is the bottom rung of a ladder from which we ascend to beauty itself."[21] Using art as a tool to rise to union with God is called the *anagogic* process. It is particularly important in the Roman Catholic and Orthodox traditions.

Abbot Suger, the great medieval abbot at the Church of St. Denis in Paris, had these words inscribed on the front portal of the church, words that illustrate the anagogic process:

> Whoever thou art, if thou seekest to extol the glory of these doors,
> Marvel not at the gold and the expense but at the craftsmanship of
>   the work.
> Bright is the noble work; but, being nobly bright, the work
> Should brighten the minds, so that they may travel, through the true
>   lights,
> To the True Light where Christ is the true door.
> In what manner it be inherent in this world the golden door defines:

---

21. Clement of Alexandria, quoted in Patrick Sherry, *Spirit and Beauty: An Introduction to Theological Aesthetics* (Oxford: Clarendon Press, 1992), p. 7.

The dull mind rises to truth through that which is material,
And, in seeing the light, is resurrected from its former submersion.[22]

The quintessential example of the anagogic process is the icon. The faithful focus their gaze on the icon and see through the painted image to the archetypal reality that is behind it. This is the process of *veneration*. The icon becomes a means of spiritual ascent for the faithful as they seek contemplative bliss. It represents a powerful example of eschatological hope at work.

The anagogic process illustrates the relationship between the practice of aesthetic contemplation and spirituality. As Nicholas Wolterstorff points out, "There is an inherent similarity, worth noting, between aesthetic and mystical contemplation. The art lover, like the mystic, turns away from ordinary concerns to be caught up in the bliss of contemplation."[23]

Immanence is the exact opposite of this process. Here the artist looks horizontally rather than vertically. The artist focuses on the things of this world as they reveal the God of the universe. The present moment is hallowed. Those who use and appreciate art in this way believe that the divine is present in all of life. There is no sacred/secular division. Furthermore, God may be seen in and through the things of this world, including its artwork. There is no need to transcend the artistic image to achieve union with God. This approach is consonant with Protestant spirituality. Good examples include depictions of daily life by Pieter Bruegel the Elder (ca. 1525?-1569), and dramatic sketches performed in worship that reveal the depths and intricacies of human relationships.

The dialectic between the pastoral and the prophetic dimensions of art is closely related to that between transcendence and immanence. Prophetic art is designed to show us something about reality. The artist who creates prophetic art takes a long, deep, intense look at the world and arrives at insights regarding God's word for the world. Prophetic art illuminates dark corners of the universe. Through prophetic art we encounter the ground of our being on a fundamental, existential level. We experience a new view of the human person in a sculpture by Rodin and a new view of Christ in the music of Arvo Pärt.

Prophetic art challenges us on a spiritual plane. Richard Harries notes,

22. Abbot Suger, quoted in Janet Walton, *Art and Worship: A Vital Connection* (Wilmington, Del.: Michael Glazier, 1988), pp. 33-34.
23. Wolterstorff, *Art in Action*, p. 49.

"Art first of all makes us see the 'isness' of what is before us, whether we like what we see or not." He goes on, "The capacity to see what is there, without illusion, self-indulgence, fantasy, or denigration, is integrally related to the capacity to love."[24] This is art done not only from a prophetic but also from a transcendent viewpoint.

In the case of pastoral art, we encounter works of art whose purpose is to help us deal with the reality that prophetic art has uncovered. It heals wounds and rejuvenates the human spirit. We remember David playing to Saul to calm his soul and think immediately about the role of music, art, or dance therapy in our own world. We recall murals painted on inner-city walls by disadvantaged youth that speak of hope and possibilities for growth. We acknowledge the different ways in which a beautiful image or a comforting poem has impacted our own spiritual life over the years. Using art to minister to the faithful, to overcome divisions between people, or to provide hope in a bleak situation are all examples of the pastoral function of art. They resonate with the immanent dimension of spirituality.

Love represents the true union between the prophetic and pastoral dimensions of art. To value reality in art, to portray the world with all its ills and foibles, is to love those who will see and hear prophetic art, for they should not be deceived. To comfort them, in turn, with countervailing pastoral images is a way of saying that this is not all there is, that through God's grace and mercy there is the possibility of redemption, the reality of transformation.

Finally, let me suggest that there might be an important role for imagination and creativity in the life of the Spirit. Spiritual life is an adventure. In a very real sense, it is experimental. We are constantly going down new paths, led we know not where. If we can employ our imaginations along the way, we have the capacity to envision a new reality, to grow. Historically, imagination has been a key tool in spiritual life as believers put themselves in the midst of biblical scenes and envisioned the sights, sounds, and smells associated with a parable or an Old Testament story.[25] In a religious tradition as abstract as Judeo-Christian monotheism, it is critically important that believers employ their imaginations in creative ways to keep the faith fresh and new. This does not imply a re-

24. Richard Harries, *Art and the Beauty of God: A Christian Understanding* (London: Continuum, 1993), pp. 105-6.

25. See especially the works of writers representing the *Devotio Moderna*, a late medieval movement whose classic text is Thomas à Kempis's *The Imitation of Christ*.

treat from reality; on the contrary, it represents a headlong surge into the real world.

Orthodox believers would be wary at this point. They would caution us that as we engage our imaginations in the life of faith, it is important to guard against fantasy. Orthodoxy suggests that instead of relying on the imagination to form us, we should rely on the liturgy and the art forms that act in coordination with it. This insures that our imaginative visions of the divine will not be confused with the God who is beyond every image and metaphor.

Growth in Our Life as Embodied Spirits: Arts Ministry and the Body

We have considered the relationships between arts ministry and the mind and arts ministry and the spirit. Now it is time to turn our attention to the human body. Carolyn Dietering reminds us that we are "embodied spirit and enspirited flesh."[26] The relationship between the spirit and the flesh — indeed, the entire Christian attitude toward the human body — has been a sticking point for arts ministry throughout its history. We will examine the relationship between arts ministry and the body under two headings: (1) Christian Attitudes toward the Body, and (2) Dance: The Art of Embodiment.

A Celebration of Embodiment: Christian Attitudes toward the Body

Paul is the culprit. Or, rather, the interpreters of Paul are collectively the culprits. We have heard so often that Paul favors the spirit over the body. This represents a rather superficial reading of Paul. These interpreters ignore passages like Romans 12:1: "I appeal to you therefore, brothers and sisters, by the mercies of God, to present your bodies as a living sacrifice, holy and acceptable to God, which is your spiritual worship." Here we see a call for the positive use of the body, not the denigration of the flesh.

This suggests a different interpretation of Paul's writings. Is it not possible that for Paul the flesh represents the fallen person and the spirit the redeemed person?[27] I would suggest that pitting the body against the spirit

---

26. Carolyn Dietering, *The Liturgy as Dance and the Liturgical Dancer* (New York: Crossroad, 1984), p. 9.

27. Dietering, *The Liturgy as Dance*, p. 13.

is, in fact, a dualism that is not in line with the integration of the human person called for in Scripture (including in the writings of Paul).[28]

Christianity is a religious tradition based on physicality. Marina Herrera and Elly Murphy point out, "Symbolically, the body is a reminder of our earthiness, our material nature, our rootedness in time and space."[29] The Christian tradition was founded on the material creation of the world and human beings at the beginning of history, the present redemption won for us by the incarnation and physical resurrection of Jesus, and our future hope for the resurrection of the body that we proclaim every time we say the Apostles' Creed.

If we didn't recognize the importance of embodiment prior to the birth of Christ, this event alone should drive home the point. Susan Bauer writes, "Faith in the Incarnation enables congregations to fully celebrate and affirm the physical, the body as instrument."[30]

It is unquestionably difficult for people to celebrate embodiment in our contemporary society when they are overweight, physically handicapped, constantly compared to "ideal" bodies in the media, and struggling to use their own bodies appropriately in the face of many different kinds of temptations. It may be that arts ministry can help them wrestle with some of these very issues as they seek to follow Paul's advice and offer their bodies as living sacrifices.

Dance: The Art of Embodiment

Ted Shawn, one of the pioneers of modern sacred dance, once said, "Dance is the only art in which we ourselves are the stuff of which it is made."[31] Dance is, perhaps, the only art form that literally involves *embodiment*. Other art forms also involve the body. Performance art, whether in the realm of music, visual art, or theatre, is inherently physical. Nonetheless,

---

28. This is also related to the Manichean heresy, which says that the spirit is good and matter is evil.

29. Marina Herrera and Elly Murphy, "The Religious Nature of Dance," in *Focus on Dance X: Religion and Dance,* ed. Dennis J. Fallon and Mary Jane Wolbers (Reston, Va.: The American Alliance for Health, Physical Education, Recreation, and Dance, 1982), p. 55.

30. Susan Bauer, "Dance as Performance Fine Art in Liturgy," in *Dance as Religious Studies,* ed. Doug Adams and Diane Apostolos-Cappadona (New York: Crossroad, 1990), p. 181.

31. Ted Shawn, quoted in Carla De Sola, "And the Word Became Dance: A Theory and Practice of Liturgical Dance," in *Dance as Religious Studies,* p. 155.

as we consider the relationship between the arts and the body, it is appropriate that we focus our attention on dance.

At its core, dance is movement directed toward a particular purpose. We encounter this idea first in the creation account in Genesis, where we read that a wind from God swept over the face of the waters. The very act of creation was dynamic and involved movement. Movement is scattered throughout the pages of the Bible. The nation of Israel moved through the parted waters of the Red Sea in the Exodus; God moved before the people as a pillar of fire in the desert; Joshua led the people in procession around Jericho before "the walls came tumbling down"; and God passed by Elijah on the mountain. To all of this we need to add the many specific references to dance in Scripture — Miriam dancing to celebrate the parting of the Red Sea, David dancing before the Ark of the Covenant, the victory dance for Saul and David, Judith leading a dancing procession of women; Jephthah's daughter dancing with timbrels to greet him; wedding dances in the Old Testament and at Cana, and various references to dance in the book of Psalms.[32] In fact, movement, embodiment, and dance itself are central features of many biblical narratives.

The early church recognized this and celebrated it. Ambrose writes,

> Let us not be ashamed of a show of reverence which will enrich the cult and deepen the adoration of Christ. For this reason the dance must in no wise be regarded as a mark of reverence for vanity and luxury, but as something which uplifts every living body instead of allowing the limbs to rest motionless upon the ground or the slow feet to become numb.[33]

Unfortunately, Hellenism attempted to quash the enthusiasm for dance. It is remarkable that, in the face of growing opposition, dance continued to raise its head throughout much of church history. At various points along the way there have been dance processions, dance games, circle dances, prayer dances, dances involving balls, and dances through labyrinths. Children danced, as did priests; in Shaker meetings, all the people participated in the dance. Dances were connected with death (the *Totentanz*), but also served as metaphors for Christian life (the *Tripudium* — a procession which takes three steps forward and one step back).

32. See Dietering, *The Liturgy as Dance*, Chapters 5-7.
33. Ambrose, quoted in Marilyn Daniels, *The Dance in Christianity: A History of Religious Dance through the Ages* (New York: Paulist Press, 1981), p. 18.

The Störling Dance Theater, Olathe, Kansas

A chase scene from *Underground*

The Störling Dance Theater, located in the Kansas City area, is not an explicitly Christian dance company, yet its goals and the character of its productions are very much in line with the overarching goals of arts ministry. The company's work is characterized by a unique combination of movement and storytelling. Since its first performance in 1998, the ensemble, directed by Finnish immigrant Mona Enna, has grown to the point where they perform concert-length works, including *The Prodigal Daughter*, a twist on the original parable of the prodigal son; *Her Last Prayer*, which tells the story of a teenage martyr in China; *Butterfly*, which recounts the life of a woman who contracts Alzheimer's disease; and *Underground,* an original ballet depicting stories from the Underground Railroad. Mona Enna writes,

> I'd have to say that the origins of Störling Dance Theater go way back to when I became a Christian. I was in dance school, and at the age of fourteen became a Christian in my hometown, Kokkola, Finland. One of my first desires was to use my love for dance to honor God. My pastor, Johan Candelin, encouraged me to do that and created various opportunities for me to serve the church and community. Störling today is definitely a step along a journey . . . both artistically and structurally. I started with small ideas and concerts and [they] gradually grew into larger and larger-scale work. Now Störling is doing full-scale, full-length ballets. One of our main passions is to tell new stories through dance and theater that have a relevant and hopeful message for our generation.
>
> *Underground* has clearly become the signature work of the company. It was inspired by [my husband] Jeremiah and hearing racist language and race-baiting going on more and more in our media culture in the U.S. We decided something had to be done, and so we started to pray and look for opportunities to speak out about this. The Underground Railroad jumped out at us as a story that reflected so many important things: that the issue is about good versus evil, not black versus white, that God is the hero of the Underground Railroad, which, as historians point out, "had no leader," and that if we are to overcome evil in our day, we must include God and band together with like-minded people. The kids in the cast read books on the Underground Railroad. We pray for our community, and we build community through the production. *Underground* has become a living, giving, healing experience in many, many ways. I think it also encapsulates the best of what the arts have to offer to humanity.*

*Mona Enna, e-mail to the author, 15 December 2010.

Today, dance — particularly liturgical dance — remains important in worship. Liturgical dance begins in postures, movements, and gestures. Prayer postures include standing, sitting, kneeling, hands uplifted, fingers clasped. There are processions into and out of worship, processions for communion and offerings, and procession in baptisms, weddings, and funerals. Gestures are made by the presider: the elevation of the bread and the cup, the sign of the cross, and various blessings. Worship itself is a sort of dance, a play of different movements that, taken together, form a coordinated dance of the body of Christ. It grows organically from the dance of life that is formed from the simple gestures and movements of our day-to-day existence.

What are some of the different purposes for dance in the life of a Christian, and how do these purposes relate to the developing life of the body? First and foremost, dance helps us live as whole people.[34] Carla de Sola says, "Perhaps dance's most important gift to us lies in its ability to unify us and make us whole by joining our inward life with our outward expression. This can be done when the simplest gesture is meaningfully done."[35] Dance integrates the human person. It gives expression to our affective, physical, cognitive, and spiritual capacities simultaneously. It offers hope for the redemption of holistic living itself.[36]

Dance is not only a tangible way to express the inner life of the person; it is also an opportunity to shape that life, to help it grow and mature. In fact, dance functions as a metaphor for human life and formation. As Martha Graham once said, "Dance is the symbol for the performance of living."[37] When we read these words, the text of Sydney Carter's famous hymn rings in our ears: "Dance then, wherever you may be, for I am the Lord of the Dance, said He."

Dance is also a way of communicating meaning.[38] It helps us interpret

34. Carolyn Deitering points out that "Human wholeness is a sacred gift. Reclaiming that gift, wherever it has been lost, is imperative for a Church that teaches that God has become a human person." See *The Liturgy as Dance*, p. 11.

35. De Sola, "Reflections on Dance and Prayer," in *Focus on Dance X*, pp. 60-61.

36. Gerardus van der Leeuw adds, "We must all learn once more to dance, so that once again a general consciousness of life can be created, and finally perhaps even a style of life." See *Sacred and Profane Beauty: The Holy in Art* (Nashville: Abingdon Press, 1963), p. 74.

37. Martha Graham, quoted in Barbara Kres Beach, "The Art of Worship and the Art of Dance," in *Focus on Dance X*, p. 80.

38. Susan Bauer says, "There is a body knowledge or kinesthetic intelligence that facilitates an understanding of our world and relationships with people." See "Dance as Performance Fine Art in Liturgy," in *Dance as Religious Studies*, p. 180.

the facts of our existence by relating them to the essential core of our being, the flesh and bone into which God breathed life. Albert Rouet sums this all up, saying, "As an art, dance gathers up and condenses the essential reality of the human. It moves toward the heights of human expression and toward a glimpsed fulfillment. In this way dance touches upon the sacred, that is to say, upon what is indispensable for living and what gives meaning to life."[39]

Conclusion

The life of the mind, the spirit, and the body are important elements in the formation of a fully-functioning disciple of Jesus Christ. A thoughtful and carefully crafted arts ministry should attend to each of them. In so doing, arts ministry can be an important factor in the vitally important task of uncovering our authentic identity before God and forming ourselves into the *Imago Christi* that is our chief goal and our greatest joy.

39. Rouet, *Liturgy and the Arts*, p. 149.

CHAPTER FIVE

Arts Ministry and the World

Aesthetic delight is a component within and a species of that joy which belongs to the shalom God has ordained as the goal of human existence. . . . Since it belongs to the shalom that God intends for each of us, it becomes a matter of responsible action to help make available, to ourselves and others, the experience of aesthetic delight. It becomes a norm for action.

Nicholas Wolterstorff, *Art in Action*

Imagine the church as the place for an alternative conversation. In a society of denial, as the church we speak what we know, evoke resistance and yearning, permit alternatives, authorize newness. . . . The subject of the evangelical conversation is how our life, our bodies, and our imagination can be weaned from the deathliness of the world to the newness of life in the gospel. It is a conversation to which all are invited. From our several enslavements we are summoned to a common, liberated obedience. That conversation is difficult and unfinished. It is a conversation that promises our life shall come together in wonder, love, and praise. What news!

Walter Brueggemann, *Biblical Perspectives on Evangelism*

The Arts Minister as Servant

In 1995 Elvera Voth formed the East Hill Singers. This is a chorus whose members are inmates in the Lansing (Kansas) Correctional Facility. Currently the chorus rehearses weekly and is joined once a month by volunteers from the Kansas City area. They perform a number of times each year in Kansas City and surrounding communities. Since 1995, Voth has developed two other choirs: the West Wall Singers, maximum-security inmates who perform in the prison chapel, and the Tower Singers, who rehearse and perform in the medium-security unit at the prison. The various choirs sing classical and sacred repertoire, show tunes, spirituals, and folk music.

Voth and colleagues from throughout the region have taken this choral component and expanded it into a non-profit organization entitled Arts in Prison.[1] The organization currently sponsors programs in creative writing, the visual arts, drama, yoga, and gardening for the prisoners. While it is not explicitly Christian, by its actions this organization shows us what arts ministry is all about.

After one choral performance, Frank Ward, pastor emeritus of Rainbow Mennonite Church in Kansas City, wrote, "For perhaps the first time, the audience was confronted by a group of male prisoners who challenged our stereotypes about them. Here were men singing powerfully about spiritual realities who, regardless of their failures, were undeniably human along with the rest of us."

One prisoner explained how participation in his singing group changed him: "It made me feel like maybe I'm not just being punished. I mean, I am being punished for what I did. But being in this program made me think that I can also come out . . . well, better . . . a better person." Another adds, "Before I joined the East Hill Singers, I really hadn't ever been in a situation that was a positive one. Never. I can't tell you how much it meant to me to be in this program, where it is all positive. I mean, Elvera never got mad, she never got aggravated. It's a whole new experience for me."

Arts ministry is not just for us, and Arts in Prison is a powerful and poignant reminder of that fact. Under the right circumstances, arts ministry can be a source of hope for the church and the world. It relies on the artistic process to provide the means for the service it renders. This process

1. The source for the following account is the organization's Web site: http://www.artsinprison.org (March 1, 2009).

is often misunderstood. Since artists spend so much time perfecting their craft, often in isolation from society, art is sometimes seen as a selfish and self-centered pursuit. Nothing could be farther from the truth. It is true that artists take joy in what they do. They revel in their art and attend to the minutiae of each gesture, brush stroke, or line of dialogue with keen interest. What this means is that they are focusing not on themselves, but on the work of art. Art arrests their attention and turns them from pure introspection, which is often necessary in the creative process, to an orientation that is open and receptive, that draws from their inner resources and allows them to give back to the world a unique and unrepeatable vision.

That vision impacts the lives of other people. When artists take up the task of ministry, whether in connection with a church or an organization or simply as individuals concerned with the potential benefits of their art to the wider world, they become, first and foremost, servants. In the foregoing example, Voth and her colleagues are clearly functioning in this role as they work in the prison population. It is important to note that the prisoners themselves also become servants in and through their artistry. Their art shows their own value and worth as human beings made in the image of God. It discloses the dignity of the human person to all who encounter this art and helps make human dignity a tangible reality in their own lives.

As we have seen in the preceding two chapters, arts ministry means attending to the intersection between God and the arts and the intersection between human formation and the arts. Arts ministry recognizes that art is a communicative language expressing the transcendent and immanent aspects of the divine. Through the medium of arts ministry the arts become a factor in developing the life of the mind, the spirit, and the body; they help us uncover our fundamental human identity and transform us into the *Imago Christi*.

Alongside and in conjunction with these priorities, arts ministry also means service. Here we are focused on art as *ministry*, turning our attention from the inner life of the artist, from a focus on God and human formation to the outer life, where we examine the various ways in which artists and arts ministers are embedded in the world. There are four significant aspects to the relationship between arts ministers and the world that we will address in this chapter. These include arts ministry and

- *evangelism* — the relationship with those who are not yet committed to the path of Christian discipleship;
- *community* — the relationship with people of faith;

- *social justice* — the relationship with those at the margins of society; and
- *the cosmos* — the relationship with creation itself.

It is important to recognize that these four facets of arts ministry are not mutually exclusive. They are interdependent, relating organically to one another in much the same fashion as our own interior relationships of mind, spirit, and body.

Arts Ministry and Evangelism

In his quote at the head of this chapter, Walter Brueggemann reminds us that evangelism is, first and foremost, a conversation. In a world of shouting and political rancor, of culture wars, litigation, and denominational tensions, Brueggemann brings us back once again to the possibilities engendered by simply talking with one another.[2]

Robert Hutchins calls this the "Great Conversation" and identifies it with the intellectual tradition of the Western world.[3] Perhaps, in reality, it is a conversation that pre-dates the Western world or civilization itself. Perhaps it is a conversation that finds its origins in the great Trinitarian dialogue out of which the cosmos itself was birthed.

"In the beginning was the Word." So John opens his epic proclamation of the gospel (the "good news") of Christ. Since the time of that dramatic prologue (itself an artistic expression), the church has engaged in an ongoing conversation with the surrounding culture and with faithful believers from every time and place. This conversation has many different purposes. It recounts the deeds of God in and through salvation history (the *kerygma*). It calls people of faith to their covenantal duties and challenges their assumptions about their own personal commitments and social responsibilities. It confronts the world and refutes the claims to ultimacy that are attached to every new commodity or icon of contemporary culture.

The Bible is the first and primary setting in which we encounter this conversation. As Walter Klaiber reminds us, the conversation "is closely

---

2. L. DeAne Lagerquist adds, "*Conversation* derives etymologically from a 'turning together' and even hints at the life-altering turns we know as conversion." See *Translucence: Religion, the Arts, and Imagination*, ed. Carol Gilbertson and Gregg Muhlenburg (Minneapolis: Fortress Press, 2004), p. xi.

3. Robert Hutchins, *The Great Conversation* (Chicago: Encyclopaedia Britannica, 1952).

connected with the announcement of God's eschatological salvific activity by means of which he turns the fortune of his people for the better and in particular helps the suffering, the desperate, the prisoners, and those with disabilities to new life."[4]

Luke picks up on this idea, citing repeated proclamations of the kingdom of God. After the resurrection of Jesus, the content of this announcement turns in a Christological direction in the book of Acts. In the Pauline letters it focuses specifically on the missionary task of preaching the gospel message. Today, we call this conversation *evangelism.*

Potential Problems with Art and Evangelism

Before going on, we should note several potential problems with evangelism that relate to the arts:

(1) The practice of evangelism involves a call to individual salvation that does not always lead to a life of social responsibility. Aylward Shorter reminds us that "evangelization applies not only to individuals but to their culture."[5] Frank Senn notes that individual salvation often focuses on human emotion and excludes the *kerygma,* the proclamation of the works of God in the world. "The church's witness becomes individual testimony to what God has done for me," Senn says, "whereas true apostolic witness is to what God has done in Christ for the life of the world."[6]

(2) Evangelism is frequently seen in relation to church growth. In practice this often means *proselytism* — the attempt to win over members of another tradition to a local congregation. This exacerbates the problems associated with denominationalism and further divides the Christian community.[7] Brueggemann says, "In our moments of sanity . . . we know that the issues of evangelism do not concern the health of the institutional church. The issue is rather that the life of creation, the fabric of the human community, is deeply in jeopardy among us."[8]

4. Walter Klaiber, *Call and Response: Biblical Foundations of a Theology of Evangelism,* trans. Howard Perry-Trauthig and James A. Dwyer (Nashville: Abingdon Press, 1990), p. 24.

5. Aylward Shorter, *Toward a Theology of Inculturation* (Maryknoll, N.Y.: Orbis Books, 1988), p. 29.

6. Frank Senn, *The Witness of the Worshipping Community: Liturgy and the Practice of Evangelism* (New York: Paulist Press, 1993), pp. 46, 50.

7. Senn, *The Witness of the Worshipping Community,* p. 55.

8. Brueggemann, *Biblical Perspectives on Evangelism: Living in a Three-Storied Universe* (Nashville: Abingdon Press, 1993), p. 46.

What do these concerns have to do with arts ministry? Plenty. First of all, as we have already seen, the arts play a pivotal role in the emotional appeal of evangelism. Thus, they can easily become part of the problem when they focus solely on individual feelings and never integrate the convert into a full life of discipleship and social involvement.

Second, churches are increasingly creating entertainment-based worship services focused on emotive music and drama.[9] The underlying purpose of these services is often described as evangelism, when, in actual practice, it could sometimes be nothing more than proselytism. As with the idolatries we encountered earlier, this illustrates the fact that art can be used to achieve both positive and negative goals in the church.

Finally, art that is employed strictly for the purpose of saving souls can easily lose its integrity as art and be stripped of the very important purposes for which it is employed in human living. It no longer enriches through its sheer beauty, informs or forms us through its ability to make visible the invisible, or joins us together in communities of appreciation and gratitude. It all too easily becomes a tool that is lacking in thoughtfulness or real depth and, as such, is misused.[10] This makes it even more imperative that we ground our worship and witness in a thoroughgoing understanding and appreciation of what constitutes an authentic and healthy relationship between art and evangelism.

The authentic evangelistic conversation fulfills a number of different purposes and takes a variety of forms. First of all, it works through the medium of discursive language and theology. This is expressed most directly in evangelistic preaching — an art form in its own right. Preaching is the medium that has pride of place in the evangelistic enterprise. Alongside

9. Walter Kallestad, pastor of the Community Church of Joy in Phoenix, writes,

> The only way to capture people's attention is entertainment, I thought. If I want people to listen to my message, I've got to present it in a way that grabs their attention long enough for me to communicate the gospel. It was an epiphany, a breakthrough understanding for me. So our church strategy revolved around the gravitational force of entertainment for evangelism. [It's important to note that this article discusses how Kallestad later changed his mind on this point.]

"Showtime, No More!: Could Our Church Shift from Performance to Mission?" http://www
.christianitytoday.com/le (11/26/2008); *Christianity Today International Leadership Journal*.

10. H. R. Rookmaaker says, "When art is used as a tool for evangelism, it is often insincere and second-rate, devaluated to the level of propaganda. I would call this a form of prostitution, a misuse of one's talents." See *The Creative Gift: Essays on Art and the Christian Life* (Westchester, Ill.: Cornerstone Books, 1981), p. 113.

evangelistic preaching, however, the fine arts and human creativity are the most natural vehicles with which to communicate the gospel in a way that speaks powerfully to contemporary people.

Whether the medium of communication is preaching or art (or preaching *as* art), at the center of the conversation we find God. This is the good news. God has provided the Holy Spirit so that we can talk with one another, engaging in holy communication that points us in the direction of the saving love of Christ. The bad news is that we often garble the communication through our own lack of receptivity toward and clarity about the message. As has been suggested so often, our Babel (or babble) stands in opposition to the divine Pentecost.

Before we apprehend the gospel message "with ears that can hear," we need to be able to re-imagine it. The surrounding culture has provided us with a set of assumptions regarding Christianity. We tend to think and talk using those assumptions without first stopping to listen, without opening ourselves to the power of the original salvation story.

We are afraid of this kind of openness for two reasons. First, we simply do not want to work that hard. Uncovering the meaning of the gospel message and applying it to our lives takes time and effort. It requires us to change, with all the risks that frightening word implies. As a result of the gospel, we must become increasingly real and authentic in our encounter with God, the world, and ourselves.

To be receptive to newness and growth, we have to become vulnerable. We have seen that the arts provide access to places within the human person that are not touched in any other way. They help to make us vulnerable. Evangelists were among the first to recognize and capitalize on this possibility. John Wesley teamed up with his brother Charles, who wrote thousands of hymns for use in the early Methodist evangelistic meetings and services. Dwight Moody saw this same need very clearly when he persuaded Ira Sankey to leave his job and steady income with the IRS and join him to lead the hymn-singing at his revivals.

The gospel message inhabits us. So does art. Both the gospel and art have the capacity to help us change every aspect of our lives: body, spirit, and mind, our relationships with God, with those around us, and with the world itself. As Wesley and Moody both realized, emotion plays a pivotal role in these changes. It is a powerful motivating force behind our desire to alter the way in which we live. We are often at our most vulnerable when we experience the depths of emotion that come through contact with beauty, as well as through the anguish and pain that the arts can express.

Thus, while it is correct to say that the arts speak to the whole person, it is their capacity to move us emotionally that often provides the impetus for change and growth in other dimensions of our life.

At different times and in different circumstances, art employs the affections in at least four different ways. First, art enables us to vicariously experience the pain and alienation of the world. A particularly whimsical example of this is the way in which the private and public sufferings of the silent film star Charlie Chaplin illustrate the universal human condition. Chaplin, perhaps the first great comedic film star from the early twentieth century, lived a difficult life off-screen. Because of the early death of his father and his mother's illness, Charlie had to make his own way in the world before the age of ten. He soon found himself in vaudeville, where he developed a reputation as a comedian. Chaplin's brand of comedy was wide-ranging, encompassing slapstick and social criticism. With his trademark top hat and his melancholy demeanor, he created the character called "the Little Tramp," in the process personifying the trials and heartbreak of ordinary people living through difficult times.

Second, art provides countervailing, life-giving images to combat the destructive images coming from our society. We are bombarded by gratuitous sex, violence, and coarse language in the popular media. The results of the destructive and repressive policies of governments and social systems are all too apparent when we turn on the evening news. Arts ministry combats these images by providing alternatives that focus our attention on the holy and remove us, however temporarily, from the sphere of influence arising from the profane culture in which we live. In place of the fluctuating images of devastation and corruption coming from our television screens, we turn to beautiful paintings hung on our walls, paintings that form us over time and therefore require careful selection at the outset. As we are formed by these paintings, we are empowered to return to our profane culture and work toward its transformation.

Third, art provides pastoral experiences that soothe the hurts of the world. One example of this is the manner in which art therapists use the drawings and paintings of patients as a key to unlocking issues that have been causing pain and stunting the growth of those under their care.

Finally, art provides what Abraham Maslow calls "peak experiences,"[11] experiences that motivate us and inspire us to re-enter the fray, encounter-

11. Abraham Maslow, *Toward a Psychology of Being* (New York: D. Van Nostrand, 1968).

ing the problems and temptations we meet with renewed vigor and cour-age. The theologian Paul Tillich offers a unique illustration of the power of peak experiences. Tillich was a soldier in the trenches of World War I. To take his mind off the war, he studied pictures of great art that he encoun-tered in magazines. After the war ended, he traveled to Berlin, where he went to the Kaiser Wilhelm Museum to see the original paintings. He de-scribes the power of that experience:

> On the wall was a picture that had comforted me in battle, *Madonna with Singing Angels,* painted by Sandro Botticelli in the fifteenth century.
>
> Gazing up at it, I felt a state approaching ecstasy. In the beauty of the painting there was Beauty itself. It shone through the colors of the paint as the light of day shines through the stained-glass windows of a medieval church.
>
> As I stood there, bathed in the beauty its painter had envisioned so long ago, something of the divine source of all things came through to me. I turned away, shaken.
>
> That moment has affected my whole life, given me the keys for the interpretation of human existence, brought vital joy and spiritual truth.[12]

As many commentators have noted, this is a remarkable account from the life of a theologian of the stature of Paul Tillich. It is also a wonderful example of the power of art to open us to "the divine source of all things." As we enter into this conversation with art, we are "converted," baptized into a new way of relating to God and the world around us.

"I Love to Tell the Story"

The first task of evangelism is to tell the dramatic story of salvation history, the narratives that are foundational to the life of faith. Narratives of faith take the place of countervailing stories that try to provide meaning in our lives, stories that culminate in material gain, athletic conquest, personal power, or national pride, stories provided by the surrounding secular cul-ture that, in the end, are inadequate. As Walter Brueggemann says, "The reason they are less than adequate stories is that they lack the life-giving

---

12. Tillich, quoted in *Paul Tillich on Art and Architecture,* ed. John Dillenberger (New York: Crossroad, 1987), pp. 234-35.

power of holiness out beyond ourselves to which we must have access if we are to live fully human lives."[13]

The gospel itself is extraordinarily dramatic. Beyond the floods, shipwrecks, sea monsters, fires, and earthquakes, there is the sheer drama of creation and the image of God indwelling the world in the person of Jesus Christ. The drama of the gospel suggests that the dramatic arts of theatre and film, as well as the literary arts, are particularly appropriate and powerful means of telling once again the age-old story.

In his excellent study titled *Storytelling: Imagination and Faith*, William J. Bausch notes a number of characteristics of story. Here I would like to list several of these characteristics that make stories particularly appropriate vehicles for the evangelistic conversation:

1. Stories provoke curiosity and compel repetition.
2. Stories are a bridge to one's culture and roots.
3. Stories help us to remember.
4. Stories restore the original power of the word.
5. Stories evoke in us right-brain imagination, tenderness, and therefore wholeness.
6. Stories promote healing.
7. Stories provide a basis for hope and morality.
8. Stories are the basis for ministry.[14]

As Bausch explains,

> Propositions are statements on a page; stories are events in a life. Doctrine is the material of texts; story is the stuff of life. "He was rejected" is a clear and firm statement of fact, and there it rests. "He came unto his own and his own received him not" is a bit more catchy and poetic. But "there was no room for them in the inn," with its contextual richness of a cave, angels, Magi, shepherds, and an exotic star, is story. It will not let us forget, as time has demonstrated, the person written about: his life, rejection, and death. Theology is a secondhand reflection of such an event; story is the unspeakable event's first voice.[15]

---

13. Brueggemann, *Biblical Perspectives on Evangelism*, p. 11.

14. William J. Bausch, *Storytelling: Imagination and Faith* (Mystic, Conn.: Twenty-Third Publications, 1984), pp. 29-63.

15. Bausch, *Storytelling*, p. 28.

Storytelling takes many forms. It comes to us in spoken, written, or enacted narratives. By whatever means it is conveyed, when human beings enter into the narrative details of a story, the possibility for transformation occurs as they imagine themselves anew in and through the lens of the characters they see in front of them.

Arts Ministry and Community

It is important to counterbalance the emphasis on the individual — often encountered in evangelistic art — with a strong focus on the relationship between art and community. As we move from a consideration of art and evangelism to an examination of art and community, we see that arts ministry can be an important bridge between the private and public spheres of Christian life and witness.

The danger in an exclusively private approach to arts ministry is that the individual Christian and the local church can lose all connection with the church universal. This is what happens so often when contemporary worship becomes the sole alternative available in a local parish. The artistic traditions in these services are limited to styles derived from North American popular culture coming exclusively from the last twenty-five years. The message of this art is often based on an appeal to the individual. When these services become the norm, not only do we overbalance our worship in the direction of the individual, but we find that we are no longer worshipping with believers from ages past or with those who live in other parts of the world. The doctrine of the communion of the saints is very much at risk.

The alternative is to view art as one of the signposts of our common life. If arts ministry employs language and images that are inclusive, it can provide a home for everyone. One aspect of inclusivity involves relating worship and ministry to the setting of the local culture. Roman Catholics call this *inculturation,* while Protestants typically employ the term *indigenization.* Both terms mean that we accommodate the (artistic) language of *native* cultures into our own faith and practice.

However, we also need to bear in mind that to be truly inclusive, art should not be restricted to any one cultural tradition. Inculturation should not mean restricting ourselves *only* to the local tradition. Indigenization should not become a way of segregating people into cultural ghettoes where they have no contact with the outside world. Rather, true inclusivity refers to the underlying principle that art should create access to the breadth and depth of our faith, access that is possible only if we take full advantage of the artistic resources we have been bequeathed by our predecessors, our contemporaries, and those who live apart from us.

In his classic book *Life Together*, Dietrich Bonhoeffer says, "Our community with one another consists solely in what Christ has done to both of us."[16] One of the ways that Christ acts in both of us is through the medium of artistic experience, a gift of grace that unites the Christian community in holy fellowship.

As art works on us individually, we are formed into new people. This process of human formation establishes possible connections between people that were not there previously. Not only do we develop common bonds in terms of our character and identity, but we also learn to enjoy and share our enjoyment of common objects of beauty. As Frank Burch Brown says, "Beautiful works of art . . . constitute extensions and expressions of who we are. Much of our shared delight as humans is artistic in nature."[17]

This shared enjoyment of beauty can lead to shared bonds of love between human beings. As Brown explains, "Because the love and enjoyment of other human beings is both enhanced and interpreted through art, it is partly by appreciating what others have made artistically that we can love one another."[18] In light of this, let us heed the call of the gospel and love one another, for love (as well as beauty) comes from God. In our mutual experiences of beauty, we discover once again the richness of our common humanity.

That richness is enhanced by the power of arts ministry to help us cross barriers that keep people apart. This includes generational, cultural, denominational, theological, and disciplinary barriers. As Doug Adams reminds us, "Worship with all the arts involves those who remember through hearing and those who remember through seeing and those who remember through eating and dancing. Such worship helps churches grow by bringing together persons of all different ages, races, genders, and classes."[19]

We also have to acknowledge that sometimes the arts *are* the barrier for many people. When theological distinctions between denominations

16. Dietrich Bonhoeffer, *Life Together* (San Francisco: Harper, 1954), p. 12.

17. Frank Burch Brown, *Good Taste, Bad Taste, and Christian Taste: Aesthetics in Religious Life* (New York: Oxford University Press, 2000), p. 116.

18. Brown, *Good Taste, Bad Taste, and Christian Taste*, p. 116.

19. Doug Adams, *Postmodern Worship and the Arts* (San Jose, Calif.: Resource Publications, 2002), p. 1.

Kingdom Kidz: Puppets for the Lord
St. Andrews United Methodist Church, Milton, Pennsylvania

Donna Bridge and the Kingdom Kidz' presentation at a Chinese Overseas Mission Church

Donna Bridge was in her final year as a kindergarten teacher when she invited a friend into her classroom to present a storytelling session using puppets. This was her first introduction to puppetry. Following that, in December 1999, while she was on staff as the Children's Ministry Coordinator at St. Andrews United Methodist Church in Milton, Pennsylvania, a member of the congregation presented Bridge with some puppets she found at a yard sale. That day the Kingdom Kidz Puppet Ministry was birthed. Bridge soon assembled a team of volunteers and began work on their first project: a presentation at the church's block party the following June.

Since that initial venture, the ministry has continued to grow and prosper. In 2008, children and adult volunteers presented 152 different performances. Along with Bridge, who serves as the director of the ministry, a board of directors and eighteen volunteers support the ministry. Along the way the ministry team has attended puppet festivals and acquired the resources needed to do black-light puppetry, a form of puppetry in which the entire performance venue is darkened and fluorescent puppets glow under ultra-violet light, allowing for a wide variety of special effects and creative opportunities not otherwise available in typical puppetry.

After the third year of the ministry, Bridge asked the volunteers what direction they envisioned for the ministry. The overwhelming response was to move out beyond the confines of their church and share the ministry on a broad basis. This progressed to the point that they now perform only a few times a year in their own church, and have expanded the ministry to include both sacred and secular venues. They eventually incorporated and have achieved non-profit status. Over the years, Kingdom Kidz have performed for worship services, puppet dinner theatre, children's day services, church retreats, community police nights out, local Lions' Club events, school events, and festivals. Recently they presented programs in conjunction with a public television station and the local community hospital. They discovered that allowing the audience to handle the puppets themselves at the end of a presentation spurs even greater interest in the ministry.

According to Bridge, Kingdom Kidz exists "to present to kids of all ages the Gospel of Jesus Christ in a creative and challenging manner, as well as presenting social and moral issues in a secular setting for all ages. . . ."* The entire ministry takes very seriously the calling to surround everything they do with prayer and to rely on God's guidance at every turn. Devotions are part of every rehearsal. The ministry shows evidence of a deep commitment to discovering how their puppetry can be of service to Jesus Christ.

*Donna Bridge, e-mail to the author, 4 July 2009.

are blurred, oftentimes the arts are one of the principal differences that separate churches from one another in the eyes of the laity. One church employs the music of popular culture, while another uses classical repertoire; one has a liturgical dance company, while another considers dance to be sinful; one creates elaborate banners and showcases visual art, while another believes in whitewashed walls and denigrates symbolism; one integrates film into their worship services, while another finds this to be an unnecessary distraction. These distinctions have the potential to divide congregations from one another and to create rifts within individual congregations. As arts ministers in these congregations soon discover, it is virtually impossible to avoid offending someone's aesthetic sensibilities regardless of what position a church takes. In this ecclesiastical and social context, it is particularly important to acknowledge the many ways in which the arts can help us bridge the barriers between people, thereby enriching the unity of Christ's church.

Generational Barriers

Arts ministry is often limited to youth. Congregations tend to be forgiving of low artistic standards and supportive of creative ventures in worship and ministry as long as young people are involved. While this limitation is unfortunate (as is the assumption that we do not need to hold young people to high standards), it does drives home a point that the church has long understood: adults will follow the lead of their children. In the words of Isaiah, "and a little child shall lead them" (Isa. 11:6b).

John Calvin was well-acquainted with this in sixteenth-century Geneva. He wanted to teach a new repertoire of congregational psalmody to the congregation, and he used the children to do it. The children's choir at St. Pierre in Geneva became mentors for the Genevan church, learning new tunes and texts, singing them both within and outside of worship, thus enabling their parents to gradually learn them as well.

Stereotypically, particular styles or forms of art have often been associated with different generations. Whether or not the stereotype is accurate, it is often assumed, for instance, that elderly parishioners appreciate nineteenth-century hymnody and realistic visual art, and have a natural resistance to dance in worship. Members of the baby-boom generation enjoy praise choruses, soft rock, and drama. Young people, meanwhile, are attracted to hard rock music and "alternative" music. They are more fully sensory in their approach to worship and naturally gravitate toward film.

These stereotypes break down quickly in conversations with real people. Stereotypes like this tend to create generational barriers based on artistic forms and styles. The problems with this approach become most apparent in churches that plan different worship services to appeal to different generations. The lack of intergenerational interaction creates the potential for conflicting visions of what it means to be the church. In addition, it creates a climate where the values and wisdom of older generations are no longer available for the benefit of those who are younger, and vice versa.

The arts can help the church transcend these barriers. Today we find intergenerational sacred dance companies involving young children and their grandparents, art shows that feature the works of children, youth, and adults, choirs that include adolescents and adults, and drama troupes that employ actors of all ages. Intergenerational ministry can be hampered by the fact that seniors, adults, young people, and children often feel uncomfortable when they are artificially thrown together in order to create intergenerational opportunities. "Youth Sunday" is a typical case in point. Often the only people in the congregation who genuinely appreciate this tradition are the parents of the young people who are participating. One wonderful aspect of arts ministry is that there is a common purpose and a common set of skills germane to that purpose which people of all ages can embrace. A working example of this is Declare His Glory Dance Ministry at Sunrise Church, a United Methodist congregation in Colorado Springs. This is an intergenerational ensemble whose ages range from seven to senior-citizen age. They participate together in Bible study, prayer, and rehearsal; they dance in worship, at senior residences, and in concerts at the church.

Clearly, the arts have the capacity to unite people across the generational divide. At a time when youth culture is increasingly becoming enshrined in the church through the medium of contemporary worship, it is especially important to find venues where members of different generations can develop common interests and share insights with one another. Arts ministry is uniquely positioned to assist in this process.

Cultural Barriers

The arts have the potential to cross two different kinds of cultural barriers: barriers within the Western church and barriers between the Western and the non-Western world. Within the Western church we have witnessed cultural barriers — between adherents of historic or "classical" art forms (particularly music) and those who advocate for popular culture, and between different racial, ethnic, and socio-economic groups.

The classical-popular divide is a cultural barrier that is crossed only with the greatest of difficulty. Nonetheless, it is possible to do so provided that education and pastoral ministry are valued by the leadership of the local church. For art to be an agent of unity rather than disunity, two factors are particularly important. First, both classical and popular advocates must be willing to work toward mutual understanding. This means understanding one another's art forms, not just their motivations for employing these styles. Second, there must be a desire to undergird art with theological reflection. Debates about this topic involve theology more than they do art. Without thoughtful and mutually respectful education, it is hard to bridge this barrier. With these caveats, however, I believe it is still possible to say that there are individual artworks and styles of art (especially from folk traditions) that can cross stylistic lines and be a source of unity in the church. In many cases the non-musical arts are particularly effective ways to provide this unity.

Divisions between diverse racial, ethnic, and socio-economic groups are increasingly being crossed as subcultures intentionally expand their repertoire and worship using the materials common to other groups. In many congregations, homogeneous artistic style is no longer seen as the ideal. Here we can take a cue from ecumenism, which learned the importance of building on the basis of strong religious traditions before seeing how these traditions could be shared. Similarly, building from the strength of vibrant ethnic artistic traditions can provide the resources necessary to cross over and experiment with other artistic styles.

Outside the Western world, the arts are often allied with Christianity. Worship in Africa practically demands dance. Latin America has a thriving visual arts culture. The Christian arts faced a difficult beginning in the non-Western world owing to the oppressive cultural evangelism of nineteenth-century missionaries. The situation is no less challenging today because of the ubiquity and hegemony of American popular culture. Nonetheless, much indigenous music, art, and dance has made its way into the worship lives of cultures throughout the world. From Korean Presbyterians to Argentinean Roman Catholics, there has been an upsurge in indigenous artistic activity during the past century. In the United States, non-Western artistic expression is rapidly becoming a more important part of the worship and cultural life of many mainline churches, including those churches that have little or no ethnic population.

Subcultures often find occasion to express themselves in and through arts ministry. An African-American gospel choir, a mariachi band, pottery from New Mexico, dances from Appalachia, films from France — all these point to the vitality of different subcultures as they integrate themselves into arts ministries in new and exciting ways. An arts ministry that seeks out the resources of different cultures can, in fact, teach an important lesson in cross-cultural sensitivity to the entire church. It can bring the wisdom of different subcultures to the church at large.

Denominational Barriers

Our culture is highly mobile. So, too, are the members of our churches. Denominational loyalty, which used to run so deep, is often replaced by church-shopping as more and more cherishers of choice search for the "perfect fit."

Fortunately, the arts are not restricted to one denomination or another. They easily cross these barriers and appeal to people who would, ordinarily, not have been associated with one another. Lutheran chorales are found in Catholic hymnals. We understand that there is nothing "Methodist" about the gesture of a dancer or the metaphors in a poem. Color, line, and texture are not Protestant or Roman Catholic categories. As such, the arts have great potential as a focal point for ecumenical activity. They can unite Christians who are divided by historical or denominational rifts.

This ability to cross denominational barriers is also one of the services provided by sacred arts organizations as they seek to overcome the isolation of individual artists. Christians in the Visual Arts, for instance, brings together visual artists from a wide variety of different denominations and enables them to identify with one another and pursue their common interests without reference to denominational barriers.

Theological Barriers

Just as there is nothing "Methodist" about a gesture, so there is nothing conservative or liberal about it, either. Ecumenism travels only as far as theology allows. The arts offer an opportunity to go farther, to connect us with those with whom we have significant doctrinal disagreements, to enable us to worship with them and share their passion for the beauty of a painting or an elegant liturgical dance. This is a rare experience in our fractured ecclesiastical world and deserves to be cultivated.

Professional Barriers

Finally, we come to professional barriers. In recent years, it has become harder and harder for people to talk with one another. Engineers can't understand psychologists; stockbrokers can't relate to pharmacists. Seemingly no one can understand doctors. As the world becomes more and more specialized, each profession develops its own language and ways of thinking. Arts ministry offers the possibility of crossing these barriers. This happens as people from differing professional backgrounds come together in community to create and appreciate common art forms. It also occurs as the arts relate to one another in the context of the church's life and mission. Historically, worship has been the locus for a variety of different art forms, operating either independently or in concert with one another. This is no less true today. Dancers work with musicians and theatre artists. Poets interact with composers and visual artists. In addition to these cross-disciplinary opportunities within the arts, there are additional possibilities for integration between arts ministry and other church ministries such as religious education or evangelism.

Shared delight and the ability to bridge a wide variety of religious, cultural, and artistic barriers make arts ministry an important resource for enhancing community in the local church. Relationships between individuals and groups become more cohesive and loving, and the church's bonds of unity are fostered, making them available as a source of pastoral healing during the inevitable times of conflict and stress that are bound to come to every local congregation at some point in its history.

Arts Ministry and Social Justice

Art helps integrate people into the Christian community. In turn, it nurtures the ability of that community to encounter the world in prophetic terms that offer hope for transformation and renewal. As we have done earlier, we will first consider the question of whether or not art functions as a force for social justice. Following that we will ask the related question of how art might function in this capacity.

Beauty and Goodness

At the root of the question of art and social justice lies the larger issue of the relationship between beauty and goodness. These two words have a long and complex history together. In the Bible we see them linked in Psalms 29 and 96, where we read this classic exhortation: "Worship the Lord in the beauty of holiness" (KJV). Western philosophy views the connection between beauty and morality under the broad heading of axiology. Here aesthetics, the study of value in relation to beauty, is related to ethics, the study of moral values (one might say moral beauty). Plato was one of the first Western philosophers to take up this issue. He wrote extensively on the impact that the arts, particularly music, have on human behavior, and the important role that music plays in creating a good society. Plato believed that music has a profound influence on character development, and thus it should be regulated carefully.[20]

The late medieval world continued to develop beauty and goodness as two elements of the transcendental properties of being, aspects of God's character that, in turn, were found together in everything that exists. Clearly, the relationship between beauty and goodness is complex. To unpack it further, we need to first look at the meaning of the term *ethos*.

Quentin Faulkner has written about ethos in relation to musical thought in the church. He defines *ethos* as the way that "music cooperates in the formation of good human character."[21] By extension, this same concept can be applied to the other arts as well. For instance, William Dyrness points out that in the seventeenth century, people who studied "moral" paintings were thought to become better people.[22]

---

20. For a good discussion of Plato's view, see Donald Walhout, "Music and Moral Goodness," *The Journal of Aesthetic Education* 29, no. 1 (Spring 1995): 9-10.

21. Quentin Faulkner, *Wiser than Despair: The Evolution of Ideas in the Relationship between Music and the Christian Church* (Westport, Conn.: Greenwood Press, 1996), p. 66.

22. William Dyrness, *Visual Faith: Art, Theology, and Worship in Dialogue* (Grand Rapids: Baker Academic, 2001), p. 58.

Concerts with a Cause

The Georgia Guitar Quartet performing in 2010 at a concert by Concerts with a Cause, St. John United Methodist Church, Augusta, Georgia

In 2003, St. John United Methodist Church in Augusta, Georgia, dedicated a new three-manual mechanical-action pipe organ built by the Dobson Organ Company of Lake City, Iowa. As a way of presenting this organ to the community, they began a new concert series. Under the leadership of music director and organist Jamie Garvey, this series has developed two focal points:

The ancient Christian understanding of ethos says that by imitating the ideal order of cosmic harmony through music, human beings can in some small way tune themselves to the harmony of the spheres and regain the state of their souls prior to the time of their fall from grace in the Garden of Eden. John Dryden articulated this eloquently:

From Harmony, from heav'nly Harmony
This universal Frame began;
From Harmony to Harmony

(1) presenting music of great beauty that is not otherwise available in the Augusta community, and (2) raising money for local service organizations. Donors underwrite the costs of the series each year, and a "love offering" is taken at each concert. As of the 2009-10 season, $87,346.65 has been provided to thirty-one local service organizations. Among the many recipients have been Habitat for Humanity, the Golden Harvest Food Bank, the Boys and Girls Clubs of Augusta, the United Methodist Children's Home, the Alzheimer's Association of Augusta, and the Friendship Community Center.

While organ music remains a central focal point of the series, there have been a wide variety of different musical offerings over the years. Some examples include the Manhattan Piano Trio with Eugenia Zuckerman, the Atlanta Sacred Chorale, the Georgia Guitar Quartet, a performance of the Brahms Requiem with Joseph Flummerfelt conducting, and an evening with Don and Emily Saliers. Concerts typically average 300 audience members; the biggest audience — a crowd of 1800 — came for the Brahms Requiem.

The ministry expresses its primary mission in the following terms: "Christianity has always been associated with great works of art and beauty, expressing the inexpressible and transcending the earthbound. It is our prayer that these concerts will help you find God here. As we gather, we also hope to benefit service organizations which are doing good work for the Kingdom of God in our community."* In this mission statement Concerts with a Cause is explicitly relating art and social justice, making real the connection between beauty and holiness.

*See http://www.stjohnaugusta.org (May 1, 2009).

Through all the compass of the Notes it ran,
The Diapason closing full in Man.[23]

Medieval writers note that the emotions should be under the control of the mind. The good life, the life they believe the gospel envisions for God's people, is a life of calm, tranquil nobility. The principal task of music

23. John Dryden, "A Song for Saint Cecilia's Day," in *The Poems of John Dryden*, Vol. III, ed. Paul Hammond and David Hopkins (Harlow, Eng.: Pearson Education, 2000), pp. 185-91.

and the arts is to impact the life of the mind and to enable the mind to be in charge of the emotions. Music or art that stimulates the emotions is, in fact, considered to be a moral problem, not a positive contribution to mature living.

In the wake of Renaissance humanism, the arts were once again seen as a source of emotional stimulation, a viewpoint also shared by the sixteenth-century reformers. Luther believed that music forms good character, governs the feelings, quiets and cheers the soul, and forms fine and skillful people.[24]

As time went on, belief in the positive role that art plays in expressing the emotions continued and intensified in the literature of aesthetics. Immanuel Kant noted that we are more likely to do our duty if we are happy than if we are disheartened or morose. Being downcast is enervating, while joy is energizing. Music and art help us keep our spirits up, thus contributing to our overall sense of duty and responsibility.[25]

From his vantage point in the twentieth century, the composer Paul Hindemith added, "Music has to be converted to moral power. We receive its sounds and forms, but they remain meaningless unless we include them in our own mental activity and use their fermenting quality to turn our souls towards everything noble, superhuman, and ideal."[26]

We should stop briefly and note the two different emphases that have been suggested thus far: (1) the Greek and medieval idea that the arts are a means of impacting the mind so as to control the passions and keep them in check, and (2) the modern notion that sees the arts as a means of arousing the emotions so that we will be motivated to do good works.

In both cases, the prior question of whether or not the arts have an impact on morality is answered in the affirmative. The real issue is *how* this happens, not *whether* it happens.

If we grant art a role in ethical life, we need to ask one further question: To what extent is moral goodness or badness intrinsic in an artwork? The concern is not simply whether art impacts human behavior, but whether and to what extent art can be said to possess ethical qualities itself. Donald Walhout amplifies this thought: "What we mean by a morally good or bad work is one whose whole makeup, whose total impact, whose

---

24. For a good discussion of Martin Luther's thought on music, see Carl F. Schalk, *Luther on Music: Paradigms of Praise* (St. Louis: Concordia Publishing House, 1988), especially pp. 31-49.

25. See Walhout, "Music and Moral Goodness," pp. 13-14.

26. Paul Hindemith, quoted in Walhout, "Music and Moral Goodness," pp. 14-15.

very nature makes a positive or negative contribution to the moral threshold of a humane society."[27]

On the surface, it seems obvious that works of art are *things*, morally neutral in themselves, taking on moral implications only as they form associations in the mind of the observer. This implies a learned reaction by the observer and a certain common storehouse of meaning between the artwork and the observer.

Nonetheless, the question stands. Are there, in fact, associations that are so common within a particular culture that individual works of art can be said to be morally good or bad? This is the issue that is at the center of the censorship debate. It is also an important question for arts ministers to ask. Granting that more or less universal moral implications might be perceived by significant segments of the population, arts ministry must function in a pastoral mode, with thoughtfulness and sensitivity to the sheer power of the arts to impact human behavior in either a positive or a negative direction.

Instrumental Value and Intrinsic Value

If the arts do, in fact, have the capacity to be moral, is this the primary reason that they should exist as a vital part of a church's ministry? Is a painting, or a play, or a dance valuable because it has a positive impact on human character?

Those who answer "yes" are sensitive to the "instrumental" value of art. In other words, art is important as an instrument (or means) that enables human beings to achieve some higher purpose. This argument is often encountered as a rationale for keeping the arts in the public schools in times of budget crisis. The arts are viewed as a tool to increase the intelligence and social skills of schoolchildren. Similar arguments are applied to the role of art in the church. Art becomes important in relation to ecclesiastical goals, not because of any special value it has in the life of the individual or the community. The arts help worshippers experience a "high" that binds them to the community. Likewise, art keeps Sunday-school children occupied and allows them to have a good time at church. Some of the goals are quite lofty. As this and the preceding chapter point out, art has the capacity to help us become mature disciples. Likewise, it is hard to imagine worship that is totally devoid of art.

27. Walhout, "Music and Moral Goodness," p. 12.

These later goals, in particular, appear so self-evident that there would seem to be no logical alternative to the instrumental theory of value. As with most things in human life that appear self-evident, this is not the case. The contrasting view is that the significance of art transcends any of the particular goals it helps us achieve. Art has intrinsic value in human life. It offers sheer delight, providing a sense of fulfillment and satisfaction that do not require any practical rationale. Its justification, as is the case with all of creation, is simply that "God has willed it to be."[28]

In the end, there is no reason why the instrumental and the intrinsic theories of art need to be mutually exclusive. Both make important contributions toward understanding why we engage in arts ministry.

Art as a School for Ethical Sensitivity

Whatever else it does, art clearly has an impact on human intuition. Intuition, in turn, is a factor in many moral decisions. As William Dean reminds us, "The tough ethical problems have to do with getting oneself and others to be sufficiently sensitive to realize that love and justice are demanded in a particular situation."[29]

Being sensitive to the moral implications and consequences arising from a potential course of action is one of the most important personal and social skills we possess. Is it possible that aesthetic sensibility and moral sensibility may be related through their shared reliance on human intuition?

The fact that many Nazi prison camp administrators loved art and music suggests that intuition arising from aesthetic contemplation does not guarantee moral behavior. Human beings have the power of choice, and they can decide how and under what circumstances they will apply the sensitivity they have gained through exposure to the arts. Let us be clear, though. This is not an argument for being insensitive. It is simply a way of recognizing that we live in a fallen world. Given the moral pressures brought to bear by the world, it is *even more imperative* that we develop every resource at our disposal to become aware of the needs of those around us. Living a life surrounded by beauty and creativity has the potential to

28. Hans R. Rookmaaker, *The Creative Gift* (Westchester, Ill.: Cornerstone Books, 1981), pp. 113-14.

29. William Dean, *Coming to a Theology of Beauty* (Philadelphia: Westminster Press, 1972), p. 167.

act on us for good by heightening awareness of our surroundings and deepening our capacity to respond to what we see and hear.

Living an ethical life means, first and foremost, living in right relation: right relation to God, to ourselves, to other people, and to the cosmos. Living in right relation means starting from a view of the world that is honest and unprejudiced. It means being rooted in the reality of the situation, not coloring that reality to make it appear as we would like it to appear. Seeing things as they are, making distinctions between the essential and the inconsequential, is a moral imperative. When we view life in this way, we are developing a moral vision of the world. Cast in these terms, art is a powerful lens through which we can view the world from a moral perspective. It provides us with a vision that is often uncompromising and lays bare the brute facts of our existence.

The alternative is to view life through rose-colored glasses. Unfortunately, much of the "religious" art (music, dance, drama, etc.) that we employ in the Western church does this all too well. Richard Egenter notes that attempts to awaken a superficial or sentimental religious response from the viewer/listener may be morally suspect. They reduce the profound to the trivial, replacing authentic artistic creativity with cheap effects. He says, "Reality has first been smoothed out and only then given artistic expression. A picture of this kind, by avoiding all disturbing facts and jarring notes, creates a gentle, placid atmosphere in which there is an element of complacency which can very rapidly become a means of cheap stimulation. . . ."[30]

Authentic religious art not only engenders an honest view of the world; it communicates that view to the observer. The insights of the artist can become a significant factor in developing the moral vision of the individual or community that employs his or her art in worship and witness. It is important that the content of this artistic vision corresponds to the depth and complexity of the world around us, not to the triviality and superficiality of our own limited vision.

Art as a School for Ethical Imagination

William Dean says, "The heart of moral inadequacy is a failure to imagine fresh interpretations, or appearances, and to contrast these with the reali-

---

30. Richard Egenter, *The Desecration of Christ,* trans. Edward Quinn, ed. Nicolete Gray (Chicago: Franciscan Herald Press, 1967), p. 42.

ties of a situation. . . . If the ability to conceive of fresh interpretations of real situations is lost, ethical sensitivity and discernment are cut off at their source."[31]

Artists engage our imaginations as they take us on a tour through the alternative world of meaning they have constructed. In this imaginary world, it is possible to envision new relations between people, new relations with the environment, and new relations with the divine. Old habits of mind and behavior are suspended, and we can re-envision what it might be like to live in a world of justice and peace, in a city whose main street is the "river of the water of life" (Rev. 22:1). As the facts on the ground in our own world become more violent and life itself becomes more tenuous, it is increasingly important to be able to envision these other possibilities.

James Empereur talks about the importance of breaking free from the tyrannies of the past and imaginatively reconfiguring the web of power in which we are caught. He notes, "We are less overwhelmed by unjust situations and structures when we have an alternative world of meaning." Empereur points out that, having separated ourselves from the world in which we live and reconstructed that world according to a different set of priorities, we can then re-enter our own world with renewed vigor and insight, and "we can responsibly engage it."[32]

Sometimes we are afraid of this kind of work. It seems like an exercise in fantasy and unreality. In fact, it is one of the most important means of acting responsibly in the real world. Without the ability to engage our ethical imagination, to distance ourselves from the sources of oppression and reconfigure them in our imaginations, we might very well miss the opportunity to act on these new images in the real world.

Art as a School for the Will

John Navone reminds us of the importance of beauty for the development of the human will:

> Beauty, in fact, is at the heart of all human motivation, decision, and action; for we do not decide and act unless we are moved by the attractive-

---

31. Dean, *Coming to a Theology of Beauty,* pp. 169-70.
32. James Empereur, "Art and Social Justice," in *Art as Religious Studies,* ed. Doug Adams and Diane Apostolos-Cappadona (New York: Crossroad, 1990), pp. 175-76.

ness of a particular good. . . . Life without beauty would be unmotivated, mere drift, and less than truly human. . . . Without the attractiveness of beauty, intellectual, moral, and religious goods are bereft of their power to transform human life.[33]

There are, in fact, several different ways in which the arts function as a school for the will. First, as Navone points out, living a good life, defined as a life guided by proper ethical decisions, can be a dry and unappealing proposition. It suggests a life lived under the law rather than under grace, a life that is defined by saying "no" to the temptations of the world rather than saying "yes" to the wonders of God's kingdom. For the good life to be attractive, for it to hold out a vision that has the power to motivate us, it must, in some way, be beautiful.

This does not mean that we have to be constantly surrounded by beautiful artifacts or works of art. It certainly does not mean that we depend on beauty to save us.[34] What it does mean is that beauty is an important, indeed a necessary component of the good life. As Nicholas Wolterstorff says at the head of this chapter, beauty is "a component within and a species of that joy which belongs to the shalom God has ordained as the goal of human existence."[35]

For human beings to live lives of high ethical character and conviction, they have to be properly motivated. For most people it is not enough to simply suggest that motivation arises from duty. There must be something desirable about the end they are seeking. The beauty of the ethical life, beauty as part of what it actually means to *experience* this life, can be an important factor in providing the necessary motivation.

Second, both art and ethical living require discipline. The artist develops certain habits and practices them over time. Artists learn to work with their materials and fashion them into coherent shapes and forms. They redeem the time spent in preparation by investing it with meaning and sig-

33. John Navone, *Toward a Theology of Beauty* (Collegeville, Minn.: Liturgical Press, 1996), pp. 24-25.

34. While I think that in absolute terms this is true, it is still worth reading Alexander Solzhenitsyn's article titled "Beauty Will Save the World" in *The World Treasury of Modern Religious Thought*, ed. Jaroslav Pelikan (Boston: Little, Brown & Co., 1990), pp. 623-30, where he argues that the "whimsical, unpredictable, unexpected branches of Beauty" may, in the end, yield more fruit than truth and goodness.

35. Wolterstorff, *Art in Action: Toward a Christian Aesthetic* (Grand Rapids: Wm. B. Eerdmans, 1980), p. 169.

nificance, by developing their own unique expressive language that cooperates in the creation or re-creation of beauty.

Living a life based on moral conviction similarly requires the formation of habits. This takes practice over a long period of time. It is often arduous work. In the process of living, as in artistry, servanthood becomes the central focus. Just as artists serve a vision of beauty that sometimes takes over their entire being for a time, so the pilgrim on the path of servanthood and discipleship is taken over by a vision of holiness:

> Christ be with me,
> Christ within me,
> Christ behind me,
> Christ before me,
> Christ beside me,
> Christ to win me,
> Christ to comfort
> and restore me.[36]

The vision of which St. Patrick writes, that we sing to the stirring tune of "St. Patrick's Breastplate," is a vision of discipleship that is all-encompassing, involving discipline and beauty, empowered by the abiding presence of Christ, who is there "to comfort and restore me." It is a vision that grows out of the possibilities of human formation inherent in the arts and offers the hope of moral action in the larger social spheres in which we all live.

The Artist as Witness and Advocate

Finally, we look at the artist as witness and advocate. As Empereur suggests, many artists live on the margins of society. As such, they have a certain distance from the society that enables them to see it more clearly and act as critics. In the context of their criticism, artists bear witness to an alternative world of meaning that holds human dignity as a core value.

Empereur continues, "Art can bring us together in ways that social programs, government policies, or ideological designs cannot. Art can

---

36. St. Patrick, "I Bind unto Myself This Day," trans. Cecil Alexander, *The Hymnal 1982* (New York: Church Hymnal Corporation, 1982), #370.

help us to find solidarity in the beautiful rather than in systems. Art speaks for those who will not speak or who cannot speak. Art can help us take the first step in building bridges between hostile powers."[37]

Unfortunately, the alternative scenario is also possible. In the wrong hands, art can be oppressive. As is the case in many totalitarian regimes, it serves as a projection of power and a means of solidifying a repressive ideology. The potential for this to happen makes the prophetic responsibility of the artist even more important. In the dual roles of *witness*, confronting the unjust social systems created by human civilizations, and *advocate*, voicing the concerns of those who are crushed by these systems, artists serve both the culture and the church. Judith Malina, co-founder of "The Living Theatre" in New York City, wrote about it this way:

> The role of the artist in the social structure follows the need of the changing times:
>
> > In time of social stasis: to activate
> > In time of germination: to invent fertile new forms
> > In time of revolution: to extend the possibilities of peace
> > > and liberty
> > In time of violence: to make peace
> > In time of despair: to give hope
> > In time of silence: to sing out[38]

This is a role that the church itself is often reluctant to embrace. Perhaps, over time, arts ministry can challenge the church to reconsider the centrality of this calling to its life and mission in the world.

Arts Ministry and the Cosmos

Beyond their connections with human communities, we should not forget that arts ministers are engaged with the cosmos itself. "Dust to dust and ashes to ashes." So we repeat sorrowfully on Ash Wednesday each year. Instead of thinking of this as a fateful pronouncement on our expected de-

37. Empereur, "Art and Social Justice," p. 168.
38. Judith Malina, "The Work of an Anarchist Theatre," in *Reimaging America: The Arts of Social Change*, ed. Mark O'Brien and Craig Little (Philadelphia: New Society Publishers, 1990), p. 40.

mise, we might look on it as a proclamation — indeed, a celebration — of how we are rooted in creation and enjoy its manifold gifts. Just as human beings were called to be gardeners in Eden, cultivating and caring for the world, so arts ministers can be gardeners (literally or figuratively) in the setting of the local church.

This has a variety of different implications. Nicholas Wolterstorff notes that all human beings have a spatial and a causal connection to the created world.[39] They exist in a particular place and interact with the things around them.

In addition, artists are embedded within creation by virtue of the fact that the materials they employ in their creative work are the same materials from which they themselves are fashioned. They share a direct, physical connection with their artistry. This is obviously true of dancers, but in more subtle ways applies also to other art forms and the processes of human creativity itself. We do not live in a vacuum. God has provided us with the created world as the context for our very being, as the means for the sustenance of our lives, for our ability to work and play, to give birth and grow, to hope and to love.

As we look at the world around us, we are inspired by the sheer abundance and extravagance of the natural world and led to praise the God who is the source of all beauty:

> I sing the goodness of the Lord,
>   that filled the earth with food;
> he form'd the creatures with his word,
>   and then pronounced them good.
> Lord, how thy wonders are display'd,
>   where e'er I turn mine eye;
> If I survey the ground I tread,
>   or gaze upon the sky![40]

For most people this is probably what comes to mind when they first think of beauty: the natural beauty of a sunset or a mountain range, the amazing variety of God's creatures or the mind-numbing reaches of inter-

---

39. Wolterstorff, *Art in Action*, p. 70.

40. Isaac Watts, "Praise for Creation and Providence," in *Divine Songs for Children*, 1715, quoted in Erik Routley, *A Panorama of Christian Hymnody* (Chicago: GIA Publications, 1979), p. 125.

stellar space. In the context of arts ministry, we think first of the beauty of a poem or the graceful movement of a dancer, not the world of nature. Yet, I would suggest that these forms of aesthetic beauty and human creativity are rooted in the larger context of natural beauty, to which they ultimately owe their existence. In fact, aesthetic and natural beauty exist in a relationship to one another that is mutually edifying and enlivening to both the community of faith and the wider human community from which it is drawn.

Richard Harries says, "Experiences of beauty, whether in nature or in art, are among the most precious and powerful given to us. Beauty has the strange effect of at once beckoning us to itself, and pointing beyond itself to that which seems tantalizingly unattainable. It draws us to itself and through itself."[41]

As arts ministers we should keep this in mind. Among other things, this means that arts ministry can take as its object the natural world, not just the world of human creativity. It explores the interconnections between the two, in the process cultivating new and unexpected landscapes and vignettes.

Calvin Johansson reminds us, "The material world is a gift from God, has potential, and is fundamentally good. Consequently, the artist must respect it."[42] As artists work with their materials, as they get to know them intimately and spend time being attentive to the inner properties and tendencies of those materials, they come to respect and even love the materials themselves. They enter into a relationship with wood, stone, fabric, color, gesture, and sound that is endlessly inquisitive and takes great joy in every new discovery. This is a lesson to all of us about how we should relate to the world in which we live. Wendell Berry teaches us this lesson through the words of his character Hannah Coulter as she walks along the Shade Branch River:

> One of the happiest moments of my walks is when I get to where I can hear the branch. The water comes down in a hurry, tossing itself this way and that as it tumbles among the broken pieces of old sea bottom. The stream seems to be talking, saying any number of things as it goes

41. Richard Harries, *Art and the Beauty of God: A Christian Understanding* (London: Continuum, 1993), p. 42.

42. Calvin M. Johansson, *Music and Ministry: A Biblical Counterpoint* (Peabody, Mass.: Hendrickson, 1984), p. 10.

along. Sometimes, at a certain distance, it can sound like several people talking and laughing. But you listen and you realize it is talking absolutely to itself. If our place has a voice, this is it. And it is not talking to you. You can't understand a thing it is saying. You walk up and stand beside it, loving it, and you know it doesn't care whether you love it or not. The stream and the woods don't care if you love them. The place doesn't care if you love it. But for your own sake you had better love it. For the sake of all else you love, you had better love it.[43]

Indeed. Perhaps, at the end of the day, one of the most important functions of arts ministry is to bring a little piece of that created world into our everyday existence, to help us notice it in a new way and to love it "for the sake of all else you love." As we become more responsible partners with the created world, both ecologically and aesthetically, we will have more and more to celebrate. The rose garden that is our lives and our ministry will surely be enhanced if it is located in the presence of real roses.

Conclusion

Arts ministry involves us in a web of relations with the world around us that is simultaneously exciting and challenging. In our artistry and our ministry we are called to proclaim the gospel message through evangelism, deepen our bonds with one another in community, advocate for the widow and the poor as we practice social justice, and take delight in the beauty of the garden, the cosmos in which we have been placed. As we seek to open our lives and our ministries to these tasks, we are blessed by the presence and promises of God, promises founded in creation itself and leading us toward a time when "all things will be made new." As Christians and as artists this is both our hope and the substance of our existence here on earth.

---

43. Wendell Berry, *Hannah Coulter* (Berkeley, Calif.: Shoemaker & Hoard, 2004), p. 85.

CHAPTER SIX

Arts Ministry and Human Creativity

He brings forth living beings endowed with souls, such exactly as He wishes, and He graces each one, as an artisan, as a master, with all that He desires and wishes To Him be glory and power, now, always and forever and ever. Amen.

Symeon the New Theologian, *Hymns of Divine Love*

Living creatively is much more than artistic activity. It is living all of life in such a manner that we fulfill the potential of our humanity.

Calvin Johansson, *Music and Ministry:*
A Biblical Counterpoint

There is a powerful, awe-inspiring creativity manifest in our world — and indeed, in ourselves: the new, the novel, the unforeseeable, the previously unheard of, break forth roundabout us and in our midst; and human life continues to be sustained from beyond itself. This serendipitous creativity provides grounds for our hope for the future.

Gordon D. Kaufman, *In the Beginning . . . Creativity*

Creation and Destruction

In the small town of Whitwell, Tennessee, stands a boxcar, and inside that boxcar are eleven million paper clips, representing every man, woman, and child killed by the Nazis in the Holocaust. The boxcar is the centerpiece of a children's Holocaust memorial, created by children and teachers from Whitwell Middle School between 1998 and 2001.[1]

The children came up with the idea of collecting paper clips during a special Holocaust education course sponsored by the school, a course intended to teach them about the importance of tolerance. They began their collection in recognition of non-Jewish Norwegians who, faced with the order to force Jews to wear yellow stars on their clothing, began wearing paper clips on their own lapels in protest. The children decided to build on this idea and create their own memorial to the Holocaust using paper clips. As the word spread about the students' project, paper clips began arriving from all over the world, many with personal notes attached. Among those who donated paper clips were groups of German schoolchildren.

Soon the students began searching for an appropriate way to store and exhibit the paper clips. With the help of Peter and Dagmar Schroeder, White House correspondents for a group of German newspapers, they initiated a search for an original German railcar in which to store the paper clips. After many fruitless inquiries, a special boxcar was found, a car that, in all likelihood, had been used to transport Jews to concentration camps. With generous assistance from many people and organizations, the railcar was transported from a German railway museum to Tennessee, first by rail, then by ship, and finally on a flatbed car, where it traveled from Baltimore harbor to Tennessee. The date on which this final journey was made was September 11, 2001. The Schroeders write,

> As the memorial, a symbol of tolerance, rolled slowly through the countryside, terrorists struck the United States. . . . The students of Whitwell Middle School mourned with the rest of the world. For three years, they had worked to fight hate and intolerance. They watched the tragedy on TV with tears in their eyes. Nobody could talk. Finally, one girl spoke

---

1. For the complete story of this memorial, see Peter W. Schroeder and Dagmar Schroeder-Hildebrand, *Six Million Paper Clips: The Making of a Children's Holocaust Memorial* (Minneapolis: Kar-Ben Publishing, 2004).

up. "If I had not known why we were building a memorial," she said, "I would know it now."[2]

So would we. As the foregoing story illustrates, we live in an age that teeters precariously between creativity (illustrated by the children's memorial) and destruction (represented by Hitler and the terrorists). There are many signs of this tension. There are currently an estimated 27,600 nuclear weapons in the stockpiles of the world's arsenals.[3] During the last century we have witnessed the wholesale slaughter of human beings in Russia (Stalin killed anywhere from 7 to 43 million, depending on the source), Germany (Hitler killed eleven million), Cambodia (Pol Pot killed 1,700,000), and Rwanda (500,000), to name but a few of the more high-profile genocides. Human beings have also had an adverse impact on the natural world. Earth's population is tripling, from 2.7 billion people in 1930[4] to a projected 8 to 9 billion people in the year 2030.[5] This alone has strained the resources of our planet. Climate change, produced in part by greenhouse gasses, threatens supplies of food and water, increases the chances of coastal flooding, intensifies natural disasters, and rapidly extinguishes many species. Under these circumstances, it is no wonder that Thomas Merton began his essay entitled "Theology of Creativity" with these chilling words: "The most obvious characteristic of our age is its destructiveness."[6]

Yet, during this same era, we have also witnessed an extraordinary outpouring of human creativity and ingenuity. Human beings have learned how to fly, lit the world with artificial light, acquired the ability to manage deadly diseases, discovered how to communicate instantly with one another across and between continents, unraveled the secrets of the human genome, created the capacity to store and utilize entire libraries of information at the click of a button, made global travel routine, sent human beings to walk on the moon, and launched spacecraft that have escaped the solar system and are traveling right now in interstellar space.

So too, in the arts, the past century has been a time of extraordinary

2. Schroeder and Schroeder-Hildebrand, *Six Million Paper Clips,* p. 47.

3. Carnegie Endowment for International Peace, 2007-8.

4. "Historical Estimates of World Population," U.S. Census Bureau, Population Division/International Programs Center, 2008.

5. "World Population to 2030," United Nations Department of Economic and Social Affairs, Population Division, 2010.

6. Thomas Merton, "Theology of Creativity," in *The Literary Essays of Thomas Merton,* ed. Patrick Hart (New York: New Directions, 1981), p. 355.

productivity and imagination. This is the century of George Balanchine and Rudolf Nureyev, of Evelyn Waugh and Georges Bernanos, of Frank Capra and Ingmar Bergman, of Igor Stravinsky, Arnold Schoenberg, Georges Rouault, I. M. Pei, Rainer Maria Rilke, and Václav Havel.

In reality, creativity and destruction have always been closely related. Soon after humanity's expulsion from Eden, we read the story of the brothers Cain and Abel. It is remarkable that so soon after the original creation mandate in the Garden, we are faced with the bald, hard fact of Cain's murder of his brother.

Right from the beginning, human actions, and specifically human creativity, had consequences in the world. Early in the book of Genesis we encounter the story of Adam naming the animals (Gen. 2:19-20). Adam named the animals one by one, and whatever name Adam gave an animal was its name from that time forward.[7] Recently Beverly Shamana noted, "We have forgotten that our creative gifts have the power to transform the world."[8]

Evidently this transformation can be in the direction of hopefulness, peace, and productivity, or in the direction of rancor, tension, and devastation. After all, it took real creativity to murder millions of innocent people in the death camps of World War II and not alert the Allies to what was really going on. It takes real creativity to construct nuclear weapons and put them on individual missiles that can be delivered with pinpoint accuracy to multiple targets simultaneously.[9]

In light of the dual potential of creativity, Matthew Fox asks the question that should be on all our minds and lips: "Will we use our creativity to destroy or to bless with?"[10] He goes on to suggest what is really at stake: "Whether our species is sustainable or not depends on our wresting creativity back from the brink of its demonic potential."[11] In this setting, arts ministry has never looked so important.

---

7. This is a good example of what many commentators call "performative language," language that actually changes things in the world.

8. Beverly J. Shamana, *Seeing in the Dark: A Vision of Creativity and Spirituality* (Nashville: Abingdon Press, 2001), p. 127.

9. Matthew Fox, *Creativity: Where the Divine and the Human Meet* (New York: Jeremy P. Tarcher, 2002), p. 6. Fox adds, "Our creativity is not only where the Divine and the human meet but also where the Divine and the demonic meet" (pp. 35-36). He continues, "The capacity for evil in our species is so profound because our creativity is so deep" (p. 37).

10. Fox, *Creativity*, p. 6.

11. Fox, *Creativity*, p. 11. He goes on, "I reconstruct Christianity and culture around the

In a sense, creativity actually requires destruction. Picasso once said, "Every act of creation is first of all an act of destruction."[12] Creativity means breaking new ground. It requires us to leave behind old ways of thinking and old habits. In so doing, our old routines and ideas are disassembled. They become obsolete and are revised in favor of fresh insights and patterns of living.

This chapter will explore the creative process, a process that involves fulfilling our mandate to be a fruitful people, living with a sense of openness and wonder, and learning how to develop new structures and new possibilities in our individual and collective lives. In particular, of course, we will look at human creativity through the lens of the arts and, specifically, of arts ministry. Our examination encompasses four subjects: (1) exploring the imagination; (2) exploring the meaning, significance, and context of human creativity; (3) working toward a tentative, provisional theology of creativity; and (4) addressing the issue of how arts ministry might foster, express, and embody human creativity.

Dry Bones: The Imagination in Christian Life and Witness

"The hand of the LORD came upon me, and he brought me out by the spirit of the LORD and set me down in the middle of a valley; it was full of bones. He led me all around them; there were very many lying in the valley, and they were very dry. He said to me, 'Mortal, can these bones live?' I answered, 'O Lord GOD, you know'" (Ezek. 37:1-3).

After Auschwitz and the killing fields of Cambodia, it is not so hard to imagine walking among a field of dry bones as it once was. If anything, this makes the question that God asks Ezekiel even more telling: "Can these bones live?" This question, uttered in the midst of the valley of dry bones, makes the human imagination the principal conversation partner with God.

The Bible is not primarily a discursive book of doctrines that teaches us how to think and how to live. It is a book that speaks to our imaginative

---

number-one survival issue of our time: the sustainability achieved when creativity is honored and practiced not for its own sake but for justice and compassion's sake. This is the way of the Holy Spirit, who is the Spirit of Creativity and compassion."

12. Pablo Picasso, quoted in Rollo May, *The Courage to Create* (New York: W. W. Norton, 1975), p. 60.

capacities. "The kingdom of God is like a mustard seed" (Matt. 13:31). "Awake, O harp and lyre! I will awake the dawn" (Ps. 57:8). "And the four living creatures, each of them with six wings, are full of eyes all around and inside. Day and night without ceasing they sing, 'Holy, holy, holy, the Lord God the Almighty, who was and is and is to come'" (Rev. 4:8).

The imagination offers us the possibility of contact with God through the medium of metaphor, story and symbol. It also offers us a source of power and hope in our own lives, in our communities, and in the wider world beyond.

The imagination begins in fantasy and ends in reality, a journey that involves risk. Urban Holmes notes that we are on a pilgrimage. He says, "We expect a pilgrimage to be characterized by imaginative meaning, full of ambiguity. A pilgrimage is a risky thing, for we cannot be sure what will be encountered."[13] As we progress on our personal and corporate pilgrimage, we find ourselves moving into strange and unexpected lands. The imagination creates new worlds for us to explore. C. S. Lewis presents an enduring example of what such an imaginary kingdom might look like:

> "Further up and further in!" roared the Unicorn, and no one held back. They charged straight at the foot of the hill and then found themselves running up it almost as water from a broken wave runs up a rock out at the point of some bay. Though the slope was nearly as steep as the roof of a house and the grass was smooth as a bowling green, no one slipped. Only when they had reached the very top did they slow up; that was because they found themselves facing great golden gates. And for a moment none of them was bold enough to try if the gates were open. They all felt just as they had felt about the fruit — "Dare we? Is it right? Can it be meant for *us*?"
>
> But while they were standing thus a great horn, wonderfully loud and sweet, blew from somewhere inside the walled garden and the gates swung open.[14]

Or, as in the vision of Daniel, our journey may lead us to an encounter with a man unlike any other man:

13. Urban T. Holmes III, *Ministry and Imagination* (New York: Seabury Press, 1981), p. 126.

14. C. S. Lewis, *The Last Battle* (New York: Collier Books, 1956), p. 176.

On the twenty-fourth day of the first month, as I was standing on the bank of the great river (that is, the Tigris), I looked up and saw a man clothed in linen, with a belt of gold from Uphaz around his waist. His body was like beryl, his face like lightning, his eyes like flaming torches, his arms and legs like the gleam of burnished bronze, and the sound of his words like the roar of a multitude. (Dan. 10:4-6)

Rather than removing us from reality, these images connect us directly to the source of life and vitality in God. They speak to fundamental human needs and offer hope for redemption. Leland Ryken notes, "Often it is the most obviously fantastic literature that touches most powerfully and at the most points on actual experience."[15] He adds,

The unreality of the imagination has another quality to commend it. It has arresting strangeness — a strangeness that compels our attention because it is something other than the ordinary. One of the main functions of the arts is to overcome the deadening effect of the routine, the commonplace, the cliché. The imagination is always searching for freshness of expression.[16]

The reality we encounter through the world of the imagination has many different layers of meaning. It has depth and texture. Imagination takes images from the material world and uses them to evoke that which is beyond all speech and all imaging. In so doing, connections are formed between human experience and the divine mystery. This fosters a sense of wonder and awe and spurs our devotion.

Ultimately, the healthy, integrated human imagination provides hope. It frees us from our feeling of being trapped in a corner, of giving up on the future. It does this by providing alternative paths, helping us envision the different roads we might take on our pilgrimage. These alternative avenues represent transformation, taking our past experiences and expectations and turning them on their head, forging new structures and new opportunities. Northrop Frye says, "The fundamental job of the imagination in ordinary life, then, is to produce, out of the society we have to live in, a vision

---

15. Leland Ryken, *The Liberated Imagination: Thinking Christianly about the Arts* (Wheaton, Ill.: Harold Shaw, 1989), p. 119.

16. Ryken, *The Liberated Imagination,* p. 109.

of the society we want to live in."[17] Michael Card adds, "None of us can accomplish anything without first imagining it."[18]

As we engage with God imaginatively in and through the medium of arts ministry, it is important to keep two things in mind. First, the human imagination itself needs to be redeemed. It can send us in the wrong direction just as easily as it can find the right path. Second, the imagination needs to be exercised. Urban Holmes says, "The imagination is something we *train* by saturating ourselves in the imaginative works of others."[19] Through disciplined exercise of the imagination, we have the opportunity to engage in creative ministry, to help us hear the voice of God calling us home.

The Meaning and Significance of Human Creativity

Tree tops ebb and flow as shadowed patterns of old lace
silent bell rusts in toppling steeple
doors swing on broken hinges
when wind whispers around roof beams
a holy place open to echo vespers

time passes quickly
in such self made labyrinths
if creativity is not sought

otherwise you are what you are
maze after maze . . . exactly
like the first . . . . . . never ending

art is as necessary as air
silent . . . . invisible
written on the face of time
history stamping page after page
and He is in every evening sky

17. Northrop Frye, *The Educated Imagination* (Bloomington: Indiana University Press, 1964), p. 140.
18. Michael Card, *Scribbling in the Sand: Christ and Creativity* (Downers Grove, Ill.: InterVarsity Press, 2002), p. 55.
19. Holmes, *Ministry and Imagination*, p. 105.

showing us that Christ
is what this is all about

When our lofty dreams are dead and gone
will we have made a worthy journey?

Marie Asner, "In His Image"[20]

Will we, indeed?

What Is Creativity?

We turn now from our brief foray into the human imagination to examine the phenomenon of human creativity. In his book *Creativity: Theory, History, Practice*, Rob Pope defines creativity as "the capacity to make, do, or become something fresh and valuable with respect to others as well as ourselves."[21] Calvin Johansson defines the word "creative" as "that which breaks new ground imaginatively and with integrity."[22]

Taking these two definitions as a point of departure, we might posit that creativity involves an object that is made, an action, or an ongoing process of becoming. Further, it has certain standards associated with it, including freshness, value, imagination, and integrity.

Creativity in the Church: A Brief History

For centuries the church debated whether human beings actually engaged in creative work. The debate was largely semantic. The real issue was whether it was appropriate to call works creative when they emerged not *ex nihilo* ("from nothing") but through a rearrangement of existing ideas or materials.

There was a tendency in the early church to define the word "creativity" strictly, relating only to its *ex nihilo* manifestation. Everyone acknowledged that only God could create *ex nihilo*, an event that occurred in the

---

20. Marie Asner, "In His Image," unpublished poem, commissioned by Michael Bauer, © 1993. All rights reserved. Used by permission.

21. Rob Pope, *Creativity: Theory, History, Practice* (London: Routledge, 2005), p. xvi.

22. Calvin M. Johansson, *Music and Ministry: A Biblical Counterpoint* (Peabody, Mass.: Hendrickson, 1984), p. 15.

beginning of time and continues through the ongoing creative activity of God sustaining and shaping the universe. There was no real debate about the capacity of human beings to do anything really "new" themselves, but there was a genuine concern for making and doing as generic categories. Anything that was made or done was an example of what the Greeks called *ars*. Whether or not artistic products were actually called "creative," they were nonetheless examples of *ars*. Note that, in this way, the early church avoided making any distinction between art and craft. The two were not thought of apart from one another.

Throughout the Middle Ages, creativity continued to be associated with its *ex nihilo* manifestation. This was expressed particularly in mystery, where the unexplained, incalculable power of the divine breaks into the universe and impacts human affairs. Renaissance humanism began to change this focus. Humanists believed in rational analysis. Slowly, creativity began to be linked with human beings and, especially, with the power of human reason to solve problems. The new paradigm for creativity became problem-solving. This represented a profound change from earlier attitudes. As Urban Holmes says, "The power of ambiguity, a sensibility to life, and the relation between beauty and goodness came to be lost to the God at the end of a syllogism."[23] By the time of the Enlightenment in the seventeenth and eighteenth centuries, the emphasis on problem-solving as the locus of creative activity was extended to encompass the need for humans to create something *new*, not only new artifacts but entirely new styles. Thus was born the category called the "fine arts," a designation that continues to be employed to this day. Creativity was a term reserved for ideas or artifacts that broke sufficiently with tradition so as to warrant this lofty designation.

One aspect of this focus on innovation was to separate the arts from other creative endeavors and give them a special place of honor. Crafts and trades, which merely had to do with making or doing, were no longer thought of in relation to the arts. The ultimate consequence of this development was that the bond between the artist and the craftsman was severed. This had profound consequences both for craft and for fine art. The work of the craftsman was denigrated when creativity was no longer considered part and parcel of everyday life and ordinary human activities. As a result, the craftsman could not produce works of true inspiration. On the other hand, the work of the artist was no longer considered practical in any

23. Holmes, *Ministry and Imagination*, p. 2.

meaningful sense; it was separated from real life and took on an ornamental function.

The nineteenth century continued this line of thinking and created the cult of the artist. A new hierarchy was born. The lonely, isolated artist working at the fringes of society, forging a new style, was accorded the status of "genius" or "hero." Merton refers to "the myth of the genius as hero and as high priest in a cult of art that tends to substitute itself for religion." He continues, "Here what matters is no longer art or the work of art as such. Here art stands out as the monument of genius, not as the symbol of a transcendent spiritual reality but as the ikon of the artist himself."[24]

The constant pressure to create new styles grew throughout the Romantic era. This, in turn, led artists to separate themselves from their audience, forming an aesthetic chasm that grew wider with each passing generation. As untrained audiences (and congregations) in the twentieth century gradually stopped identifying with the artworks produced by the great figures in the art world, an opening was created into which popular culture inserted itself. Creativity, once again, was re-defined. It became associated with artworks that were commercially successful — artworks that created and energized fads. Popular culture, in turn, created its own set of artistic heroes. This became a factor in the church just as much as it did in the rest of Western culture.

Over the past century, the explosion of creative activity in the social, scientific, and artistic arenas meant that change came with increasing rapidity to the modern world. Two parallel developments ensued: (1) specialization, which occurs as the sophistication and complexity of individual disciplines make it necessary for people to narrow their focus; and (2) the realization in some quarters that meta-narratives (overarching, unifying themes) exist, with the potential to bind these individual disciplines into larger, coherent wholes. This later development offers hope for the re-integration of the fine arts with the more basic structures of human creativity. We may be working toward a time when it is once again possible to experience the unity of making, doing, and becoming that was lost during the Renaissance and the Enlightenment.

Meanwhile, in non-Western cultures, a deep appreciation for creative work has always been integral to the development and self-understanding of the people. Many African languages have no word for "art." Instead, they employ a variety of different words for creative activity, for making and

---

24. Merton, "Theology of Creativity," p. 360.

doing.[25] The ornamental and practical dimensions of life co-exist alongside one another. As these cultures impact the West and, specifically, the Western church, there are additional reasons for hope.

Toward a Theology of Creativity

Creativity begins and ends with God. In Genesis we read about the beginning: "In the beginning when God created the heavens and the earth, the earth was a formless void and darkness covered the face of the deep, while a wind from God swept over the face of the waters" (Gen. 1:1-2). And in Revelation we read about the end and the new beginning: "Then I saw a new heaven and a new earth; for the first heaven and the first earth had passed away, and the sea was no more. And I saw the holy city, the new Jerusalem, coming down out of heaven from God, prepared as a bride adorned for her husband" (Rev. 21:1-2).

These are the poles within which we can begin talking about a theology of creativity: creation and new creation, alpha and omega, Creator and Eschaton. Between these two poles we experience the mystery of God's creative activity, and we explore the various dimensions of what it means to be co-creators with God. Creativity is shrouded in mystery just as the earth was once cloaked in darkness. Creativity is shrouded in mystery just as the path to our ultimate destiny with God is often opaque and difficult for us to discern. Yet here we are, standing between these two great mysteries, awash in the blessings afforded by God's abundant gift of creativity.

The initial mystery is simply that anything exists at all. God chose, and the world came into being. Gordon Kaufman calls this "serendipitous creativity."[26] He goes on to paraphrase the prologue to John's Gospel: "In the beginning was creativity, and the creativity was with God, and the creativity was God. All things came into being through the mystery of creativity; apart from creativity nothing would have come into being."[27]

The second mystery is that God chose to redeem the world from its travails and suffering, to birth a new creation amid the problems and calamities of our current circumstances. Jeremy Begbie says that we should actually be talking more about *re*-creation rather than about creation itself.

---

25. Shamana, *Seeing in the Dark,* p. 133.
26. Kaufman, *In the Beginning . . . Creativity* (Minneapolis: Fortress Press, 2004), p. 56.
27. Kaufman, *In the Beginning,* p. ix.

He envisions the re-creative work God is doing even now and suggests that we have a role to play in this process: "Whether through paint or sound, metaphor or movement, we are given the inestimable gift of participating in the re-creative work of the Triune God, anticipating that final and unimaginable re-creation of all matter, space, and time, the fulfillment of all things visible and invisible."[28] Thomas Merton adds, "We all have an obligation to open our eyes to the eschatological dimensions of Christian creativity . . . 'all creation is groaning' for the final manifestation of this finished work, the only work that has an eternal importance: the full revelation of God by the restoration of all things in Christ."[29]

Not to be overlooked in the face of the creative and re-creative activities of God is the fact that divine creativity did not stop on the seventh day of creation, only to return at the end of time. Instead, God continues to care for creation as long as history endures. The name we give to this process is *creatio continua*. The ongoing task of shepherding creativity throughout history is the work of the Holy Spirit, the Creative Spirit who stands astride history and makes all things new.

There are two dimensions to the Spirit's work in regard to creativity. The first dimension has to do with the evolutionary quality of our universe. Change is constant, both here on earth and throughout the cosmos. New stars are constantly forming from clouds of gas, old stars are imploding, and new species of living organisms are born and die in an extraordinary drama that we are only beginning to understand. Creation itself is engaged in a great dance. The Holy Spirit — the Creative Spirit — is the choreographer of this dance, a dance that is improvisatory at the same time that it is full of pattern and order. The second dimension of the Creative Spirit involves us.

Human Creativity

Human beings are, at root, creative people. As we have seen, the reason for this is our creation in the *Imago Dei*, the "image of God." Roger Hazelton asks the primal question: "Must there not be some continuity, some common denominator of meaning, between what man does in the arts and

28. Jeremy Begbie, "The Future: Looking to the Future: A Hopeful Subversion," in *For the Beauty of the Church*, ed. W. David O. Taylor (Grand Rapids: Baker Books, 2010), p. 181.
29. Merton, "Theology of Creativity," p. 370.

Garden Ministry
Asbury United Methodist Church, Bettendorf, Iowa

Asbury UMC garden plots

In 2001, Dave Phillips was present at a church meeting at which new ideas for outreach ministries were explored. At the meeting, Dave suggested that the church should begin a garden ministry. He describes his thought process this way:

> At the time I guess I was going through a midlife crisis and doing some soul-searching; our boys had graduated from high school, and looking back on my life, I asked myself, What really have I done during my life to make my little corner of the world a better place than when I came into it? What have I done to make a difference in the lives of people around me?
>
> I grew up on a farm, and we had a big garden. At the time, I didn't enjoy gardening that much, as it was "work." Later, after I got married, we always had some garden space, and gardening became one of my favored pastimes.*

*This and subsequent quotes in this case study are from Dave Phillips in an e-mail to the author, 27 June 2009.

Soon he approached his friend Dale with his desire to start a garden ministry, and the idea was off and running. They decided to announce this new ministry to the congregation in a novel way, Dave explains:

> I dressed up as a farmer/gardener. I borrowed some bib overalls (I think from Joe Douglas), a straw hat from Gene Miller, tied a red handkerchief around my neck, stuck a handkerchief in my back pocket, got a hoe, and walked down the aisle at the 8:30 A.M. service (to the chuckles of many in the congregation) and informed people of the new outreach ministry that was being started.

That first year the garden included twelve 20' × 20' plots that were worked by twelve members of the congregation (the twelve "garden disciples"). The purpose of the garden was to provide fresh vegetables for people who didn't have access to them. Initially they decided to give the produce to three organizations: Lend-A-Hand, a low-income apartment complex in downtown Davenport, Iowa; John Lewis Coffee House, a community kitchen serving the poor and homeless in downtown Davenport; and Valley Shelter, a shelter for displaced youth. They harvested and distributed 2,400 pounds of produce.

As the years went on, they acquired additional plots in different parts of the community, including the backyards of congregation members. The ministry was supported financially through a combination of efforts, including a line item in the church's budget, spaghetti luncheons featuring sauce made from tomatoes that were harvested from the gardens, annual gifts from the local Optimist Club, and free-will donations from congregational members who took home a small percentage of the produce on Sunday mornings.

The gardens grew to a maximum size of 1¼ acres, which proved to be hard to sustain. They have since been reduced to about an acre. Dave describes the scope of the project as it developed over the course of about seven years: "Almost 170,000 pounds of fresh vegetables have been distributed to over 30 different organizations to include food pantries, homeless shelters, and community kitchens."

Seven dedicated gardeners and about twenty other volunteers have become involved over the years. Several years ago the gardeners recorded their hours on-site when they gardened. That year they collectively spent somewhere between 1,700 and 2,000 hours gardening. Dave explains the many blessings of this ministry:

> Through the working of his Holy Spirit, many individuals in our community have become involved in the ministry, [including] those who have made land available for our use, businesses who have provided us substantial discounts on required purchases, and members of an antique tractor club who have plowed our plots to ready them for planting.
>
> A wonderful thing about our ministry is that it affords many opportunities to get involved — i.e., gardening, distributing the harvested produce, and freezing harvested produce for later distribution during the winter months.
>
> Our Garden Ministry is responding to God's command in Isaiah 58:10: "Feed the hungry." With God's continual blessing, our ministry is taking "a bite out of hunger" in the Quad Cities and is touching the lives of thousands of needy people.

what God does in creation?"[30] Dorothy Sayers answers the question affirmatively: "The characteristic common to God and man is apparently that: the desire and the ability to make things."[31] Once again, this is not to say that creativity exhausts the meaning of the *Imago Dei*, but that it is a fundamental and irreducible aspect of our creation in the image of God.

Creativity is not properly thought of as an optional activity. It was commanded by God in what has become known as the *creation mandate*.[32]

---

30. Roger Hazelton, *A Theological Approach to Art*, quoted by James Romaine in *It Was Good Making Art to the Glory of God*, ed. Sandra Bowden and Ned Bustard (Baltimore: Square Halo Books, 2000), p. 190. Answers to this question are not universally positive. Calvin Seerveld says, "There are no biblical grounds either for the usual talk about artistic 'creation.' Comparisons between God as a capital A Creator Artist and man as a small, image-of-God creator artist are only speculative and misleading" (quoted in Bowden and Bustard, *It Was Good Making Art to the Glory of God*, p. 190). Once again, as it was in the early church, I think the debate is largely semantic.

31. Dorothy Sayers, quoted in Bowden and Bustard, *It Was Good Making Art to the Glory of God*, p. 90.

32. Merton says, "All time and all history are a continued, uninterrupted creative act, a stupendous, ineffable mystery in which God has signified his will to associate man with himself in his work of creation. . . . If man was first called to share in the creative work of his

As Calvin Johansson reminds us, "Man creates as a result of the responsibility cast upon him in the creation mandate. Formed by God, every man is given the task of responding to His call to be a co-creator." Johansson goes on to quote Psalm 8: "You made him little lower than the heavenly beings and crowned him with glory and honor. You made him ruler over the works of your hands. . . ."[33] Ultimately, creativity is not optional activity because it is *life-giving*. In the absence of creativity, human beings lose the will that they need to remain vital and productive, either within their own private lives or as members of society.

The ability to be creative is a gift that is innate and virtually universal.[34] It is a gift that can be developed. First of all, it depends on the quality of our interactions with the world around us.[35] As we live our lives, we have a series of encounters with reality. These encounters can be quite intense. They might involve the wonder or awe we experience when we are in the presence of great natural or artistic beauty. They might be occasioned by interpersonal conflict or a deep, passionate love. Creative encounters come in a wide variety of different forms. They can be chaotic; they can be peaceful and meditative. Some are more powerful than others.

In any case, experiencing our human and natural environment in detail, allowing ourselves the time and attentiveness to take in the rich textures of the world around us, requires an element of courage.[36] We feel the tension and ambiguity that is so characteristic of the human condition. In so doing, we travel on a path not yet taken, toward an end that is only dimly in sight.

---

heavenly Father, he now becomes involved in the 'new creation,' the redemption of his own kind and the restoration of the cosmos." See "Theology of Creativity," pp. 368-70.

33. Johansson, *Music and Ministry,* p. 15.

34. There may be some extenuating circumstances that temper this claim. For example, brain injuries can impact our capacity for creativity.

35. Kathleen R. Fischer says, "Through the creation of poems, legends, mosaics, carvings, paintings, songs, and sculptures, the artist, in a sense, makes the world stand still long enough for us to glimpse its mystery." See *The Inner Rainbow: The Imagination in Christian Life* (Mahwah, N.J.: Paulist Press, 1983), p. 57

36. Rollo May says, "Every creative encounter is a *new* event; every time requires another assertion of courage. What Kierkegaard said about love is also true of creativity: every person must start at the beginning. And to encounter 'the reality of experience' is surely the basis for all creativity. The task will be 'to forge in the smithy of my soul' . . . to make something of value for human life" (*The Courage to Create,* p. 26). Matthew Fox adds, "Creativity takes courage — courage to explore one's deepest self and to let in the depths of the world's struggles and joys, torments and agony" (*Creativity,* pp. 71-72).

When we fashion a response to these encounters, we exercise the creative gift we have been given. The response takes our own unique distillation of the world around us and translates it into a creative form that can be offered to others and back to God.[37] As we fashion our own unique creative response, we are empowered by the Creative Spirit, who is both guide and interpreter. What we produce may or may not correspond to the traditional forms found in the fine arts. It will nonetheless be artistic by virtue of the creative process that birthed it.

John de Gruchy says, "Artistic creativity is not only God-given but one of the main ways whereby the power of God is unleashed, awakening both a thirst for justice and a hunger for beauty."[38] This is a way of saying that human creativity has a role to play in the church, in the lives of individual Christians, and in the world itself. It is a channel enabling the wisdom and authority of God to find expression in the here and now, in the rough-and-tumble of human life and human institutions.

The Creative Act

The creative act is a two-stage process. In the first stage, vulnerability is important. Artists must open themselves up to the world and experience it in all its depth and intensity. They explore not only the objects and events in the world around them, but also their own internal state of being and their relationships with God, other people, and the cosmos. Thomas Merton says,

> It is the renunciation of our false self, the emptying of self in the likeness of Christ, that brings us to the threshold of that true creativity in which God himself, the creator, works in and through us. . . . this is creativity in a new and spiritual dimension, which is its full Christian dimension. And this applies not only to the artist but to every Christian.[39]

This initial stage of the creative endeavor is often accomplished in solitude. Ideas that are based on primary observations have a gestation period

---

37. Note that creativity does not come with a guarantee. As Rollo May reminds us, "We cannot *will* to have insights. We cannot *will* creativity. But we can *will* to give ourselves to the encounter with intensity of dedication and commitment" (*The Courage to Create*, p. 46).

38. John W. de Gruchy, *Christianity, Art, and Transformation* (Cambridge: Cambridge University Press, 2001), p. 241.

39. Merton, "Theology of Creativity," p. 370.

of their own. This period is characterized by relaxed awareness. It is a time of preparation and rehearsal, making way for the new insights that will follow. When insights come, they are frequently unexpected. They seem to originate outside of our own consciousness, as if through a direct, existential, and deeply personal contact with the source of creativity itself. It is important to realize that creative insight is not a substitute for labor, discipline, and the frustration born of the struggle between the artist and his or her materials. Instead of taking its place, insight works in concert with discipline to produce an honest product.

The second stage of the creative endeavor involves the creative act itself, the realization of ideas in the world of human experience. At times of deep, creative engagement there is often a sense of joy, an ecstatic response to the presence of the new in our midst. The distinction between subject and object is temporarily transcended. We are one with our surroundings. Life at these moments is experienced as integrated and whole. It exists almost beyond the limitations of space and time. We are fully functioning, alive to the moment, open to new possibilities, non-judgmental, and full of wonder.[40] This is a deeply satisfying experience. In this respect, creative and spiritual experiences bear a close resemblance to one another.

True creativity, developed in vulnerability and realized in the birthing of new objects, actions, or a new quality of living, requires freedom; yet this is not untrammeled freedom, not freedom without responsibility or purpose. The Dutch art historian and aesthetician Hans Rookmaaker describes artistic freedom this way:

> Freedom is positive. It means being free from tradition, from the feeling that everything you do has to be original, from certain fixed rules said to be necessary in art — but also from the thought that to be creative you must break all kinds of rules and standards.
>
> Freedom means also that there are no prescriptions for subject matter. There is no need for a Christian to illustrate biblical stories or biblical truth, though he may of course choose to do that.[41]

Creativity is the result of openness to new ways of thinking, new approaches to solving problems, new methods, new materials, new para-

---

40. Rollo May notes that the creative act yields "a sharpened perception, a vividness, a translucence of relationship to the things around us. The world becomes vivid and unforgettable" (*The Courage to Create*, p. 51).

41. Hans Rookmaaker, quoted in Card, *Scribbling in the Sand*, p. 136.

digms. It would be easy for this focus on the new to make us think that tradition is no longer of value. This is clearly not the case. As Roger Scruton points out, "Real originality does not defy convention but depends on it. You can only 'make it new' when the newness is perceivable, which means departing from conventions while at the same time affirming them. Hence originality requires tradition if it is to make artistic sense."[42]

Perhaps what is new involves simply applying what we have learned in one context to a different context altogether. Perhaps what is new comes from taking the materials we have received from our tradition and re-arranging them in an innovative fashion so that they serve a different function from the one that was originally intended. Newness can mean different things to different people in different settings.

Whatever it means in any particular setting, it is clear that newness for its own sake is not necessarily appropriate or creative. We can easily mistake newness for authentic creativity. Merton, in his typically prophetic voice, says, "When everything is creative, nothing is creative. When nothing is creative, everything tends to be destructive, or at least to invite destruction."[43] When we do not discipline our thinking by applying standards or norms to creativity, we run the risk of acting in ways that are actually destructive of our ends.

The Cross

The cross is an important symbol of both divine creativity and human destruction. It presents us with a "creative role of suffering"[44] that simultaneously shows us the full force and face of evil and yet exhibits the redemptive power of God. This has much to say to us as creative people. First of all, it means that we must take seriously our vocation to depict evil in the world. Evil must be exposed to the light of day and shown for what it is. Art must be unremittingly honest in its portrayal of human depravity.

At the same time, we need to celebrate the victory over death that was won on the cross by our Lord and Savior Jesus Christ. This should be done without any sense of triumphalism or sentimentality. It should be an expression of unremitting joy.

42. Roger Scruton, quoted in Pope, *Creativity*, p. 24.
43. Merton, "Theology of Creativity," p. 358.
44. Merton, "Theology of Creativity," p. 370.

Sanctifying the Ordinary

Finally, human creativity should lead us to sanctify the ordinary. The German composer Hugo Distler wrote about music-making at home: "The sense and duty of all domestic and social music-making has always been, or at least should have been, to uplift the everyday, to let it become once again richer in associations, to 'sanctify' it in a true sense."[45] This is true of every aspect of human creativity. It is what Pieter Bruegel did in his paintings and what Aaron Copland did in so much of his music.

Why the everyday? Why not seek out experiences that titillate and excite, that thrill and move us? Why should we be focusing our creative output on the common, unremarkable features of our lives? There are several different answers to this question. One involves the Incarnation. God came to us in the person of Jesus Christ, "sharing our common lot." In so doing, God "baptized" the ordinary and said to us that the context of our lives is significant and worthy of our attention and creative efforts.

God is immanent in these very ordinary experiences, closer to us than we are to ourselves. The ordinary stuff of life thus has the potential to hint at the presence of the divine in our midst. Karl Rahner notes that "the very commonness of everyday things harbors the eternal marvel and silent mystery of God and his grace."[46]

Kathleen Fischer sounds a warning about what happens when we lose this important perspective: "When matter and spirit are split asunder, everydayness is no longer a vessel of mystery; it is a source of ennui, discouragement, boredom."[47] This is clearly a reality for many in our culture and in the church today.

How does human creativity respond to this loss of mystery? It seeks out ways to give the Creative Spirit access to our lives once again, thereby creating the conditions where epiphanies can occur, where God can be experienced anew under the guise of the mundane.

45. Hugo Distler, *Thirty Pieces* preface, trans. Mark Bergaas, in "Hugo Distler: 1908-1942," *The American Organist* (April 1982), p. 175.

46. Karl Rahner, *Belief Today* (New York: Sheed & Ward, 1967), p. 14, quoted in Fischer, *The Inner Rainbow*, p. 8.

47. Fischer, *The Inner Rainbow*, p. 9.

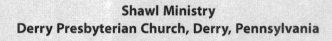

Shawl Ministry
Derry Presbyterian Church, Derry, Pennsylvania

Members of the Derry Presbyterian Church Shawl Ministry

Fabric arts of different varieties are an integral part of arts ministries throughout the country. Many Episcopal churches have embroidered their altar rails and liturgical furniture. Lutheran churches often sponsor quilting ministries. Derry Presbyterian Church in Pennsylvania provides an excellent example of a shawl ministry. Sue George, the coordinator of this ministry, describes its birth and its powerful impact:

> You could say it all started with a sheep-covered baby blanket. During the summer of 2003 I picked up my knitting needles to make a small blanket for my new nephew Tommy. Not long after I finished making that blanket, a Derry church member handed me a book, *Knitting into the Mystery: A Guide to the Shawl-Knitting Ministry* [by Susan Izard and Susan Jorgensen; see bibliography] that told the story of how shawl ministry began and how to set up a program of your own. It was that book that gave impetus to the formation of Derry's own shawl ministry in January 2005. The book told heartwarming stories about knitting and crocheting shawls for [people] who may be ill, or grieving, in a nursing home or homebound, recovering or in need of comfort.

What makes the gift of a shawl so powerful is the gentle prayer blessing that each shawl carries with it. In this age of greed and it's-all-about-me, many recipients can't believe someone would take time to do this special thing just for them. Their shawl becomes a tangible sign of God's love and comforting presence. In the past four years, we've given away more than 500 shawls through our program. They've traveled to recipients in boxes and bags. They've been draped over babies after their baptism and comforted college students living far from home. They've given strength to those in the hospital and those near death. Wherever they go, they bring the prayers of a caring group of women who gather to bless them within a quiet circle.

We began by making just shawls, and in the past four-and-a-half years, have expanded the program to include small white blankets for infants (given at their baptisms), soft caps for chemotherapy patients (a pattern was developed by one of our group members), and lap-robe-sized blankets for our graduating high school seniors (made in their high school colors). The size of the group has changed over time. Early on, twenty or more ladies filled the room at each meeting, and that's narrowed down to a core group of about a dozen. There are also some who knit and crochet for us and never attend our monthly gathering. One dear lady was the mother of one of our church members. She lived in New Jersey and would send us garbage bags full of completed shawls a couple times a year. She was glad to participate in our group from afar, since she couldn't find a group locally. The deacons and pastor keep us up-to-date on who needs a shawl, and the deacons most often make the deliveries. This partnership between the knitters and delivery persons allows for more people in the church to be involved and to discover for themselves the impact of the ministry.

We make shawls and send them wherever there's a need. One person in England found us online and requested a shawl, which we shipped to her. One of my favorite "pay it forward" stories was the shawl we made for a woman who attended another church in our community. She was so touched by our gift that it became the impetus for her to form a group in her own church. Now that congregation is making and sending out shawls to folks we would never find out about.*

*Sue George, e-mail to the author, 27 June 2009.

Summary: A Theology of Creativity

Any theology of creativity must take account of the creative work of God at the beginning, middle, and end of history, of our story. It should acknowledge that human beings are creatures made in the image of God with a mandate to go into the world and be creative. This is not optional work. It is not something we do only when we have the time or the money.

Creativity involves sustained attention to ideas, to the natural world, to the human community, and to the artifacts that are the products of creative endeavors. It functions best when we are vulnerable to the world around us and open to the work of the Creative Spirit in our lives. Periods of sustained attention are followed by moments of insight and, on occasion, ecstasy.

Creativity is often developed in solitude, and yet it requires disciplined training that can come only from contact with other creative people. Creative work, in turn, needs to be done in an environment that is free, yet one that also demands responsibility. It respects and builds on tradition and continues to seek the new. It acknowledges human depravity and also celebrates Christ's victory.

Creativity values the materials of art and the stuff of this world as potential means of hinting at divine transcendence. It sanctifies the ordinary by looking for God under the guise of the material world and cherishes epiphanies of the immanent God wherever they may be found.

The Creative Enterprise

Western culture in the twenty-first century does not always value creativity. As a society of specialists, we tend to delegate certain "special" people to be creative on our behalf. These are people with training, talent, or fame. We celebrate their work, which seems far removed from anything that we can do or imagine ourselves.

This is a direct result of the nineteenth-century creation of the artist as genius. When this occurred, artists became more like God and were separated from the lives and concerns of ordinary people. It was not accidental that many medieval artists did not sign their works. Until we reached the High Middle Ages, most art and music were anonymous. During the Renaissance, as human beings rose in stature, the name of the artist became more important. The iconic stature of individual artists has grown steadily from that time until our own.

It may be that limiting the scope of our imagination to the "fine arts" (an Enlightenment term) has also contributed to this problem. John Dewey gives us an important reminder about artistic endeavor: "The intelligent mechanic engaged in his job, interested in doing well and finding satisfaction in his handiwork, caring for his materials and tools with genuine affection, is artistically engaged."[48] If arts ministry involves only dancing, sculpting, playing an instrument, or producing a film, then many of us will feel left out; there is no room for the talented mechanic or the creative homemaker. If the fine arts are the only creative option available to us, then we have a hole in our collective souls, because many of us have experienced the fine arts as children, but long ago left them behind and simply don't have the time to pursue them with any degree of seriousness.

The question remains before us: Is creativity ordinary or extraordinary? Should art be limited to specialists, or are there avenues for all of us to pursue creativity in the context of our own lives? The approach taken in this book is unequivocal. We are all creative people, and we all must develop our own unique creative gifts if we are to become the people God intended us to be. Ananda Coomaraswamy puts it this way: "It is not that the artist is a special kind of person, but that each person is a special kind of artist."[49]

When we engage in creative pursuits, we are fulfilling the potential of our humanity. Abraham Maslow says we are in the process of self-actualization. I would refine that somewhat, because I do not believe that actualizing our potential is strictly a matter of our own efforts. Instead, I would say that we are in the process of discipleship. We have access to a Spirit who inspires, guides, and empowers every creative act in our lives.

Think about cooks. Good cooks employ the right tools in their kitchen. They know what kind of knife to use when cutting bread and what kind of knife to use when cutting an onion. They value their tools and search out just the right tool for each job that needs to be done. They also know the various vegetables and meats and grains they are selecting as they prepare each new dish. They not only know the ingredients; they come to love them. They know how to examine food at the market and determine what will work best for the meal they are preparing. They develop a language all their own: blanching, broiling, basting. In fact, the number

48. John Dewey, *Art as Experience* (New York: Perigee Books, 1980), p. 5.
49. Ananda Coomaraswamy, quoted in Carolyn Dietering, *The Liturgy as Dance and the Liturgical Dancer* (New York: Crossroad, 1984), p. 6.

of individual, discrete bits of knowledge that go into fine cooking is staggering. Yet this is not all that is required. A critical part of what it means to be a good cook is developing an intuitive understanding that enables an individual to cook "according to taste."

Cooks also know how to present food to bring out the tastes, the colors, and the textures of a meal in just the right proportions. As the film *Babette's Feast* so richly demonstrates, when all of this comes together, the result is an artistic experience.[50] It is beautiful to see, to smell, to touch, and to taste. There are many good reasons why feasting plays an important role in biblical narratives, but one reason that should not be overlooked is *the food!*

Everything we have just described involves creativity. Clearly, cooking is an artistic endeavor. Interestingly, it is also an art form that is virtually universal. We all cook, even if we only wander into the kitchen and make a sandwich or fry an egg. The difference is that we do not all engage in discipleship when we cook. Not everyone pays close attention to the tools of the trade. We do not all spend time with individual ingredients or experiment with different combinations to create something fresh and interesting. For some of us, making a sandwich (and the same one each time, at that) is the greatest adventure we will ever have in the kitchen.

This is where arts ministry comes in. The point is not that everyone needs to become a great cook. In fact, this wouldn't be appropriate. It would mean that each individual is not developing his or her unique gifts and interests. But cooking remains part of everyone's life — as do many other "life tasks." Since this is true, arts ministry should help all of us to enrich our lives through the application of creativity to the common, everyday tasks in which we are engaged. It should also cooperate with the work of the Creative Spirit to inspire, encourage, and empower us to develop our own unique gifts and interests in the other areas of our lives.

These gifts might include gardening, woodworking, collecting, keeping a well-ordered house or apartment, sewing, investing, or playing a sport.[51] In passing, it is important to note that the opposition so often ex-

---

50. *Babette's Feast,* Gabriel Axel, 1987.

51. Hans Rookmaaker adds, "Creativity means growing bulbs, designing a new car, building a computer, discovering certain relationships within molecules, or writing a sermon. All these activities and a thousand more, like town planning, architecture, road construction, but also office work and cooking. All of these can be done in a creative way." See *The Creative Gift: Essays on Art and the Christian Life* (Westchester, Ill.: Cornerstone Books, 1981), p. 74.

pressed between sports and the arts can be overcome by viewing them as two different approaches to the same goal: the development of our creative potential as human beings.

As we develop our creative potential in other ways, we may find the urge to become more creative in the kitchen as well. Creativity has a way of spilling over from one area to another in our lives.

In addition to the foregoing options that all involve *making* or *doing,* there are also activities that open us up to the possibilities of life and help us to grow. These activities involve *becoming.* We read books to learn more about something that interests us. We attend concerts, exhibitions, plays, or movies not only to be entertained (although the refreshment of the human spirit is certainly an appropriate activity in and of itself) but also to learn and to be enriched. Learning and appreciation are not just passive activities. They require discipline, time, and attention. Learning and appreciation are themselves creative acts. They are acts that assist us in the process of transformation and, in turn, give us the tools to help transform the world around us.

Who is creative? All of us are — the entire human race. It is the task of arts ministry, in conjunction with the other ministries of the church, working under the leadership of the Creative Spirit, to help nurture this creativity in the life of God's people and in the life of the world around us.

Creative Living

Creativity is a process, a way of life. A truly creative life is a life that is open to God. It is a life that is constantly in the process of changing and growing, a life that glorifies God by exhibiting all of the many and variegated talents and gifts with which God has blessed us.

Living life in a dynamic fashion as men and women who are open to change is a creative process. It is refusing to believe that the present way of doing things has to remain constant forever. Growth is too scary for many people to seriously contemplate. The old joke is told about how many Christians it takes to change a light bulb: four — one to change the bulb and three to ask, "Who said anything about change?" Change is indeed scary. For when change and growth occur, people let go of their old ways. In a very real sense, they die through the process of growth.

People and communities that are living creatively are in the process of becoming. There is an open-ended quality to their journey that does not accept the finality of yesterday's answers. Beverly Shamana says that creative life involves "our willingness to surrender, to let go of control over outcomes, to see things differently, to value risk, and to live willingly with ambiguity."[52]

Ultimately, the object of creative living is our own lives.[53] Over time, we are charged with the task of fashioning our lives into works of art. Some will create a masterpiece; others will make something cheap and trivial. The choice is ours. Living creatively means making good choices, choices that create meaningful relationships with God, other people, and the world around us.

Human relationships involve creative living at the highest level. Many different creative skills are needed to forge healthy relationships. We learn how to listen and be attentive to others' needs and concerns. We learn how to forgive and how to celebrate, how to console and how to challenge, how to weep and how to laugh. Speaking specifically of the marriage relationship, Matthew Fox says, "Every day, surely every week and every season, adaptation is required. . . . A dance ensues. An art is required in building and maintaining any meaningful relationship."[54] As Fox suggests, this way of relationship can also apply to parenting, to being the child of a parent, to friendship, and to collegial relationships.

Problems crop up in human relationships just as they do in the rest of life. It is important to nurture creativity if we want to be good at solving the problems we meet on our own interpersonal journeys. Creativity enables us to recognize problems and separate those that are significant from those that are not. It gives us the capacity to imaginatively envision different approaches to issues and allows us to test these out to ascertain their potential outcomes. Creativity helps us recognize commonalities between different problems and apply what we have learned in one instance to a seemingly unrelated circumstance. As such, it is an important resource and should be cultivated at every turn.

One of the serious problems that besets all of us is that we get into ruts periodically. These can be short-lived, or they can dominate our entire lives. At root, ruts are the result of a lack of discipline. They occur when we absolve ourselves of our most basic human responsibilities and give the

---

52. Shamana, *Seeing in the Dark*, p. 64.

53. Matthew Fox says, "Our ultimate act of creativity is giving birth to who we are" (*Creativity*, p. 32).

54. Matthew Fox, *Creativity*, p. 215.

power over ourselves to something that is not ultimate. We're in a rut because we don't have the energy, creative intuition, or knowledge to do anything else. We open the box of frosted cereal again this morning because we've opened a hundred — or a thousand — boxes of this same cereal before. On some minimal level, it satisfies our basic need for sustenance, and we get a little sugar fix from the sweetened cereal that we enjoy. We may never have decided that this was a habit we should cultivate. We simply did it because it was easy and we didn't have to invest ourselves in it. Pretty soon we go from having a bowl of this cereal every morning to letting that cereal become a bigger part of our diet than we would ever choose if we sat down and thought about it. We find ourselves sitting on the couch in front of the television eating this cereal as an afternoon snack, or eating it in bed before we go to sleep.

This is how habits turn into addictions, how the creative dimension of our lives gets snuffed out like so many birthday candles. Living with addictions is the opposite of creative living. When an addiction takes over, it dictates how we live. Suddenly we're not making free, creative choices about our lifestyle; instead, we're controlled by external forces that disrupt the dance of life, causing us to stumble and get in our own way. There are many potential examples, from food to sex, to drugs and alcohol, to the vicarious living that happens when we park ourselves in front of the television.

In place of ruts and addictions, we need to develop holy habits and rituals that empower us in the direction of a balanced, healthy lifestyle. Matthew Fox suggests that true creativity may, in fact, be a necessary antidote to addiction.[55] Creative living involves ordering our lives through discipline and the guidance and power of the Creative Spirit so that we are bringing order out of chaos and living in an integrated fashion with God, with ourselves, and with the world around us.

The presence of ruts and addictions in life reminds us that, while we are all creative people, not all that we do is creative. There are a number of different criteria to employ as we examine the creative life. First of all, true creativity has integrity. It is an honest pursuit that is not based upon deception or fraud. In the process of being creative, we show the world who we really are. We exhibit our character.

Second, truly creative living requires commitment. It is not a cheap or easy pursuit. It is not always convenient or easily accessible. We must practice creative living — it is not something that we simply fall into. We can-

---

55. Matthew Fox, *Creativity,* p. 18.

not succumb to the notion that we are being truly creative when we refuse to refine or deepen our creativity.

Creative living often doesn't lead to instant gratification. We are frequently denied immediate satisfaction in the process of achieving a level of satisfaction that is lasting. This is difficult, because it goes against the grain of our current culture. We listen to music that makes no demands on our intellect and provides all its pleasures within a three- to five-minute time span. We want our projects to be completed as quickly as possible. We live in a world of sound bites and fast food. God calls us away from all this, calls us to take creative living seriously, to discipline ourselves by undergoing the training we need to maximize our gifts, and to take time to live in a creative fashion rather than submitting to the demands of modern society.

For all of us, creative living is a key element in becoming a whole person. Here it's appropriate to quote again from Marie Asner's poem: "Time passes quickly/in such self made labyrinths/if creativity is not sought/otherwise you are what you are/maze after maze . . . exactly/like the first . . . never ending."[56] Lifestyles that are dominated neither by routine nor by the expectations of a mechanistic society are expressions of this fundamental quality of creativity. They give us hope and possibilities for redemptive living.

Creativity and the Community of Faith

Creative products are not produced in isolation. Creativity requires community to be whole and holy. In addition, art and creativity build on the institutions and prior work that have come before. Without earlier artists and craftspeople to show the way, it would not be possible to develop the stylistic maturity or technical skills required to make creative products today. Harold Best says, "Linked in countless ways, we imagine and make. Shut off from these communities, we become quite helpless. . . . We cannot create out of nothing. Our abilities to imagine and craft . . . are dependent and limited."[57]

By their very nature, both community and creativity involve intimate expressions of faith. They are both very personal. There is a direct relationship between the degree of intimacy we sanction in our communities and

56. Marie Asner, "In His Image."

57. Harold Best, *Music through the Eyes of Faith* (San Francisco: HarperCollins, 1993), p. 34.

the creative potential of our work.[58] We create because we have had the opportunity to engage the world in depth, to form an intimate relationship with the object of our attention and with the materials we use to produce art. This spills over into our relationships with people in the context of human community. It informs and forms us as a creative people.

The relationships we have in our churches are vitally important. As Urban Holmes points out, "The Christian congregation needs to find the means of being an intimate community. For it is only in the intimate community that we can . . . discover the infinite richness of life that can make the very banality of everyday living not only tolerable but meaningful."[59]

The Iona Community, off the coast of Scotland, is an example of one such community, a "Christian ecumenical community working for peace and social justice, rebuilding of community and the renewal of worship."[60] Out of the context of this community, the Wild Goose Resource Group (WGRG) has emerged over the years. The WGRG has created a wide range of musical and liturgical resources that are employed by churches and individual believers all over the world.

Similarly, L'Abri, the community formed first in Huemoz, Switzerland, by Francis and Edith Schaeffer in 1955, has also been a place where faith and art have found a comfortable home together.[61] The annual arts week in Huemoz, as well as the many performances, lectures, and classes that have considered questions about the relationship between art and the Judeo-Christian tradition, are testaments to the power and creative potential of art when it is embedded within a vibrant community.

Creativity flourishes in this type of community for other reasons as well. The community can play a critical role in developing and shaping creativity. It is difficult for artists and craftspeople to refine creative abilities without aesthetic criticism and accountability. By providing these things, the community can play a positive role in forming the creative gifts of its members.

---

58. Matthew Fox notes, "When we practice intimacy, we are developing our powers of imagination and creativity. When we ignore intimacy, we are contributing to the powers of destruction" (*Creativity*, p. 187).

59. Holmes, *Ministry and Imagination*, p. 206.

60. See the Iona Community Web site: http://www.icna.org.uk.

61. See the L'Abri Web site: http://www.labri.org. Other prominent examples of intentional Christian communities integrating faith and art include the Grünewald Guild (see Appendix One), St. John's Abbey in Collegeville, Minnesota, and Holden Village in the state of Washington.

In every community, artists and craftspeople need support. They take risks in their work, and sometimes they fail. They need the freedom to risk and fail that only a community can provide, especially a faith community that bases its life on the rich outpouring of love, grace, and mercy that it receives from God. Within certain limitations, this freedom extends to the opportunity for artists and craftspeople to express minority opinions in their art, to stretch the bounds of the faith tradition within which they're working. Certainly this must be done with sensitivity to the pastoral dimension of ministry and in coordination with the pastoral leadership of the community. But, given these caveats, this kind of important creative work can channel the word of God to the community and beyond.

Risk is also a factor for untrained laity who are trying out new, creative ideas or working on creative projects. If these projects involve artistry or craftsmanship, they often place these laypeople in the position of beginners at first. This means their self-image can be threatened. Those who have been in that position know how important a supportive community is to the success of each new creative venture.

Artists and craftspeople are accustomed to being isolated in their work. This makes community all the more important. Bernice Johnson Reagon, the founder and original leader of the African-American vocal ensemble Sweet Honey in the Rock, expressed it this way:

> It is important to gather together to nurture and feed as a community committed to being a presence in a society beyond our own meager lives. . . . First, there is a home base; there is a place that you can go back to for shelter, rest, and reorientation. It is from there that you move into the world offering your message and work — sometimes to people who will throw rocks at you, throw you in jail, or slam doors in your face. Facing work of this intensity, we do not have to apologize for needing to return to home base. . . . It is important to have a safety zone to refuel where you can eat your dinner with others who understand and will protect your need to be vulnerable.[62]

The work that artists do in community is not just for their own personal gratification. It is not necessarily even just for the local community.

---

62. Bernice Johnson Reagon, "Nurturing Resistance," in *Reimaging America: The Arts of Social Change,* ed. Mark O'Brien and Craig Little (Philadelphia: New Society Publishers, 1990), p. 7.

It is given life and expression there, but any time that creative products are made, there is the potential for them to be shared more widely and freely, shared with anyone who needs them — shared just as a cup of water or a morsel of food is shared with those who have none. Nourishment for the body, the mind, and the soul are all important parts of the Christian mission. Artists and craftspeople play an important part in this mission through their compassion and their artistry.

Sharing the results of creative projects means that artists and craftspeople have the opportunity to speak and dance and paint and sing for those who cannot do these things themselves. Everyone is creative in some way, but no one can be creative in every way. I would love to be an accomplished dancer. In my dreams I am a combination of grace and power. I think to myself that surely, with the proper training, this must be possible. Unfortunately (or perhaps fortunately), this is true in my dreams but not necessarily in real life. Instead of spending time and resources developing skills as a professional dancer myself, I rely on trained dancers to open up this dimension of creative expression for me. When artists and craftspeople share their creative efforts, it makes it possible for others to experience a creative facet of life that would not otherwise have been available to them in the same way.

Sharing creative projects also makes it possible to articulate suffering for those who cannot do so themselves. Creativity can speak for the voiceless and the powerless. Sometimes the most powerful political statements are made in highly creative ways. Some years ago I attended an exhibition of visual art created by political prisoners. The exhibition was held at the museum for the International Committee of the Red Cross in Geneva, Switzerland. The sheer creativity of the works I saw has remained with me ever since. It was a powerful testament to the true meaning of freedom created by people who were, in every other respect, anything but free. These works exhibited the prophetic dimension of creativity.

Creativity can protest, but it can also heal. In recent years drum circles have become increasingly popular as a means of providing the possibility of self-expression to those who are unable to express themselves in other ways because of the particular circumstances of their lives. In these circles, everyone is given his or her own drum. Participants create rhythm both independently and in response to the rhythm of the group. In so doing, they find a voice, a way to express themselves, and they learn what it is like to work cooperatively with others. This shows us a pastoral, healing role for creativity.

Recovering Our Creativity

When we were young, creativity was not an issue. We were naturally curious and unabashedly creative. We could try new things and experiment to our heart's delight. But somewhere along the line, we became adults.

Society doesn't like it when adults act like children. There are acceptable behaviors and unacceptable behaviors; as we grow up, we are taught which is which. Unfortunately, this means that the creative impulse has been driven out of most of us. We no longer feel free to take risks. We don't want to look stupid or feel embarrassed. C. S. Lewis has a unique perspective on this problem:

> When I was ten, I read fairy tales in secret and would have been ashamed if I had been found doing so. Now that I am fifty, I read them openly. When I became a man, I put away childish things, including the fear of childishness and the desire to be very grown up.[63]

If only we could all put away "the fear of childishness and the desire to be very grown up"! We have been led to believe that we must act according to someone else's standards. Instead of answering the call to be creative, going out on a limb and trying something new, we say "Not me, not yet, not good enough."[64]

Thomas Merton reminds us why recovering our creativity is so important: "The restoration of our creativity is simply one aspect of our recovery of our likeness to God in Christ. . . . Creativity becomes possible insofar as man can forget his limitations and his selfhood and lose himself in abandonment to the immense creative power of a love too great to be seen or comprehended."[65]

We need to find ways that we can recover our sense of innocence, of abandonment, and of creative freedom. In recent years a wide-ranging literature has been published to help us with this issue. The most famous of these books are the "Artist's Way" publications by Julia Cameron. A somewhat more orthodox Christian version of *The Artist's Way*, entitled *The Creative Call*, has been written by Janice Elsheimer.[66]

63. C. S. Lewis, "On Three Ways of Writing for Children," quoted in Shamana, *Seeing in the Dark*, p. 109.

64. Shamana, *Seeing in the Dark*, p. 15.

65. Merton, "Theology of Creativity," p. 368.

66. Janice Elsheimer, *The Creative Call: An Artist's Response to the Way of the Spirit*

Cameron and Elsheimer take similar paths to reawakening a sense of curiosity and play in adults. They adopt a project method involving a variety of different tasks that force the adult to engage his or her creative side in new and yet familiar ways. Examples include writing a thank-you letter to someone who encouraged you along the way, keeping an artist's daybook in which you simply write each day, writing about the dreams and talents you had as a child, writing a list of sounds you heard today, and writing a response to the pronouncement you heard growing up: "You don't have enough talent to be a . . ."

Reawakening our creative spirit can happen in solitude, but it is helpful if the community supports this activity. It should, in fact, be a primary goal of arts ministry to assist in this project. Whether we play games, go fishing, take up a hobby, or follow the prescriptions in *The Creative Call,* the joyful task of becoming creative again is one of the most important paths we will pursue in our adult lives. Who knows? Perhaps there is hope for me as a dancer yet. . . .

Conclusion

Creativity is a blessing and a privilege bestowed on us by a gracious Creator God. Its importance cannot be overstated. In the twenty-first century, our growth — indeed, our very survival as individuals, as a community, and as a species — depends on our exercising creativity for the benefit of all. If we commit to this process, we will grow more deeply into the image of Christ, the New Adam who names us and calls us into a creative future.

(Colorado Springs: WaterBrook Press, 2001). See also Julia Cameron, *The Artist's Way: A Spiritual Path to Higher Creativity* (New York: Jeremy P. Tarcher, 1992).

CHAPTER SEVEN

Arts Ministry and Worship

Liturgy is not simply doctrine well dressed and ornamented. The truth revealed in such a gathering is truth in the form of music heard deeply enough to make us the music; stories told so well that we become part of the story . . . prayers prayed with such integrity that we become prayerful; and meals celebrated so graciously that we are nourished and become ourselves bread for others. This is the supremely transforming art. It is the holiness of God that lures us, delights us, and, in time, transfigures the world before us.

Don Saliers, *Worship and Theology*

A liturgy given not so much for the sake of the Church but for the sake of the world must attract the world to what is lifted up. In other words, it must be something of great Beauty.

Alejandro Garcia-Rivera, *Living Beauty*

Ritual Moments

It is appropriate to begin a discussion of the arts in worship with a procession. In this case, it will be a special procession, a procession of the arts. The processional music is the canticle "Song of the Three Children."[1]

1. "Song of the Three Children," in *The Grail*, ed. Gregory Polan (Chicago: GIA Publications, 1963). The text is Daniel 3:57-88 (Vulgate); the music is by A. Gregory Murray.

188

A. Gregory Murray

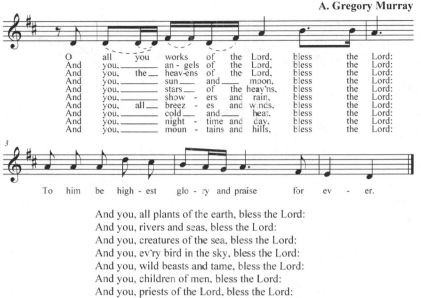

O all you works of the Lord, bless the Lord:
And you,—— an - gels of the Lord, bless the Lord:
And you, the — heav-ens of the Lord, bless the Lord:
And you,—— sun — and — moon, bless the Lord:
And you,—— stars — of the heav'ns, bless the Lord:
And you,—— show - ers and rain, bless the Lord:
And you, all — breez - es and winds, bless the Lord:
And you,—— cold — and — heat, bless the Lord:
And you,—— night - time and day, bless the Lord:
And you,—— moun - tains and hills, bless the Lord:

To him be high - est glo - ry and praise for ev - er.

And you, all plants of the earth, bless the Lord:
And you, rivers and seas, bless the Lord:
And you, creatures of the sea, bless the Lord:
And you, ev'ry bird in the sky, bless the Lord:
And you, wild beasts and tame, bless the Lord:
And you, children of men, bless the Lord:
And you, priests of the Lord, bless the Lord:
And you, servants of the Lord, bless the Lord:

While the congregation and cantor alternate through this lovely litany, members of the choir enter the sanctuary led by dancers. The choir members are all carrying various artworks: paintings, pottery, poems, a clarinet, an African drum, a flute, and pieces of literature. A giant red cloth stretches from aisle to aisle, wafting over the heads of the congregation as it is held high by the dancers leading the procession. Eventually, the symbols of beauty come to rest with the red cloth at the foot of the altar.

Thus began a service of worship at a conference in Kansas City sponsored by Imago Dei: Friends of Christianity and the Arts. There are special times in the life of the church, like the one described above, when the power, grace, and beauty of worship, enacted through the medium of music, architecture, visual art, poetry, dance, drama, or some combination of them, fosters what can only be described as an ecstatic experience. These are moments when the City of God and our human abode mix and comingle, when life is lived with one foot on earth and one foot in heaven. On these occasions, the everyday, mundane realities of life are transfigured, and we briefly glimpse the great feast that has been prepared for us since the beginning of time. Although it is not possible to control or manipulate the divine presence, these experiences show us, through the medium of worship and the arts, how the mystery and wonder associated with living in direct, existential contact with the invisible God can become a tangible, palpable reality in our lives. They can bring us to tears.

The Jewish liturgical scholar Lawrence Hoffman calls these "ritual moments."[2] Moments like this bind the worshipper to the community in which the experience occurs and, ultimately, to God. A ritual moment may be facilitated by the work of a dancer transporting the congregation to new heights while interpreting a vocal solo or an anthem. It may be experienced when light hits the image on a stained-glass window in just the right way, and we are reminded of the luminescence of God. It may happen when the organ is playing a stirring arrangement of the last stanza of the closing hymn, and the choir enters with an exhilarating descant. For many people, ritual moments are kindled anew each week as they repeat the age-old pattern of approaching the table, moving arms and body into familiar positions that speak to them of continuity with the church through the ages, and of the unfolding rituals of their own lives and the life of their community. Indeed, ritual moments may involve any number of artistic or liturgical stimuli, singly or in combination with one another.

Ritual moments are embedded within actual rituals, repeated patterns that help make life meaningful. These patterns involve thought and action, periods of waiting and periods of fulfillment, reflecting the rhythms of life itself. Rituals occur in everyday experience when we have our breakfast in the morning, or water our plants. They are habits that help us mark and make sense out of the normal events of our days, weeks, and years. We often think about the word "ritual" in the context of public worship, a time when the rhythms of life and of salvation history itself are reflected in the structures of the liturgy. Ritual moments enliven rituals in the same way that the sun breaking from behind a cloud enlivens us on a rainy day, or an unexpected taste enables us to savor a moment at a meal.

When ritual moments occur in public worship, they often are connected with art. Their chief function is to act as a means of helping the congregation become aware of the divine presence in their midst. God is not being summoned to earth; rather, the God who is already here is more easily seen, heard, and felt by the faithful because their own intuitive sense is heightened, and they become more vulnerable to God's activity in their lives. Through whatever means they occur, ritual moments operate as pow-

---

2. Lawrence Hoffman, *The Art of Public Prayer: Not for Clergy Only* (Washington, D.C.: Pastoral Press, 1988). See especially Chapters One and Two.

erful markers in human memory, enabling past events to move and energize life in the present and enabling present experiences to shape our future.

Ritual moments are especially important when the hectic schedules of day-to-day life leave parishioners intuitively and emotionally impoverished. People may work throughout the week in an office job, on a factory floor, or in a service industry where the work itself is not especially redemptive or fulfilling. Their thoughts may be focused on the criticisms of their boss or simply on the list of tasks they need to accomplish. When they come to church after experiencing the cumulative effects of a long week, it is often difficult for them to clear their minds and hearts of the baggage they bring with them to worship and allow the Holy Spirit to infiltrate their imagination. In this setting, ritual moments help them experience the divine presence at times when this might not otherwise be possible.

Because of the potential significance of ritual moments in both individual and communal life, the goal of creating an environment conducive to experiencing ritual moments often becomes a chief motivating force behind the work of the arts minister. This means that arts ministers must become sensitive to the subtle nuances of the liturgy, to the ways in which it gives birth to the various sacred arts, and to the purpose and role of ritual moments in the lives of the faithful.

In the present chapter, we will consider this important work under three headings: (1) Worship as Art — an examination of the ways in which worship itself is an art form; (2) Artful Worship — a look at how the enactment of worship can be enhanced; and (3) The Arts in Worship — a discussion of some of the roles the fine arts play in public worship.

Worship as Art

Worship is itself a work of art.[3] In his classic work *Sacred and Profane Beauty*, the Dutch aesthetician Cornelius Van der Leeuw says, "Look at the

---

3. Don Saliers says, "Christian liturgy is an art, but not, in the first instance, a 'work of art.'" See "Liturgical Aesthetics: The Travail of Christian Worship," in *Arts, Theology, and the Church*, ed. Kimberly Vrudny and Wilson Yates (Cleveland: Pilgrim Press, 2005), p. 188. Following Wolterstorff, Saliers defines a work of art as "an entity made or presented in order to serve as an object of aesthetic contemplation" (p. 189). This could lead to a protracted discussion that I will avoid here, adding only my belief that there are other purposes for which artworks are employed. Personally, I have no problem with viewing Christian liturgy as a "work of art."

liturgy; among the forms of Christian art, it is the transcendent and dominant one."[4] While we are accustomed to thinking about the role of the arts *in* worship, we may not have considered the notion that worship *is* a form of art. In a very real sense, this is more fundamental to our consideration of arts ministry than any discussion of visual art or drama or dance.

How are worship and art related to one another? One way they relate is on the level of human experience. Both worship and art enable us to experience ourselves, other people, the world around us, and God in new ways. They help us view reality "up close and personal" by forcing us to stop and pay attention to the minutiae of our lives. As the liturgical theologian Paul Hoon says, "Art and liturgy . . . are not only *ways of experiencing reality.* They are also distinctive *visions of reality;* they become *declarations of the nature of reality;* they consequently *prescribe the nature of man's response to reality.*"[5]

As an example, consider the prayer of confession. Here the church looks at human failures, lost opportunities, and broken relationships. Parishioners pray for forgiveness for their own personal mistakes, their lack of understanding and compassion. They pray also for the manifold ways in which the community, the nation, and the world have lost their way. This is a common liturgical experience shared by millions of worshippers each week. Yet, for many people, the sense that they are broken and in need of the compassion and care of Christ washes over them only when the words of the prayer are amplified by the poignant singing of a hymn:

> Precious Lord, take my hand,
> Lead me on, let me stand,
> I am tired, I am weak, I am worn.
> Through the storm, through the night,
> Lead me on to the light,
> Take my hand, precious Lord,
> Lead me home.[6]

So often it is the coincidence of spoken liturgy and related artistic experiences within a single worship service that brings the full meaning and

---

4. Cornelius Van der Leeuw, *Sacred and Profane Beauty: The Holy in Art* (Nashville: Abingdon Press, 1963), p. 110.

5. Paul Waitman Hoon, *The Integrity of Worship: Ecumenical and Pastoral Studies in Liturgical Theology* (Nashville: Abingdon Press, 1971), p. 273.

6. Thomas Dorsey, "Precious Lord" (New York: Unichappel Music, 1938).

import of an image home to people as they sit in their pews. The form and content of a prayer or a litany combine with the expressive power of other art forms to stake their claim on our affective, spiritual, and intellectual life. We find that we can no longer avoid confronting our failures or celebrating our joys. When prayer, readings, and the sermon are integrated with singing, dancing, drama, or the visual arts, we are surprised to learn lessons that are seemingly self-evident, yet lessons we would not have learned without the presence of liturgical art. These "ritual moments" occur because of the coordinated activities of liturgy and art, and yet, ultimately, they are founded on the reality of God's presence with us.

As liturgy and art relate to one another through their common grounding in reality, they also share a search for transcendence. Albert Rouet says, "Art and liturgy are invited to join forces in a realm beyond themselves. Their rapprochement is transcendence."[7] In the context of this meeting between art and liturgy we experience the mystery of participating in that which is beyond either art or liturgy — indeed, that which is beyond the normal reality that we experience on a day-to-day basis.

Human beings need to know that there is something besides just themselves and their mundane existence, something that exceeds their own imagination and offers the prospect of unifying the disparate parts of their existence, bringing order to chaos. This is possible only when they become aware of the presence of transcendence in their midst, when they have direct, existential contact with the One who is beyond all their images and concepts. Paul Hoon expresses a similar idea when he says, "No artistic experience and no religious experience are finally satisfying unless they somehow speak to man's intuition that there is *wholeness of meaning* at the heart of things."[8] Worship and the liturgical arts both share this same goal. They both have the capacity to lead us toward transcendence and the possibility of integration that results. In this context they seek to make the invisible center of all things visible, and from that center they help us reorient our lives.

How they accomplish this goal may seem counter-intuitive, but it is the only real option available to them. Art and worship both rely heavily on the senses, the sensual dimension of human living. When we worship

---

7. Albert Rouet, *Liturgy and the Arts*, trans. Paul Philibert (Collegeville, Minn.: Liturgical Press, 1997), p. xiii.

8. Hoon, *The Integrity of Worship*, p. 271. Hoon amplifies this point somewhat, saying, "Both art and liturgy can function to bring man to engagement, even to communion with reality in a way so vital that one can speak of it as priestly" (p. 281).

and engage the world artistically, we involve and sometimes overlay the visual, the aural, the gustatory, the tactile, and the olfactory senses in a multidimensional panoply that is richly textured and enlivens those who are open to its power. Both liturgy and art build on God's self-revelation through matter, through the stuff of this world. They help us discern hints of transcendence in the midst of life, in the midst of nature itself — through water and light, in oil, wood, and stone, in sound and gesture.

As an extension of their common sensuality, their grounding in the particular, art and worship are united as actions. Action, by its very nature, is dynamic and vital. Through liturgical and artistic actions, human beings are directly and intimately involved in the world. The artist creates an artifact that is used in a way that encourages an active response. Both the initial creative work on the part of the artist and the appreciation and use of the work in the life of an individual or a community constitute significant actions. Similarly, liturgy is an act, initially on the part of God, that involves a human response. It is not just a matter of standing outside of life and looking in, participating in a conversation about theology or the world. In fact, it is not a time when we meet together to talk *about* anything. It is a time when we practice living in the presence of the God who created, redeemed, and sustains all of life, who calls us from the boundaries of our existence into a vital, transformed life. In a very real sense, God is the artist who acts liturgically in our world and engages us in order to elicit a change in our behavior and our understanding.

As we act in the world, we take risks. Both worship and art recognize and value risk-taking. There is nothing safe about either liturgy or art. In a passage that is so often quoted that it has become practically iconic, Annie Dillard says,

> Does anyone have the foggiest idea what sort of power we so blindly invoke? Or, as I suspect, does no one believe a word of it? The churches are children, playing on the floor with their chemistry sets, mixing up a batch of TNT to kill a Sunday morning.[9]

Art is similarly explosive and can engage us with equally devastating force. Because of the risks involved in attending to art and worship, there is a very real possibility that change may occur, whether we are ready for it or not. Change comes both in the lives of individual people and in the social

9. Annie Dillard, *Holy the Firm* (New York: Harper & Row, 1984), p. 4.

systems and structures that bind people together. This is frightening to many people, yet potentially hopeful for all.

One of the most potent means of effecting change through art and worship is by employing their mutual ability to captivate the person in the pew. Liturgy and art are mutually enchanting. They work independently and together with one another to connect the worshipper with the ultimate source of enchantment, the God who at the end of the ages promises to liberate us into a kingdom of light and beauty, a kingdom where suffering is banished, where we will sing together and join in an extraordinary feast whose richness and abundance exceed our imagination.

The Drama of Worship

Albert Rouet once said, "The liturgy is an art which uses other arts."[10] This is the touchstone for the next part of this discussion. It sends us on a search for the relationship between liturgy and individual art forms in hopes that this will provide a more complete picture of how worship functions as art. We begin with drama.

Our lives are made up of a succession of stories, one after the other, marking the events, places, and people we encounter on our own personal journey. Perhaps it is for this reason that storytelling is so central to the ministry of Jesus. As he tells stories to his disciples, his stories become part of our story.

You remember the account of the man who was beaten and left for dead on the roadside. As Jesus weaves his tale, we watch the prominent and "religious" members of society look the other way, marvel at the warmth and compassion of the outcast who takes him to an inn, and wonder about how we ourselves respond to those in our midst who have been left for dead because of AIDS, abuse, or homelessness. This Gospel lesson teaches, inspires, challenges, and moves us. The story of the Good Samaritan (Luke 10:30-37) is a creative literary form (the parable) used by Jesus to make an important theological and ethical statement. As it calls readers or listeners to employ their imaginations, to engage the narrative in terms of their own lives and experience, it truly becomes a work of art.

Whether we hear this narrative when it is read to us on Sunday morning from the pulpit or see it enacted in worship, we are caught up in its twists and

10. Rouet, *Liturgy and the Arts*, p. 1.

Friends of the Groom: Theatre Coming to a Church Near You
Cincinnati, Ohio

The Friends of the Groom production of *The Lion, the Witch, and the Wardrobe*

In 1980 Tom Long, a recent theatre graduate of the University of Cincinnati, gathered a group of friends and asked them to play parts in a Christian musical he was writing. The group chose their name as a reference to the image of Christ as the bridegroom in the New Testament — appropriate, since they're committed to proclaiming the Christian message in their unique way. Long tells the story of how things developed from the first play till now:

> We produced the play with six adults and one crew member, and toured it to three other churches. The next year we did a new play — this time with a cast of eleven. By the third year, a number of clergy were interested in helping the group become a formally established organization.
>
> Three Episcopal rectors encouraged their congregations to support the

group as a ministry, contributing about $1,300 each. One of the three put us in touch with an attorney who donated her time to help us become a non-profit corporation with a board of directors. At the same time, we picked a name for ourselves, got some stationery printed, and in March 1982, Friends of the Groom was born.

The group has continued to develop since that time. Interest in the group increased dramatically after we performed at an Episcopal Diocesan convention in the fall of 1982. In 1983 we took another large step forward by forming a team of five regular performers who cleared their summer calendars in order to be available as a traveling company. In the fall of 1983, we received first place in a national chancel drama competition sponsored by the Episcopal Foundation for Drama in St. Louis.

That first summer we performed about 10 or 12 times. Each performance led to more performances, particularly when we appeared at conferences or large gatherings. Today we perform 160-190 times a year, normally reaching 16-18 states and about 10-12 denominations. Our traveling team is composed of three actors who all live in the Cincinnati area. The performing is heaviest on the weekends, with two overnight trips planned each month. We continue to rehearse at St. Thomas Episcopal Church, but the members of the group come from a variety of churches and denominations.

Friends of the Groom is supported financially by an annual direct-mail fund drive and by performing fees. I work as the full-time director, with two part-time office staff. The actors are also paid, but only work part-time. Throughout our history, we've had several things going for us: (1) The Holy Spirit. I don't think any of us had a clear vision for how the group would grow. The Lord gradually and surely led us forward, and each new development grew naturally from the one before it. (2) A group of wonderful friends with flexible schedules who have been willing to devote a lot of time, talent, and faithful witness to the group. (3) A loving and supportive congregation. St. Thomas has contributed money, space, encouragement, a friendly audience, and its prayers.*

---

*This is taken from the Web site of Friends of the Groom: http://www.fog.homestead.com.

turns. The details of the story are immediately compelling. We become personally involved as the tale unfolds.[11] We are left without excuses.

The story of the Good Samaritan is an excellent example of drama within the liturgy. The larger question is this: In what way is the liturgy itself a drama? Throughout the Middle Ages, many commentators attempted to answer this question by reading a subtext into the liturgy, an underlying dramatic account, generally taken from events in the life of Christ.[12] Now known as historical typology or liturgical allegory, these accounts gave the faithful something familiar to hold on to as they viewed the mysterious rites of the church. Examples vary widely, from the literal interpretations of Nicholas Cabasilas, who believed that the texts of the liturgy referred directly to the acts they signified (i.e., the Eucharist refers to the sacrifice of Christ), to the more colorful writings of Amalarius of Metz, who thought that virtually every part of the liturgy referred to either a theological or a historical reality: the altar cloth is the burial cloth of Christ, the two candles carried before the gospel are the law and the prophets, the stole represents the yoke of Christ, the opening collect is Jesus' visit to the temple as a child, the epistle represents John the Baptist's teaching, and so on.

Today, viewing liturgy as metaphorical drama continues to resonate with the Orthodox tradition, which invests deep meaning in the individual actions and setting of liturgy, and to some extent with the Roman Catholic tradition — in particular, its view of the priest acting as Christ for the gathered assembly. It is clear to many that worship is deeply and passionately dramatic and that it is metaphorical at its very core. Worship connects the larger narrative of *kairos* (sacred time, as recorded in the events of salvation history) with the everyday dramas of *chronos* (our own story, bound by time).

As Don Saliers reminds us, "Worship in the gathered community of faith takes the form of enactment."[13] On a mundane level, there are scripts,

---

11. Paul Hoon adds, "The experience of immediacy, further, can become an experience of *engagement*. The test of good theatre . . . is always whether it involves, not merely whether it entertains" (*The Integrity of Worship*, p. 271).

12. Important figures in the Eastern Church include Cyril of Jerusalem, Theodore of Mopsuestia, Pseudo-Dionysius the Areopagite, Maximus the Confessor, Germanus of Constantinople, and Nicholas Cabasilas. Significant Western authors are Amalarius of Metz and William Durandus. For further information, see Paul Rorem, *The Medieval Development of Liturgical Symbolism*, Grove Liturgical Study no. 47 (Bramcote, Nottingham, England: Grove Books, 1986).

13. Saliers, *Worship Come to Its Senses* (Nashville: Abingdon Press, 1996), p. 85.

sets, a musical score, costumes, and actors who are engaged in telling the story. More important is the manner in which worship involves us in the dramatic quality of salvation itself. Each time we gather as the community of faith, we enact once again the "old, old story." Protestants resonate most with the drama of worship when this story is proclaimed from the pulpit. Preaching and the reading of Scripture uncover the ongoing tensions between death and life, justice and mercy, suffering and exaltation, and sin and redemption that are part of the human/divine drama and become constituent parts of worship. Jeremy Begbie points out that promise and fulfillment — involving dramatic tension and release — are part and parcel of the unfolding story of salvation.[14] The dénouement of the Christian story and, by analogy, of liturgy itself, occurs on the cross as Jesus dies for our sins. His death and resurrection are made real for us at the Eucharistic table. This is the ultimate drama that the liturgy enacts as we gather to break bread and to become, once again, the body of Christ.

The Poetry of Worship

For a long time, the history of worship was seen largely as the history of its words. While this is no longer an exclusive focus of liturgical studies, nonetheless the text of liturgy remains an important part of the worship experience, a lens through which we can view not only liturgical history but also the practice and impact of liturgy in our own time.

As noted earlier, almost one-third of the Hebrew Bible is poetry. Historic liturgy is similarly laden with poetic language and poetic devices. This is not accidental. As Michael Driscoll reminds us, "Discovering God and enacting our relationship with God and one another through liturgical worship means the words must be more like poetry than prose."[15]

Poetry involves metaphorical communication that has the capacity to touch us at the core of our being. Metaphors are non-literal, non-discursive forms that speak to us on a variety of different levels. They are multivalent. Metaphorical language is often understood as the creation of a new mental reality. As we view one object in terms of another, our perception and under-

14. Jeremy S. Begbie, *Theology, Music, and Time* (Cambridge: Cambridge University Press, 2000). See especially Chapter Four.

15. Michael A. Driscoll, "Musical Mystagogy: Catechizing through the Sacred Arts," in *Music in Christian Worship: At the Service of the Liturgy,* ed. Charlotte Kroeker (Collegeville, Minn.: Liturgical Press, 2005), p. 33.

standing are forever altered. We no longer see the individual objects; we see the relationship between them as a new phenomenon. For example, think of viewing Jesus as "the sacrificial victim" (a discursive, technical description); then think of Jesus as the "Lamb of God" (employing poetic, metaphorical language). Both descriptions express similar theological content, but they differ markedly in their relative richness and expressive power.

In Christian worship, metaphors occur in rapid succession. Their meanings pile on top of one another so fast that we often miss the fact that they are metaphors at all. Read aloud Psalm 91:3-4 and see if you catch all the metaphors there: "For he will deliver you from the snare of the fowler and from the deadly pestilence; he will cover you with his pinions, and under his wings you will find refuge; his faithfulness is a shield and buckler."

The metaphorical and poetic dimensions of Christian liturgy are a challenge for many people who have little direct contact with poetry outside of Sunday morning services. This is especially noticeable in the work of lectors and cantors, who are charged with proclaiming the Word in liturgy. Their primary experiences with language are often literal, prosaic, colloquial, and occasionally banal. Worship not only includes poetry and metaphorical speech; its fundamental approach to and understanding of God are poetic. Without a similar sensibility to poetic ways of thinking and understanding, it can be difficult to engage God on the deepest level, much less to proclaim God's Word in public worship.

This represents one of the deepest divisions between contrasting traditions of worship in the contemporary church. Historic liturgy, as expressed in so-called traditional worship, is rich in poetic meaning. It values ambiguity and the suggestive quality of metaphor, viewing this as a strength, not a weakness. By contrast, contemporary worship often features prosaic language. It is more literal, admits of less ambiguity and, therefore, of less mystery. It has the potential to reduce God to the level of human comprehension, rather than letting God be God. In many contemporary worship services, prosaic, colloquial language (along with colloquial dress and environment) is virtually the only means of address that is employed. This is not merely a matter of style. The choices between being prosaic and poetic are not arbitrary. They define the ways in which we view reality, the approach we take to thinking about ourselves, our neighbors, God, and the world around us. Although it is not debated with anything approaching the fervor of the dialectic between "traditional" and "contemporary" worship music, the distinction between poetic worship and prosaic worship may be just as significant. Marshall McLuhan is still right: "The medium is the message."[16]

The Dance of Worship

We are all, at heart, dancers. In varying degrees our lives consist of movement. The Judeo-Christian tradition defines us as people who are on a journey. We move forward, backward, and side to side as we integrate our walk with that of our neighbor. We reach up and down in our search for the summit and ground of our existence. Movement is central to our identity as members of the Christian community. It is a prime characteristic of our individual and communal lives. Ultimately, our solo and ensemble movements constitute a wonderful, intricately choreographed dance with God.

Our own personal liturgical dance begins with simple movements and gestures. We move into and out of the worship space; we greet one another with gestures of peace. According to our tradition, we move forward to receive the Eucharist or to baptize a child. The pastor, in turn, walks back into our midst to introduce the newly baptized infant to his or her new church family. We may stand or sit, bow, kneel, raise our arms in praise, lay on hands, or make the sign of the cross. The presider greets us with arms wide open in a sign of welcome or raises one hand as a gesture of blessing. Don Saliers points out that "In some respects our bodily movements, gestures, and dispositions may be the most deeply theological aspects of communal worship."[17]

Sometimes in worship we move individually, and sometimes we move in concert with the entire community, either in carefully choreographed processions or more random, even spontaneous movements (for instance, in charismatic worship). Life abounds in movement, and movement is at the center of ritual. In fact, ritual is a way of enacting movement. It does not allow us to remain in one place on our life's journey, but forces us to choose, to move forward on our pilgrimage with God. Thus, the patterns of our worship are, at their most fundamental level, a dance — the dance of

16. Marshall McLuhan's famous declaration — "The medium is the message" — was discussed at length in his book *Understanding Media: The Extensions of Man* (Cambridge, Mass.: MIT Press, 1964).

17. Saliers, *Worship Come to Its Senses*, pp. 163-64.

life. They remind us of who we are and help us to avoid the illusion of stability and stasis in our lives. They also remind us that we are whole people, full of the vitality that comes only from enspirited flesh.

The experience of embodiment is fundamental to human existence. Even for those who are physically handicapped there is a relationship between embodiment and incarnation, between the fact that we feel the wind on our cheek and the sun on our face and the fact that God came to live an embodied life among us.

Dance allows artists to express these most basic facts of our existence, to express in movement what it means to be an embodied, enspirited people. Albert Rouet says, "As an art, dance gathers up and condenses the essential reality of the human. It moves toward the heights of human expression and toward a glimpsed fulfillment. In this way dance touches upon the sacred, that is to say, upon what is indispensable for living and what gives meaning to life."[18]

As we experience liturgy, we experience what it means to be a nomadic people, to live on the move, always ready to pull up stakes and proceed to the next destination. The liturgy encourages and embodies this posture toward life. In and through it we learn to dance with God and with one another.

The Art and Architecture of Worship

Ever since Bezalel and Oholiab constructed the tabernacle, Judeo-Christian worshippers have valued a sense of space, a physical location that in some way defines not only where we are, but who we are. The spaces of our lives establish a temporary environment (the tabernacle, after all, was mobile) that is bounded by the present moment and yet connects us in some way with our past and our future.

As we inhabit worship spaces, we establish certain patterns and habits. We always sit in the fifth pew from the front, right on the aisle, and, consequently, relate to a particular group of liturgical "neighbors." We become accustomed to a way of being in the room physically. As Don Saliers notes, "The bodily memory of having knelt at an altar rail or of sitting in a specific place becomes part of the theological significance of the rites."[19] The

---

18. Rouet, *Liturgy and the Arts*, p. 149.
19. Saliers, *Worship Come to Its Senses*, p. 159.

physicality we discussed in our earlier consideration of dance is thus connected to the physical dimensions and character of the spaces in which we worship. Both in some way embody the faith.

Janet Walton says that when we build a church, we proclaim "a commitment to a long-term Christian engagement."[20] I think this is true not only with respect to the fact *that* we construct churches, but also with respect to *how* we construct our churches. There is a difference between constructing a building that is flimsy and one that is solid, between constructing a building that is meant to speak only to a single generation and one that has the potential to allow God's voice to be audible down through the ages.

Of course, this begs the question. There is an inherent tension between building temporary spaces for pilgrim people (i.e., the tabernacle) and constructing more permanent spaces as a witness to our seriousness of purpose (i.e., the temple). This is an irresolvable conundrum with which each succeeding generation must struggle. The real challenge may be to come up with imaginative solutions that speak to both of these concerns simultaneously.

Buildings not only confine us; they also provide an environment that has the potential to liberate us. It is a cliché to say that we form buildings and then buildings form us, but it is nonetheless true. The visual environment in which we worship is a particularly good example of this. Our theology, our relationships with others, our affective and ethical lives — all are impacted by the various visual environments in which we live. We need to remember the importance of the choices we make as we select permanent furnishings and artwork, as well as seasonal paraments, vestments, flowers, and other environmental aids to our worship. They impact who we will become as individuals and how we will live into our shared future. They bear witness to our commitments and our self-understanding as Christian people.

A good example involves flowers. In this book we have developed the metaphor of the rose to represent arts ministry. Why are roses important in our spaces of worship? In sanctuaries that are often devoid of natural beauty, they remind us of our connection to creation and to the doctrine of creation that is often overlooked in favor of images in stained glass or statuary that devote attention exclusively to the redemptive process. They sug-

20. Janet Walton, *Art and Worship: A Vital Connection* (Wilmington, Del.: Michael Glazier, 1988), p. 42.

gest that we take seriously our mandate to cultivate creation and create form out of chaos.

Whether by way of flowers or art, whether in the lines and angles of a room or the character of its furnishings, faith is expressed in and through the architectural and visual environment of worship. There is often a direct relationship between the theological convictions of individual faith traditions and the buildings in which they meet for worship. Nicholas Wolterstorff points out the convergence (or "fittingness," as he calls it) between "the clean white interiors of the American colonial churches and the highly organized, rational character of the religious self-understanding of those who built them."[21] Likewise, many commentators have made the case that Gothic architecture and Scholasticism have a certain synergy.

It is important to note that liturgy itself has an architectural dimension. Liturgy has form and function that often mirrors the form and function of the spaces in which it is set. Its architectural dimensions are generally so specific that they are not easily portable to another location. They work in *this* space in a different way than they would work elsewhere. This is a lesson the Methodists learned as they moved westward across America in the nineteenth century. The old forms of Anglican liturgy that John Wesley valued so highly did not fit as well into the new framework of outdoor worship, of the sawdust trail and the mourner's bench. Its new architectural context led to a fundamentally new worship service and, I would argue, a new self-understanding of the people who worshipped in this setting.

The Music of Worship

At its most basic level, music involves rhythm. Music helps organize our lives by coordinating us with the dimension of time. This is no less true of liturgy. One way to view liturgy is by looking at its rhythms. Albert Rouet says, "Liturgy is a journey marked by a rhythm."[22] Paul Hoon points to the rhythm of the readings, of confession/absolution, of processional/recessional, of offering, thanksgiving, fraction (breaking the bread), and communion.[23] We could also talk about the rhythm of the seasons of the

---

21. Nicholas Wolterstorff, *Art in Action: Toward a Christian Aesthetic* (Grand Rapids: Wm. B. Eerdmans, 1980), p. 118.

22. Rouet, *Liturgy and the Arts*, p. 18.

23. Hoon, *The Integrity of Worship*, pp. 286-87.

church year and the rhythms of our lives as we pass from one stage of life to another.

Liturgies mark these various rhythms in unique ways. We baptize and confirm; we marry and bury; we follow a lectionary cycle that immerses us in the whole range of salvation history. Within individual worship services, different readers have their own sense of pacing and rhythm. They exhibit other musical characteristics in their reading as well, including inflection, pitch, and articulation.

Music, like other art forms, is constitutive of our theology. Different kinds of music provide different theological messages. This is not just tied to text. It is true for purely instrumental music as well. Thus, the music we select for worship will impact our theology as well as our spirituality. As Don Saliers points out, "To persist in using tensionless, easy-listening music will, over time, produce tensionless spirituality. To have a steady diet of music which is pompous, romantically self-assertive, or grandiose will affect and effect a pompous or self-indulgent ethos of prayer and participation."[24]

The patterns and rhythms of life pulsate through our music and through our liturgies. They speak to us of the God who is at the center of every pattern and every moment of time, the God who loves us into being and seeks us at every juncture, in every season of our lives.

Summary

As a way of summing up this brief consideration of worship as art, let me invite you to consider what worship would look like in the absence of story and metaphor, of poetry, movement, space, and rhythm. Thus denuded of its artistic elements, worship would be at risk of losing its sense of enchantment. If worship itself did not function artistically, it would tend to *disengage* us from our involvement with the world around us and from God.

Artful Worship

The Roman Catholic document *Sing to the Lord* says, "Faith grows when it is well expressed in celebration. Good celebrations can foster and nourish

24. Don Saliers, "Liturgical Musical Formation," in *Liturgy and Music: Lifetime Learning*, ed. Robin A. Leaver and Joyce Ann Zimmerman (Collegeville, Minn.: Liturgical Press, 1998), p. 388.

faith. Poor celebrations may weaken it." What does it mean to celebrate the rites well? What could it possibly mean to celebrate poorly? The document itself provides one answer to this question, reminding us that the goal of liturgical worship is to make it possible for everyone to "praise and beseech the Triune God more powerfully, more intently, and more effectively."[25]

Worship that accomplishes this goal may be said to be artful worship. Liturgy is complex. There are many details to be considered and many tasks to be accomplished for a worship service to occur in an orderly fashion, to say nothing of its being compelling. This means that the process of planning and executing artful worship is deeply collaborative. Liturgy is the result of a community effort; it is not a solo affair. Many people with varied skills must be involved for it to happen at all, not the least of which is the assembly itself.

Planning and Enactment

In the planning and executing of worship there is a dialectic between focusing on "correct" style — the technical requirements of liturgy — and needing to enter into the mystery of worship with honesty and humility, allowing the Spirit to speak to the depths of our being. Focusing all our attention on rules or rubrics can distract us from the more essential focus on God. As Albert Rouet reminds us, "A strict adherence to rubrics may reduce the liturgy to a mechanical exercise."[26]

Artful worship is similar to artistic performance. For example, when dancers or musicians perform, they first pay attention to the technical details of their craft. They learn how to execute a plié or how to play a scale. They practice this skill until they can do it with ease. In time they learn to apply these skills in the context of different dances or pieces of music. When they finally arrive at a performance, they are no longer focused on technical skills per se; their attention is riveted by the aesthetic of the dance or the piece of music they are performing.

It is the life-giving quality of the music or dance itself that matters. Having prepared well, artists care much more about whether or not the piece comes across as compelling than about whether they missed a few notes or

---

25. United States Conference of Catholic Bishops, *Sing to the Lord: Music in Divine Worship* (USCCB, 2007).

26. Rouet, *Liturgy and the Arts*, p. 26.

didn't hold a perfectly straight line long enough within a combination. It's true that if technical problems happen *too* frequently in performance, they distract from the central artistic goal. Nonetheless, technique is not the point. Art is about beauty and truth. It is about the sorrows, joys, challenges, and vitalities of life itself. Artists understand that a performance is not an exercise designed to impress the audience with their technical prowess. It is not an opportunity for them to be worshipped as some sort of heroes.

In liturgy this attitude is, if anything, even more important. Worship is all about giving life to people and praise to God. It is about icons showing the way to God, not idols standing in our path to block access to the divine. To be truly artful, worship needs to be focused on the essentials, the inner meaning and significance of what is occurring. It needs to be focused on God.

This is not meant to excuse poor preparation or sloppy execution. It is not meant to suggest that as long as we dedicate worship to Jesus in our hearts, anything goes. Not at all! As Michael Driscoll reminds us, "We must tend to the aesthetics of worship. . . . Good liturgy is requisite to rich symbolic participation and contemplation."[27] Thoughtfulness and careful consideration given to the details of worship create an avenue by means of which the Spirit can work through us. They help us become more transparent and increase our ability to function as icons for those around us. Artful worship involves loving God and neighbor *so much* that our love overflows to encompass the liturgy itself. We enter into worship with a loving concern for the many small details and individual tasks that go into making an artful, beautiful, and compelling service.

Developing Liturgical Habits

Don Saliers is right when he says, "The liturgy is itself a country we must learn to dwell in."[28] Over the years we have forgotten that worship is a learned activity. As worship and evangelism have been conflated, there has been an attempt in many quarters to "dumb down" worship so that it is immediately accessible to everyone. The notion that we have to learn how to dwell in the country of liturgy has been lost. If we are to hope for a rejuvenation of worship — including the enactment of artful worship and the use

27. Driscoll, "Musical Mystagogy," in *Music in Christian Worship,* p. 34.
28. Saliers, *Worship Come to Its Senses,* p. 139.

of the fine arts in worship — it is important that we recover this idea and make sense of it in the current liturgical climate.

Learning occurs outside of worship as a means of preparing for full participation in worship, and also in worship, as a by-product of simply spending a significant amount of time in the pews. Participation in liturgy can involve learning on many different levels. As parishioners worship, they are learning about the primary relationships in their lives. With respect to God, they are learning something about theology. They experience divine mercy and eschatological anticipation. They learn what it means to hope and what it means to have faith in the face of mystery. In a very real sense, they come to learn the language of heaven. With respect to their own character and identity, worship helps form parishioners in the image of God, and helps them learn the lessons of morality and truthfulness, of graciousness and generosity. In regard to others, parishioners learn about issues of justice, forgiveness, love, and compassion. They come to understand something about the structures and institutions that govern the common life of the community. In terms of the world, they learn how to be effective gardeners, tending to creation in light of the mandate first given to us in another garden so long ago.

All of this learning is, in a sense, contingent. It is contingent on the ability of parishioners to enter into worship with a set of common, shared assumptions and, to a degree, a common language of worship. Let me give some specific examples. First of all, when we plan worship, we usually assume a certain fluency with the basic narratives of the Judeo-Christian experience:

"In the beginning when God created the heavens and the earth. . . ." (Gen. 1:1)

"I have set my bow in the clouds, and it shall be a sign of the covenant between me and the earth." (Gen. 9:13)

"I will make of you a great nation, and I will bless you, and make your name great, so that you will be a blessing." (Gen. 12:2)

"I am the LORD your God, who brought you out of the land of Egypt, out of the house of slavery; you shall have no other gods before me." (Exod. 20:2-3)

"The LORD is my shepherd, I shall not want." (Ps. 23:1)

"For a child has been born for us, a son given to us; authority rests upon his shoulders; and he is named Wonderful Counselor, Mighty God, Everlasting Father, Prince of Peace." (Isa. 9:6)

In these passages and so many others are contained the substance of the Judeo-Christian story, the account of salvation history that explains why we are gathering for worship. We easily forget that this story is *learned*. Increasingly in the current cultural climate this learning cannot be taken for granted. Those who enter our worship services often feel like they are in a foreign country, where the basic narratives of the faith are assumed, not explained. It is a place where we seem to be, literally, preaching to the choir.

Worse yet is the notion, encountered in all too many services, that learning the narratives of the faith is not really important. In many liturgies today the Old Testament is rendered irrelevant by the very fact that it is left out of corporate worship. Sometimes, in the interest of preaching to a particular theme, there will be no gospel reading. Personal relationships are the dominant issue in worship, and a few very basic theological ideas are presented over and over again with little concern for increasing depth of understanding. In churches where this is occurring, the issue of biblical literacy seems to be almost beside the point.

Even in services that incorporate the lectionary readings, there is an additional assumption to consider: that parishioners understand the cultural context of liturgy. On a mundane level, this means that everyone in the congregation is supposed to be able to read and speak the native language. In an increasingly multicultural setting, this is not something we can always take for granted. On a deeper level, it assumes a certain fluency with the musical and symbolic languages of worship. This is challenged when we look around ourselves and see arcane symbols that seem to require explanation. We hear songs (either from popular culture *or* hymnody/chant from the tradition) that are unknown to us, sometimes written in strange and unfamiliar styles. We can appreciate them on a certain level, but to understand them fully would require a measure of aesthetic education (for either popular or traditional repertoire). In addition, many if not most parishioners have never learned to appreciate the vocabulary of dance and liturgical gesture, or the rich, metaphorical language of poetry. These various artistic languages are all set in a formal liturgical context that can be obscure and bewildering. There is nothing worse than being part of a congregation and not knowing what to do or when to do it. Clearly, the literary and artistic languages of worship are *learned activities*.

In the early church, the catechumens (those preparing to be baptized) were ushered out of worship early in the service each week. What they learned of Christianity and of worship they learned outside of liturgy itself.

The modern era has substituted religious education and the family for the ancient catechetical process, but taken together these do not seem to provide adequate attention to the lessons that need to be learned. The resulting situation is one where, rather than teaching about the faith and the language of worship outside of liturgy, all the teaching is done at the eleven o'clock service on Sunday morning. When this becomes impossible, liturgy is altered, minimizing the need to understand the rich history and narratives of the Judeo-Christian story or the languages of worship. The Roman Catholic "Rite of Christian Initiation of Adults" (RCIA) is an exception to this. Here, building on primal Christian tradition, both theology and liturgy are the subject of formal education as preparation for full liturgical participation.

In order for the faithful to participate in worship with all their heart, soul, and mind, they must be formed in certain habits or dispositions appropriate to liturgy. These include learning the basic narratives and the underlying theology of the faith, as well as growing in their ability to appreciate and participate in the various liturgical arts they encounter in full-bodied sensual worship. They are not only learning *about* the faith; they are learning and growing in their own affective, intuitive, intellectual, spiritual, and even physical lives.

As mentioned earlier, this learning can occur both within and outside of worship. In fact, the best approach is a combination of extra-liturgical and liturgical stimuli that lead participants to growth and maturity in the faith as whole people. In this way, habits are formed and practiced over and over again each time people come to worship or attend catechetical classes. Thus learning happens through a variety of different means, some of which are didactic and intentional, others of which are indirect and intuitive.

These habits carry over into the rest of life. They are practiced much as pianists practice their instrument or actors practice delivering a soliloquy. Worship itself becomes a rehearsal, a time when parishioners learn to be the people God created them to be so that they can be God's people in the world. Tangentially, it is also a time when they experience the richness of the metaphors and liturgical forms that make up the substance of the liturgy itself.

Just as these liturgical habits carry over into our daily lives, so public, corporate worship leads in turn to the rehearsal and performance that is the rest of our lives. Rouet says, "Liturgy is beauty because it dares to make the least action beautiful. . . . In making such an action beautiful, it teaches how to ennoble corresponding gestures in ordinary life. Ordinary life receives a vocation to such beauty, if we come to love both life and beauty itself!"[29]

The Arts in Worship

As we consider the arts in worship, we will, of necessity, focus our attention to a certain extent on special services, services held at festivals or conferences, services whose purpose is to highlight the use of the arts in worship. In some ways this is a shame. The only reason for this is that the arts are frequently held at arm's length from the regular liturgical practice of the community. In many churches they come to full expression only on special occasions. In addition, the arts are often relegated to purely functional status, unrelated to the inner dynamic of beauty and truth that liturgy conveys at its depths. In his "Letter to Christian Artists," John Paul II offers an alternative vision:

> I appeal especially to you, Christian artists: I wish to remind each of you that, beyond functional considerations, *the close alliance that has always existed between the Gospel and art* means that you are invited to use your creative intuition to enter into the heart of the *mystery of the Incarnate God* and at the same time into *the mystery of man.*[30]

If art is purely functional (or thought of as ornamental and, thus, expendable), then the liturgical arts become an exceptional activity, not the norm. Janet Walton describes the impoverishing consequences:

> When art is not understood as a significant component of a church's expression of itself, the vitality of the church is weakened. Prosaic architectural designs are accepted in place of more imaginative structures. Vestments, vessels, and furniture are ordered without thought about the specific characteristics of a particular local context. Music is treated as a functional component of worship rather than as a rich resource for understanding and transformation. Visual art is considered as decorative rather than an integral part of the liturgical experience. Processions are viewed as utilitarian. . . . Dance, drama, and poetry, if used at all, are re-

29. Rouet, *Liturgy and the Arts,* p. 79.

30. John Paul II, *Letter of His Holiness John Paul II to Artists* (Boston: Pauline Books and Media, 1999), pp. 30-31.

served for special occasions instead of becoming a regular consideration in the planning of worship.[31]

To the extent that the creative use of the arts is a normal part of your worship setting, then the following examples will be routine for you. If not, then perhaps these examples will begin to awaken your imagination and help you understand what might be possible not only on special occasions, but also in the most mundane and restrictive circumstances.

"Let us go to the house of the Lord": Art and Environment

Art sets the context for worship. This includes our total sensory environment: sound, sight, taste, touch, and smell. It creates a setting in which beauty can be expressed and admired.

The document *Environment and Art in Catholic Worship* makes an important connection between beauty and worship:

> Liturgy's climate is one of awe, mystery, wonder, reverence, thanksgiving, and praise. So it cannot be satisfied with anything less than the *beautiful* in its environment and all its artifacts, movements, and appeals to the senses. . . . In a world dominated by science and technology, liturgy's quest for the beautiful is a particularly necessary contribution to full and balanced human life.[32]

Beauty matters. It matters in life, and it matters in worship. Marva Dawn reminds us that "our increasingly ugly world makes it all the more imperative for worship to remind us of God's beauty."[33] Almost every commentator I know says that beauty in liturgy is not intended for the same purpose as that in the museum or the concert hall. It is not offered as the object of contemplation for the purpose of achieving aesthetic delight.[34] Amplifying this point, John Witvliet says, "Liturgical art, much of

---

31. Walton, *Art and Worship*, p. 69.

32. National Conference of Catholic Bishops, *Environment and Art in Catholic Worship* (Chicago: Liturgy Training Publications, 1993), no. 34.

33. Marva Dawn, *Reaching Out without Dumbing Down: A Theology of Worship for the Turn-of-the-Century Culture* (Grand Rapids: Wm. B. Eerdmans, 1995), p. 249.

34. Wolterstorff posits three criteria for aesthetic quality: unity, internal richness (variety), and intensity. He notes that most liturgical art, whose principal goal is not aes-

it participatory in character, is the art of a community, at the service of its liturgical actions and not at the service of aesthetic contemplation."[35] With the greatest respect for my colleagues and forebears who hold this position, I find myself differing from it. I believe that there is no fundamental opposition between aesthetic contemplation and the contemplation of God. In fact, aesthetic contemplation is a gift from God. God establishes this as a value and gives us the intuitive capacity and ability to learn, thereby enabling us to engage in aesthetic contemplation. As we turn our attention to the beauty that surrounds us in liturgy and spend time contemplating it, we are led to the source of all beauty — God. When we have the thrill of singing a rousing hymn in the company of an assembly that really sings, or feel the sense of awe engendered by a holy space, we are at that very moment experiencing aesthetic contemplation. At these moments the vault of heaven opens, and we can perceive a direct existential contact with the divine.

Union with God is, for many in the Christian tradition, the ultimate goal of liturgy. Aesthetic contemplation does not replace this goal or supersede it, but it is an important means by which our *awareness* of this union, our perception of the workings of the Spirit, comes alive. Heightening our awareness of God's presence in our midst seems to me to be central to the act of praise, central to confession and lament, central to receiving forgiveness and approaching the table. We go through a variety of ups and downs in our spiritual lives. It is critically important for us to remain faithful regardless of whether or not we *feel* God's presence. Living in the presence of God *and being aware of it* would seem to be an appropriate goal for all of life. I think it is very much the point of liturgy and very much the point of ensuring that the climate in which liturgy occurs, and the liturgy itself, are as beautiful as we can possibly make them.

The procession with which we opened this chapter reminds us of our need to offer beauty back to the Author of all beauty whenever we gather for worship. Every gift with which we have been endowed should be returned to God in a loving sacrifice of praise and thanksgiving. Beauty in worship will nourish us and attract the world to God's abundant harvest. It

---

thetic satisfaction, needs more unity and intensity than internal richness (*Art in Action*, p. 185).

35. John Witvliet, "The Worship: How Can Art Serve the Corporate Worship of the Church?" in *For the Beauty of the Church*, ed. W. David O. Taylor (Grand Rapids: Baker Books, 2010), p. 56.

The Network of Biblical Storytellers
Indianapolis, Indiana

Mei-Lin Po performs at a festival gathering of the Network of Biblical Storytellers

will entice us into a deeper and more fully committed relationship with the One in whom true beauty resides.

"Be transformed by the renewing of your mind": Art and the Word

"As a deer longs for flowing streams, so my soul longs for you, O God." A lector begins reading the familiar verses of Psalm 42. "My soul thirsts for God, for the living God." Between these verses, a second reader shares a poem about an Alzheimer's patient: "Here" by Jennifer Armstrong.[36] Back

36. Jennifer Armstrong, "Here," *Christianity and the Arts* 7, no. 2 (Spring 2000): 24, used in conjunction with Psalm 42 with permission of the author.

Story is at the heart of biblical religion. In 1977 a young Ph.D. student named Tom Boomershine was in the process of writing a doctoral dissertation that took account of the manner in which oral culture was a factor in the development of biblical texts. Around this same time, he was struck by a car, and his legs were seriously injured. As he convalesced, Boomershine reflected on the story of the healing of the paralytic found in the Gospel of Mark. During his lengthy recovery, he discovered for himself the power of committing scriptural stories to memory.

After receiving his Ph.D., Boomershine led the first of many workshops. Out of these workshops grew a core of people who became committed to the idea of learning and telling biblical stories. In 1977 this group officially formed the Network of Biblical Storytellers (NBS). Since that time the network has grown and developed in a variety of different ways. A decade after its founding, the organization began sponsoring annual conferences (now called "festival gatherings"), which have been held each year since then in locations around the country. Storytelling trips overseas began with a trip to Russia in 1988 and subsequently have included trips to the Holy Land and other destinations. In 2006 an Academy of Biblical Storytelling was established "to provide a process of support and training in both the performance and [the] teaching of biblical stories."* The organization also maintains a directory of storytellers.

*Taken from the Network of Biblical Storytellers' Web site: http://www.nbsint.org.

and forth they go, each reading reflecting and commenting on the other in a soulful dance that helps us hear both texts with new ears:

Psalm 42/"Here" by Jennifer Armstrong
Antiphonal Reading

1. As a deer longs for flowing streams,
   so my soul longs for you, O God.

   He's watching TV when I arrive.
   It's Monday noon, our weekly lunch date.
   We'll walk up to the corner restaurant
   and he'll have a BLT and a milkshake.

2. My soul thirsts for God, for the living God.
   When shall I come and behold the face of God?

   It never changes.
   But he changes all the time, terribly.
   Alzheimer's scatters his life
   like a baleful wind tears at sand and stone.

3. My tears have been my food day and night,
   while people say to me continually,
   "Where is your God?"

   A few shrubs and shreds of memory cling
   to the scoured cliff face of his mind.
   How long till they too are whirled away?
   Will he know who I am today?

4. These things I remember, as I pour out my soul:
   how I went with the throng,
   and led them in procession to the house of God,
   with glad shouts and songs of thanksgiving,
   a multitude keeping festival.

   My greeting is tentative — "Daddy?"
   He looks up, filled with delight.
   "Oh boy!" he cries like a child getting
   a marvelous treat (my father, a child).

5. Why are you cast down, O my soul,
   and why are you disquieted within me?
   Hope in God; for I shall again praise him,
   my help and my God.

   He's happy today I tell myself
   with a stern inner shake.
   I turn off the Travel Show
   and we walk outside.

6. My soul is cast down within me;
   therefore I remember you from the land of Jordan and of Hermon,
   from Mount Mizar.

7. Deep calls to deep at the thunder of your cataracts;
   all your waves and your billows have gone over me.

8. By day the LORD commands his steadfast love,
   and at night his song is with me, a prayer to the God of my life.

   He stops and stares in amazement.
   His face is as open and filled with wonder
   as a baby taking his first long drink of sun and sky.
   I look too, at the crocus pushing up through wet leaves,
   the yellow forsythia shaking free of winter,
   the squirrels chasing bushy tails around tall trees.
   "You never know where you'll be,"
   he whispers reverently.
   "First I was in Africa and now I'm here."

9. I say to God, my rock, "Why have you forgotten me?
   Why must I walk about mournfully because the enemy oppresses
       me?"

10. As with a deadly wound in my body, my adversaries taunt me,
    while they say to me continually, "Where is your God?"

    I take my father's hand.
    I can't speak.
    I silently pray
    that today
    I too may
    be here.

11. Why are you cast down, O my soul,
    and why are you disquieted within me?
    Hope in God; for I shall again praise him,
    my help and my God.

This could be called an example of *midrash*, the ancient Jewish rabbinical practice of adding brief interpolations that comment on verses of Scripture.[37] It is one among many creative ways to proclaim the Word and

---

37. Note that the term *midrash* is, in reality, much more complex and rich than I am suggesting here.

help the faithful hear it from a fresh perspective. The Word can be accompanied by projected visual images; it can be proclaimed by a lector who memorizes and delivers the text of Scripture in a dramatic soliloquy;[38] it can be enacted by a drama team. There are many possibilities, each of which is motivated by a desire to help the congregation enter into the text attentively and with renewed appreciation for its power and possibilities. The arts bear much responsibility for this process. They refresh our imagination by presenting well-worn truths in new forms, by helping us see with new eyes and hear with new ears the ageless story of prophets and priests, of kings and shepherd boys, of angels and a baby in a manger.

In addition to proclamation, the arts play an important role in the exegesis (interpretation) of Scripture. Many parishioners and pastors alike would be surprised to learn that art, including artworks without a text or any explicit referential images, has a vital role to play in helping us understand and apply the words of Scripture to our lives. An interesting example of this is the so-called *resonance,* a practice in some European churches of allowing the organist to improvise following the sermon. Once the pastor has finished his exposition of the text for the day, the organist exegetes the same text using the medium of music. Through this combination of proclamation and exegesis, people's theology is formed, and the connection between information and formation is strengthened.

"Do this in remembrance of me": Art and the Sacraments

Before approaching the table of the Lord, we leave aside our grievances with one another and unite together as the body of Christ. Carla de Sola has choreographed a simple movement that expresses this unity in a beautiful and natural way. It involves the congregation leaving their seats and walking through the chancel, greeting one another with raised arms and the touching of palms. This occurs while everyone is singing the Taizé refrain *Dona nobis pacem* ("Lord, give us peace"). The singing and movement can go on comfortably for several minutes while a soloist intones a text over the top of this refrain:[39]

---

38. This genre of proclamation is supported by the work of the Network of Biblical Storytellers (see Appendix One for further information).

39. Jacques Berthier, *Music from Taizé, Volume II,* p. 26. Copyright © 1984, Ateliers et Presses de Taizé, GIA Publications, Inc., exclusive North American agent. All rights reserved. Used by permission.

Do - na no - bis pa - cem Do - mi - ne

Art plays an important role in sacramental celebration. The gestures of the presider, the liturgical furnishings of table and basin, the vessels employed to administer the Eucharist, the poetry of the Eucharistic prayer, the music that accompanies the celebration, the visual art and architecture that provide its physical context, the sight and aroma of incense, the movement of the people — all these are significant artistic elements that support and enhance the administration of the rites.

Sacraments are themselves uniquely artistic, because they represent the visible sign of an invisible and spiritual reality. This is very much what art does. Perhaps this is why art has such an affinity for sacramental celebration. Both are rooted in the material world — in oil and water, in grain and the fruit of the earth, in gesture and movement, in sound and sight, in taste and touch — yet both point to another world beyond our earthly existence. While art is not itself a sacrament, it operates in a sacramental fashion throughout the liturgy and in the context of human life itself.

> All our meals and all our living
> Make us sacraments of thee,
> That by sharing, helping, giving,
> We may true disciples be. Alleluia.
> Percy Dearmer, "Draw Us in the Spirit's Tether"

"To whom be glory forever and ever": The Language of Prayer and Praise

The arts provide a deeply meaningful avenue of approach to the divine. We ground our worship in praise and thanksgiving. The very act of giving praise suggests a personal involvement with God that is facilitated by the arts. It is hard to give authentic praise to God while just going through the motions. The arts help stimulate and enliven us at times when we don't have the emotional or physical resources to invest in worship. They literally pick us up, in the process reorienting our energy and attention from ourselves to God. The arts also help us bare our souls, bringing God's grace to bear on the trials and struggles of our lives. They give us a vehicle to express our sorrows and our frustrations, to lay our pain and loneliness before the throne of mercy. They help us to pray and teach us to lament.

This includes the struggle to praise God when we don't feel like offering praise. Alejandro Garcia-Rivera notes that "lament protests the loss of joy and delight of life that makes possible praise and thanksgiving."[40] While art can enliven us and provide an affective dimension to our praise, it can also sustain us in times that are dry and seemingly fruitless.

Sometimes it is possible to hold on to beauty when other values have passed us by. I suspect that, for many, beauty nourishes their existence in the interim times when it is difficult to name the source of their being. This is a way of saying that there is a relationship between beauty and hope. When we have lost the way on our journey to our true home in the kingdom of God, beauty is there. It can point us in the right direction, reminding us once again where we came from and where we are going. There is a sense in which beauty is founded on hope, and hope finds its true end in beauty.

The way from hope to beauty and back again is the way of prayer. Jeri Gerding says, "Art and prayer both involve trusting a process. What they share in common is that we don't know what's going to happen until we begin. We cannot control the outcome."[41]

The process of traveling the path of prayer begins with *anamnesis* — ("do this in remembrance of me"). The contemporary church tends to live its liturgical life in the present. The past has been devalued as the old forms, structures, and symbols of the faith have gone by the wayside. Anamnesis protests this trend. It represents something more than simply recalling the events of salvation history. It is a way to make those events come to life, connecting us with our forebears in the community of the saints.

One example of this occurred at Crossroads Reformed Church in Overland Park, Kansas, on All Saints' Day one November. On this day, family and friends of all the church members who had died the preceding year

---

40. Alejandro Garcia-Rivera, *Living Beauty: The Art of Liturgy* (Lanham, Md.: Rowman & Littlefield, 2008), p. 157.

41. Jeri Gerding, *Drawing to God: Art as Prayer: Prayer as Art* (Notre Dame, Ind.: Sorin Books, 2001), p. 19.

were invited to come to worship. Wooden candlesticks were constructed on bases of varying heights so that there was one candlestick for each deceased member. The sanctuary was arranged in a flexible manner with chairs; this allowed the large candlesticks to be located throughout the congregation.

During the prayers of the people, the choir surrounded the congregation and, to the accompaniment of handbells weaving a light tapestry of sound in the background, individual choir members sang over and over again the opening phrase "For all the saints" from Ralph Vaughan Williams's famous hymn of the same title. They sang simultaneously, at random times and tempi. While this was occurring, the names of all the deceased were read from the book of the dead, one at a time. As each name was read, a family member or friend came forward, lit a candle from the Christ candle, and returned to light one of the candles around the sanctuary. After the final name was read, the hymn "For All the Saints" was sung in its entirety to conclude the service. The environment and music combined to evoke the image of a cloud of witnesses that was felt by all as a powerful ritual moment.

Liturgical anamnesis like this leads inexorably to eschatology. We remember who God is and what God has promised. In so doing, we remember into the future. Once again, the arts have something to offer. They give us a foretaste of bliss, a hint of what it must be like to experience sheer delight. C. S. Lewis describes this in *The Last Battle*, when the children and Tirian (the last king of Narnia) have arrived in Aslan's country and are sampling the beautiful fruit of its trees:

> What was the fruit like? Unfortunately, no one can describe a taste. All I can say is that, compared with those fruits, the freshest grapefruit you've ever eaten was dull, and the juiciest orange was dry, and the most melting pear was hard and woody, and the sweetest wild strawberry was sour. And there were no seeds or stones, and no wasps. If you had once eaten that fruit, all the nicest things in this world would taste like medicines after it. But I can't describe it. You can't find out what it is like unless you can get to that country and taste for yourself.[42]

If we remain faithful throughout the process of remembering and hoping, of anamnesis and eschatology, eventually we will be led by the Spirit to a place where the Author of beauty calls us by name, where our

---

42. C. S. Lewis, *The Last Battle* (New York: Collier Books, 1956), p. 137.

dreams are realized by the One who loves us and provides for us a place where beauty will fill us to overflowing, where we will, indeed, taste for ourselves of this fruit.

"Grow in the grace and knowledge of our Lord": *The Path of Discipleship*

The second-century church father Irenaeus once said, "The glory of God is man fully alive."[43] It is in worship more than anywhere else that we are enlivened, that we take up our walking sticks and begin treading the path to glory. This journey takes time. Albert Rouet reminds us that "liturgy requires craftsmanship . . . the work of the liturgy is to make people into the people of God."[44] This is a long process. It requires laying our lives open to God over and over again to break down our inherent resistance to change and growth. This is one reason why it is so important to be in church each week.

Fortunately, we have resources that help us along the way. One good example is icons. To encounter an icon is to find a road sign on the path of discipleship. Icons are markers that show us the way, not by depicting the image of a believer, but by venerating the faith of the saints. The saints, as we know, "are models of those who see goodness, truth, and beauty clearly."[45] By making the interior life of the saint visible, the iconographer gives us a model of discipleship, a guide on our journey of faith. Here private devotional life and public worship become indistinguishable. One runs into the other in a holy play of paint on wood.

The liturgical arts are all about transformation. They foster vulnerability and entice people to return to liturgy over and over again by virtue of their beauty. The *shema* is the foundation of Jewish worship. Jesus quotes it in Matthew 22:37 and calls it the first and greatest commandment: "Love the Lord your God with all your heart, and with all your soul, and with all your mind." The path of discipleship and human formation in liturgy is a path toward this holistic life. It involves the whole person: heart, soul, and mind. The arts involve us on each of these levels. They help us to think and to feel, to love and to discern, to rejoice and to reflect.

43. Irenaeus, "Adversus Haereses," 4.20.7, quoted in Garcia-Rivera, *Living Beauty*, p. 73.
44. Rouet, *Liturgy and the Arts*, p. 5.
45. John Dykstra and John H. Westerhoff III, *Sensing Beauty: Aesthetics, the Human Spirit, and the Church* (Cleveland: United Church Press, 1998), p. 62.

"Serve one another in love": Service and Mission

A wedding service is a time when the couple is blessed by God and sent on their way by the Christian community toward a life of mission and service. One particular wedding illustrated the manner in which liturgy and art could function together in this process. Following the ring ceremony, in the midst of the service, the bride and groom recessed to the middle of the sanctuary, accompanied by two soloists singing the first two verses of "Lord of All Hopefulness."[46] This hymn features a text that speaks of the progression of the Christian life from the morning of life to its evening. It is sung to the same tune as "Be Thou My Vision." As the couple recessed, the entire congregation was invited to stand, leave their seats, and surround them in the center of the nave.

The ritual that followed is one of the oldest in Christendom, but one that for some reason is rarely performed at weddings: the laying on of hands as a means of commissioning the couple for the journey ahead. The congregation all connected physically by touching the couple or the people in front of them. After several pastoral prayers, the congregation was invited to offer spontaneous prayers. These prayers lasted for almost five minutes, after which there was a final collect and a processional back to the front, with everyone singing the final two verses of "Lord of All Hopefulness." I can personally testify to the power of this moment from the inside of that circle — a circle of life if ever there was one.

Art prepares us to serve by sending us into the world with the knowledge of what is real. It forms us as creative people in the liturgy and equips us to employ our creative gifts in the service of the God who made them and nurtures them throughout our lives.

Conclusion

Albert Rouet says, "The real question is not if this liturgy pleases you, not even if you find it beautiful. The real question is whether the liturgical rites move people forward to walk with God and to move toward God."[47]

One person will not like every species of rose as much as their neigh-

46. The text of "Lord of All Hopefulness" is by Ian Struther (Oxford: Oxford University Press, 1931); the music is Irish Traditional.
47. Rouet, *Liturgy and the Arts*, p. 19.

bor will. For most of us, though, walking through a rose garden is an experience that has the potential to captivate and enchant. Liturgy is like that. Not everyone will resonate with precisely the same liturgical form or style, just as not everyone will appreciate a work of art in the same way. Nonetheless, in the liturgy, as in the rose garden, our best efforts are required, and the possibility of transformation is present at every turn. Art is integral to this process of human and liturgical transformation. It is one of the greatest gifts we have been given.

CHAPTER EIGHT

Toward a Theology of Arts Ministry

What do we love, if it be not beauty?

Augustine

The world in which we live needs beauty in order not to sink into despair. It is beauty, like truth, which brings joy to the heart of [people] and is that precious fruit which resists the wear and tear of time, which unites generations and makes them share things in admiration. . . . Remember that you are the guardians of beauty in the world. May that suffice to free you from tastes which are passing and have no genuine value. . . .

Pope Paul VI, Closing Message of the
Second Vatican Council to the Artists

How Do the Arts, Beauty, and Creativity Impact Human Life?

Within the span of two days during one recent Lenten season, I experienced two contrasting liturgical references to the Holocaust. The first occurred in a morning prayer service celebrated at a conference held by the American Guild of Organists. The psalm in this service was a solo organ work, a setting by Paul J. Sifler entitled *The Despair and Agony of Dachau as Envisioned by Psalm XXII.*[1] The music could only be described as jar-

1. Paul J. Sifler, *The Despair and Agony of Dachau as Envisioned by Psalm XXII* (Hollywood, Calif.: Fredonia Press, 1975).

ring. Waves of intense dissonance were coupled with unsettling rhythmic figures. The overall effect was one of utter despair. If I had not known the title of the piece, I might have guessed that it was about the Holocaust simply by listening to it. In the end the piece left the group hanging, as if a question was still in the air.

Two days later, in the context of a parish liturgy, I experienced an anthem that was also based on the Holocaust. The primary message this anthem tried to convey was hope and confidence in God despite the horrors of the camps. It was a sweet piece in a major key with virtually no hints of angst or pathos.

The contrast between these two experiences was stark and startling. I feel sure that the two pieces conveyed quite different messages to their respective hearers, messages that were not dependent on text or titles but that came through loud and clear in the music itself. To be fair, the two groups were very different, and there is no doubt that it would have been impossible to present both musical pieces in either setting. Nonetheless, the fact remains that these works had a profoundly different impact on the lives of the people in attendance.

A defining question for the arts minister is this: How do the arts, beauty, and creativity impact human life from a Christian perspective? As the foregoing anecdote illustrates, this question is not merely theoretical. Artistic choices matter; they have a practical effect on the lives of people in the church and in the surrounding culture. Following on the heels of this question is a related issue: How can arts ministry support and foster an appropriate role for the arts, beauty, and creativity? Finally, how can arts ministers make choices that reflect the values of goodness, truth, and beauty and help people move in the direction of ever-greater maturity?

Let's not be naïve. These topics are the most difficult issues in arts ministry. They are difficult for a variety of different reasons. First, the aesthetic and theological ideas surrounding these issues are unfamiliar to many artists and laypeople and almost as many pastors. Second, the implications of these ideas are potentially threatening and divisive. Beauty turns out to be not so beautiful depending upon how it is defined. Nonetheless, it is material that cannot be avoided, either in this book or in arts ministries throughout the church. The treatment of these topics here will seem shallow to some and rigid to others. As in the church as a whole, the audience to whom the questions are addressed determines, in part, the character of the answers.

The next two chapters consider these fundamental issues. In this chapter we will focus on three issues: (1) art as meaningful communication, (2) the perennially important and controversial question of beauty, and (3) the task of making artistic judgments in the church. These three issues are foundational and must be taken into account by every arts minister. As we think together about these questions, perhaps we will begin to see the hints of what a theology of arts ministry might look like. Hinting at this topic is a very artistic approach to take. It is open-ended and offers promise for future development. It plants seeds in the hope that some will grow into mature plants, perhaps even roses.

Art as Meaningful Communication

The arts can be a form of meaningful communication. This statement is not obvious to everyone, nor is it lacking in controversy.[2] Most parishioners, if asked, would probably indicate that the purposes of the arts are to move them emotionally and to make their worship experience more vivid. If they took the time to think deeply about the subject, they might see the potential for the arts to proclaim the Word or to enliven the celebration of the sacraments. Without at least a modicum of education in theological aesthetics, it might not occur to them that the arts actually speak a theological language of their own or have the potential to be sacramental.

Laypeople typically consider nonverbal art forms meaningful only through their association with words. This is why people talk while the prelude and postlude are played at church each Sunday. They do not understand that meaningful communication might be occurring. They would never consider talking when the pastor is speaking, but when the organist is playing, it is somehow acceptable.

For many laity, the principal purposes of the arts in their lives are to help them escape from the everyday grind of reality, to move them on an emotional level, to give them a pleasurable way to pass the time, or to provide an ornamental dimension to what would otherwise be for them a more drab and colorless world. These are all, within limits, perfectly acceptable and important reasons to have art in our lives. They are not, how-

---

2. Harold Best says, "Art and music are morally relative and inherently incapable of articulating . . . truth speech. They are essentially neutral in their ability to express belief, creed, moral, and ethical exactitude or even worldview." See Harold M. Best, *Music through the Eyes of Faith* (San Francisco: HarperCollins, 1993), p. 42.

First Presbyterian Church Theater
Fort Wayne, Indiana

A scene from *Tuesdays with Morrie,* based on Mitch Albom's best-selling book, produced by the First Presbyterian Church Theater during the 2010-2011 season

"Drama is one means to reassert the terrible importance of each human soul. Art and religion, twin manifestations of the creative human spirit, must seek to arouse and repair our ability to dream dreams splendid enough to create a world more consistent with our divine image. . . . What kind of theater can serve such purposes? Theater that does not flinch from looking straight at life."*

> Statement of Purpose
> First Presbyterian Church Theater

First Presbyterian Church in Fort Wayne, Indiana, has long sponsored theater as a significant component of its ministry. In 1968 they opened a theater fa-

*This and subsequent quotations are taken from the Web site of the First Presbyterian Church Theater: http://www.firstpres-fw.org/the_arts/theater.

cility underneath their new building. Following a later renovation, this theater now seats 290 and boasts an annual series of seven shows, including musicals, comedies, and dramas, each of which has a run of eight performances. An average year sees a total attendance of anywhere between 7,000 and 8,500 audience members. The lobby of the theater is an art gallery that features six or seven exhibitions each year. There are two full-time theater employees on the payroll of the church. Roughly 10 to 20 percent of the participants in the productions are church members, while a large percentage of the ushers and other support personnel are church members. Church office staff handle phone reservations and ticketing, the maintenance staff of the church clean the facility, and the church business office handles the finances of the theater.

A twelve-member drama committee selects the shows to be presented each year. Criteria include the following: "Shows deal with one of two issues: how human beings treat one another, or how an individual wrestles with universal questions in the never-ending quest to glimpse the face of God. FPT's choice of material is driven by the quality of the writing. Only great plays can explore complex issues." Playwrights whose work has been produced at First Presbyterian Theater include Shakespeare, Molière, Henrik Ibsen, Mark Twain, Edward Albee, Thornton Wilder, David Mamet, Christopher Durang, Gilbert & Sullivan, Andrew Lloyd Webber, Lillian Hellman, Neil Simon, A. R. Gurney, Robert Anderson, and Arthur Miller.

At the heart of this extensive theater program is a vision for the role of theater in the life of the church and the wider community. The statement of purpose, adopted first in 1973, sums up this vision with inspiring and challenging words:

> It is part of the business of the church theater to face its own members and society with those things we would rather not face, in order that, once recognized, they leave us free to act and to work for richer relationships, for an interaction of people based on the willingness to deal honestly with what really lies beneath our habits and customs. . . . The church is only ready for religion, only ready for drama, when it can open itself to the implications of dramatic revelation; when the congregation can accept the world of the imagination and can risk being excited, risk being frightened, risk being changed. Such risk is near the very heart of the Christian message.

229

ever, the only options. As Jeremy Begbie comments, "The belief that the arts are always aimed at creating illusion, or that they can express nothing more than emotional states, or that they can never be more than ornamental — all these are regrettable misunderstandings which can only impoverish the Church's life and mission."[3]

Meaningful communication is missing from the lay vocabulary of the arts. Mortimer Adler, one of our greatest American philosophers, says, "Mind is the realm in which meanings exist and through which everything else that has meaning acquires meaning."[4] In other words, meaning is not intrinsic. It does not adhere within an object, whether it be liturgy, dance, drama, poetry, music, or anything else. Meaning occurs as the result of a mental process through which human beings engage their environment and imaginatively construct connections between different parts of their experience. The artistic connections that are formed in the minds of believers don't occur in a vacuum. The cultural context, the history and traditions of the local congregation, and the background the believer has in the arts are all factors that influence the possibility of forming meaningful associations.

Nonetheless, there must be some quality within an artwork that gives it the capacity to become the object of attention and to form associations within the mind of someone who comes into contact with it. Art that is bland and devoid of any variety or intensity is not likely to form or retain strong connections with most people over time. However, even art that is striking, that arrests the attention, is not enough. Those who form these associations must have the aptitude and the requisite desire to pursue this goal in the first place. As congregations encounter works of sacred art, they need to develop aesthetic and affective skills. They also need to be open to new experiences. Parishes need leaders who can help them in this task, including pastors and arts ministers who will foster an environment of receptivity, inquiry, and curiosity.

It is important that we not underestimate the significance of the question of meaning and its role in the life of faith. The notion that the arts can mean something to people has been under attack for a long time. Think for just a moment about the consequences of this question: What if the arts do

---

3. Jeremy S. Begbie, *Voicing Creation's Praise: Towards a Theology of the Arts* (Edinburgh: T&T Clark, 1991), p. 258.

4. Mortimer Adler, *Art, the Arts, and the Great Ideas* (New York: Macmillan, 1994), p. 46.

not communicate meaningfully to people in the pews? What then? If art no longer functions as a medium of meaningful communication, it is reduced to the level of entertainment, a passing diversion that can and will be employed for any purpose we choose. This is precisely what has happened in much of the church.[5] If the arts do not form meaningful connections in the minds and hearts of parishioners, then there can be no question about what art is appropriate for worship or ministry; anything that meets the immediately perceived needs of the people will do. If, on the other hand, the arts do serve as a vehicle for the formation of meaningful associations, then the entire dynamic of the discussion is different; then the church has to ask questions about what meaning is being communicated and how it is being communicated.

Clearly, a lot is at stake. The Roman Catholic document *Music in Catholic Worship* discusses the question of meaning in relation to music:

> In addition to expressing texts, music can also unveil a dimension of meaning and feeling, a communication of ideas and intuition which words alone cannot yield. This dimension is integral to the human personality and to growth in faith. It cannot be ignored if the signs of worship are to speak to the whole person.[6]

Music (and, I would add, by extension, the other arts as well) has the capacity to facilitate the creation of meaning. In the words of Fred Pratt Green's wonderful hymn "When in Our Music God Is Glorified," there is a

---

5. Certainly entertainment and the decorative arts have an important role to play in the life of Christian people. Theodore Prescott makes a valuable contribution to this topic when he notes that communication is only one role for the arts and a role that may lead to the creation of much bad art in the service of Christian truth. I would add that art's potential ability to communicate meaning is precisely the point at which it has been at odds with modern culture. Few have questioned art's ability to provide a decorative quality to human life or to help refresh us when it functions as entertainment. The problem comes when we claim that art has a didactic function, that it fosters meaning and teaches us something about God and ourselves. I believe that this function of art must be redeemed and put into service once again so that it can bear fruit. See *It Was Good Making Art to the Glory of God,* ed. Ned Bustard (Baltimore: Square Halo Books, 2000), p. 144.

6. *Music in Catholic Worship,* quoted in Jan Michael Joncas, *From Sacred Song to Ritual Music: Twentieth-Century Understanding of Roman Catholic Worship Music* (Collegeville, Minn.: Liturgical Press, 1997), p. 42. It should be noted that this document has now been superseded by *Sing to the Lord: Music in Divine Worship* (United States Conference of Catholic Bishops, 2007).

"new dimension in the world of sound."[7] I want to suggest that this "new dimension" is the dimension of meaning, the formation of new connections in the mind and experience of the perceiver. The messages we receive through these connections are, indeed, integral to human formation and to our capacity to live as whole people.

Language

The Christian church developed in a Greco-Roman cultural milieu. Palestine itself was under the influence of Hellenism. As the church moved westward into Asia Minor and beyond, it encountered an increasingly Greek approach to thought and discourse. From that time forward, Christianity built its theological and ecclesiastical edifice on a Greco-Roman foundation that privileges discursive language and reason. The *logos* became central not only to a Christian understanding of the role and person of Jesus Christ, but also to the manner in which theological criticism and debate would occur. This was very different from the Semitic culture indigenous to the Near East. Semitic people were concerned with images, metaphor, and poetic speech to a much greater degree than their Greek counterparts. The one exception to this is the development of the icon in Hellenistic culture. Here the Greeks showed a remarkable ability to incorporate images in a significant way into their theological understanding and ecclesiastical practice.

The prevailing Western preference for discursive language over images seems to say that God functions in an abstract world of reason, not in the nitty-gritty of our lives in this world. It suggests that the mind is superior to the body, that reason is superior to intuition, and that the invisible is superior to the visible. As William Dyrness reminds us, this is not a biblical approach.[8] It is dualistic thinking that originates in Plato and was imported into Christian theology. It is not true to the doctrines of creation or the Incarnation, both of which speak of the fundamental goodness and reality of the stuff of this world.

Artistic language, on the other hand, depends on image and metaphor

---

7. Fred Pratt Green, "When in Our Music God Is Glorified" (Carol Stream, Ill.: Hope Publishing Company, 1972).

8. William Dyrness, *Visual Faith: Art, Theology, and Worship in Dialogue* (Grand Rapids: Baker Academic, 2001), p. 145.

as its mode of discourse. It relies on the intuitive capacity of the human person. The point of artistic language is to help make the invisible visible, "the disclosure of ultimate reality in and through finite form."[9] It is interesting to compare the different approaches taken by artistic and discursive language. How do these two alternatives function theologically?

Theologians often warn artists that nonverbal art forms cannot make definitive or detailed truth claims. While on one level this is correct, it is nonetheless important to acknowledge that, from a theological standpoint, discursive language cannot do this, either. The difference between the two is relative. It would be good for theologians to keep in mind that when speaking about God, all language — whether verbal or nonverbal — is, by definition, metaphorical. Thus, using artistic images to express theological ideas is simply substituting one kind of metaphor for another. In fact, it is not difficult to argue that if the theologian's principal task is to say something truthful about God, then the metaphorical language of the arts provides the most powerful and *accurate* approach to the task. In any case, it is a necessary component in any comprehensive theological program. Frank Burch Brown reminds us that, "if theology seeks to understand and reflect critically on faith, and if much that is vital to faith is poetic and imaginative, then a theology incapable of appreciating and interpreting what is poetic and imaginative about faith will have no way of finishing its job."[10]

Rather than simply focusing on their differences, we should from the outset examine the characteristics that discursive and artistic theological languages have in common. Wilson Yates notes, "Art can serve as a model of theological creation through the insights it offers regarding the process and structure of creation and through the artistic elements it provides theologians to construct theology. . . . We can see the structure of art as insightful for understanding the structure of a work of theology, we can see how certain elements of art are a necessary part of theology, and we can see theology as necessarily artful."[11]

The question has often been asked — Is art a language at all? The arguments over this issue are serious and complex.[12] Answers do not come eas-

---

9. Begbie, speaking of Tillich's ideas in *Voicing Creation's Praise*, p. 256.

10. Frank Burch Brown, "How Important Are the Arts, Theologically?" in *Arts, Theology, and the Church*, ed. Kimberly Vrudny and Wilson Yates (Cleveland: Pilgrim Press, 2005), p. 43.

11. Wilson Yates, *The Arts in Theological Education* (Atlanta: Scholars Press, 1987), p. 121.

12. Many writers have addressed this question. Some comparisons that seem important

ily. Without in any way trying to minimize the difficulties involved, I would suggest the following reasons for giving at least a provisional "yes" in response to this question. First, art has certain recognizable elemental properties: line, rhythm, color, texture, character, plot, rhythm, and so on. Second, there is a standard syntax that governs the relationship between these elemental properties. While the "rules" of art change from time to time, it remains true that each new style has its own set of conventions that govern how works in that style are produced and how they arrange these various structural building blocks. Third, at least within a given culture, there is a storehouse of common, shared meanings that unite the artist and the consumer of art and enable meaningful communication to occur. These shared meanings relate in part to artistic conventions and in part to metaphorical relationships, some of which are stock and well-worn and some of which are fresh and engage the imagination of the viewer, reader, or listener in new ways.

Because of the presence of these three factors, I believe it is possible to argue with some confidence that artistic language exists. Notice that, just as in the case of discursive language, the presence of artistic language does not imply understanding. If a phrase is spoken to me in Chinese, I will not understand the meaning of the phrase because I do not speak Chinese. However, no one will deny that language is present, even though I am not

---

to me are as follows. In the first chapter of his book *Music and Mind* (Lewiston, N.Y.: Edwin Mellen Press, 1990), Harold E. Fiske points out the following similarities between music and language that I am, in turn, going to posit of all the arts:

(1) The arts and language both have their origin outside the real world — they originate in the brain of the sender and are reconstituted in the brain of the receiver.

(2) Both the arts and language involve the ability to recognize certain patterns. This skill requires a number of cues, strategies, and some invariable features common to the artist, the speaker or performer, and the hearer.

In the same vein, John Sloboda, in *The Musical Mind: The Cognitive Psychology of Music* (Oxford: Clarendon Press, 1985), adds these similarities:

(3) Language and music [the arts] are both universal in the sense that all human beings, except those with certain disabilities, have the capacity to attain linguistic and musical [artistic] competence.

(4) Both the arts and language can create a virtually unlimited number of sequences.

(5) Language and the arts both seem to be learned rapidly by children.

(6) In both cases it is easier at first to receive artistic communication than to produce it.

(7) Both art and language have a mixture of some universal and some cultural traits.

Finally, both the linguist Noam Chomsky and the music theorist Heinrich Schenker point to a common characteristic of music (the arts) and language: they both have surface features and deep structure.

able to understand it. This is often the case with artistic language, where a "storehouse of common, shared meanings" is held in common with some but not with others. When this happens, language is present, but meaningful communication is not.

What Meaning Is Disclosed?

If, in fact, art can disclose meaning, then the next question to ask is this: *What meaning is disclosed?* "Art for art's sake," the dictum of much modern art, would seem to suggest that artistic meaning is self-contained. At the very least this approach limits the sense in which art grows out of and is connected back to the world in which we live. John Dewey, the American pragmatist philosopher and educator, struggled with the relationship between the arts and ordinary human life. He was very much concerned with the manner in which art is walled off from the rest of life. Accordingly, he wrote, "A primary task is thus imposed upon one who undertakes to write upon the philosophy of the fine arts. This task is to restore continuity between the refined and intensified forms of experience that are works of art and the everyday events, doings, and sufferings that are universally recognized to constitute experience."[13]

Dewey could well have been writing about arts ministry. If art is, indeed, disconnected from life, if it has nothing to say that is relevant to human relationships, individual morality and social justice, social and political systems, or theological and philosophical truth, then why bother with it? If its sole value is entertainment, then why expend all the time and energy needed to perfect it? If it is intended only to provide a diversion for bored people, then why go to the trouble and expense of constructing an arts ministry in the first place?

Clearly, churches in which entertainment *is* the primary rationale for their arts ministry need to do some serious self-examination. Hopefully, such churches are in the minority. Meaningful communication still seems to be an important part of many arts ministries.

What meaning is disclosed by art? In the end, it is the nature and character of reality, including the person and work of the Triune God, the reality of the human situation with all its joys and sorrows, disappointments and ecstasies, coupled with an existential awareness of the wonders of the

13. John Dewey, *Art as Experience* (New York: Perigee Books, 1980), p. 3.

cosmos. Art discloses what grace enables, what God first imprints in the mind of the artist through talent, experience, intellect, training, and intuition. Most important of all, art discloses an *idea:* the reality of the natural, human, and divine world as perceived by the artist. As Richard Harries says in his fine study *Art and the Beauty of God,* "Above all it [art] is the expression of a quest for truth, of an honest attempt to see and state things as they are, in poetry, drama, art, or music. In art as in the universe, it is in the end truth that speaks to us and truth which brings us up short."[14]

How Does Art Disclose Meaning?

If this is the intended content of artistic disclosure, if this represents *what* art discloses, then we must turn to the question of *how* the artist achieves this end. How does art disclose meaning?

Deductive versus Inductive Methods

Wilson Yates suggests two possible answers to this question: the inductive method and the deductive method. We begin by looking at the deductive approach, which Yates explains this way:

> In the deductive approach, the arts are seen as a cultural source that should yield insights that are useful in the explication of certain Christian doctrines. The beginning point is with doctrine, not with the work of art, and the attraction of the work depends on whether it enhances or deepens the doctrinal claims. . . . The focus rests on how a work of art helps us elaborate, or illustrate, or better understand a given doctrinal perspective.[15]

An example of this would be the famous "Passion" or "Good Samaritan" typological windows at Chartres Cathedral that illustrate the intrinsic relationship between Old Testament and New Testament narratives in order to portray the idea that God's plan of salvation is consistent and trustworthy. Likewise, Bach's *Fugue in E-flat Major,* BWV 552 for organ, is a good

---

14. Richard Harries, *Art and the Beauty of God: A Christian Understanding* (London: Continuum, 1993), p. 149.

15. Yates, *The Arts in Theological Education,* p. 140.

example of the deductive approach. Through its use of three flats and three fugal sections, it is a formal, artistic depiction of the doctrine of the Trinity.

Yates goes on to speak of the second option, the inductive approach:

> Here the theologian begins with the work of art and experiences it in light of its own claims and insights quite apart from whether those insights fit a particular doctrinal assumption. . . . In this process there is an openness to the revelatory power of the arts and an insistence that the theologian treat a work of art as a potential source in helping create and shape doctrine.[16]

Prophetic art is, by definition, an example of the inductive approach. Here is an example, drawn from Thomas Merton's poem "The Original Child Bomb":

> There was discussion about which city should be selected as the first target. . . . It was decided Hiroshima was the most opportune target, as it had not yet been bombed at all. Lucky Hiroshima! What others had experienced over a period of four years would happen to Hiroshima in a single day! Much time would be saved, and "time is money!"
>
> When they bombed Hiroshima they would put the following out of business: The Ube Nitrogen Fertilizer Company; the Ube Soda Company; the Nippon Motor Oil Company; the Sumitoma Chemical Company; the Sumitoma Aluminum Company; and most of the inhabitants.[17]

Merton's poem has an ironic tone that hints at a distinctive approach to the issues raised by Hiroshima. It is not intended strictly to illustrate any Christian doctrine, but meant to help us rethink the connections between our faith and our political choices. Laity and artists in the church would often be surprised by the idea that art can shape doctrine. The notion that artists create works that actually alter our understanding of God, humanity, or the cosmos — rather than simply illustrating the theological or doctrinal thinking of the church — is, for many, a new idea.

Catherine Kapikian relates a story about her work as an artist at Wesley Theological Seminary in Washington, D.C., that illustrates this point:

16. Yates, *The Arts in Theological Education*, p. 140.

17. Thomas Merton, "The Original Child Bomb," in *The Collected Poems of Thomas Merton* (New York: New Directions, 1977), p. 295.

Integrating art and theology occupies much of my adult life. Sometimes it is awkward. In a late afternoon appointment with my former academic dean, the sun filtered through the half-open blinds, slanting rigid parallel lines across his elongated tabletop. He sat at one end, I at the other. Surrounding us on three sides were walls embedded with shelves of floor-to-ceiling books, in their own way rigid and unyielding, their spines echoing the reflected parallel lines of light. The tension mounted. In a moment of exasperation, I yelped, "I am an artist first." Leaning into the table as his hand hit it, he retorted, "But you are a theologian too." Caught off-guard, I peered at him in disbelief. "Really?" I said. "Yes, really."[18]

Artists need to remember that they function as theologians, not simply as illustrators. Art speaks about the divine just as much as theology does and therefore is capable of shaping theology.

Formal, Referential, and Experiential Meaning

One classical approach to the question of "how" art speaks meaningfully involves the formal, referential, and experiential dimensions of artistic communication. The three categories are not mutually exclusive. Individual artworks can cross the line and simultaneously represent two or more of the categories.

On a *formal* level, art speaks through the syntax of the artwork, developing analogies between, for instance, the color red in a painting and the passion of Christ, or musical dissonance and human sin. The recipient of this artwork needs training if formal communication is to be meaningful. Unless the viewer knows about the relationship between red and Christ's passion, this connection may not be immediately apparent.

Referential meaning involves a more direct form of communication that does not require a comparable level of training. It involves a one-to-one correspondence between something in the artwork and something in the real world.[19] A painting of the New Church at Delft by Hendrick van Vliet and the sound of a bird call in the music of Messiaen are good examples.

18. Catherine Kapikian, *Art in Service of the Sacred* (Nashville: Abingdon Press, 2006), p. 135.

19. *Mimesis* is the word that Plato and Aristotle use for imitation. This involves a depiction of the universal (perfect) qualities of an object in the real world, as opposed to copying, which is an attempt to replicate the image of the object. Referential meaning could occur as the result of either mimesis or copying.

The last category, *experiential* meaning, occurs when an artwork is embedded in the soil of everyday actions and experiences. Work songs and folk dances are examples of experiential meaning in artworks that lend significance and dignity to the patterns and rituals of daily life.

Art's Symbolic Character

All artworks share in one fundamental characteristic of artistic language: its symbolic character. Symbols from sacred art remind us of our history. They provide countervailing images that combat the prevailing secularism that is all around us. When we hang them in our homes or on our church walls, they become an abiding presence in our lives, forming us over time into their image. The power of symbols in our lives has the potential to enliven and deepen our spiritual sensitivity and our human sensibilities.

As Janet Walton says, "Sounds, shapes, words, texture, movement arranged into artistic forms invite participants into a world of knowing where literal interpretation is replaced by the logic of symbols and where immediate recognition is replaced by an exploration of layers of meaning."[20] Jeremy Begbie gives an example of artistic symbolism involving music. He points to the fact that music involves the presentation of waves of tension and resolution caused by elements such as rhythm, meter, harmony, and timbre all working on different levels simultaneously. Begbie views this as an analogy for the biblical doctrine of eschatology. Often our view of eschatology is dominated by a uniform model leading to a single, unambiguous event at the end of human history. Begbie believes that musical language suggests a more subtle and variegated explanation of eschatology than that which is available through words alone.

For Begbie, eschatology involves patterns of promise and fulfillment that are working on multiple levels simultaneously throughout salvation history. Human hopes interweave with promised responses from God over the course of time. Musical development likewise creates evolving patterns of tension and resolution that symbolize repeated fulfillment throughout salvation history on the part of God, a sign of the inexhaustible self-communication of divine mercy and love.[21]

---

20. Janet Walton, *Art and Worship: A Vital Connection* (Wilmington, Del.: Michael Glazier, 1988), p. 78.

21. See Jeremy S. Begbie, *Theology, Music, and Time* (Cambridge: Cambridge University Press, 2000), Chapter Four.

This is an excellent example of the *analogic* function of art, the manner in which art acts as a metaphor or analogy for human experience.

To Whom Do the Arts Disclose Meaning?

The next question involves identifying the object of artistic communication. To *whom* do the arts disclose meaning? One of the principal medieval responses to this question is the claim that art is "the bible of the illiterate." John of Damascus says,

> There are some people who find fault with us because we bow down before and worship images. . . . Certain events that actually took place and that were seen by human beings have been written down for the remembrance and instruction of those of us who were not alive at that time, in order that, though we did not see them, we may still obtain the benefit of them . . . by hearing and believing them. But since not everyone is literate, nor does everyone have time for reading, our ancestors gave their permission to portray these same events in the form of images, as acts of heroic excellence.[22]

One interesting feature of John's argument is the assumption that the "illiterate" can "read" the theological language present in imagery. It is clear that this varies greatly with the imagery in question. Today, it often requires as much or more education to read the theological language present in images than is required to read discursive language. Much has changed since the seventh and eighth centuries, when John was writing. Gutenberg invented the printing press, making literature affordable. In the developed world, free education taught the public to read. Several centuries later, television came along, devaluing the written word and the forms of discourse that it enabled. In the twenty-first century, the image is once again replacing the word as the dominant mode of communication.[23] This means that image-based communication — artistic communication — is rapidly becoming the province of the culture at large. In an earlier culture

---

22. John of Damascus, *The Orthodox Faith,* quoted in Jaroslav Pelikan, *Imago Dei: The Byzantine Apologia for Icons* (Princeton: Princeton University Press, 1990), p. 1.

23. See Mitchell Stephens, *The Rise of the Image, the Fall of the Word* (Oxford: Oxford University Press, 1998).

that valued the word, images were the bible of the illiterate. In a contemporary culture that values images, they become everyone's bible.

Obstacles to Comprehension of Meaning

Charles Rosen suggests several problems that inhibit artistic comprehension:

(1) Frustration at the absence of the familiar or at the presence of a style we do not understand often leads to powerful emotions that can inhibit our ability to think rationally.
(2) The reverse of this is also true — too much familiarity can lead to a comfort level that overlooks problems because they have always been there. There needs to be some challenge. As Rosen says, too much familiarity allows us to settle comfortably into error. The name he gives to widely accepted error is *tradition*!
(3) People have different abilities to discern artistic patterns and relationships. It is not possible to assume that all the faithful have the same shared pool of artistic associations or backgrounds. This is particularly true in a mobile culture in which many parishioners move repeatedly and migrate from one denomination to another.[24]

Quentin Faulkner adds that the constant presence of art in our lives is an impediment to meaningful communication. Ubiquitous images and musical stimuli that confront us through the media, in shopping malls, and in so many of the everyday realities of our lives in Western culture teach us *not* to pay attention to any one work of art. Faulkner notes that we are not only uneducated artistically; we possess a "philistine confidence of ignorance" that exacerbates the problem.[25]

The issue of meaning in relation to art is critically important in the context of arts ministry. In the process of working to overcome these various obstacles, meaning emerges as we make connections between different parts of our artistic and lived experience and integrate what we have learned into our individual and corporate lives. If it is to flourish in the life

24. Charles Rosen, *The Frontiers of Meaning* (New York: Hill & Wang, 1994), Chapter One.

25. Quentin Faulkner, *Wiser than Despair: The Evolution of Ideas in the Relationship between Music and the Christian Church* (Westport, Conn.: Greenwood Press, 1996), p. 202.

of the church, arts ministry must take seriously the question of meaning in all its many dimensions. Arts ministers must evaluate the products of their efforts in light of their meaningfulness to people whose artistic lives are in their care.

On the Objectivity of Beauty

Meaningful arts ministry involves beauty. Beauty itself has traditionally been the province of the field of aesthetics. As we begin to unpack a few of the many implications of aesthetics for arts ministry, it is helpful to bear in mind the underlying, often unstated relationship between aesthetics and theology. This relationship becomes explicit in different ways in the work of individual authors. Aesthetics, after all, is neither more nor less than the sum total of the implications arising from the underlying philosophy or theology of the aesthetician. If God is seen as an objective reality, then the aesthetics arising from this theology will tend toward objectivity. If, on the other hand, God is seen as somehow contingent or the result of human calculation, then aesthetics will lean in the direction of subjectivity. This fundamental distinction is central to practical decisions about aesthetic standards for art in public worship or in the wider life of the church and the world. Its implications are often unnoticed by those who make these decisions.

The fact that God is considered beautiful means there is the potential for beauty itself to be seen as objective. The classic question is this: Do we think an object is beautiful because we love it, or do we love it because it is beautiful? Many patristic and medieval theologians gave the second response. For them, beauty is *not* in the eye of the beholder. We love things because they are objectively beautiful; they are not beautiful simply because we love them.

One contemporary voice supporting and amplifying this notion is Richard Harries: "I readily admit that what strikes us as beautiful does indeed arouse powerful feelings: feelings of pleasure, delight, wonder, and longing. But . . . such feelings are not in themselves grounds for ascribing beauty to the object which evokes them. Such feelings are the effect which something beautiful has on us. They are the results of beauty, not part of its defining characteristics."[26]

---

26. Harries, *Art and the Beauty of God*, p. 25.

In the Middle Ages, the ability of theologians to view beauty as objective was based on three related principles: (1) the ultimate source of all beauty located in the beauty of an objective God, (2) the doctrine of "the transcendental properties of being," and (3) the confluence of unity, variety, and intensity as aesthetic categories. We have already discussed the idea that God is beautiful (see Chapter Three). We turn now to consider the other aspects of this grand theo-aesthetic equation.

The "Transcendental Properties of Being"

After completing each day of creation, God paused and said, "It is good." As Richard Harries points out, the Septuagint — the Greek version of the Hebrew scriptures used by Jesus and the early church — translates the word "good" as "kalon." It is not accidental that this word also has a relationship to beauty.[27] In other words, the Greeks believed there was a primal relationship between goodness and beauty. William Dyrness notes, "Throughout Scripture, words for beauty and goodness overlap, and their realities are often indistinguishable because they both express God's own goodness and his integrated purposes for creation. When God said of creation, 'It is very good,' was he making an ethical judgment? An aesthetic one? Clearly he intended both."[28]

God's beauty is intimately connected to God's goodness and truth. This famous trio — *the good, the true, and the beautiful* — is known collectively as the doctrine of the "transcendental properties of being."[29] The good, the true, and the beautiful all originate and receive their fullest expression in the transcendent God, who resists every human attempt to be confined to our imperfect moral, intellectual, and aesthetic concepts. They are thus designated as "transcendental properties." By means of God's grace and generosity, these same qualities are present to a degree in everything that exists, every "being" in the cosmos. The doctrine of the transcendental properties of being has roots in the Bible as well as in the Platonic and Neo-Platonic tradition, and was developed by theologians over a

---

27. Harries, *Art and the Beauty of God*, pp. 35-36. See also the discussion in John Navone, *Toward a Theology of Beauty* (Collegeville, Minn.: Liturgical Press, 1996), pp. 35-36.

28. Dyrness, *Visual Faith*, p. 151.

29. For the ancient Greeks, the coincidence of the beautiful and the good had a special name: *Kalokagathia*.

For the Joy of Singing:
The Kaw Valley Shape Note Singing Association
Kaw Valley, Kansas

A KVSNSA "Sing" in progress at the Kansas State Fiddling and Picking Championships in 2010

Sometimes arts ministry is a simple expression of the joy of engaging in an art form with friends, family, and colleagues. It can foster community and serve as a ministry to those who participate. For members of the Kaw Valley Shape Note Singing Association in Northeast Kansas, singing is their passion — in particular, singing tunes from the *Sacred Harp,* the most popular of the more than one hundred oblong tune books published in America during the first half of the nineteenth century.

On the first Sunday of most months since 1992, a group of singers gathers, usually in a local church, to sit in a square and sing the hymns and anthems that are the heart and soul of the shape note singing tradition. Different singers are given the opportunity to select the songs to be sung, give the opening pitch, and get everyone started. After a tune is selected, typically the group sings through the "fa," "sol," "la," and "mi" syllables that are familiar to sacred harp singers everywhere. Then it is time to sing the piece through with text. While the singing is not intended as a performance, it is always good to hear a tune come together easily.

Susan Green, one of the founding members, writes,

> We first met when the Kaw Valley Fiddling and Picking Championships [in Kansas] brought up Charles Whitmer from Texas, I think in 1992, to teach a singing school as part of the Fiddling and Picking weekend. . . . Joe Douglas and Joe Casad were there at Charles's singing school, so I announced that we were trying to get a singing going in Kansas City, and they drove over for one of our singings, and that was the core of the group that turned into Kaw Valley.
>
> We've done singing schools at lots of churches and for some college classes. We've had some all-day singings, where guests came from out of town . . . and then we co-sponsored the Arrow Rock (Missouri) all-day singing for probably five years.

Current member Lara West adds,

> We offer people the opportunity to explore their musical and cultural heritage in a participatory way. In addition, singing with us may still help people to learn to read music, just as the original shape note singing schools did. Our main activity is our monthly sing. In addition, we usually sing during the Kansas State Fiddling and Picking competition weekend in August, and we often sing at one or more Christmas events. The most common places for us to sing Christmas events at are the Shawnee Indian Mission in the Kansas City area and Missouri Town 1855, a living history site in Lee's Summit [Missouri].*

To hear a sample of their singing, visit the group's Web site: www.kaw shapenote.org.

---

*Susan Green/Lara West, e-mail to the author, 16 November 2010.

long period of time, culminating in the work of the scholastics in the thirteenth century.

Gesa Elsbeth Thiessen says, "For the early Christians beauty, truth, unity [which is sometimes added to the list], and goodness in the world are always seen as signs of divine revelation, of God's beauty, truth, unity, and goodness. . . . The good, the true, and the beautiful cannot be thought of apart from one another, as God in Godself is supreme beauty, goodness, and truth."[30]

Truth, goodness, and beauty are wed in both the divine and the human spheres. Dividing them from one another comes only at a price. As one example, consider what happens when we try to separate beauty from truth. According to Richard Harries, "True beauty is inseparable from the quest for truth. When the attempt to produce something beautiful is separated from truth, the result is sentimentality."[31]

John Witvliet points out some of the many problems inherent in sentimental artworks: "Sentimental art invites worshippers into a mode of engagement that ultimately cheapens, rather than deepens, the enactment of their covenantal relationship with God. Sentimental artworks . . . avoid depicting evil honestly, generate a kind of emotional self-indulgence, and fan an aversion to costly action and engagement." He goes on, "Christian worship seems to be a perennial magnet for attracting sentimental artworks — melodies, images, metaphors, rhythms, and palettes of color that succeed at making worship pleasant and utterly innocuous."[32]

One of the traditional approaches to thinking about the *transcendental properties of being* is to note that in the Godhead, beauty is the radiance of goodness and truth. What this really means is that without beauty, truth and goodness can become sterile, legalistic, and cold. Truth by itself does not have the ability to entice or allure the believer. This is an ever-present danger in religious traditions that devalue beauty. They need to be enlivened once again by beauty so that they mirror the abundant, rich qualities that characterize the Judeo-Christian God, qualities that are communicated to human beings through divine revelation and epiphany. As John

---

30. See *Theological Aesthetics: A Reader,* ed. Gesa Elsbeth Thiessen (Grand Rapids: Wm. B. Eerdmans, 2004), pp. 12-13.

31. Harries, *Art and the Beauty of God,* p. 49.

32. John Witvliet, "The Worship: How Can Art Serve the Corporate Worship of the Church?" in *For the Beauty of the Church: Casting a Vision for the Arts,* ed. W. David O. Taylor (Grand Rapids: Baker Books, 2010), p. 60.

Navone says, "Beauty is the enabling power of the truly good to draw us out of ourselves for the achievement of excellence."[33]

Unity, Variety, and Intensity

Building on the notion of the transcendentals, we need to put flesh and bones on the idea of beauty, to seek out a definition of beauty that has the power to guide our actions and our aesthetic choices. One of the most important definitions of beauty offered by the Western world is the idea that beauty possesses the greatest degree of unity, variety, and intensity coexisting at one time and in one place. If all these are present, by definition, we have located a beautiful object.

Nicholas Wolterstorff offers a classic presentation of these three qualities. He asks, What are the criteria for determining aesthetic excellence? His answer involves three principles: unity, variety, and intensity:

Unity: "For any object whatsoever which lacks unity to a significant degree, its lack of unity is for everyone an aesthetic defect in that thing. . . . For any object whatsoever whose character has unity to a significant degree, its unity is for everyone an aesthetic merit in the object."

Internal richness, variety, complexity: "For any object whatsoever whose character lacks internal richness to a significant degree, its lack of richness is for everyone an aesthetic defect in that thing. . . . For any object whatsoever whose character possesses internal richness to a significant degree, its internal richness is for everyone an aesthetic merit in that thing."

Intensity: "For any object whatsoever which is aesthetically bland, its blandness is for everyone an aesthetic defect in that object. . . . For any object whatsoever which is aesthetically intense, its intensity is for everyone an aesthetic merit."[34]

Wolterstorff is building on a long tradition dating back to Plato and Aristotle, whose chief Christian exponents include Augustine and Aqui-

33. Navone, *Toward a Theology of Beauty*, p. 25.

34. Nicholas Wolterstorff, *Art in Action: Toward a Christian Aesthetic* (Grand Rapids: Wm. B. Eerdmans, 1980), pp. 164-67.

nas. "Beauty must include three qualities," Aquinas asserts: "integrity or completeness — since things that lack something are thereby ugly; right proportion or harmony; and brightness — we call things bright in color beautiful."[35]

From a biblical standpoint, there are a variety of instances where unity, variety, and intensity all make an appearance together. Perhaps the most significant of these is the doctrine of the Trinity itself. In the Trinity infinite variety is joined with infinite unity and infinite intensity, leading to infinite beauty.

Unity, variety, and intensity, as defining properties of beauty in works of art, are objective because they can be measured. They are open to public examination. Neither the viewer nor the listener need take anyone else's word for it. They are criteria that anyone with the proper training can employ. Augustine was imbued with the notion that the categories of measure, weight, and number (biblical principles derived from wisdom literature) were prime examples of the importance of measurement. Taken together, they have the potential to provide an objective quality to aesthetic judgments. This is based on the assumption that trained viewers will arrive at similar conclusions when they are viewing the *gross* aesthetic characteristics of an object. This rarely involves subtle judgments between objects. It is my experience that many of the practical aesthetic comparisons we make in the church involve artistic choices that are strikingly different. I believe that trained observers will be virtually unanimous in noticing these differences.

For example, rhythm, melody, harmony, and form are the basic building blocks of music. In musical terms, they constitute what Augustine was referring to when he spoke of measure, weight, and number. Anyone educated in music theory can examine these characteristics and look for the relative degree of unity, variety, and intensity present in each of these building blocks as found in any particular piece of music. Robert O'Connell sums up Augustine's approach to the issue of objectivity in aesthetic judgment: "Reason remains [for Augustine] the ultimate judge of what is beautiful. . . . It is, in fact, a judge more ultimate and trustworthy than even the most ancient and revered authorities on the subject."[36]

---

35. Thomas Aquinas, *Summae Theologiae* Ia. *33-43,* quoted in Thiessen, *Theological Aesthetics,* p. 106.

36. Robert O'Connell, *Art and the Christian Intelligence in St. Augustine* (Cambridge, Mass.: Harvard University Press, 1978), p. 69.

Writing hundred of years later, Thomas Aquinas, while affirming this approach, muddied the waters when he said, "Beauty . . . has to do with knowledge, and we call a thing beautiful when it pleases the eye of the beholder."[37] At that moment Aquinas stood with one foot in the medieval world and one foot in the modern world. On the one hand, he represented the culmination of a long-standing school of Christian theology that affirmed the objectivity of beauty. Yet, he pointed to the potentially subjective idea of locating aesthetic value in the vicissitudes of individual preference and taste. It is important to note that Aquinas had not yet made the leap to modern aesthetic subjectivism. For him, it was the sensitive, trained observer — the observer who possessed *knowledge* — who mattered, not the neophyte. Nonetheless, at this point we begin the long, slow progression through history that ends with the notion of aesthetic relativity and each person's opinion about the arts being equally valid. In his song "Everything Is Beautiful," Ray Stevens includes this very concept in the first verse:

There is none so blind as he who will not see.
We must not close our minds; we must let our thoughts be free.
For every hour that passes by, you know the world gets a little bit
   older.
It's time to realize that beauty lies in the eyes of the beholder.[38]

It is one thing to say that "everything is beautiful in its own way" and quite another to say that "beauty lies in the eye of the beholder." The distance that Ray Stevens travels between these two aesthetic poles represents the span between the medieval world and our own. It is a journey that encapsulates the struggles we still face today in arts ministry.

Making Artistic Judgments

The choice between thinking about beauty as an objective category and thinking about beauty as a subjective category is critically important in the day-to-day decisions that are made in arts ministries. It raises one of the

---

37. Thomas Aquinas, *Summae Theologiae* Ia. 2-11, quoted in Thiessen, *Theological Aesthetics*, p. 88.

38. Ray Stevens, "Everything Is Beautiful," from the album *Everything Is Beautiful*, Barnaby Label (New York: CBS Records, 1970).

most pervasive and difficult issues for the arts minister: the issue of artistic quality. This is a particularly vexing issue as it relates to the integration of artistic materials from popular (i.e., secular) culture into the church, especially given the fact that a significant percentage of churches engaged in arts ministry in North America today base their ministry on popular culture.

As we begin to look at the issue of quality and how it relates to arts ministry in these churches, I want to introduce a distinction between two words that are often used interchangeably: "beauty" and "prettiness."[39] The two concepts are not identical. During the Middle Ages, the church was focused on beauty. The Renaissance witnessed a gradual shift away from beauty toward prettiness. Ever since the Renaissance, the church has been caught in a murky struggle, trying vainly to assimilate these two closely related concepts into one overarching synthesis. I think it would be healthier for all concerned if the differences between the two were carefully noted so that we could once again employ the concepts of beauty and prettiness in an appropriate fashion.

Let me contrast beauty and prettiness on a number of different levels. Keep in mind as I do this that there is some degree of overlap between these two terms, and in some areas the differences are differences of degree, not of kind. Nonetheless, I believe there is some validity to this approach: it is worth pursuing to see where it will lead us and by what route we will travel.

My first point is that beauty is an intrinsic quality. Objects are beautiful or ugly by virtue of how they are constructed. Something is beautiful regardless of whether or not anyone else thinks it is beautiful. On the surface this contradicts the notion that meaning is a construct of the human brain, not an intrinsic quality. This seeming contradiction would stand only if beauty could not be measured. But since, in the Western tradition, beauty is a function of its unity, variety, and intensity, that gives it the potential for objectivity, because a beautiful object can be broken down into its constituent parts and each part can be analyzed and measured according to these three criteria.

Prettiness, on the other hand, depends upon a human reaction. People will always disagree about whether or not a particular combination of sounds or colors or words is pretty. These judgments are culturally conditioned and subject to change as fads come and go or as we move from one

---

39. For further treatment of the difference between beauty and prettiness, see Richard Harries, *Art and the Beauty of God,* pp. 47-49.

place to another in our world. Prettiness has to do with taste, whereas people with completely divergent tastes can all acknowledge beauty. Prettiness attempts to answer the question "What do you like?" Beauty attempts to answer the question "What is well constructed?"

According to the Western formulation, intrinsic qualities that, by definition, make an art object well constructed are unity, variety, and intensity, all existing on a high plane simultaneously. This means that a piece of art possessing these qualities, like Picasso's *Guernica,* can be beautiful without being pretty at all.

Beauty expresses the "depth dimension" of reality; it relates to concerns that are truly ultimate. The message that beauty delivers makes a claim about what we should value in life, a claim that we should be concerned with quality, not only in our artistic products but also in the different choices we make as we live our lives. This message is one that we may not understand in the same way we understand the morning newspaper, but it is nonetheless important. It represents a new vision of wholeness and holiness that we often miss in our electronic generation.

Prettiness also teaches a message, but it is a different message altogether. Prettiness is a measure of how much we have bought into our culture. To be concerned with prettiness is to be concerned with that which satisfies, that which gives us a pleasurable feeling and makes us comfortable. Prettiness is what the advertising agencies use to make us desire a certain product or buy into an artificial dream. Prettiness creates an outward picture of tranquility. Prettiness is the white picket fence around a perfect house in the suburbs. It is a Monet impression of the surface of life among the bourgeois on a Paris street. Prettiness is what we go shopping for in our malls, and what we hear piped in through the speakers while we are making our selections.

The expression that comes out of our mouths when we are confronted with a pretty object is "Aaaah." The expression that comes out of our mouths when we are confronted with a beautiful object is "Aha!" The pretty object warms the heart. The beautiful object generates new insights into the nature of reality, into our identity before God and God's identity both within and infinitely beyond our lives.

Beauty requires something of us. It demands that we be held accountable for learning and growth. In order to hear the message of beauty, we have to learn its language. To some extent that means we need to learn its artistic language.

As we hear the message of beauty, we are confronted with the question of whether we need to change from the people we are now into new people. This change requires openness and vulnerability on our part. We must let go of our well-worn patterns and habits. We must move out of "all the old familiar places" and learn to find our way in a country where the streets and the avenues all look different. There is a vague sense of apprehension that we must either overcome or learn to live with as we proceed on our journey. Even the road maps are different. They are not always clearly marked; rather, they require us to use intuition to reach our goal. We would be wise in these circumstances to rely on trained guides in much the same way as mystics throughout history have relied on spiritual directors to show the way.

There is, on the other hand, a certain conformism and leveling that accompanies prettiness. It does not take any special skills or training to recognize that something is pretty. This brings people from the same cultural context together. The shared experience of prettiness is one of its special appeals. It fosters the bonds of community because everyone can participate equally in the warm feelings generated by a pretty object. This bonding increases the likelihood that individuals will remain part of the group in which they experienced the pretty object.

Prettiness can contribute to a church's being perceived as user-friendly — or, in the parlance of the day, seeker-sensitive. Prettiness attracts prospective worshippers and helps them overcome their reluctance to participate in the life of a new group by forging immediate bonds between them and the older, established members of the group. In addition, prettiness has the capacity to cross many cultural barriers. Young and old, rich and poor, educated and uneducated, even believers and non-believers all can appreciate a pretty song or laugh at an amusing moment in a dramatic sketch. All of us can share the warm feelings that result from this common experience.

Where does this leave us? We have a choice to make in our ministry in the church. Prettiness is a value that is most often associated with popular culture. Beauty is a value most often associated with classical culture. This is not an absolute distinction, but it does reflect a general trend. The distinction between the two is summed up when we think of the word "culture." Originally, "culture" referred to the highest achievements of human civilization (i.e., beauty). Now this same word is used to denote the sum total of *all* the achievements of human civilization (i.e., prettiness). The choice of which cultural model to follow reflects our image of who we want to be and what we think about God, and it directly impacts what our arts ministry will look like.

This choice requires discernment. John Witvliet has written about the need for discernment in worship and ministry. His comments apply especially well to the related questions of how to judge art and how to integrate art into the ongoing life of the community of faith. He suggests the following requirements:

(1) *Openness:* Witvliet writes, "Discerning people are always willing to give a person, a movement, or a worship style a fair hearing." This, of course, includes a new artwork. It may apply either to the artistic products I have defined as pretty or to those that are beautiful.

(2) *Choosing and being consistent:* Existentialism (and, I might add, Christian moral philosophy) teaches us that we must choose and accept responsibility for our choices once they have been made. To suggest that every artwork is equally good or equally appropriate in the setting of a particular Christian community is not theologically defensible.[40] It would be like saying that truth and goodness do not matter, that all actions and all ideas are equivalent.

(3) *Knowledge:* Witvliet says, "To make good choices, we need to be learners, readers, questioners." We need to be on a path of growth that encompasses the aesthetic, affective, cognitive, and spiritual dimension of our lives. Specifically, to make good choices about artistic quality, we need to be growing in our knowledge about art, its forms and structures, its language and symbols.

(4) *Pastoral quality:* Learning to be pastoral in the context of arts ministry is vital. Decisions regarding artistic quality are integrated into the day-to-day life of the church. These decisions have a direct impact on the church's ability to function as the body of Christ. It is *not* sufficient to make aesthetic judgments and then act on them without reference to the effect of these judgments on the community.

(5) *Community:* Witvliet notes that (aesthetic) discernment happens best in the context of community. "None of us by ourselves has the per-

---

40. Calvin Johansson writes, "Who is to say that a particular piece of music is creative? If one agrees that standards are a matter of taste and that one taste is as valid as another . . . then that is the end of it. Carried to its logical conclusion, all music (and everything else, for that matter) is of equal value. Such a stance is intolerable for a Christian because it implies that instead of being in a fallen condition all men are perfect, that God has given to every man similar gifts, all used equally well, that the world is devoid of any value system. . . . Such a philosophy belongs to the absurdists who deny value, achievement, or authority. It is not a viable option for the Christian." See Calvin M. Johansson, *Music and Ministry: A Biblical Counterpoint* (Peabody, Mass.: Hendrickson, 1984), p. 19.

spective to see the whole picture." We all can sharpen one another's aesthetic insights by examining works of art together, rather than simply relying on our own judgment.

Ultimately,

(6) *discernment* is a gift of the Spirit.[41]

Integrating Aesthetics into Christian Faith and Practice

Over the centuries, churches have taken radically different paths when it comes to the question of how to integrate aesthetic theories into Christian faith and practice. Surveying the landscape of arts ministry, I would like to suggest five different approaches to this question that are operative in the contemporary church. These approaches are inspired (very loosely) by Richard Niebuhr's classic study *Christ and Culture*.[42]

Let me be clear: the primary question that is addressed here is the aesthetic issue we have been discussing. It is important to note that there are other important aspects to the question of integrating art into faith and practice *besides* the aesthetic question. As Don Saliers reminds us, "No judgment about the aesthetics of liturgy can be made on *purely* musical or artistic grounds alone."[43]

For instance, there is the question of whether or not a particular artwork is *fitting* within any particular setting. This question alone raises many different related issues. *Sing to the Lord*, the Roman Catholic document we mentioned earlier, lists three criteria that relate to the issue of fittingness: liturgical, pastoral, and musical.[44] Although the five approaches I will suggest touch on liturgical, pastoral, and aesthetic issues, their clear emphasis is on the third of these three criteria — the aesthetic criterion. A more thoroughgoing attempt to develop a theology of arts ministry would, no doubt, develop all three of these criteria at length.

However limited, I have found the following list to be a helpful lens to use when I look out over the landscape of the church.

41. John D. Witvliet, "The Virtue of Liturgical Discernment," in *Music in Christian Worship: At the Service of the Liturgy*, ed. Charlotte Kroeker (Collegeville, Minn.: Liturgical Press, 2005), pp. 83-97.

42. H. Richard Niebuhr, *Christ and Culture* (New York: Harper & Row, 1951).

43. Don Saliers, *Worship and Theology: Foretaste of Glory Divine* (Nashville: Abingdon Press, 1994), p. 195.

44. *Sing to the Lord* (United States Conference of Catholic Bishops, 2007).

First, it is possible to say that we should not have any art in church or, at least, that we should intentionally reduce the amount of beauty that we employ in our worship. This was Ulrich Zwingli's basic position in the sixteenth century. He expelled music from worship and eliminated all visual images in the interest of avoiding idolatry. He really wanted to eliminate public worship; he thought that worship should be done in spirit and in truth in solitude. He knew that this was not practical, so he stripped it down to the essentials, which meant eliminating the music and visual art that he considered to be particularly distracting and lacking in biblical support. Note that even in this circumstance, Zwingli retained an architectural setting for worship, the language of poetry, especially as embodied in the Psalms, and the artistry that was embedded in his sermons. Nonetheless, there is no question that the Zwinglian service was radically different from its predecessor, the late medieval Roman Catholic mass.

When we examine the goals of this approach, we see that increased attention is focused on the left brain, the discursive mode of communication between human beings and God. The Word with a capital "W" is of paramount importance. Ethics and boundaries are emphasized. The church produces upstanding men and women with a clear sense of right and wrong. At the same time, holiness becomes strictly a matter of ethics, while the dimension of awe, the *mysterium tremendum* of worship and ministry, is lost.

For Zwingli (who was himself a superb musician and might lay claim to the title of the greatest musical theologian in all of history), there *is* a place for cultural expression, but its place is in the home, not in the church. This creates a *de facto* division between the sacred and the secular dimensions of life. Zwingli's notion is particularly interesting in light of the reformers' stated goals of *eliminating* a sacred/secular division and viewing all of life as sacred and belonging to God. I'm going to label this approach *anaestheticism*. Just as an anesthetic gradually deadens a person's physical sensitivities, so *anaestheticism*, the de-emphasis of beauty in the church, deadens our spiritual sensitivities. Today, many churches similarly limit or reduce the presence of beauty in their worship and ministry.

The second approach requires that we make a distinction between beauty and prettiness. Exponents of this philosophy may value the staying power of a piece of art over time, the opinion of experts, or the standards developed by the academic community, standards such as unity, variety, and intensity. In whatever fashion they arrive at their decision, somehow they decide which artworks embody beauty, and they exclusively employ this repertoire in liturgy and ministry. As Frank Gaebelien says, "Nothing short of the best will do as the standard for criticism. The God who gave us in his Son the one and only example of a perfect human life as our pattern of obedience has on the lesser level of the arts given us the high products of genius as examples of excellence."[45]

I am going to label this approach *aestheticism*. When beauty is the criteria for selecting artworks for the church, people are exposed to art that has the potential to teach them something about value and about the kind and quality of decisions they should make in their Christian lives. True beauty generates a depth of meaning that is not easily exhausted; it has the capacity to qualitatively improve the ministries in which we work. It can stand up to repeated exposure and have something new to say each time. Choosing beauty is a choice *for* objective standards and *against* the meaninglessness of total relativity in art and in the moral circumstances with which we are confronted on a daily basis. Beauty teaches us something about the idols of our society. It unmasks for us the fiction of commercialism as an ultimate value and fosters abundant, new, mature life for all those who can speak its language.

There are also challenges associated with choosing beauty. As I said earlier, beauty requires something of us. We must learn its language in order to participate fully in its benefits. Many people will choose not to make the effort. We may lose parishioners in our churches. Many of those who remain will do so with a sort of stoic acceptance of their fate. They will simply assume that sacred art has to be like this. They will acquiesce to the selection of beautiful artworks simply because they don't want to fight the status quo. To choose beauty in the presence of those for whom beauty has no meaning may be to actually *choose* lack of meaning as a value. This is a telling critique that applies to many churches in which arts ministry is outwardly thriving.

In regard to the question of meaning, artists who accept this approach achieve a solid grounding for artistic values. The aesthetic quality of worship and ministry is enhanced, and the transcendent character of the divine is made available to the willing worshipper. On a practical level, many professional artists are comfortable in this setting because it offers them an opportunity to work with great art and to re-create the thrill of exciting li-

45. Frank Gaebelein, *The Christian, the Arts, and Truth: Regaining the Vision of Greatness* (Portland, Ore.: Multnomah Press, 1985), p. 103.

turgical experiences. Meaning emerges for them in direct proportion to their contact with artworks of depth.

Along the way, professional artists often encounter the charge of elitism. It is important to keep in mind the distinction between elitism and excellence. Elitism involves the claim that there is a privileged artistic language, a language or style that holds pride of place because it is approved by a privileged class of people (usually trained artists, so-called experts, often called "snobs" by those who are not in this class). Elitism represents the rule of the mighty over the powerless.

Excellence, on the other hand, involves the insistence that art itself must hold up to a certain set of norms that have been established and developed over time through rigorous practical trials, thereafter established in a series of theoretical constructs that are not arbitrary and that are, within broad limits, publicly verifiable.

For those who accept aestheticism as their standard, this distinction between elitism and excellence is important to understand and to articulate in the course of their ministry.

Next we come to institutions who respond to the question "What artworks should we employ in church?" by saying, "Give the people what they want." In other words, they choose prettiness.

Those who follow this approach will achieve many positive results. Giving people what they want and what they like will tend to make them happy. It may increase church attendance and generate quantitative growth in the church's programs. There will be an aura of success that surrounds churches that value prettiness. This will give arts ministers in these churches a positive self-image relative to their work. In addition, many people will, for the first time, experience a new dimension in their faith life and, specifically, in their worship life. People who for years have gone to church and never felt anything may be moved by what happens in the service. This will undoubtedly have important ramifications for every area of their Christian walk. Community will develop through the experiences of warmth that the congregation shares. The power of the arts will evoke memories and recall associations with positive experiences in people's lives. A personal relationship with God may develop where none had existed before. There may be a renaissance in church life, a renaissance based on the subjective experience of a pretty object.

But there are also dangers associated with the choice of prettiness. The art objects that are generating all these good feelings may not have a high degree of integrity in their construction. Their inherent weaknesses may not enable them to continually perform the same function they performed when they were first introduced into the church. Repeated experiences with these art objects in worship often leads to the congregation paying increased attention to the details of the object. Much of this attention is on an intuitive, unconscious plane; nonetheless, it is virtually impossible for a poorly constructed item to retain its value for a congregation *ad infinitum*.

Perhaps an even greater danger is that some members of the congregation may be lulled into a sort of catatonic state by pretty objects. Prettiness does not encourage people to look beneath the surface of the object and see what else is there. This prompts an important question: Do we want to produce Christian people who don't look beneath the surface of their culture, who don't see the idols that are all around them, who have become blind to reality because they've spent so much time focusing on their personal feelings? After we have used pretty artworks to lure these people into the church, what happens to them then? This is one critique that could be leveled at the church growth movement today.

I'm going to label this approach *cultural relativism*. It is a particularly potent force in any church where the main purpose of worship is to bring the unchurched into the fold. It is important to note that evangelism as the principal purpose for worship is a relatively new phenomenon, dating only from the days of frontier religion in America during the nineteenth century. When success and meaningfulness are measured in numbers of converts, it should come as no surprise that artworks selected for worship conform as closely as possible to the cultural traditions of those to be converted.

Next we examine variety as an organizing principle. Speaking about music, Paul Wohlgemuth sums up this approach when he says, "As you guide your ship of church music through a stormy sea of change, may you not ride on only one wave! We communicate with the greatest number of people if we keep a balanced repertoire before them, and the repertoire must give each person the opportunity to experience something spiritual for the immediate present."[46]

Variety offers worshippers a diversity of artistic styles in the setting of one local parish, sometimes in the setting of one worship service. This approach recognizes that there is a risk in choosing either aestheticism or cultural relativism. In either case, people are excluded. Aestheticism ex-

---

46. Paul W. Wohlgemuth, *Rethinking Church Music* (Carol Stream, Ill.: Hope Publishing Company, 1973), p. 30.

cludes people who appreciate prettiness but not beauty. Cultural relativism excludes people who appreciate beauty but not prettiness.

The name I am going to give to variety is *critical pluralism*. This tradition, instead of simply providing what the majority of people want, recognizes that there are different factions in the church that appreciate different styles of art or worship; thus it is imperative to provide a stylistic diet that keeps everyone satisfied. Variety rests on the theological principle called *adiaphora*, which means that we should allow for variations in liturgical rites when those variations don't have any bearing on salvation. In practice, I suspect the principal reason that people employ variety in the church today may be the same as at other times in church history: to avoid unnecessary political conflict in the congregation.

At this point we should stop and ask if it is possible to obtain the benefits of prettiness and the benefits of beauty without sacrificing either our aesthetic values or the lives of our congregations in the process. Some would answer "yes," pointing to growth as the means to achieve this goal — growth in the direction of greater maturity, including aesthetic, affective, cognitive, spiritual, and theological maturity.

Hebrews 5:13-14 says, "For everyone who lives on milk, being still an infant, is unskilled in the word of righteousness. But solid food is for the mature, for those whose faculties have been trained by practice to distinguish good from evil." Notice the various component parts of Paul's concept. First, the immature lack certain skills. In regard to the arts, this could include the skills required to appreciate and find meaning in aesthetic objects. Second, movement from immaturity to maturity is a function of practice. It is not something that can be done quickly; rather, it takes time and effort.

Choosing growth means that if we attract people to the faith with prettiness (milk) and then leave them at this initial stage in their development, we are not practicing good discipleship or, in the end, being particularly loving. On the other hand, it is not acceptable to provide a steady diet of beauty (solid food) for those who have no appetite for it, those for whom it has no meaning. There must be growth in the direction from prettiness to beauty, growth from a diet of milk to a diet of solid food. It is important to recognize that this kind of aesthetic growth does not imply the elimination of prettiness so much as the addition to the repertoire, over time, of artworks of great beauty and depth. Thus, growth has the potential to effectively reverse the historic shift from beauty to prettiness that occurred as Western civilization moved from the Middle Ages to our own time.

Of course, artworks of depth can *also* be pretty. In fact, the search for artworks that embody beauty *and* prettiness is an important task for the arts minister. In this instance, prettiness provides the initial attraction that arrests the attention of the viewer or listener; meanwhile, the depth dimension inherent within the work has time to act, thereby creating opportunities for increased maturity. As John Witvliet suggests, arts ministers should "appreciate the remarkable skill of poets and musicians who accept the challenge to be both profound and accessible at the same time, which is a lot more difficult than simply being one or the other."[47] Gradually, as this process plays out in the life of the church, the congregation comes to value not only prettiness but also depth.

As beauty is increasingly incorporated into the church, it subverts the values derived from our secular culture. It subverts the idols that try to entrap the Christian community and, in so doing, helps form people into the image of Christ and sets them on the path to true spiritual maturity.

The key is to provide opportunities for growth at every turn. Those who practice this approach must be honest and open about what they are doing. They must start by acknowledging the level of aesthetic maturity in the congregation, or there is no hope of growing. Yet even as they are at the initial stages of their journey, they must help the people in the pews to understand that they are in fact on a journey, that the Christian life is not static.

This final approach is by far the hardest route an arts minister could choose. It demands that people be open and vulnerable. It forces mature artists who know what is beautiful to use artistic products that are not well-constructed because they correspond at that time to the congregation's aesthetic sensitivity and capacity for openness. This is extraordinarily difficult and frustrating. It also raises the potential issue of dishonesty if arts ministers are not open about the rationale behind the choices they are making.

Despite the challenges of this approach, it can become a source for human change and development. In order for this approach to be successful, aesthetic education is required. This may mean formal adult or youth education classes. Education also happens informally simply through the choices made about which musical repertoire, visual images, dramatic sketches, or liturgical dances to include in worship and in arts ministry outside of wor-

47. John Witvliet, "The Worship: How Can Art Serve the Corporate Worship of the Church?" in Taylor, *For the Beauty of the Church*, p. 48.

ship. In this instance, rather than simply seeing the arts as a reflection of who we are, we see them as a function of who we will become. The arts thereby become a way for the Christian community to move forward in its collective journey. I call this final approach *developmentalism*. Meaning is achieved through qualitative growth, not just quantitative growth. Arts ministers pursue this approach by learning as much as possible about their congregation's interests, abilities, and capacity for change, and using this information to devise an artistic program that is simultaneously fulfilling and challenging.

There are two significant gains achieved by using the developmental approach: arts ministry takes on a pastoral dimension by remaining in contact with the artistic language skills and felt needs of the people, and arts ministry takes on a prophetic dimension by calling the people to move forward and not allowing them to remain comfortably in one place.

These, then, are the five options:

1. *Anaestheticism:* restricting the use of beauty in the church.
2. *Aestheticism:* employing only the most well-constructed art in the church.
3. *Cultural Relativism:* choosing whatever art the people want.
4. *Critical Pluralism:* providing a mixture of artistic styles.
5. *Developmentalism:* assisting the congregation in the process of growth.

The choices made by individual arts ministries will significantly impact the character and configuration of everything they do. At first, rather than trying to make a normative judgment about which of these approaches to pursue, it may simply be important for an individual ministry to locate itself, to understand what it is already doing and what effects various choices might have on the lives of those engaged in the ministry. Only then can the ministry begin to critically analyze alternative possibilities.

Conclusion

The issues of whether or not the arts constitute meaningful communication, the meaning of beauty from a Judeo-Christian perspective, and the role of aesthetic judgment are all critically important issues for the arts minister. The historic dialogue regarding these issues has been intense, reflecting their significance in ecclesiastical life. They are by no means the only issues to consider in a theology of arts ministry, but they do provide a starting point for reflection and further expansion. We now turn our attention to the practical sphere, where we will focus on the question of how to initiate and develop arts ministry in the setting of the local church.

CHAPTER NINE

The Practice of Arts Ministry

Both the church and the artist share in common a search for ways
to speak the truth, to live more authentically. The church needs
the help of artists to understand human life and to express the
depths of truth, both human and divine. Artists need the church,
a community that recognizes the importance of truth as well as
the vitality of art and will provide the space and resources for interaction with it. Not only do the church and artists share a mutual goal, the embodiment of truth, but they depend on each other
to accomplish it.

Janet Walton, *Art and Worship: A Vital Connection*

A Model

From 1995 to 2003 I was Organist and Minister of Arts at Crossroads Reformed Church in Overland Park, Kansas, a suburb of Kansas City. It is a
small Reformed Church in America congregation founded by people of
Dutch descent. At that time we averaged around 100 worshippers split between two Sunday services, and we had a very limited budget. One of the
reasons I like talking about this particular arts ministry is that it allows me
to note that successful arts ministry can happen in small churches as well
as large congregations. It can flourish in denominations that have a rich
history of the arts and in traditions like the Reformed tradition that have a
long history of iconoclasm and reticence regarding many art forms. I'm

going to describe this ministry in some detail, because I think it is a good illustration of some of the possibilities that are available in virtually every local church today.

The arts ministry we developed in this church included the music ministry, a visual art and environment team, a resident liturgical dance company called the Miriam Dance Ensemble, and, on occasion, a drama troupe we named City of Light.[1]

In regard to staff, I directed the arts ministry as a whole as well as serving in the music ministry. We had a choral conductor, a trumpeter-in-residence, and a staff choreographer. Over the years, we struggled to find someone to direct the drama ministry, with limited success. We also had an arts ministry board that met at least twice a year, including one retreat per year.

During this time the arts ministry produced three weekend arts festivals at the church and a weekend arts retreat at Conception Abbey, a Benedictine monastery near Kansas City. Programs sponsored by the arts ministry included tours of church architecture in the Kansas City area; a docent-led tour of medieval sacred art at Kansas City's Nelson-Atkins Museum of Art, followed by a Renaissance sacred art tour the next year; several showings of sacred films with commentary by the film critic of one of our local newspapers; liturgical dance workshops; writing and journaling workshops; poetry readings; jazz services and concerts; visual arts workshops for young people; and finally, guest lecturers talking about a wide variety of topics ranging from the history of frescoes to sacred space.

In the music ministry we purchased a grand piano as well as new handbells and commissioned an anthem from K. Lee Scott entitled "A City Radiant as a Bride," which is now part of his *Requiem*.[2] In addition, we formed a new handbell choir and continued to develop our choral program, including sponsoring music education classes during the thirty minutes prior to many of our choir rehearsals.

The visual arts ministry produced a full set of indoor banners for the liturgical year and some additional outdoor banners for our parking lot. There were several exhibits of the work of local artists as well as a number of exhibits of creative products or collections drawn from our own congregation.

---

1. The ministry was called *Imago Dei*, a name later transferred to a regional sacred arts organization that continues to be active in the Midwest at the present time.

2. K. Lee Scott, *Requiem* (Chapel Hill, N.C.: Hinshaw Music, 2006).

I taught a series of adult education classes entitled P.A.C.T. (the "Partnership for Arts and Christian Theology") that educated the congregation about the relationship between Christianity and the arts. During this time, in addition to the classes, there were six sermons preached about various topics related to the arts.

In the literary and dramatic arts we commissioned poems from Marie Asner, a noted local poet, and sponsored regular poetry services that incorporated historic and contemporary Christian poetry. We also staged a full-scale medieval drama entitled *The Shepherds,* along with various other smaller dramatic sketches.

This was all done with a modest budget and very part-time staff. As we developed this ministry, we discovered that the real issue was not lack of money or time; it was a question of how creative we could be in our thinking and imagining.

In light of this example, I want to suggest that arts ministry is an option in virtually every congregation. The real question is not whether it is possible, but how arts ministry can grow in the soil of the church. As we consider this question, we will break it down into two parts: theory and practice. In local churches this division is especially important. There is a tendency to proceed directly to practice without prior reflection. Too often, ministries take a "ready, shoot, aim" approach to their work. They create programming without thinking through the questions that the programs are meant to address. This is particularly problematic in the area of worship. Time is devoted to planning the logistics of worship rather than thinking about the meaning and significance of what we do when we gather to offer praise, confession, lament, and thanksgiving to God.

The same temptation is present in arts ministry, with equally disastrous results. Given the various suspicions and misunderstandings about arts ministry that are prevalent among laity and clergy alike, an approach that considers only practice can kill fledgling arts programs before they have a chance to root themselves in the institutional life of the church.

Theoretical Considerations

This discussion of theory will consider three different topics: (1) basic principles, (2) potential pitfalls, and (3) key considerations of the arts minister.

A Christian Arts Camp
Fellowship Lutheran Church, Tulsa, Oklahoma

**Lauren Leifeste learns to play the organ
at the Christian Arts Camp**

Bible School and summer camp are a traditional part of the annual Christian education program at many churches. Fellowship Lutheran Church in Tulsa, Oklahoma, has put a different twist on this idea by sponsoring summer arts camps for young people.

The camps began in 2000 with a focus on music. Two five-day camps have run parallel to one another each year: a primary camp open to five-year-olds through those entering third grade, and an advanced camp for those entering the fourth grade through those entering the eighth grade.

Over the years the musical offerings (choir, instrumental music lessons, instruction in Orff instruments and handbells) have expanded to include instruction in visual arts (quilting and crocheting, clay art, sketching, set design, banner-making, watercolor painting, calligraphy) creative writing, theatre (including the production of musicals), and liturgical dance. Students above the eighth grade are admitted into a pipe organ class. This class utilizes churches throughout the area and teachers drawn from the Tulsa chapter of the American Guild of Organists.

Students in the primary camp engage in all the camp activities: choir; bells and chimes; art; music and movement. Students in the advanced camp choose electives to pursue on a more intensive basis.

Approximately half the camp participants come from Fellowship Lutheran Church, while the other half come from the community at large. In a typical year the camp hosts roughly eighty children, split more or less evenly between the two age groups. There are three primary administrators on staff at the church, in addition to which the camp hires ten to twelve instructors and involves the services of fifty-five to sixty-five volunteers.

Vicki Smith, co-coordinator of the camp, writes, "Our purpose is to serve the children of the greater Tulsa Community by inspiring and developing children's skills for Christian service."* As has been the case so often in church history, children become arts ministers when they are treated with respect and challenged to become full participants in the church's life and witness.

*Vicki Smith, e-mail to the author, 3 November 2010.

Basic Principles

Among many different options, we will examine several principles as foundations of arts ministry: thoughtfulness, playfulness, and the pastoral/prophetic dialectic.

Thoughtfulness

As I said a moment ago, it is critically important to surround arts ministry with an environment of thoughtfulness. This takes three forms: study, conversation with one another, and prayer, our conversation with God. All three of these occur in the context of community. They should be pursued together, including as wide a range of potential participants as possible. In so doing, we learn and grow ourselves, and discover something of what it means to be the body of Christ. We lead by learning. The model of arts ministry that results will be fitted to the circumstances of the particular institution in which it is developed. It will have the potential to grow organically, taking into account the gifts and interests of the community of faith and the opportunities present in the local area.

Patricia O'Connell Killen points out that "Reflection is the act of deliberately slowing down our habitual meaning-making processes to take a closer look at the experience. . . ."[3] This is strikingly similar to what happens in the artistic process. Art enables a detailed examination of a particular scene taken from one moment in time. Thus, process and product coalesce. Arts ministry takes on a reflective character as it exercises its own native capacity to focus attention on the minutiae of human experience.

There is, of course, a price to pay for being thoughtful, just as there is a price to pay for doing arts ministry. Reflection takes time. It requires human capital. In a society that values getting everything immediately, it is not always easy to argue in favor of reflection. Nonetheless, it is important. When a ministry has taken the time to be thoughtful in its initial planning stage, then when it needs to make decisions about issues like financing, it can do so carefully and wisely. Thoughtful planning maximizes the chance that the ministry will yield fruit and be supported by the wider community.

3. Patricia O'Connell Killen, "Assisting Adults to Think Theologically," in *Method in Ministry: Theological Reflection and Christian Ministry*, ed. James D. Whitehead and Evelyn Eaton Whitehead (Kansas City: Sheed & Ward, 1995), p. 105.

Playfulness

Play is undervalued in the church. We have a tendency to be very serious about Christianity. The previous discussion about thoughtfulness and reflection might lead us in this direction. However well-intentioned, the tendency to take an overly solemn approach to Christian life and witness can blind us to the importance of play in the community of faith. Jesus calls us to enter the kingdom as little children. What does this mean? First of all, it means that we are free to imagine new worlds, new ways of being in our own world, new ways of being ourselves. Imagination is the raw material of play. It is faith's partner in the dance of life.

When we are at play, we delight in the object of our attention. In the movie *Chariots of Fire*, the Scottish runner Eric Liddell throws back his head and runs, fueled not so much by adrenaline (or technique, for that matter) as by pure joy. In those moments he says he can "feel God's pleasure."[4] Arts ministry needs to be a place where we can learn the language of delight, where we can throw back our collective heads and leave reason behind for a moment, celebrating the wonder of a climactic moment in a drama, an exquisitely written line of poetry, or the whirl of a dancer twisting and turning across the floor, seemingly unfettered by space or time.

Playfulness suggests participation. We are most actively at play when we are engaged in creating art in some way. However, playfulness is not the exclusive property of those with special gifts and opportunities. As Eric Liddell runs, we can all vicariously "feel God's pleasure." That is the beauty of art and the possibility of arts ministry. On some level it communicates to everyone with ears to hear its joys and pains, its hopes and dreams, its excitement and wonder.

As we engage in arts ministry, as we work through the various administrative details and tasks associated with its formation and development, it is important to seek out opportunities to play. We should not cease our efforts to reflect, but we should recognize that, without play, thoughtfulness is sterile. It is play — existential experience with the sacred arts — that makes reflection meaningful and sets the tone for all we will do in our ministry.

---

4. *Chariots of Fire* (Enigma Productions, 1981).

The Dialectic of Pastoral and Prophetic Ministry

To Judeo-Christian people, the God who is pictured in Scripture is anything but a static, passive figure. God did not form the world and then leave it to its own devices. The God of Scripture is a God who embraces change, who subverts the status quo in the knowledge that history itself is moving inexorably toward its own fulfillment. The Lord of history embraces change and growth as the proper model for human formation.

Human beings are on a pilgrimage here on earth. This requires moving from place to place and adapting to each new environment, including the environment of liturgy. As Carolyn Dietering reminds us, "True ritual is *living* ritual, containing the past, embracing the present, and allowing the future to unfold. Ritual which does not grow, naturally and organically with the faith of the people who practice it, loses its claim to be ritual. It becomes ritualism. Meaningful form gives way to formalism."[5]

From a biblical perspective, it is impossible to imagine human life as standing still. We are on a journey, moving either in the direction chosen by God that results in a more abundant life, or in a direction that we ourselves choose, a direction that invariably leads to our own demise. There is no third option. Standing still, whether in worship, in arts ministry, or in the context of our lived experience, is an idolatrous myth created by people and institutions whose primary motivation is self-preservation and the preservation of the status quo. This myth is ultimately self-defeating. As you can tell, this is an unabashed advertisement for the *developmental* approach I outlined in the previous chapter.

The arts create an environment that makes change more palatable. Because the arts involve creative responses to the world, they can be catalysts to help us engage the world in a spontaneous, fresh, innovative fashion. However, when the arts themselves change (especially in the context of liturgy), people get uneasy. Michael Card says that "creative worship is one response to the heartbreaking beauty of God."[6] This may be true, but it is not always easy for worshippers to either comprehend or embrace. Change is hard. It demands that we take risks.

There are two further challenges that make this even more difficult. First, individual people within any congregation will be at different places

---

5. Carolyn Dietering, *The Liturgy as Dance and the Liturgical Dancer* (New York: Crossroad, 1984), p. 7.

6. Michael Card, *Scribbling in the Sand: Christ and Creativity* (Downers Grove, Ill.: InterVarsity Press, 2002), p. 32.

in their journey with respect to change. Some will have just come through times in their lives that were chaotic or heartbreaking. They may very well feel the need for stability in their experiences at church. Other people will need new opportunities to express their faith. New challenges will be welcomed in response to a new set of questions.

The second problem is mobility. Congregations themselves are not static. People come and go, which means that the underlying profile of a particular congregation with respect to change will alter over time.

In the face of the change required by arts ministry, we need to remember that resistance is a normal reaction from the faith community. We should expect it and not be discouraged or confounded when it appears. Instead, we should be thankful for it because it helps us to know where people are in their thinking and self-understanding. Many people will be unhappy but not express their feelings. They should be encouraged to do so, since it is much healthier for the entire ministry if people trust leadership enough to express their ideas and feelings. We should greet these expressions with pastoral sensitivity and recognize that, in the end, love demands that we help people to grow.

Artists know from their own experience that growth does not happen in a straight line. As they work with their artistic materials, there will be periods when it seems like they are moving backwards or not making any headway at all. Then, all of a sudden they will have a burst of creative energy, and new ideas will emerge. These are insights from the artistic process that should help the arts minister understand the process of growth within a congregation. There should be no expectation that growth will be constant or proceed at a regular pace. It will not. Simply knowing that should help the process go more smoothly.

There are two ways that the arts function in relation to change. First, they encourage an experimental approach to ministry, to worship, and to the life of faith itself. They are a means of supporting and encouraging receptivity to God's remarkable self-revelation. Janet Walton explains, "When applied to liturgical practice, originality is expressed in fresh insights, evocative images, energizing architecture and environments, spirited music, forms that are on the cutting edge of acceptability. Old answers do not satisfy new questions. . . . Worship requires beauty which anticipates a spirit of adventuresomeness and openness as a witness to the uncharted ways of God."[7]

7. Janet Walton, *Art and Worship: A Vital Connection* (Wilmington, Del.: Michael Glazier, 1988), p. 62.

Second, the arts are grounded in tradition. Art forms do not emerge out of nowhere. They are based on the creative efforts and insights developed by generations of earlier artists. As such, they foster continuity and the conservation of ideas that were successful. The great challenge is to assimilate this rich tradition into the present situation in such a way as to make it come alive again.

In the contemporary church, where there is a need both to innovate and to conserve, we are faced with the responsibility of doing arts ministry in a dialectical fashion. The dialectic is between pastoral ministry that sympathizes with the concerns and fears of people who need stability in their lives, and prophetic ministry that pushes people beyond their comfort zone to enable them to grow. It is analogous to the dialectic experienced each week in worship between the *ordinary* of the liturgy (parts that do not change from week to week) and the *propers* of the liturgy (the parts that do change).

Doing things the same way all the time, whether in worship, ministry, or living itself, can be stultifying. It has the potential to snuff out the sparks of faith that are implanted at great cost by the Holy Spirit. On the other hand, constant change is distracting. It causes us to lose our focus on God and transfer it to the artworks we employ in worship and ministry. In other words, both sameness and frequent change are problems.

Marva Dawn summarizes the issue well: "A dialectical tension is required that must be carefully maintained by worship planners — to maintain a liturgical form, whatever style that might involve, that actually frees worship participants to focus on God without being distracted by either novelty or monotony."[8] As we move between these two poles, we need both patience and persistence. We need to search for shared artistic and religious values, speak to questions that animate the entire community, and look for artistic forms and styles that are meaningful to people who inhabit the various subcultures that exist in the church. We should assume that people can learn from one another's values, sense the import of fresh questions, and be enlivened by new artistic languages, some of which require not only exposure but a modicum of education. If we practice both patience and persistence consistently, we will create the conditions in which a congregation can learn to trust us. This is critical if arts ministry is to succeed.

8. Marva J. Dawn, *Reaching Out without Dumbing Down: A Theology of Worship for the Turn-of-the-Century Culture* (Grand Rapids: Wm. B. Eerdmans, 1995), p. 246.

Success in arts ministry is based on the assumption that people can grow. The assumption that growth is impossible is itself idolatrous, because it does not recognize the human condition. We are people made in the image of the God who initiated a redemptive process that embodies change and growth as fundamental principles. To say that we cannot change, that we cannot grow, is to admit that sin has won. It is to proclaim that we are a people without hope, without the means to grow, and without a future. It is utterly and completely unbiblical. It is simply not an acceptable position for the church to take.

By definition, arts ministry requires change. Sometimes this change will occur in worship, and sometimes it will happen elsewhere. In whatever setting it happens, art is all about changing perceptions by showing us the world in a new way. Arts ministry without change is a contradiction in terms. The real question is not *whether* change will happen, but *how* it will happen. It is a question of process, not product.

Theodor Seuss Geisel (more commonly known as Dr. Seuss) wrote a classic in the field of aesthetics entitled *Green Eggs and Ham*. The metamorphosis that takes place in this book is heartening for arts ministers. Sam, the hero of the story, is faced with the challenge of eating green eggs and ham, a combination he finds distasteful without having ever tried it. He opens with the exclamation "I do not like green eggs and ham!" By the end of the story, he has changed his approach: "Say! I like green eggs and ham! I do! I like them, Sam-I-am!"[9] It turns out that simple exposure, in combination with the qualities of thoughtfulness and playfulness, changed Sam to the point where he was empowered to try something new and, in so doing, discovered that green eggs and ham were not so bad after all. Patience and persistence won the day. The same thing can happen in the church. If we are thoughtful in our approach to introducing art in the church and playful in our presentation, people can discover for themselves the delightful qualities of art that at one time might have eluded or even frightened them.

This is the delicate balance we need to achieve in arts ministry. We must be thoughtful and playful, pastoral and prophetic as we engage with others who have their own unique histories and sensitivities. This dialectical approach to arts ministry can be practiced over time just as one practices the clarinet or a pirouette. Under the guidance and direction of the Spirit, it can bear much fruit in the life of the church and beyond.

9. Theodor Seuss Geisel, *Green Eggs and Ham* (New York: Beginner Books, 1960).

Potential Pitfalls

There are many potential pitfalls to avoid in the creation and development of arts ministry. I have selected five to discuss here: (1) art as a manipulative tool; (2) relevance: acquiescing to the messages of secular culture; (3) the allure of perfection and the temptation of cheap grace; (4) the cult of personality; and (5) stressing results over faithfulness. Each of them has the potential to undermine the goals and theological foundation of arts ministry.

Art as a Manipulative Tool

The question of the appropriate use of beauty has many dimensions. One facet of this issue is the way art is misused in both the church and the wider culture when it becomes a manipulative tool.

As we have already noted, Bernard of Clairvaux believed that excesses in materials, craftsmanship, size, and quantity of art create sensory saturation that manipulates the worshipper.[10] Hundreds of years after he lived, Baroque churches were designed for this very purpose. They used a combination of ostentatious architecture and visual art to overwhelm worshippers with images of the divine, in the process giving them the sense that they were actually caught up in heaven.

Harold Best points out the problem with this way of thinking: "Whenever we assume that art mediates God's presence or causes him to be tangible, we have begun the trek into idol territory."[11] Best suggests that this is what many church musicians do on Sunday morning. Musicians think that creating the right mood or emotional state in the worshipper will somehow cause God to be present in the service.

Rather than calling God into our midst, art often manipulates our senses, leaving us disordered and disoriented. The church may be built to make us think we are in heaven, but we are, in fact, still on earth, with all the problems and anxieties we had when we entered the door. A combination of architecture, music, paintings, and sculpture may be designed to give us the feeling that God is present, but ultimately God's presence to us

---

10. See Bernard's discussion of excesses in Conrad Rudolf, *The "Things of Greater Importance": Bernard of Clairvaux's Apologia and the Medieval Attitude toward Art* (Philadelphia: University of Pennsylvania Press, 1990), pp. 57-70.

11. Harold Best, *Unceasing Worship: Biblical Perspectives on Worship and the Arts* (Downers Grove, Ill.: InterVarsity Press, 2003), p. 166.

is a matter of divine sovereignty.[12] It is not something that is under our control. Although we cannot control God, we need to keep in mind that the manner in which we *sense* the divine presence in our worship life is also important. This varies with the turns and twists of our individual and corporate relationship to God. Any use of the arts as a means of channeling our relationship with God in a particular direction *could* be seen as an example of manipulation.

The question we must ask here — and it is a difficult question — is whether or not, *by definition,* almost every artistic product is not in some sense manipulative. From the Renaissance to the present, most Western art has been and is, at least in part, intended to move our affections, to impact our emotional life. It is often difficult to separate our affective response to artworks from our response to divine initiatives, particularly when both occur in the context of worship.

Is the issue of manipulation simply one of intent? Are we freed from the charge of manipulation if we offer worship to God sincerely and without any ulterior motives? I am never comfortable with this approach. It does not recognize the unintended effects that occasionally result from our actions. Sometimes we manipulate people without ever consciously attempting to do so.

What, then, constitutes artistic manipulation? Perhaps the key to unlocking this riddle is to look at the relationship between art and reality. Art that is non-manipulative is art that assists us in the process of living in right relation with ourselves, other people, God, and creation itself. Anything that causes these various relationships to be disordered is by definition manipulative and idolatrous.

---

12. The *Constitution on the Sacred Liturgy* (Gallagher translation) from Vatican II makes a more explicit statement about divine presence:

> Christ is always present in His Church, especially in her liturgical celebrations. He is present in the sacrifice of the Mass, not only in the person of His minister, "the same now offering, through the ministry of priests, who formerly offered himself on the cross," but especially under the Eucharistic species. By His power He is present in the sacraments, so that when a man baptizes it is really Christ Himself who baptizes. He is present in His word, since it is He Himself who speaks when the holy scriptures are read in the Church. He is present, lastly, when the Church prays and sings, for He promised: "Where two or three are gathered together in my name, there am I in the midst of them."

Relevance: Acquiescing to the Messages of Secular Culture

Simone Weil once said, "To be always relevant, you have to say things which are eternal."[13] The contemporary church has become saturated with a concern for relevance. This is often couched in the desire to meet "felt needs." In and of itself, there is nothing wrong with this notion. It is person-centered Christianity that takes seriously the plight of the individual believer. In a sense, this is nothing more than traditional pastoral theology and ministry at work.

The underlying question is this: What does the individual really *need*? This may be quite different than what they *want* at the moment. Finally, who will make this determination? This issue frequently arises in arts ministries that interact with popular culture. Products of popular culture are, almost by definition, what people in the congregation want, because they are popular. Does this mean that they are also what the congregation needs to further their growth and maturation process in the faith?

Speaking about music and preaching, Marva Dawn suggests some of the aesthetic and religious implications of this focus on relevance:

> Most movements to attract new members emphasize an appeal to the tastes of the public, stressing that music should be like that found in the outside world and that sermons should minister to worshippers' "felt needs." . . . How will we teach Christianity's specialness if the music in our worship services imitates the superficiality and meaninglessness of the general world and our sermons talk about subjects that those in the pew can learn from psychologists, sociologists, and the local television station? . . . Our music must contain the *substance* of the faith, the heritage of the Church's uniqueness, the character-forming truths of Christianity.[14]

This same question could be asked of the other arts as well. In North America, much of the creative use of the arts is occurring in churches that focus on popular culture. I believe that in many cases churches have collectively forgotten about (or never realized) the way that art works. *Artistic forms and styles imply underlying theological messages.* It would be impossible to overestimate the importance of this statement. Unfortunately, we

---

13. Simone Weil, quoted in Os Guinness, *No God but God: Breaking with the Idols of Our Age* (Chicago: Moody Press, 1992), p. 169.

14. Dawn, *Reaching Out without Dumbing Down*, p. 46.

have not learned to listen to what these forms and styles say to us. As we become sensitive to those messages through increased education in the arts and theology, the most important question becomes this: How can we be relevant and yet avoid prostituting ourselves to the prevailing secular culture? The answer we give will play a large part in determining the way in which our arts ministry impacts the life of the community of faith.

The Allure of Perfection and the Temptation of Cheap Grace

Artists in our society are taught to seek perfection. The culture encourages them to develop technique to the point that they avoid all errors. This becomes a virtual creed of artistic behavior for many young artists. The idea that a recording company would issue a compact disk containing wrong notes or rhythms is beyond the pale.

The modern notion of perfection is based on the exaltation of technique. Technique is a particularly seductive source of temptation to the artist. There is so much emphasis on technical perfection in the arts that technique itself often becomes a substitute for the true meaning of an artwork, or even for artistic expression itself. When we are concerned primarily with technique, we only have to ask how an artwork communicates meaning; we don't need to address the issue of what the artwork is trying to communicate.

In contemporary society, perfection is often confused with excellence. From the standpoint of Christian anthropology, perfection is an ill-fated standard in this world because it does not reflect the reality of the human person, who is out of sync with God and yet ultimately destined for union with God.

The other side of this equation is "cheap grace." This is all too prevalent in arts ministries. Here the artist is not held to any standard at all. Technical flaws are overlooked simply out of charity, especially since the artist is offering his or her gifts to God.

Once again, we find that the right course lies somewhere in between these two extremes. Artists must be held to a standard. Standards are important as a means of presenting artists with a goal, something objective against which they can judge their work. But in the world of pastoral ministry, the standard that really matters may be *growth*, growth that reflects the outer reaches of the artist's capability at the time. It is in this reaching, in this stretching to be the best that we can be, that excellence — defined as an *objective* standard of beauty, becomes a tantalizing possibility. Nonetheless, the closer we get to the goal of excellence, the more we should understand that the products of our artistry will never be "perfect." In fact, perfection is often the enemy of excellence. In the search for an abstract and disembodied perfection, we often lose sight of the very human qualities that make true excellence possible.

The notion of encouraging artists to come ever closer to a standard of excellence is particularly problematic in the case of children. There is a tendency in the church to undervalue children's capabilities. "Cute" becomes the standard, rather than teaching children and challenging them to use their abilities at full stretch. Art in the church should not just serve the needs of children. Rather, children in the church should use art to serve the needs of the community. They should be arts ministers themselves. In so doing, they are formed for lifelong praise of God. In the end this will serve children's real needs on a much more profound level.

The Cult of Personality

One of the shifts that occurred in the Western world after the eighteenth century was a change in the role and status of the artist. The Artist (with a capital "A") was put on a pedestal and worshipped by the public as a superhuman figure, a modern-day version of Michelangelo's *David*.

This was bound to have an impact on the church. In recent times we have seen singers, actors, and small ensembles emerging as the central focal point of worship, often to the detriment of "full, conscious, active"[15] congregational participation. On a larger scale, this is magnified by television and the recording industry, both of which create famous performers. In this setting, narcissism is often a problem. A celebrity-based understanding of worship and ministry engenders vicarious living and passivity on the part of the congregation. It is opposed to the biblical standard of humility and signals the death knell of true creativity.

Stressing Results over Faithfulness

At the root of many contemporary problems in the church is the issue of how to define success. Often this boils down to the question of assuring the survival and financial health of the local congregation. Numbers become a critical part of the equation of ministry, both the number of wor-

---

15. *Constitution on the Sacred Liturgy*, par. 14.

shippers and the number of dollars they give in the offering plate each Sunday.

In order to ensure an aura of success defined in these terms, it is important to keep the congregation comfortable. This has broad and potentially insidious implications for arts ministry. Often arts ministries start from humble beginnings. Since the ministries are new, involve unfamiliar artistic expressions, and impact worship, they have a tendency to threaten people. This conflicts directly with the need for comfort that is often expressed by church leaders who feel responsible for achieving an aura of success in their congregations. The absolute requirement to achieve comfort in the congregation means accepting the call to pastoral ministry and rejecting the need for prophetic ministry. Thus the dialectic between pastoral and prophetic ministry is broken. This can be a major roadblock for the budding arts ministry.

As Marva Dawn reminds us, "The danger to the Church is enormous and, strangely, often not obvious. Quality suffers when the main concern is quantity. . . . How destructive it is to genuine discipleship to measure the success of the Church by the numbers of people attracted rather than by the depth of faith and outreach nurtured."[16]

Rather than functioning in a prophetic role, the arts often become part of this program designed to achieve comfort, as Harold Best notes:

> We can easily make an idol out of the results we want our art to produce. Here is where artistic action and thinned-out versions of evangelization and seeker sensitivity can be such comfortable bedfellows. But I quickly add that popular art forms and careless versions of seeker sensitivity are not the only culprits. Many "fine arts Christians," the classicists, wag their fingers at the seeker-sensitive popularists without realizing that the kind of seeker sensitivity that depends on Bach and Rembrandt rather than Graham Kendrick and Thomas Kinkade is just as flawed. Why? Because in either case, effectiveness is the intermediary . . . anyone using any kind of art can compromise the gospel by choosing art primarily for the results it produces, rather than to glorify God.[17]

When results are placed ahead of faithfulness, idolatry has taken hold of a community. How should we define success in the church and in arts ministry specifically? Perhaps we need to return to fundamental theologi-

16. Dawn, *Reaching Out without Dumbing Down,* pp. 51-52.
17. Best, *Unceasing Worship,* p. 168.

cal goals such as the glorification of God and the sanctification of human beings. If this is happening, numbers should not be the issue; praise and holiness should be our standard.

In order to play a constructive role in the church, arts ministry must walk carefully through the minefield of this and the other potential problems we have identified. Only by naming them and taking them seriously can we avoid their pitfalls and craft a ministry based on the true beauty and creativity with which God has endowed us.

The Arts Minister: Key Things to Consider

Goals and Tasks

Before they can actively engage in their ministry, it is helpful for arts ministers to have a sense of the appropriate goals of their ministry, and how they might prepare themselves to realize those goals. Urban Holmes says, "The fundamental issue in ministry today is the recovery of a sense of enchantment and the ability to be enchanting."[18] This is clearly a goal that arts ministry can adopt. Among the many possible alternatives, it is one that virtually everyone in the church can agree upon. Thus it has the potential to be a unifying goal, a source of integration and inclusiveness.

Holmes goes on to say, "The world is disenchanted, not necessarily because God has died, has withdrawn, or has been discovered to be an illusion, but because, among the large majority of people, that data which would lead us to conclude that God is present in our experience is quite unconsciously, but effectively, not seen."[19]

Art heightens our awareness of the divine presence that is all around us. It helps us experience the mysterious, ineffable quality of the divine through sound and light, poetry and story, gesture and dance. Praise and worship are our direct response to this revelation.

Beyond this, arts ministry has two different but related tasks. William David Spencer identifies them as "lighting the world and shepherding the flock."[20] Arts ministry helps us see things as they are. It illuminates the

18. Urban T. Holmes III, *Ministry and Imagination* (New York: Seabury Press, 1981), p. 8.

19. Holmes, *Ministry and Imagination,* p. 56.

20. William David Spencer, *God through the Looking Glass* (Grand Rapids: Baker Book House, 1998), p. 155.

meaning and significance of the events and artifacts of our collective lives and brings the light of the gospel to bear on the problems we confront on a daily basis. In its shepherding role, arts ministry works as a vehicle for the expression of compassion by providing images that combat the fragmentation and alienation of contemporary life.

I have always liked the notion that arts ministers function as the artistic shepherds of their flocks. I do not know exactly what this means or how to enact it, but the concept is important. Rather than simply focusing on specific programs or ensembles or artistic products, arts ministers must focus on *people*, on the various ways that the arts impact their lives not only within the church but in every aspect of their living, be it in the home or in any of the other cultural settings in which they find themselves.

Within this broad framework, there are many specific goals that need to be established by individual ministries in light of their own unique circumstances. The process of working these out will determine the direction and orientation of the ministry. This is important work that must be continually revisited as each ministry grows and develops.

Gifts

Gifts, or charisms, from God are the source and foundation of all arts ministries. Romans 12:4-8 reminds us that we are all members of one body and that this body has a variety of different gifts. Arts ministry recognizes the diversity of creative gifts given to all God's people. It celebrates the plurality of artistic genres and fosters an environment where individual gifts are encouraged and developed in the church.

The fact of our giftedness and the way we express this in ministry is not something unusual or extraordinary. It comes from our baptism and is available to all. Baptism, says Thomas Franklin O'Meara, "initiates a person into charism and evangelical action, into a community which is essentially ministerial."[21] Our baptism is not a passive adoption that guarantees eternal life; it is an active adoption into a community that is on the path of discipleship, a path that mirrors the public ministry of Jesus. It grounds our creative gifts in the activity of God in Christ and sends us out into the world to use those gifts for the good of all.

---

21. Thomas Franklin O'Meara, *Theology of Ministry* (New York: Paulist Press, 1983), p. 141.

Education

While we are born as creative people and baptized into a community of faith, we are not born knowing how to be artists or how to engage in arts ministry per se. This means that we must be educated and trained in the various tasks that will be required of us. There are several different aspects to this education.

First, we need some theological acumen. This does not mean that we need to become professional theologians. It means that we should gradually become aware of the major theological questions regarding beauty and the arts, and that we should pay attention when sources come across our path, sources like the Bible, books about Christianity and the arts, periodicals, workshops, conferences, and teachers.

Second, we need to develop our own creative potential. There is no sense in forming an arts ministry if we ourselves are not going to be growing as creative people. The challenge is for everyone directly associated with arts ministry to find a creative outlet and to be intentional about developing it. Water your artistic or creative seed by giving it regular practice, and provide the sunshine that comes from being vulnerable to the work of the Creative Spirit, so that your seed can sprout and flourish in the rich ground of the church.

Next, we need to grow in our appreciation of the arts. No one brings equal depth to their grasp of all the fine arts, to say nothing of the many other outlets for human creativity that exist in the church. Arts ministers need to be open to the diverse approaches to God and reality that are engendered by different art forms. They should help those under their care to be similarly open and receptive, to learn how to appropriate the church's artistic tradition and develop their own intuitive capacities.

The laity will need to grow in the cognitive, affective, and, on occasion, psychomotor dimensions of their lives in order to participate fully in this ministry. This should not come as a surprise. Learning is already a part of the laity's normal experience in church. There are many skills that the laity learn and take for granted as they participate in worship each week. These skills were not inborn any more than were the skills of appreciation that I am discussing now. Skills of appreciation can be taught just as naturally and become a resource that the congregation can draw on as it encounters new and unfamiliar art forms.

Finally, arts ministers need to become aware of how the church works. Ministry is not done in isolation. It happens in the context of the Christian community. Arts ministry needs to be responsive to the different ways that the church enacts itself in its polity (governance), and in the social dynamics of the congregation. Without this awareness, arts ministry is not likely to have a long history or much of an impact on the church.

Practical Considerations

We now turn our attention to the birth and development of arts ministry in the church. There are other institutions that support arts ministries, including sacred arts organizations, museums, professional companies, and universities, but this discussion will be directed toward arts ministry's primary manifestation in the local faith community. I will treat this topic by looking first at how to lay the foundations for arts ministry and then by offering some thoughts about its subsequent development.

Please keep in mind that there are many different models of arts ministry. There is no privileged form or process. In a discipline that places a premium on creativity, the last thing we need is a rigid set of rules. What follows are a few thoughts based on practical experiences I have had over the years. If you find them helpful, that is all to the good. If not, feel free to be as creative as possible and invent your own model.

Before we start, it is important to address the question of the constituency for arts ministry. Who is involved with arts ministry in the local church? Thus far we have identified practitioners of the traditional fine arts, and we have talked about the creative potential of all God's people. Within this latter category I would like to turn our attention briefly to the specific issue of craftspeople.

A Preliminary Note about Craft

Since the Enlightenment there has been a division between the fine arts and craft. Craftspeople are often considered poor second cousins to artists. Often, beautiful artifacts that serve a practical purpose are not considered worthy of aesthetic contemplation. Utility is viewed as an aesthetic *defect* in an object. It is only when objects are no longer used for their original purpose that we stop to admire their ornamental qualities.

This division is unfortunate and certainly not biblical. Bezalel and Oholiab, the craftsmen of the tabernacle, along with all those who later worked on the temple, belie this elitist attitude. They were highly trained and valued for their skill and insight.

The division between art and craft is especially unwarranted in the context of arts ministry. Many of the people who engage in arts ministry in the church do so through the medium of crafts. True creativity overcomes the dichotomy between art and craft. Craft is born from the life of ordinary people. It grows from human experience, serves fundamental human needs, informs our living, and helps us achieve our ends.

Indeed, the standards and level of excellence embodied in fine craftsmanship are in no way less than those in the fine arts.[22] What may be different is the *higher* degree of connection with the local community (and, potentially, the community of faith) that occurs with craftspeople. Unlike artists, craftspeople have not moved further and further away from the tastes and aesthetic sensibilities of the community over the past several centuries. Craftspeople thrive in the local setting, sharing its values and mores. Cecilia Davis Cunningham elaborates:

> To be a potter today is to say that plastic cups, machine-stamped utensils, and mass-produced vessels are not enough. To be a potter, or any other craftsperson, is to opt for certain basic values that have informed our common humanity and seem worth nurturing. . . . Every craftsperson deals with the basic materials of the earth, works with tools that are part of a long, common heritage, sets out criteria to establish the craft, accepts a discipline of work, and, into this fundamental framework, inserts the self as worker.[23]

There is an intrinsic relationship between craftspeople, folk religion, and folk piety.[24] Craftspeople articulate the self-understanding of a com-

---

22. Thomas Aquinas says, "For a craftsman as such is commendable, not for the intention with which he does a work, but for the quality of the work." This quotation comes from Jean-Louis Crétien, *Hand to Hand: Listening to the Work of Art*, trans. Stephen E. Lewis (New York: Fordham University Press, 2003), p. 97.

23. Cecilia Davis Cunningham, "Craft: Making and Being," in *Art, Creativity, and the Sacred*, ed. Diane Apostolos-Cappadona (New York: Crossroad, 1989), p. 8.

24. Urban Holmes writes, "There is an integrity and authenticity to *folk piety*, just as there is to folk tales, fairy stories, and myths. They go hand-in-hand: the story and its piety. Both have the ability to convey transcendence with an incredible freshness, not only in spite of their essentially conservative nature, but because of it." See *Ministry and Imagination*, pp. 199-200.

munity in much the same way that folk religion and piety give us a glimpse of its living religious traditions. Craftspeople take this lived tradition and embody it in the material forms of their craft. Thus, to truly know a community, it is important to know something about their crafts.

Craftspeople form the backbone of the congregations in many churches. Compared to the attention the church has given to those who work in the fine arts, the church has often ignored craftspeople, and so they do their work in the private spaces of their lives or with other craftspeople outside the context of the church. Notable exceptions include the practice in many Lutheran churches of quilting and the similar practice of needlepoint that is often associated with Episcopal congregations. Circles of quilters meet in many congregations and work throughout the year to fashion lovely quilts that are subsequently donated to charity or mission work. Likewise, needlepoint circles meet to create kneelers for communion rails and chancel furniture. This is a shining example of what can and should happen more often as craft is embraced as an integral part of arts ministry.

It is now time to look at how, in union with artists, craftspeople, and the creative genius of ordinary parishioners, we might enact an arts ministry in the setting of the local church.

Stage One: Laying the Foundations

Someone has to get the ball rolling. In order to launch a new arts ministry, a facilitator of some sort needs to be identified. In many cases this may be the Director of Music, who is, ordinarily, the only professional artist on staff. Otherwise, facilitation could fall into the hands of another artist or simply a supporter of the arts in the congregation. Let's say that this person is you.

Arts ministry is developed within an institution. This offers both opportunities and challenges. Institutions, by their very nature, have their own culture, their own mission, and their own unique personalities. Every church has a particular set of idiosyncrasies that makes it distinctive in some way.

From the outset, it is important to understand something about the characteristics that make your church what it is. This means getting to know the structure and governance of the church and also getting to know the people who set the direction for the faith and witness of this particular congregation. Often these people will be members of the clergy, but in some instances committees or even individual parishioners may be the locus of authority and vision within a given congregation.

It is important for you to have their immediate support for whatever you are planning. Communication is a big key to the success of a new ministry. You should keep both the leadership and the congregation informed throughout the process of developing a new arts ministry.

You may or may not want to begin by launching a new ministry right away. Often it is better to plan a project of some sort and let the ministry grow out of the project rather than the other way around. This could be an adult education class on some aspect of Christianity and the arts. It could be a drama that is created for worship, a mural that is painted in the Sunday school hallway, a garden that is planted on the side lawn, a cooking class that is sponsored by the church, or a trip to hear a sacred music concert in the community. There are innumerable options.

While planning this initial event, you should get to know something about the congregation's background, tastes, and interests in regard to the arts. Often the leaders in a congregation may think they know the people's tastes and backgrounds when this is not really true. What music do parishioners listen to on their car radio or when they are relaxing at home? What paintings do they hang on their walls? Who has studied dance or taken an art appreciation course? Who has written poetry or acted in a play? In fact, in all likelihood, no one in the congregation really knows the artistic profile of the congregation as a whole.

To acquire this information efficiently and effectively, I suggest the use of a simple questionnaire, one that assesses the gifts, interests, training, and tastes of the congregation. You will see one example of an arts questionnaire in Appendix Two. It can easily be adapted to other situations. It could be included in a monthly newsletter or administered during the offering of a service. It takes only a few minutes to complete. Encourage as many parishioners as you can to participate. The information that you glean from this process will be invaluable for a long time to come. It will help you identify the artistic gifts that already exist in the congregation and provide a snapshot of their aesthetic sensibilities.

It would also be appropriate to teach an adult education course on the arts. Allow the class to help you lay the groundwork for arts ministry. For instance, you might teach about creativity and beauty. Identify areas of life in which people are already being creative, and have them present these to the class. Help people learn how to dream. Give them a blank piece of paper and encourage them to create their ideal job or their perfect vacation. Ask them to talk about and present examples of things they have collected in their lives — be it pottery or coins or chess sets or knickknacks or dolls. Have them envision possibilities for creative work in the church. Take the class to an art gallery or a concert or a dance recital. Bring music and visual art and poetry and movement into the classroom via recordings, slides, picture books, and so on. Have guest lecturers present the creative dimension of their lives or art forms. Engage the class in writing their own poetry or making their own drawings. Let them share their recipes and bring examples to pass, show off their woodworking or their knitting or the way they tie their own fishing flies. Help them learn to play again, to rediscover what it means to wonder at the world. The possibilities are virtually endless. What's more, these classes are enjoyable for the teacher and the students. It is easy to engender enthusiasm for this kind of a class, which in turn makes it a good springboard for a fledgling arts ministry.

In the process of experiencing the creative dimension of living, introduce the participants to a few basic theological notions like the ones we have already discussed: holistic living, along with the doctrines of creation, incarnation, and eschatology. Show them transcendent and immanent examples of sacred art. Help them see how art functions as a prophetic form. Slowly integrate their own artistic experiences and understanding into a coherent vision of how creativity and beauty can be used appropriately in the church and in their homes. This necessarily involves giving them some sense of the limits of art and the power of art to work for good or evil in the world depending on how it is used. Finally, help them understand that they are all artists in their own right and that the liturgy itself is an art form in which they are co-participants.

When you administer the questionnaire and teach the first class, you will begin to identify a group of people who have a particular interest and/or background in one or another of the arts or crafts. Bring these people together to sound them out about their interest in creating an arts ministry at the church. This will be the core of your arts committee. I would follow this up with a more extended meeting, perhaps in a retreat setting where they are not worried about picking up the kids from baseball practice or sending the next fax. The purpose of this retreat would be to iron out many of the details of what the initial arts ministry might look like.

Each time this group gets together, engage in prayer, include one concrete experience with sacred art, and hold an efficient organizational and planning session. If you can find copies, a very good resource to employ with this group is the book *Full Circle* by Nena Bryans, the book that initially inspired the current study.[25] Bryans not only provides ideas about arts ministry but also presents quotations from significant theologians and artists who discuss the relationship between art and faith.

It is also important to identify and catalog the work in arts ministry that has been done at this church in the past and the work that is ongoing in the present. Virtually every congregation has a history of arts ministry whether they know it or not. Uncovering and naming these activities helps to legitimize the notion of arts ministry in the initial stages of the discussion. While identifying these ministries is important, the participants in existing ministries should be welcomed as partners with the new arts ministry that is forming, not forced to see themselves under its umbrella.

At some point the time will be right to make initial decisions about the direction you would like the ministry to take. This requires identifying and discussing different models of arts ministry. One key decision that needs to be made early in the process involves whether or not your arts ministry will restrict itself to presenting sacred art or simply present any art as part of its mission. Both models are possible, but they make different assumptions and travel in very different directions over time. Another decision involves work within liturgy and work outside of formal worship. A mission and vision statement should be written that address these and related issues.

Based on the decisions you make, you should begin considering a name for the new ministry. Naming is a highly creative activity whose significance should not be underestimated. While naming is not absolutely necessary, I have found that a name gives a sense of identity and belonging to those whose commitment is still fragile. It helps solidify their own connection to the ministry and energizes them for the work that follows. It also helps to identify the ministry to others in the congregation and beyond who may not see it as a distinct offering of the church simply because they are unaccustomed to the idea of arts ministry in the first place.

As the seeds of an idea are planted and a direction begins to emerge, programming will be a natural part of the discussion. Although this may seem counter-intuitive, I would suggest starting outside of worship for the first year's programs. Worship is an area that is near and dear to the hearts of the faithful. Introducing new creative and artistic elements into worship

25. Nena Bryans, *Full Circle: A Proposal to the Church for an Arts Ministry* (San Carlos, Calif.: Schuyler Institute for Worship and the Arts, 1988).

at the beginning can be inflammatory. Parishioners need to be prepared for what will happen in worship through education and through establishment of an environment in the wider ministry of the church that is open to the arts. Look for opportunities to enhance the artistic quality of current ministries within the church, whether or not they currently focus on the arts. Sometimes hidden connections will emerge. The parish nurse and the spiritual life committee are both concerned with aspects of holistic living. So is arts ministry. How might these ministries relate to one another in the context of encouraging holistic life in the parish? What about the religious education program? Could there be units involving the arts that are integrated into the Sunday school or youth group activities? Simply raising these questions often leads to creative ideas on the part of the committee.

Sometimes monthly programs are a good way to begin. These might include showing a religious film and having a discussion period that follows, taking a trip to a local museum where a docent leads a tour of sacred art, sponsoring a concert of sacred choral music sung by the choir of a local college or university, planning a tour of local church architecture, presenting a class with a fine chef who demonstrates how to make creative desserts, planning an evening of poetry reading, or holding a church square dance. Once again, there are almost no limits to the possibilities once you begin to examine the options available in your area. Often you will find that the only things holding you back are the limits of your own imagination.

Finally, in this initial stage, take the results from the questionnaire and bring people with similar interests together just to see what happens. Often they will not know that others share their passions, and it will not have occurred to them that there is any role for their creative work in the church. One of the results of this can be the creation of interest groups or clubs: book clubs, cooking clubs, woodworking clubs, gardening clubs, and so on. The result of this work will be an enhanced atmosphere that is supportive of human creativity and open to new possibilities for ministry. In any case, simply becoming aware of people's artistic profiles and histories will develop their sense of community with one another by opening up new avenues of interaction within the congregation.

Stage Two: Development

As you emerge from the first year of activity, it is important to evaluate what you've done in light of your goals. It is also time to begin working to-

Religious Arts Festival
Independent Presbyterian Church, Birmingham, Alabama

The Boy Jesus by Vincent Palumbo, Master Carver at the
National Cathedral, Washington, D.C. The sculpture was
begun at Independent Presbyterian Church in Birmingham
during the 1981 Religious Arts Festival. At this festival,
children helped Palumbo chip away at the limestone.
Palumbo then took the limestone back to Washington,
completed the work the next year, and returned to
Birmingham, where it was dedicated during the 1982
Religious Arts Festival.

A religious arts festival is a time for the church to bring together the various sacred arts in a setting where both the local church and the community at large can experience the full panoply of the Judeo-Christian artistic tradition. The religious arts festival at Independent Presbyterian Church in Birmingham is one of the most well-known festivals in the United States. The festival began in 1972 as a week-long event whose purpose is "to glorify God through the rich spectrum of the arts."* The intent of the Fine Arts Committee of the church is to provide the festival as a gift to the city of Birmingham. Indeed, the festival attracts its audience from the community as much as it does from the church. The festival is administered each year by the Director of Music and Fine Arts in conjunction with approximately fifteen volunteers.

During the years of its operation, the festival has included a wide spectrum of guest speakers and artists with expertise in drama, music, dance, architecture, literature, and the visual arts. A few traditions have gradually developed. Typically, Friday night is "early music night," and Thursday night features a banquet with either a lecture or a theatre work presented afterwards. There have been concerts, special liturgies, visual art shows, dramatic presentations, lectures, readings, and dance presentations. In addition, the festival has been responsible for commissioning visual artworks, many of which are retained and displayed throughout the church and its retirement community facility. Anthems and other music have also been commissioned by the festival and are incorporated into the church's music library and worship life.

*Jeff McLelland, e-mail to the author, 30 June 2009.

ward embedding the new arts ministry in the institutional fabric of the church. This means two things: staff and budget.

By staff, I mean creating the position of arts minister. In recent years, published job descriptions for the music minister have often expanded to read "minister of music and the arts." This is one logical route to take. However, there is no guarantee that the music minister will have either the time or the interest in arts ministry needed to take on these new responsibilities. In this case the position could be independent of the music ministry, held either by a volunteer who coordinates the arts ministry or by a paid staff person.

The arts minister should be someone who can lead by listening, who can foster conversation with the goal of reaching consensus. She or he should be able to generate options that make sense for this particular congregation, and be accountable for the choices that have been made and the various tasks that need to be accomplished.

In addition to finding an arts minister, establishing a budget is another important priority. Creating a budget says to a church that this ministry is valuable. It acknowledges that paying for beauty and creative work is a legitimate part of the church's business alongside other staff positions and ministries. However small the amount may be at first, there should be a regular budget line established for this ministry early on. This will also help the ministry to have a concrete presence in the minds of the parishioners and the church leadership.

Programming during the second and subsequent years may very well enter the arena of worship. As it does this, education will be required. This should come in as many different forms as possible. An adult education class on worship and the arts could be offered; newsletter columns and bulletin notes could be written; sermons on beauty and the arts could be preached. Every opportunity should be explored to help the people understand what is being done and why it is being done.

At the outset, arts ministry might simply focus on existing liturgical ministries, with the goal of helping them perform their own functions in as artful a fashion as possible. Helping the lectors, the cantors, and the servers do their jobs well has the potential to make a real difference in the aesthetic quality of the liturgy.

In conjunction with this, focusing attention on the environment of worship is also a good way to begin. There are many creative options that could enhance worship beyond simply another banner. Using fabric itself in innovative ways, employing materials from nature like large stones and vines, and paying attention to the individual character of the seasons of the church year all make a big difference in the way the architecture of the church interacts with the liturgy.

One other dimension of arts ministry that impacts worship is the potential for the creation of new ensembles. These might include liturgical dance companies, drama troupes, or new musical ensembles. They can be intergenerational or focus on one particular segment of the congregation. Whatever their make-up, the choice of director is critical. The success or failure of the ensemble is largely a result of the background and gifts of the director. In many instances sincerity and willingness to serve are the only qualifications considered. While these are undoubtedly important, training and artistic competence should be weighted heavily when making a new hire. Students or faculty from local colleges and universities often provide good options to fill these positions.

The culmination of the program year for an arts ministry is often an arts festival. These come in a variety of different forms. Often they occur over the course of a weekend and include a variety of programs. Workshops, lectures, creative worship services, tours, concerts, and films are just some of the options for such a festival. One of the advantages of arts festivals is that they provide an easily articulated rationale for introducing creative worship to a congregation. Parishioners are likely to be more open to creative ventures when they occur on special occasions like this. This enables them to be exposed to new art forms like dance, to which they might not otherwise be so receptive.

Conclusion

Arts ministry represents an exciting opportunity for the church and for Christian people everywhere. It offers the hope of deepening the affinity between human reason, intuition, affection, spirituality, and the life of the body. It gives parishioners a new vantage point from which to view their own lives, other people, the world around them, and God, a view that is based in reality yet emanates in some mysterious way from a transcendent realm that is beyond our ability to fully conceive or replicate. Arts ministry promises a more tangible communion with the Christian community and with nature, and a heightened sense of life lived as creative people made in the image of a Creator God.

Finally, arts ministry provides a foretaste of the feast to come, a brief hint of our future existence in the City of Light, a place where beauty and celebration will be our chief goal and delight. It offers a range of tools we need to continue on our journey toward this glorious end. As we take up the challenge and opportunity of arts ministry, let us lay claim to the gift of beauty and walk with passion and wonder through the paths and contours of God's rose garden. Let us join the General Dance.

Selected Resources in the Sacred Arts

In recent years there has been a proliferation of creative ventures in support of various aspects of the sacred arts. Following is a listing of representative examples that illustrate the breadth and depth of current activity. It is by no means exhaustive. A simple listing of long-standing religious arts festivals or performing companies with accompanying descriptions would make a small book all by itself.

I found one decision in this area particularly difficult. In light of the ecumenical orientation of this book, I decided to omit denominational organizations from this listing. Many denominational organizations exist to support one or more of the sacred arts. They make a great contribution to the sacred arts landscape and provide unique and worthwhile resources of their own. I encourage readers to search online and to contact their denominational headquarters to locate the organizations that best suit their needs. I have also decided to omit sacred music organizations and academic programs from the mix simply because of their sheer numbers.

The information included in this appendix is current as of the publication date of this book. Given the normal history and development of professional organizations, both contact information and programmatic offerings will undoubtedly shift over time. All quotations included in these descriptions have been drawn directly from the institutions' Web sites.

SACRED ARTS ORGANIZATIONS

Christians In Theatre Arts

WEB SITE:	http://www.cita.org
E-MAIL:	information@cita.org
MAILING ADDRESS:	P.O. Box 26471, Greenville, SC 29616
DESCRIPTION:	"Christians In Theatre Arts (CITA) has been organized to give Christians a continent-wide support network of other believers who are also theatre artists. Whether you're leading or participating in a church drama ministry, or teaching at a high school or college, or working in the professional theatre; whether you're a performer, director, designer, or playwright, CITA is dedicated to serving you!"
FOUNDED:	1987
PUBLICATIONS:	*Christianity and Theatre:* semi-annual periodical
	CITANews: online, monthly
	Faith on Stage: Five Complete Plays
	Performing the Sacred: Theology and Theatre in Dialogue by Dale Savidge and Todd E. Johnson
OFFERINGS:	CITA Consultancy Program
	Employment listings
	Regional and national conferences
	Play and sketch contest

Christians in the Visual Arts

WEB SITE:	http://www.civa.org
E-MAIL:	office@civa.org
PHONE:	978-867-4124
MAILING ADDRESS:	255 Grapevine Road, Wenham, MA 01984

DESCRIPTION/MISSION: CIVA "exists to explore and nurture the relationship between the Visual Arts and the Christian Faith.... It is our purpose to encourage Christians in the visual arts to develop their particular callings to the highest professional level possible; to learn how to deal with specific problems in the field without compromising our faith and our standard of artistic endeavor; to provide opportunities for sharing work and ideas; to foster intelligent understanding, a spirit of trust, and a cooperative relationship between those in the arts, the church, and society; and ultimately, to establish a Christian presence within the secular art world."

FOUNDED: 1979

PUBLICATIONS: *SEEN:* semi-annual periodical

CIVA E-News: monthly

CIVA Membership Directory

CIVA Codex Series: I-VI — "a showcase for CIVA artists"

OFFERINGS: Biennial national conference

The Glen Workshop: a weeklong annual workshop/festival/symposium held at St. John's College in Santa Fe, New Mexico

European study tours

Calendar of annual and biennial sacred arts exhibitions

Traveling exhibitions

CIVA blog

Interfaith Forum on Religion, Art, and Architecture

WEB SITE: http://www.aia.org/practicing/groups

E-MAIL: Rotating

PHONE: Rotating

MAILING ADDRESS: Rotating

MISSION: "The Interfaith Forum of Religion, Art, and Architecture (IFRAA) is a Knowledge Community of the American Institute of Architects. It promotes an exchange of ideas, values, and strategic information specifically relating to the design and construction of buildings, landscapes, and works of art that serve a sacred purpose."

PUBLICATIONS: *Faith and Form:* quarterly journal

OFFERINGS: Religious Art and Architecture Design Awards: This program "was founded in 1978 with the goal of honoring the best in architecture, liturgical design, and art for religious spaces. The program offers three primary categories for awards: Religious Architecture, Liturgical/Interior Design, Sacred Landscape, and Religious Arts."

Study Tours

The Edward S. Frey Award is "given to an architect to recognize his or her contributions to religious architecture and support of the allied arts."

The Elbert M. Conover Memorial Award recognizes non-architects for their contributions to the field of religious architecture.

Conferences

The Labyrinth Society

WEB SITE: http://labyrinthscciety.org

E-MAIL: tlspr@labyrinthsociety.org

PHONE: 877-446-4520; 607-387-5863

MAILING ADDRESS: The Labyrinth Society, P.O. Box 736, Trumansburg, NY 14886

MISSION: "To support all those who create, maintain, and use labyrinths, and to serve the global community by providing education, networking, and opportunities to experience transformation."

FOUNDED: 1998

PUBLICATIONS: *TLS e-Newsletter*

Labyrinth Pathways: print journal

OFFERINGS: Online resources including the following:

World-Wide Labyrinth Locator: co-sponsored by the Labyrinth Society and Veriditas (see http://veriditas.org)

Bibliography

Labyrinth types: A guide to the many kinds of labyrinths found all over the world

Labyrinth links

Sacred Geometry: Three different ways to relate Sacred Geometry to the labyrinth

365 Club Daily Walkers

Activities for kids

Artline Project: building labyrinths along the 39th latitude

Download of a Labyrinth

Virtual Walks: Walk the labyrinth online

Labyrinths in Places: An examination of the ways that labyrinths are used

Making a Labyrinth

Events calendar

Annual gathering

Network of Biblical Storytellers

WEB SITE: http://www.nbsint.org

E-MAIL: nbs@nbsint.org

PHONE: 800-355-6627; 317-931-2352

MAILING ADDRESS: Christian Theological Seminary, 1000 W. 42nd Street, Indianapolis, IN 46208

DESCRIPTION/MISSION: "We are an international organization whose purpose is to communicate the sacred stories of the biblical tradition. Our mission is to encourage everyone to learn and tell biblical stories. At the heart and core of our Network are five general convictions that we share as a community: (1) Tell and hear biblical stories. (2) Explore the connection between the biblical stories and contemporary life. (3) Find divine power for transforming our lives. (4) Have our deepest needs met. (5) Encourage research."

FOUNDED:	1977
PUBLICATIONS:	*Scholarly Musings:* online quarterly
	The Biblical Storyteller: periodical
	Story Journey by Dr. Thomas Boomershine
	How to Learn and Tell a Biblical Story: DVD by NBS Productions
OFFERINGS:	The Academy for Biblical Storytelling provides a process of training and support in certifying biblical storytellers.
	An annual four-day festival offers keynote addresses, workshops, and storytelling events.
	The NBS Seminar is a group of professors at seminaries and colleges around the United States, full-time professional storytellers, and clergy who use storytelling as a central dimension of their ministry.
	Storyteller directory
	Storytelling tours
	Audio stories
	Video stories
	Online bookstore

Partners for Sacred Places

WEB SITE:	http://www.sacredplaces.org
E-MAIL:	partners@sacredplaces.org
PHONE:	215-567-3234
MAILING ADDRESS:	Partners for Sacred Places, 1700 Sansom Street, 10th Floor, Philadelphia, PA 19103
MISSION:	"Partners for Sacred Places brings together a national network of expert professionals who understand the value of a congregation's architectural assets, its worth as a faith community, and the significance of its service to the community at large. . . . Partners is the only national advocate for the sound stewardship and active community use of America's older religious properties. In-

formed by its research, Partners is building a shared sense of responsibility for the future of sacred places."

FOUNDED: 1989

PUBLICATIONS: "Partners for Sacred Places publishes and distributes books and pamphlets that help congregations maintain their historic buildings and raise funds to make capital improvements."

Sacred Places: quarterly journal

Your Sacred Place Is a Community Asset: A Tool Kit to Attract New Resources and Partners

The Complete Guide to Capital Campaigns for Historic Churches and Synagogues

OFFERINGS: New Dollars/New Partners for Your Sacred Place is an intensive program that gives congregations with older buildings the skills and resources to broaden their base of support.

Making Homes for the Arts in Sacred Places: "a program aimed at fostering successful partnerships between arts groups and congregations."

Economic Valuation Studies: "In 2010, Partners for Sacred Places and the University of Pennsylvania School of Social Policy and Practice concluded a pilot study of the economic impact of houses of worship. . . . We have pioneered a new quantitative approach to understanding how congregations impact local economies."

Capital Campaign Consulting

Adaptive and/or Community Use

Food in Sacred Places Initiative: "partner with other organizations on a range of options: growing food outdoors on their property; implementing community nutrition programming such as cooking or nutrition classes in their kitchens and social halls; hosting environmental education events, farmers markets, incubator kitchens, and community-supported agriculture programs on their premises."

Regional offices in Pennsylvania, Illinois, and Texas

Workshops and conferences

Information Center: This Web-based resource provides information related to the care and use of older sacred places.

Advocacy initiatives: Partners works with civic leaders, funders, and policymakers urging them to adopt policies and practices that provide new resources to older religious properties.

Quiet Garden Movement

WEB SITE:	http://quietgarden.org
E-MAIL:	info@quietgarden.org
PHONE:	+44 (0)1494 434873
MAILING ADDRESS:	The Quiet Garden Trust, Kerridge House, 42 Woodside Close Amersham, Bucks, HP6 5EF UK
DESCRIPTION/MISSION:	"Our vision is to initiate and resource a network of local opportunities for prayer, silence, reflection, and the appreciation of beauty; for learning about Christian spirituality; and for experiencing creativity and healing in the context of God's love. The Quiet Garden Movement encourages the provision of a variety of local venues where there is an opportunity to set aside time to rest and to pray. These may be: in private homes and gardens, in retreat centres or local churches, in inner-city areas, or in prisons."
FOUNDED:	1992
PUBLICATIONS:	*Quiet Places:* online newsletter
	In a Quiet Garden: Meditations and Prayerful Reflections by Brigid Boardman and Philip Jebb
OFFERINGS:	Associate Quiet Gardens
	Quiet Garden locator (worldwide)

Sacred Dance Guild

WEB SITE:	http://www.sacreddanceguild.org
E-MAIL:	admin@sacreddanceguild.org
PHONE:	877-422-8678

MAILING ADDRESS:	550M Ritchie Highway, #271 Severna Park, MD 21146
MISSION:	"The Sacred Dance Guild is an international, interfaith, non-profit organization with a commitment to advocate for the understanding of dance as a sacred art and to promote dance as a means of spiritual growth and integration of mind, body, and spirit."
FOUNDED:	1958
PUBLICATIONS:	*The Sacred Dance Guild Journal:* semi-annual periodical
OFFERINGS:	International festival
	Regional and chapter workshops
	Traveling workshops
	Sacred Dance Journey: international tours
	Sacred Dance Global Outreach
	Online:
	Events calendar
	Quotations about dancing
	Membership search

The Society for the Arts in Religious and Theological Studies

WEB SITE:	http://www.societyarts.org
E-MAIL:	Wilson Yates: wyates@unitedseminary.edu
	Kimberly Vrudny: kjvrudny@stthomas.edu
PHONE:	651-255-6190
MAILING ADDRESS:	ARTS, United Theological Seminary of the Twin Cities, 3000 Fifth Street Northwest, New Brighton, MN 55112
MISSION:	"The Society was organized to provide a forum for scholars and artists interested in the intersections between theology, religion, and the arts, to share thoughts, challenge ideas, strategize approaches in the classroom, and to advance the discipline in theological and religious studies curricula. The goal of the Society is to attract consistent participation of a core group of artists and scholars of theology and religion in order to have dialogue about

the theological and religious meaning of the arts, and the artistic/aesthetic dimension of theological and religious inquiry."

PUBLICATIONS: *ARTS: The Arts in Religious and Theological Studies:* bi-annual journal

OFFERINGS: Fellowships

Annual meeting

TEACHING RESOURCES: Syllabi exchange

Links to online collections

CENTERS

Grünewald Guild

WEB SITE: http://grunewaldguild.com

E-MAIL: office@grunewaldguild.com

PHONE: 509-763-3693

MAILING ADDRESS: 19003 River Road, Leavenworth, WA 98826

MISSION: "The mission of the Grünewald Guild, an ecumenical Christian community, is to promote and encourage creativity within individuals and congregations in response to the mystery of creation through the exploration of art and faith."

LOCATION: "The Grünewald Guild nestles amidst sweet-smelling ponderosa pine on the Wenatchee River in the Plain Valley, 14 miles north of Leavenworth Washington."

Buildings on the sixteen-acre site include the following:

"The Centrum is a remodeled Grange Hall. Downstairs, the kitchen and dining room accommodate up to 40 people a day. The main floor fellowship room is where guests relax, read, sit around the fire, or enjoy lively conversation."

"The Studio provides space for a variety of arts, including stained glass, printmaking, painting, drawing, calligraphy, ceramics, weaving, mosaic, and sculpture. We also have space for lectures, film, discussions, and other classes."

"The Fiber Arts Studio houses a large selection of looms and is where we teach weaving, quilting, and other fabric arts. The building contains five guest rooms, two bathrooms."

"The Homestead provides sleeping accommodations in five double rooms. There are two bathrooms, a hospitality area, laundry room and living room with views into the quiet forest."

"The Library was the original schoolhouse here in Plain Valley. Donated to the Guild, it now serves as a classroom and library. It also features a cozy, dorm-style sleeping loft."

FOUNDED:	1980
PUBLICATIONS:	*ArtFaith Magazine*
OFFERINGS:	Artist-in-residence program
	Internships
	Apprenticeship program
	Workshops
	Summer Program: "June through August, our Summer Program unfolds in a weeklong format, with course offerings in a wide variety of media: textiles, glass, clay, paint, ink, wood, stone, journal, and music."
	Study tours
	Retreats

EVENTS

Glen Workshop (sponsored by *Image*)

WEB SITE:	http://glenworkshop.com
E-MAIL:	glenworkshop@imagejournal.org
PHONE:	206-281-2988
MAILING ADDRESS:	3307 Third Avenue, West Seattle, WA 98119
DESCRIPTION:	"The Glen Workshop, a weeklong workshop/festival/symposium held at St. John's College in Sante Fe, New Mexico, and recently

at Mount Holyoke College in South Hadley, Massachusetts, in collaboration with *Image*. Includes writing classes, art classes, a seminar on arts and aesthetics, a retreat option. The Glen Workshop combines an intensive learning experience with a lively festival of the arts."

Calvin College Festival of Faith and Writing

WEB SITE:	http://festival.calvin.edu
E-MAIL:	ffw@calvin.edu
PHONE:	616-526-6770
MAILING ADDRESS:	Calvin College, 1795 Knollcrest Circle SE, Grand Rapids, MI 49546
MISSION:	"The Festival of Faith and Writing began as an exploration of the communities made and served by religious writing. Over the years, it has become a community itself — a gathering that encourages the many kinds of exchange that religious writing seems to occasion. Our intent is to bring together the different constituencies of this writing — authors, publishers, readers, and academics — for conversation and celebration. . . . We wish to locate, celebrate, and encourage serious imaginative writing by Christians of all denominations and communions. We welcome the work of writers in other faith traditions who acknowledge or seek spiritual understanding, grace, or transcendence."
FOUNDED:	2000 (biennial event)

MUSEUMS

Museum of Biblical Art

WEB SITE:	www.mobia.org
E-MAIL:	info@mobia.org
PHONE:	212-408-1500
MAILING ADDRESS:	Museum of Biblical Art. 1865 Broadway at 61st Street, New York, NY 10023-7505

MISSION:	"The Museum of Biblical Art celebrates and interprets art related to the Bible and its cultural legacy in Jewish and Christian traditions through exhibitions, education, and scholarship.... *MOBIA* creates an environment which encourages interfaith dialogue on the *history, meaning,* and *functions* of biblical art."
FOUNDED:	2005
OFFERINGS:	Exhibitions: "MOBIA organizes temporary exhibitions revealing the extraordinary diversity and richness of art inspired by the Bible through the centuries, including various media (painting, sculpture, graphic arts, mixed media, new media, etc.), styles, artistic movements and schools, etc.... Our goals include presenting an integrated approach that sets Biblical art and the religious traditions that fostered it within the context of history and social life; introducing the American public to subjects or types of art not often seen in other museums; and fostering interfaith dialogue by serving an audience of all religious backgrounds."

Educational offerings: "In our educational offerings, we are committed to meeting the growing need, in the immediate neighborhood and the larger New York metropolitan area, as well as nationwide via the web, for affordable arts experiences designed for children and families, and engaging lectures and symposia for adults."

Programs: "MOBIA offers concerts, lectures, film screenings, and special events to complement each exhibition."

The Rare Bible Collection

Internships: "Our interns benefit from the museum's small size by working closely with supervisors and gaining an understanding of the ways in which various departments within a museum interact."

Museum of Contemporary Religious Art

WEB SITE:	mocra.slu.edu
E-MAIL:	mocra@slu.edu
PHONE:	314-977-7170
MAILING ADDRESS:	221 N. Grand Blvd., St. Louis, MO 63103

MISSION: "MOCRA is the world's first interfaith museum of contemporary art that engages religious and spiritual themes. MOCRA is dedicated to the ongoing dialogue between contemporary artists and the world's faith traditions, and to serving as a forum for interfaith understanding. In a time when religion is viewed by many in exclusive ways, MOCRA intends to be inclusive and embracing, a center for healing and reconciliation."

FOUNDED: 1993

OFFERINGS: Exhibitions are complemented by lectures, symposia, performances, and other public presentations.

HIGHER EDUCATION

The Brehm Center for Worship, Theology, and the Arts at Fuller Theological Seminary

WEB SITE: http://www.brehmcenter.com

E-MAIL: brehmcenter@fuller.edu

PHONE: 626-304-3789

MAILING ADDRESS: Brehm Center, Fuller Seminary, 135 N. Oakland Avenue, Pasadena, CA 91182

MISSION: "The Brehm Center's mission is to revitalize the church and culture through the arts. We believe that God is the original artist, the first Creator. By engaging expert faculty, world-class artists, and visiting scholars to investigate the theory and practice of making art in ministry, we hope to inspire a new generation of culture-changers for Jesus' name. The Brehm Center and its initiatives sponsor research, community outreach, and integrated education in worship, theology, and the arts."

FOUNDED: 2001

OFFERINGS: A Brehm Center Emphasis can be pursued in tandem with any current Fuller Seminary Degree program in the schools of Theology, Psychology, or Intercultural Studies.

Theology and Arts Certificate

Master of Arts in Theology: Theology and Arts Emphasis

Master of Arts in Theology and Ministry: Worship, Theology, and the Arts Emphasis

Spirituality and the Arts Focus

Visual Faith Institute of Art and Architecture

Reel Spirituality: Faith, Film, and Culture

Online conversations

Artist-in-Residence program

Exhibitions

Conferences

Extensive coursework in theology, worship, and the arts both on-site and off-site

The Center for the Arts, Religion, and Education (CARE) at Graduate Theological Union

WEB SITE: http://care-gtu.org/

E-MAIL: info@care-gtu.org (CARE)

PHONE: 510-649-2400 (GTU); 510-849-8285 (CARE)

MAILING ADDRESS: Graduate Theological Union, 2400 Ridge Road, Berkeley, CA 94709
CARE: 2400 Ridge Road, Berkeley, CA 94709

MISSION: "Located at the Graduate Theological Union in Berkeley, The Center for the Arts, Religion, and Education's mission is to provide theological reflection and practice through educational curriculum in arts and religion and to present related arts programs that enhance the GTU community. CARE programs encourage scholarship in arts and religion through exhibitions at the Doug Adams Gallery, lectures, conferences, and grants. CARE also serves as a resource for local, regional, and national communities, including congregations, schools and colleges, and arts organizations."

FOUNDED: 1987

OFFERINGS: Ph.D. in Art and Religion

Workshops

Festivals

Conferences

Lectures

Panel discussions

Henry Luce III Center for the Arts and Religion, Wesley Theological Seminary

WEB SITE:	http://www.wesleyseminary.edu/LCAR.aspx
E-MAIL:	Various
PHONE:	202-885-8637
MAILING ADDRESS:	The Henry Luce II Center for the Arts and Religion, Wesley Theological Seminary, 4500 Massachusetts Ave. NW, Washington, DC 20016
MISSION:	"The Henry Luce III Center for Arts and Religion nurtures and guides students, churches, and artists exploring the intersection of the arts and theology. Its inviting Dadian Gallery serves as a meeting place for both contemplative reflection and communal celebration, playing host to compelling one-of-a-kind shows and spiritually themed exhibitions. A long-standing Artist-in-Residence program offers seminary students hands-on training in a variety of artistic traditions, while also providing artists with shared studio space and a spiritual home well suited to vital art-making. By producing dramatic works, concerts, artist talks, poetry readings, dance workshops, symposia, and other special events, the Center for the Arts and Religion seeks to promote dialogue between artists and theologians, and to foster inspired creativity in all forms of ministry."
FOUNDED:	1983
OFFERINGS:	Integration of the arts throughout the theological curriculum
	Certificate in Theology and the Arts
	Doctor of Ministry in Art and Religion
	Comprehensive artist residencies
	Open studio for artists-in-residence and students
	Museum-quality gallery

United Theological Seminary

WEB SITE:	http://www.unitedseminary.edu
E-MAIL:	Various
PHONE:	651-255-6137
MAILING ADDRESS:	United Theological Seminary of the Twin Cities 3000 Fifth Street Northwest, New Brighton, MN 55112
MISSION:	"Supports the educational mission of the seminary by providing students, staff, and faculty opportunities to engage the arts in learning both inside and outside of the classroom. The engagement of the arts takes place through the exhibition program, artists-in-residence, and coursework, and in lectures, worship, and the spiritual formation of our students."
	"Supports and contributes to the work of churches, faith communities, and artists by providing opportunities to explore the intersections of the arts and religion."
	"Provides a vehicle for experiencing and expressing the sacred through educational and experiential opportunities that engage the arts in relationship to the church's ministry and personal spiritual growth."
PUBLICATIONS:	*ARTS* magazine: co-published with the Society for the Arts in Religious and Theological Studies
OFFERINGS:	M.A. and M.Div. with theology and the arts concentration, D.Min. with concentration in the arts
	Integration of the arts into traditional seminary courses
	Artist-in-Residence program
	Four galleries
	Art with Soul: Annual art fair
	Summer Institute in Spirituality and the Arts
	Art studio

University of St. Andrews, St. Mary's College Institute for Theology, Imagination, and the Arts

WEB SITE:	http://www.st-andrews.ac.uk/itia
E-MAIL:	divpg@st-andrews.ac.uk
PHONE:	+44 (0) 1334 462850
MAILING ADDRESS:	School of Divinity, St. Mary's College, South Street, St. Andrews, Fife KY16 9JU, Scotland, UK
MISSION:	"The Institute for Theology, Imagination, and the Arts (ITIA) is a research institute based at St Mary's College, the Divinity School at the University of St. Andrews, Scotland. ITIA aims to advance and enrich an active conversation between Christian theology and the arts — bringing rigorous theological thinking to the arts, and bringing the resources of the arts to the enterprise of theology. As part of this, it seeks to explore the role of the imagination in the arts, as part of a wider theological interest in the imaginative aspects of our humanity."
FOUNDED:	2000
OFFERINGS:	Doctoral program
	MLitt. in theology, imagination, and the arts
	Undergraduate/graduate courses
	Conferences, seminars, colloquia
	Performances
	A publishing program including a series with Ashgate Press

Yale Institute of Sacred Music

WEB SITE:	http://www.yale.edu/ism
E-MAIL:	Various
PHONE:	203-432-5180
MAILING ADDRESS:	Yale Institute of Sacred Music, 409 Prospect Street, New Haven, CT 06511
MISSION:	"The Yale Institute of Sacred Music, an interdisciplinary graduate

center, educates leaders who foster, explore, and study engagement with the sacred through music, worship, and the arts in Christian communities, diverse religious traditions, and public life. Partnering with the Yale School of Music and Yale Divinity School, as well as other academic and professional units at Yale, the Institute prepares its students for careers in church music and other sacred music, pastoral ministry, performance, and scholarship. The Institute's curriculum integrates the study and practice of religion with that of music and the arts. With a core focus on Christian sacred music, the ISM builds bridges among disciplines and vocations and makes creative space for scholarship, performance, and practice."

FOUNDED: 1973

PUBLICATIONS: *Colloquium Journal:* annual

Prism: periodic online publication

OFFERINGS: Degree programs in choral conducting, organ, voice; early music; oratorio and chamber ensemble; church music studies; liturgical studies; religion and the arts

ISM Fellows Program: "The ISM Fellows Program offers scholars, religious leaders, and artists whose work is in or is moving to the fields of sacred music, liturgical/ritual studies, or religion and the arts an opportunity to pursue their scholarly or artistic projects within ISM's vibrant, interdisciplinary community."

ISM Study Tours

"The Institute offers a full schedule of concerts (some featuring Yale faculty and guest performers), drama, art exhibitions, films, literary readings, lectures, and multi-media events."

PERFORMANCE

A.D. Players

WEB SITE: http://www.adplayers.org

E-MAIL: various

PHONE: 713-439-0181

MAILING ADDRESS: 2710 W. Alabama, Houston, TX 77098

MISSION: "A.D. Players, founded in 1967 by Jeannette Clift George, pioneered a unique style of theater committed to producing plays and programs that uphold human value, offer creativity, and promote literacy and education."

FOUNDED: 1967

OFFERINGS: Five main-stage productions annually

Children's theatre

Theatre Arts Academy

National touring company

Internship program

Christian Youth Theatre

WEB SITE: http://www.cyt.org

E-MAIL: info@cyt.org

PHONE: 877-411-4298

MAILING ADDRESS: 1545 Pioneer Way, El Cajon, CA 92020

MISSION: Christian Youth Theatre "is dedicated to developing character in children and adults through training in the arts and by producing wholesome family entertainment, all of which reflect Judeo-Christian values."

FOUNDED: 1981

OFFERINGS: Theatre companies for children ages 4-18 located throughout the country.

Lamb's Players Theatre

WEB SITE: http://www.lambsplayers.org

E-MAIL: Office@LambsPlayers.org

PHONE: 619-437-6050

MAILING ADDRESS: Lamb's Players Theatre, P.O. Box 182229, Coronado, CA 92178

MISSION: "Lamb's Players Theatre is a professional, non-profit performing arts organization. The company's mission is to tell good stories well and be a theatre that: Probes and questions the values and choices of contemporary culture. Celebrates the joys, strengths, and diverse traditions of family and community. Explores the spiritual dimension of life. Champions the moral imagination."

FOUNDED: 1971; in 1994 the company moved to its new resident theatre in Coronado, California

OFFERINGS: Five main-stage productions annually in addition to a Christmas production

Lamb's Players Theatre Touring Company

Hip Pocket is an educational outreach program, "a multi-ethnic collaboration between local poets, actors, choreographers, and musicians designed to encourage literacy through the rhythm and power of word play in students' daily lives."

PlayWorks "introduces new material generated by, or written for, the Resident Ensemble or the LPT Touring Company."

Internship program

Summer camps

ONLINE RESOURCES

Journal of Religion and Film

WEB SITE: http://www.unomaha.edu/jrf

DESCRIPTION: "The *Journal of Religion and Film* examines the description, critique, and embodiment of religion in film. . . . The *JR&F* will consider not only films that explicitly highlight traditional religious images and themes. Although there will be analysis of films that consider such religious themes as sacred space, sacred times, savior-figures, images of god(s), and battles between good and evil, there also will be investigation of notions and assumptions that underlie everyday, 'secular,' human talk and action."

Arts Questionnaire

This questionnaire is designed to provide a brief glimpse into the artistic tastes, background, and interests of the congregation.

Name _____

Phone _____

E-mail: _____

Age Group: ☐ adult
                   ☐ high school
                   ☐ junior high

VISUAL ARTS

1. Do you create visual art yourself? If so, please check the appropriate categories:

   ☐ painting
   ☐ sculpture
   ☐ pottery
   ☐ photography
   ☐ fabric arts:
       ☐ quilting
       ☐ needlepoint
       ☐ embroidery
       ☐ knitting
       ☐ other (specify): _____

☐ woodworking
☐ jewelry-making
☐ stained glass
☐ other (specify): _____

2. Have you studied how to produce any of these visual art forms?

☐ No
☐ Yes:
    ☐ College
    ☐ Community education
    ☐ High school

3. Have you ever taken an art history or art appreciation course?

☐ No
☐ Yes:
    ☐ College
    ☐ Community education
    ☐ High school

4. Do you visit art museums?

☐ regularly
☐ on occasion
☐ never

LITERARY AND DRAMATIC ARTS

1. Have you ever participated in a play?

☐ No
☐ Yes:
    ☐ College
    ☐ Community education
    ☐ High school
In what capacity?
☐ acting
☐ costumes
☐ set
☐ lighting
☐ directing
☐ other (specify): _____

2. Have you ever engaged in creative writing?

   ☐ No
   ☐ Yes:
      ☐ poetry
      ☐ plays
      ☐ short stories
      ☐ keeping a journal
      ☐ other (specify): _____

3. Do you attend plays?

   ☐ regularly
   ☐ on occasion
   ☐ never

4. Do you read:

   ☐ poetry
   ☐ novels
   ☐ science fiction
   ☐ nonfiction
   ☐ magazines
   ☐ other (specify): _____

5. Do you watch movies?

   ☐ regularly
   ☐ on occasion
   ☐ never

6. What type of movies do you most enjoy seeing?

   ☐ art films
   ☐ comedies
   ☐ dramas
   ☐ action films
   ☐ horror films
   ☐ sci-fi films
   ☐ other (specify): _____

MUSIC AND DANCE

1. Have you ever learned to play a musical instrument?

   ☐ No
   ☐ Yes:
       What instrument did you learn to play? _____
       What instrument do you currently play? _____

2. Have you ever sung in a choir?

   ☐ No
   ☐ Yes:
       ☐ church
       ☐ community
       ☐ college
       ☐ high school
       ☐ elementary school
   Have you ever studied voice?
       ☐ No
       ☐ Yes

3. During a worship service, can you sing an unfamiliar hymn correctly on the first or second verse simply by listening and reading the musical notation of the hymn?

   ☐ No
   ☐ Yes

4. What style(s) of music do you prefer to listen to when you are at home or in the car? Please check only the styles which you listen to frequently:

   ☐ rock
   ☐ folk
   ☐ classical
   ☐ country
   ☐ pop
   ☐ jazz
   ☐ other (specify): _____

5. Do you attend concerts?

   ☐ regularly
   ☐ on occasion
   ☐ never

6. Have you ever taken a music appreciation, music history, or music theory course?

    ☐ No

    ☐ Yes:

        ☐ College

        ☐ Community education

        ☐ High school

7. How often do you dance?

    ☐ regularly

    ☐ on occasion

    ☐ never

8. Have you ever studied dance?

    ☐ No

    ☐ Yes

9. Do you attend dance recitals?

    ☐ regularly

    ☐ on occasion

    ☐ never

ARTS MINISTRY

I might be interested in the following possible ministries:

    ☐ film/discussion series

    ☐ concert series

    ☐ visual art show

    ☐ poetry ministry

    ☐ drama ministry

    ☐ dance ministry

    ☐ bell choir

    ☐ adult choir

    ☐ youth choir

    ☐ arts committee

Bibliography

Abbott, Walter M., ed. *The Documents of Vatican II*. Trans. Joseph Gallagher. New York: Guild Press, 1966.

Adams, Doug. *Eyes to See Wholeness: Visual Arts Informing Biblical and Theological Studies in Education and Worship through the Church Year*. Prescott, Ariz.: Educational Ministries, 1995.

————. *Postmodern Worship and the Arts*. San Jose, Calif.: Resource Publications, 2002.

Adams, Doug, and Diane Apostolos-Cappadona, eds. *Dance as Religious Studies*. New York: Crossroad, 1990.

————. *Art as Religious Studies*. New York: Crossroad, 1990.

Adler, Mortimer J. *Art, the Arts, and the Great Ideas*. New York: Macmillan Publishing Company, 1994.

Allen, Joseph J. *The Ministry of the Church: The Image of Pastoral Care*. Crestwood, N.Y.: St. Vladimir's Seminary Press, 1986.

Anderson, Byron. *Worship and Christian Identity: Practicing Ourselves*. Collegeville, Minn.: Liturgical Press, 2003.

Apostolos-Cappadona, Diane, ed. *Art, Creativity, and the Sacred*. New York: Crossroad, 1989.

Augustine. *The Confessions of St. Augustine*. Trans. John K. Ryan. New York: Doubleday, 1960.

Avis, Paul. *God and the Creative Imagination: Metaphor, Symbol, and Myth in Religion and Theology*. London: Routledge, 1999.

Barzun, Jacques. *The Use and Abuse of Art*. Princeton: Princeton University Press, 1975.

Bass, Alice. *The Creative Life: A Workbook for Unearthing the Christian Imagination*. Downers Grove, Ill.: InterVarsity Press, 2001.

Bausch, William J. *Storytelling: Imagination and Faith*. Mystic, Conn.: Twenty-Third Publications, 1984.

Begbie, Jeremy S. *Voicing Creation's Praise: Towards a Theology of the Arts*. Edinburgh: T&T Clark, 1991.

———. *Theology, Music, and Time*. Cambridge: Cambridge University Press, 2000.

———, ed. *Beholding the Glory: Incarnation through the Arts*. Grand Rapids: Baker Book House, 2001.

Berry, Wendell. *Hannah Coulter*. Berkeley, Calif.: Shoemaker & Hoard, 2004.

———. *Jayber Crow*. New York: Counterpoint, 2000.

———. *A Timbered Choir: The Sabbath Poems, 1979-1997*. Washington, D.C.: Counterpoint, 1998.

Best, Harold M. *Music through the Eyes of Faith*. San Francisco: HarperCollins, 1993.

———. *Unceasing Worship: Biblical Perspectives on Worship and the Arts*. Downers Grove, Ill.: InterVarsity Press, 2003.

Bonhoeffer, Dietrich. *Life Together*. Trans. John W. Doberstein. San Francisco: Harper, 1954.

Bowden, Sandra, and Ned Bustard, eds. *It Was Good Making Art to the Glory of God*. Baltimore: Square Halo Books, 2000.

Brand, Hilary, and Adrienne Chaplin. *Art and Soul: Signposts for Christians in the Arts*. Solway, Carlisle, U.K.: Piquant, 2001.

Brown, Frank Burch. *Good Taste, Bad Taste, and Christian Taste: Aesthetics in Religious Life*. Oxford: Oxford University Press, 2000.

Brown, J. Daniel. *Masks of Mystery: Explorations in Christian Faith and the Arts*. Lanham, Md.: University Press of America, 1997.

Brueggemann, Walter. *Biblical Perspectives on Evangelism: Living in a Three-Storied Universe*. Nashville: Abingdon Press, 1993.

———. *Finally Comes the Poet: Daring Speech for Proclamation*. Minneapolis: Fortress Press, 1989.

———. *The Prophetic Imagination*. Minneapolis: Fortress Press, 1978.

Bryans, Nena. *Full Circle: A Proposal to the Church for an Arts Ministry*. San Carlos, Calif.: Schuyler Institute for Worship and the Arts, 1988.

Calvin, John. *Institutes of the Christian Religion*. Trans. Henry Beveridge. Grand Rapids: Wm. B. Eerdmans, 1983.

Cameron, Julia. *The Artist's Way: A Spiritual Path to Higher Creativity*. New York: Jeremy P. Tarcher, 1992.

Card, Michael. *Scribbling in the Sand: Christ and Creativity*. Downers Grove, Ill.: InterVarsity Press, 2002.

Chinn, Nancy. *Spaces for Spirit: Adorning the Church*. Chicago: Liturgy Training Publications, 1998.

Chrétien, Jean-Louis. *Hand to Hand: Listening to the Work of Art.* Trans. Stephen E. Lewis. New York: Fordham University Press, 2003.

Collins, Patrick W. *Bodying Forth: Aesthetic Liturgy.* New York: Paulist Press, 1992.

Creaven, Fintan. *Body and Soul: A Spirituality of Imaginative Creativity.* London: Society for Promoting Christian Knowledge, 2003.

Crowley, Eileen D. *Liturgical Art for a Media Culture.* Collegeville, Minn.: Liturgical Press, 2007.

Daniels, Marilyn. *The Dance in Christianity: A History of Religious Dance through the Ages.* New York: Paulist Press, 1981.

Davies, J. G. *Liturgical Dance: An Historical, Theological, and Practical Handbook.* London: SCM Press, 1984.

Dawn, Marva J. *Reaching Out without Dumbing Down: A Theology of Worship for the Turn-of-the-Century Culture.* Grand Rapids: Wm. B. Eerdmans, 1995.

Dean, William. *Coming to a Theology of Beauty.* Philadelphia: Westminster Press, 1972.

Dewey, John. *Art as Experience.* New York: Perigee Books, 1980.

de Gruchy, John W. *Christianity, Art, and Transformation: Theological Aesthetics in the Struggle for Justice.* Cambridge: Cambridge University Press, 2001.

Dietering, Carolyn. *The Liturgy as Dance and the Liturgical Dancer.* New York: Crossroad, 1984.

Dillard, Annie. *Holy the Firm.* New York: Harper & Row, 1984.

Dillenberger, John. *A Theology of Artistic Sensibilities.* New York: Crossroad, 1986.

———, ed. *Paul Tillich on Art and Architecture.* New York: Crossroad, 1987.

Dixon, John W. *Art and the Theological Imagination.* New York: Seabury Press, 1978.

Dyrness, William. *Senses of the Soul: Art and the Visual in Christian Worship.* Eugene, Ore.: Cascade Books, 2008.

———. *Visual Faith: Art, Theology, and Worship in Dialogue.* Grand Rapids: Baker Academic, 2001.

Egenter, Richard. *The Desecration of Christ.* Trans. Edward Quinn. Chicago: Franciscan Herald Press, 1967.

Eire, Carlos M. N. *War against the Idols: The Reformation of Worship from Erasmus to Calvin.* Cambridge: Cambridge University Press, 1986.

Eliot, T. S. *Christianity and Culture.* San Diego: Harcourt, Brace, 1939.

———. *The Complete Poems and Plays: 1909-1950.* New York: Harcourt Brace Jovanovich, 1971.

Elsheimer, Janice. *The Creative Call: An Artist's Response to the Way of the Spirit.* Colorado Springs: WaterBrook Press, 2001.

Eskew, Harry, and Hugh T. McElrath. *Sing with Understanding: An Introduction to Christian Hymnody.* Nashville: Broadman Press, 1980.

Eusden, John Dykstra, and John H. Westerhoff III. *Sensing Beauty: Aesthetics, the Human Spirit, and the Church.* Cleveland: United Church Press, 1998.

Fallon, Dennis J., and Mary Jane Wolbers, eds. *Focus on Dance X: Religion and Dance.* Reston, Va.: The American Alliance for Health, Physical Education, Recreation, and Dance, 1982.

Farley, Edward. *Faith and Beauty: A Theological Aesthetic.* Burlington, Vt.: Ashgate, 2001.

Faulkner, Quentin. *Wiser than Despair: The Evolution of Ideas in the Relationship between Music and the Christian Church.* Westport, Conn.: Greenwood Press, 1996.

Fischer, Kathleen R. *The Inner Rainbow: The Imagination in Christian Life.* Mahwah, N.J.: Paulist Press, 1983.

Fiske, Harold E. *Music and Mind: Philosophical Essays on the Cognition and Meaning of Music.* Lewiston, N.Y.: Edwin Mellen Press, 1990.

Fox, Matthew. *Creativity: Where the Divine and the Human Meet.* New York: Jeremy P. Tarcher, 2002.

Frye, Northrop. The *Educated Imagination.* Bloomington: Indiana University Press, 1964.

Gaebelein, Frank E. *The Christian, the Arts, and Truth: Regaining the Vision of Greatness.* Portland, Ore.: Multnomah Press, 1985.

Gagne, Ronald, Thomas Kane, and Robert VerEecke. *Introducing Dance in Christian Worship.* Washington, D.C.: Pastoral Press, 1984.

Garcia-Rivera, Alejandro. *The Community of the Beautiful: A Theological Aesthetics.* Collegeville, Minn.: Liturgical Press, 1999.

————. *Living Beauty: The Art of Liturgy.* Lanham, Md.: Rowman & Littlefield, 2008.

————. *Wounded Innocence: Sketches for a Theology of Art.* Collegeville, Minn.: Liturgical Press, 2003.

Geisel, Theodore S., and Audrey S. Geisel. *Green Eggs and Ham.* New York: Beginner Books, 1960.

Gerding, Jeri. *Drawing to God: Art as Prayer, Prayer as Art.* Notre Dame, Ind.: Sorin Books, 2001.

Gilbertson, Carol, and Gregg Muhlenburg, eds. *Translucence: Religion, the Arts, and Imagination.* Minneapolis: Fortress Press, 2004.

Guiness, Os, and John Seel, eds. *No God but God: Breaking with the Idols of Our Age.* Chicago: Moody Press, 1992.

Halbertal, Moshe, and Avishai Margalit. *Idolatry.* Trans. Naomi Goldblum. Cambridge, Mass.: Harvard University Press, 1992.

Halewood, William H. *Six Subjects of Reformation Art: A Preface to Rembrandt.* Toronto: University of Toronto Press, 1982.

Hammond, Paul, and David Hopkins, eds. *The Poems of John Dryden, Volume III: 1686-1693.* Edinburgh Gate, Harlow, Essex, U.K.: Pearson Education Limited, 2000.

Harries, Richard. *Art and the Beauty of God: A Christian Understanding.* London: Continuum, 1993.

Heller, Ena Giurescu. *Reluctant Partners: Art and Religion in Dialogue.* New York: The Gallery of the American Bible Society, 2004.

Hoffman, Lawrence. *The Art of Public Prayer: Not for Clergy Only.* Washington, D.C.: Pastoral Press, 1988.

Holmes, Urban T., III. *Ministry and Imagination.* New York: Seabury Press, 1981.

Hoon, Paul Waitman. *The Integrity of Worship: Ecumenical and Pastoral Studies in Liturgical Theology.* Nashville: Abingdon Press, 1971.

Hutchins, Robert. *The Great Conversation.* Great Books of the Western World. Chicago: Encyclopaedia Britannica, 1952.

Irvine, Christopher. *The Art of God: The Making of Christians and the Meaning of Worship.* Chicago: Liturgy Training Publications, 2005.

Izard, Susan S., and Susan S. Jorgensen. *Knitting into the Mystery: A Guide to the Shawl-Knitting Ministry.* Harrisburg, Pa.: Morehouse Publishing, 2003.

Jensen, Robin M. *The Substance of Things Seen: Art, Faith, and the Christian Community.* Grand Rapids: Wm. B. Eerdmans, 2004.

Johansson, Calvin M. *Music and Ministry: A Biblical Counterpoint.* Peabody, Mass.: Hendrickson, 1984.

John of Damascus. *Three Treatises on the Divine Images.* Trans. Andrew Louth. Crestwood, N.Y.: St. Vladimir's Seminary Press, 2003.

John Paul II. *Letter of His Holiness John Paul II to Artists.* Boston: Pauline Books and Media, 1999.

Joncas, Jan Michael. *From Sacred Song to Ritual Music: Twentieth-Century Understandings of Roman Catholic Worship Music.* Collegeville, Minn.: Liturgical Press, 1997.

Kapikian, Catherine. *Art in Service of the Sacred.* Nashville: Abingdon Press, 2006.

Kaufman, Gordon D. *In the Beginning . . . Creativity.* Minneapolis: Fortress Press, 2004.

Kieckhefer, Richard. *Theology in Stone: Church Architecture from Byzantium to Berkeley.* Oxford: Oxford University Press, 2004.

Klaiber, Walter. *Call and Response: Biblical Foundations of a Theology of Evangelism.* Trans. Howard Perry-Trauthig and James A. Dwyer. Nashville: Abingdon Press, 1990.

Kroeker, Charlotte, ed. *Music in Christian Worship: At the Service of the Liturgy.* Collegeville, Minn.: Liturgical Press, 2005.

Küng, Hans. *Art and the Question of Meaning.* Trans. Edward Quinn. New York: Crossroad, 1981.

Laeuchli, Samuel. *Religion and Art in Conflict.* Philadelphia: Fortress Press, 1980.

Leaver, Robin A., and Joyce Ann Zimmerman, eds. *Liturgy and Music: Lifetime Learning.* Collegeville, Minn.: Liturgical Press, 1998.

L'Engle, Madeleine. *The Weather of the Heart.* Wheaton, Ill.: Harold Shaw, 1978.

Leupold, Ulrich S., ed. *Luther's Works: Liturgy and Hymns,* vol. 53. Philadelphia: Fortress Press, 1965.

Lewis, C. S. *The Last Battle*. New York: Collier Books, 1956.

Maus, Cynthia Pearl. *Christ and the Fine Arts*. New York and London: Harper & Brothers, 1938.

———. *The Church and the Fine Arts*. New York: Harper & Brothers, 1960.

May, Rollo. *The Courage to Create*. New York: W. W. Norton, 1975.

McKinnon, James. *Music in Early Christian Literature*. Cambridge: Cambridge University Press, 1987.

McLuhan, Marshall. *Understanding Media: The Extensions of Man*. Cambridge, Mass.: MIT Press, 1964.

Merton, Thomas. *The Literary Essays of Thomas Merton*. Ed. Patrick Hart. New York: New Directions, 1981.

———. *The Seven Storey Mountain*. New York: Harcourt, Brace, 1948.

Messiaen, Olivier. "Conférence de Notre Dame." Trans. Timothy J. Tikker. *The Diapason* 76 (January 1985): 10-11.

Miles, Margaret R. *Image as Insight: Visual Understanding in Western Christianity and Secular Culture*. Boston: Beacon Press, 1985.

National Conference of Catholic Bishops. *Environment and Art in Catholic Worship*. Chicago: Liturgy Training Publications, 1993.

———. *Music in Catholic Worship*. Washington, D.C.: National Council of Catholic Bishops, 1983.

Navone, John. *Enjoying God's Beauty*. Collegeville, Minn.: Liturgical Press, 1999.

———. *Toward a Theology of Beauty*. Collegeville, Minn.: Liturgical Press, 1996.

Niebuhr, H. Richard. *Christ and Culture*. New York: Harper, 1951.

Nouwen, Henri J. M. *Creative Ministry*. New York: Doubleday, 1978.

O'Brien, Mark, and Craig Little, eds. *Reimaging America: The Arts of Social Change*. Philadelphia: New Society Publishers, 1990.

O'Connell, Robert. *Art and the Christian Intelligence in St. Augustine*. Cambridge, Mass.: Harvard University Press, 1978.

O'Meara, Thomas Franklin. *Theology of Ministry*. New York: Paulist Press, 1983.

Panofsky, Erwin, trans. *Abbot Suger: On the Abbey Church of St.-Denis and Its Art Treasures*. Second edition. Princeton: Princeton University Press, 1946.

Pelikan, Jaroslav. *Imago Dei: The Byzantine Apologia for Icons*. Princeton: Princeton University Press, 1990.

Pfatteicher, Philip H. *The School of the Church: Worship and Christian Formation*. Valley Forge, Pa.: Trinity Press, 1995.

Pieper, Joseph. *Only the Lover Sings: Art and Contemplation*. San Francisco: Ignatius Press, 1990.

Plato. *The Dialogues of Plato*. Trans. Benjamin Jowett. Great Books of the Western World. Chicago: Encyclopaedia Britannica, 1952.

Pope, Rob. *Creativity: Theory, History, Practice*. London: Routledge, 2005.

Bibliography

Postman, Neil. *Amusing Ourselves to Death: Public Discourse in the Age of Show Business.* New York: Penguin Books, 1986.

Quasten, Johannes. *Music and Worship in Pagan and Christian Antiquity.* Trans. Boniface Ramsey. Washington, D.C.: National Association of Pastoral Musicians, 1983.

Rahner, Karl. *Belief Today.* New York: Sheed & Ward, 1967.

Rookmaaker, Hans. *The Creative Gift: Essays on Art and the Christian Life.* Westchester, Ill.: Cornerstone Books, 1981.

————. *Modern Art and the Death of a Culture.* Downers Grove, Ill.: InterVarsity Press, 1970.

Rorem, Paul. *The Medieval Development of Liturgical Symbolism.* Grove Liturgical Study no. 47. Bramcote, Nottingham, England: Grove Books, 1986.

Rosen, Charles. *The Frontiers of Meaning: Three Informal Lectures on Music.* New York: Hill & Wang, 1994.

Rosenthal, Peggy. *The Poets' Jesus: Representations at the End of a Millennium.* Oxford: Oxford University Press, 2000.

Rouet, Albert. *Liturgy and the Arts.* Trans. Paul Philibert, O.P. Collegeville, Minn.: Liturgical Press, 1997.

Rudolf, Conrad. *The "Things of Greater Importance": Bernard of Clairvaux's Apologia and the Medieval Attitude toward Art.* Philadelphia: University of Pennsylvania Press, 1990.

Ryken, Leland. *The Liberated Imagination: Thinking Christianly about the Arts.* Wheaton, Ill.: Harold Shaw, 1989.

Saliers, Don E. *The Soul in Paraphrase: Prayer and the Religious Affections.* New York: Seabury Press, 1980.

————. *Worship as Theology: Foretaste of Glory Divine.* Nashville: Abingdon Press, 1994.

————. *Worship Come to Its Senses.* Nashville: Abingdon Press, 1996.

Schaeffer, Francis A. *Art and the Bible.* London: Hodder & Stoughton, 1973.

Schalk, Carl F. *Luther on Music: Paradigms of Praise.* St. Louis: Concordia, 1988.

Schroeder, Peter W., and Sagmar Schroeder-Hildebrand. *Six Million Paper Clips: The Making of a Children's Holocaust Memorial.* Minneapolis: Kar-Ben Publishing, 2004.

Senn, Frank C. *The Witness of the Worshipping Community: Liturgy and the Practice of Evangelism.* New York: Paulist Press, 1993.

Schaff, Philip, and Henry Wace, eds. *The Nicene and Post-Nicene Fathers,* vol. 14: *The Seven Ecumenical Councils.* Grand Rapids: Wm. B. Eerdmans, 1956.

Shamana, Beverly. *Seeing in the Dark: A Vision of Creativity and Spirituality.* Nashville: Abingdon Press, 2001.

Sherry, Patrick. *Spirit and Beauty: An Introduction to Theological Aesthetics*. Oxford: Clarendon Press, 1992.

Shorter, Aylward. *Toward a Theology of Inculturation*. Maryknoll, N.Y.: Orbis Books, 1988.

Sloboda, John. *The Musical Mind: The Cognitive Psychology of Music*. Oxford: Clarendon Press, 1985.

Spencer, Jon Michael. *Theological Music: Introduction to Theomusicology*. New York: Greenwood Press, 1991.

Spencer, William David, and Aida Besançon Spencer. *God through the Looking Glass*. Grand Rapids: Baker Book House, 1998.

Stephens, Mitchell. *The Rise of the Image, the Fall of the Word*. Oxford: Oxford University Press, 1998.

Taylor, W. David O., ed. *For the Beauty of the Church: Casting a Vision for the Arts*. Grand Rapids: Baker Books, 2010.

Theodore the Studite. *On the Holy Icons*. Trans. Catherine P. Roth. Crestwood, N.Y.: St. Vladimir's Seminary Press, 1981.

Thiessen, Gesa Elsbeth, ed. *Theological Aesthetics: A Reader*. Grand Rapids: Wm. B. Eerdmans, 2004.

Turner, Steve. *Imagine: A Vision for Christians in the Arts*. Downers Grove, Ill.: InterVarsity Press, 2001.

Van der Leeuw, Cornelius. *Sacred and Profane Beauty: The Holy in Art*. Nashville: Abingdon Press, 1963.

Viladesau, Richard. *The Beauty of the Cross: The Passion of Christ in Theology and the Arts, from the Catacombs to the Eve of the Renaissance*. Oxford: Oxford University Press, 2006.

Von Balthasar, Hans Urs. *The Glory of the Lord: A Theological Aesthetics*. Edinburgh: T&T Clark, 1982.

Vrudny, Kimberly, and Wilson Yates, eds. *Arts, Theology, and the Church*. Cleveland: Pilgrim Press, 2005.

Yates, Wilson. *The Arts in Theological Education*. Atlanta: Scholars Press, 1987.

Walton, Janet. *Art and Worship: A Vital Connection*. Wilmington, Del.: Michael Glazer, 1988.

Whitehead, James D., and Evelyn Eaton Whitehead, eds. *Method in Ministry: Theological Reflection and Christian Ministry*. Kansas City: Sheed & Ward, 1995.

Wohlgemuth, Paul W. *Rethinking Church Music*. Carol Stream, Ill.: Hope Publishing, 1973.

Wolterstorff, Nicholas. *Art in Action: Toward a Christian Aesthetic*. Grand Rapids: Wm. B. Eerdmans, 1980.

Wuthnow, Robert. *All in Sync: How Music and Art Are Revitalizing American Religion*. Berkeley and Los Angeles: University of California Press, 2003.

ACKNOWLEDGMENTS

The author and publisher gratefully acknowledge permission to reprint the following:

Lyrics from "Dona Nobis Pacem" by Taizé. Copyright © 1984, Ateliers et Presses de Taizé; GIA Publications, Inc., exclusive North American agent. All rights reserved. Used by permission.

Lyrics from "Draw Us in the Spirit's Tether" by Percy Dearmer (1867-1936), from *Songs of Praise*, Enlarged Edition, 1931. Reproduced by permission of CopyCat Music Licensing, LLC, obo Oxford University Press.

Lyrics from "Everything Is Beautiful" by Ray Stevens. Copyright © 1970; renewed 1998. Ahab Music Company, Inc./BMI (administered by ClearBox Rights). All rights reserved. Used by permission.

Lyrics from "Song of the Three Children" (Text: Daniel 3:57-88, Vulgate), The Grail. Music: A. Gregory Murray, OSB. Copyright © 1963, The Grail, England; GIA Publications, Inc., exclusive North American agent, 7404 S. Mason Ave., Chicago, IL 60638 (www.giamusic.com; 800.441.1358). All rights reserved. Used by permission.

Lyrics from "Take My Hand, Precious Lord." Words and music by Thomas A. Dorsey. Copyright © 1938 (renewed) Warner-Tamerlane Publishing Corp. All rights reserved. Used by permission.

The poem "II (1983)" by Wendell Berry. Copyright © 1998 by Wendell Berry from *A Timbered Choir*. Reprinted by permission of Counterpoint.

The poem "Here" by Jennifer Armstrong, Musical Storyteller (www.jenniferarmstrong.com). Copyright © 2012 by Jennifer Armstrong. All rights reserved. Used by permission.

The poem "In His Image" by Marie Asner. Marie Asner retains all rights to this poem.